THEATRE

WORLD

by

JOHN WILLIS

1970-1971 SEASON

Volume 27

CROWN PUBLISHERS, INC.
419 Park Avenue South
New York, N.Y. 10016

TO
GEORGE ABBOTT

with appreciation of his genius, gratitude for his unparalleled list of contributions to theatre history, and for the years of pleasure he has given millions of theatregoers.

Since 1912 he has been involved with 115 plays and musicals, many of which rank among the theatre's best productions. He appeared in 15 plays; wrote or co-authored 30 plays and musicals; produced or co-produced 42; and as one of this century's greatest directors has been the guiding hand of almost 100 productions. The following are among the many offerings that were blessed by the "Abbott touch."

Chicago	High Button Shoes
Coquette	Where's Charley?
Twentieth Century	Call Me Madam
Three Men on a Horse	Wonderful Town
Boy Meets Girl	Pajama Game
Brother Rat	Damn Yankees
Room Service	New Girl in Town
What a Life	Fiorello
Pal Joey	Tenderloin
Best Foot Forward	Take Her, She's Mine
Kiss and Tell	A Funny Thing Happened
Snafu	on the Way to the Forum
On the Town	Never Too Late

Sada Thompson, Pamela Payton-Wright, Amy Levitt

Bert Andrews Ph

in "The Effect of Gamma Rays on Man-in-the-moon Marigolds"

Winner of 1971 Pulitzer Prize

CONTENTS

EDITOR: JOHN WILLIS

Assistant Editor, Stanley Reeves

Staff: Raymond Frederick, Maltier Hagan, Lucy Williams

Staff Photographers: Bert Andrews, Louis Melancon, Lyn Smith, Ted Yaple, Van Williams, Zodiac

THE SEASON IN REVIEW
June 1, 1970 - May 31, 1971

For a year that offered the fewest productions in Broadway history, it is difficult to express any great amount of enthusiasm. Had there not been a dearth of quality, it would be easier to write more enthusiastically. Happily for producers and theatre owners, according to Variety, grosses were the fourth highest on record; not because of larger audiences, but increased cost of tickets. The "road" hit a zenith in grosses, and for the first time almost equalled those of Broadway. The steadily decreasing number of offerings might be attributed in part to the business recession that made less money available for productions and tickets. Also, in part, it might possibly be the result of inferior scripts---a deduction made from viewing those that did open. Hopefully, next season will provide an abundance of superior native playwrights. The majority of quality scripts this season was imported--8 to be exact. There were 10 holdovers from past seasons, and an unusually small number (6) of revivals during the year. The only hit was the British mystery drama "Sleuth" with imports Anthony Quayle and Keith Baxter in bravura performances. In the musical category, the revival of "No, No, Nanette" was the only sellout, except for "Hair" that was a holdover. "Follies," a unique musical experience, and with Alexis Smith and Dorothy Collins definite assets in their Broadway debuts, arrived near the end of the season with indications that it might also become a hit.

In addition to those already mentioned, other excellent performances in new productions were given by John Gielgud and Ralph Richardson in "Home," Alec McCowen in "The Philanthropist, " Phil Silvers in "How the Other Half Loves" (all 3 plays from England), Julie Harris and Estelle Parsons in "And Miss Reardon Drinks a Little,"Danny Kaye in "Two by Two," Mildred Natwick in "70, Girls, 70" (both musicals), Lili Darvas James Earl Jones, and Earle Hyman in "Les Blancs," Cliff Gorman in "Lenny," and the entire cast of "Story Theatre/Metamorphosis." Well-deserved Tony Awards were given stars Maureen Stapleton for "The Gingerbread Lady," and Brian Bedford for "School for Wives." For supporting performances, Tonys went to Rae Allen of "And Miss Reardon Drinks a Little," and Paul Sand of "Story Theatre." Those in musicals who received Tonys were Helen Gallagher and supporting actress Patsy Kelly both in "No, No, Nanette," Hal Linden and supporting actor Keene Curtis both in "The Rothschilds." The musical "Company" (too late for awards last season) was cited, as was "Sleuth" (best play). The telecast of the Tony presentations was the most commendable ever, and should serve as a lesson for other presenters. The Drama Critics Circle citations went to "Home" for best play, "Follies" for best musical, and the off Broadway "House of Blue Leaves" for best American play.

For the second year the Pulitzer Prize went off Broadway: to Paul Zindel for his "The Effect of Gamma Rays on Man-in-the-Moon Marigolds." It also opened too late last season for competition. The number of productions off Broadway dropped to the lowest count in several years. There were fewer revivals, but a healthy number of works by new writers. Those worth mention were "Boesman and Lena" with beautiful performances by Ruby Dee and James Earl Jones, "Trial of the Catonsville 9" (transferred unsuccessfully to Broadway), "Line," and "The House of Blue Leaves" with praiseworthy characterizations by Harold Gould, Anne Meara, and Katherine Helmond who received a Derwent Award. The only musical hit was "The Dirtiest Show in Town." The most popular revivals were "A Doll's House" and "Hedda Gabler" well played in repertory by Claire Bloom, "Long Day's Journey into Night," "One Flew over the Cuckoo's Nest," and "Waiting for Godot." Other actors who should be listed for exceptional off Broadway performances are Jack MacGowran, Siobhan Mckenna, Donald Madden, Nancy Dussault, William Devane, Eric Berry, Cathryn Damon, Alice Playten, Clifton Davis, Julie Garfield, and James Naughton. Of the holdovers, "Jacques Brel. . . ." continued to be a delightful and popular musical entertainment, and "The Fantasticks" registered 4,642 performances with no prospect of closing. An encouraging report is that the fad for nudity, obscenity, and pornography is seemingly on the wane.

Lincoln Center Repertory Company (still a misnomer) had its best season, and assembled a better than usual ensemble, including stalwarts Philip Bosco and Stephen Elliott, and with David Birney, Christopher Walken, and the delightfully versatile newcomer Martha Henry, American Place Theatre presented an interesting "Pinkville" with excellent performances by Michael Douglas and James Tolkan. The Negro Ensemble Company productions were not as commendable as those in past seasons, but Ron O'Neal was outstanding in "The Dream on Monkey Mountain." The experimental Chelsea Theater Center never topped its opening production of "Saved" with an excellent cast, including James Woods who received a Derwent Award.

The New York Shakespeare Festival's summer productions in Central Park maintained the standards that have previously made it a series not to be missed. Its problem over permanent headquarters in the Public Theater complex was resolved. This prolific organization (16 productions this season) will continue its unprecedented series in the historic Village landmark, originally the Astor Library. Even the least successful of its offerings was rarely less than "interesting," and certainly worth the patronage of those who enjoy innovative theatre.

For the first time in Off-Broadway's existence, there was a strike by Equity (the actors' union) against producers and managers. Beginning Nov. 16, 1970, theatres were closed for 31 days, forcing several quality productions to end their runs. Two moved to Broadway but without the continuing success anticipated.

Notwithstanding the indisputable gloom of the season, there were some cheerful events of theatrical interest to record. Probably the most important was the change to a 7:30 curtain. It began on Jan. 4, 1971, and, relatively speaking, was enthusiastically received by theatregoers, especially commuting suburbanites, and wary urbanites who had become increasingly frightened of possible attacks en route home by predators. For restaurateurs the earlier curtain was disaster, and resulted in the closing of several popular dining places. There was a movement to effect a compromise 8 o'clock curtain. However, as the season ended it did not seem eminent because theatre attendance had increased 17% since January.

Another innovation was an acceptance by the League of New York Theatres of a "Limited Gross Agreement," initiated to cut operating costs, and increase attendance by lowering ticket prices. Its effectiveness has yet to be proved. Judging from Equity's report that only 14% of its members worked during the season, and averaged only $2500 incomes, professional theatre is at a crisis. More productions and greater audiences must be encouraged if this entertainment medium and its artists are to survive. The increase in the use of "twofers" (two tickets for the price of one) has not appreciably helped to prolong the life of legitimate productions, nor to cultivate larger audiences. Let's hope the public does not become any more indifferent to live theatre and placidly accepts only films and television.

A review of the season would be incomplete without noting the fact that "Hello, Dolly!" closed after 2,844 performances, and passed the record held by "My Fair Lady" as the longest playing musical. At the end of the season, however, "Dolly's" record was being threatened by "Fiddler on the Roof." Another event of interest was Judith Anderson in the title role of "Hamlet." She played only two performances in Carnegie Hall, but toured it during the season. Peter Brook's Royal Shakespeare Company production of "A Midsummer Night's Dream" provoked the record amount of controversy for the year.

With gratitude and support, regional theatres continue to thrive, and nurture new talent. Hopefully, they will help preserve and increase the exciting experiences that have become too rare in the legitimate theatre.

Danny
Kaye

Ruby Keeler

BROADWAY CALENDAR

June 1, 1970 through May 31, 1971

Eileen
Heckart

John Gielgud

Maureen
Stapleton

Brian Bedford

BROOKS ATKINSON THEATRE

Opened Saturday July 4, 1970.*
Jay H. Fuchs and Jerry Schlossberg in association
with John Murray present:

CHARLEY'S AUNT

By Brandon Thomas; Director, Harold Stone; Sets,
Robert T. Williams; Lighting, F. Mitchell Dana; Costumes, Richard Anderson;

CAST

Jack Chesney	Michael Goodwin
Brassett	Melville Cooper
Charles Wykeham	Rex Thompson
Lord Fancourt Babberley	Louis Nye
Amy Spettigue	Lynn Milgrim
Kitty Verdun	Andra Akers
Colonel Sir Francis Chesney	Martyn Green
Stephen Spettigue	Eric Berry
Brassett's assistant	Bruce Blaine
Donna Lucia d'Alvadorez	Maureen O'Sullivan
Ela Delahay	Elizabeth Swain

A farce in 3 acts. The time is 1892 and the action takes
place at Oxford during Commemoration Week, and at
Mr. Spettigue's house.

General Managers: George Thorn, Leonard A. Mulhern
Associate Manager: Gary Fifield
Press: Marvin Kohn, Ruth D. Smuckler
Stage Managers: Elissa Lane, Bruce Blaine

* Closed July 11, 1970 after 9 performances and 6
previews. Last revival was Dec. 23, 1953 at City Center
with Jose Ferrer, Robert Lansing, Terrance Kilburn,
Peggy Woods, for a limited engagement of 15 performances.

Louis Nye, Maureen O'Sullivan
Above: Maureen O'Sullivan, Melville Cooper

Maureen O'Sullivan, Martyn Green
Above: Lynn Milgrim, Louis Nye, Andra Akers

ANTA THEATRE

Opened Monday, September 14, 1970.*
The American National Theatre and Academy presents the American Shakespeare Festival's production of:

OTHELLO

By William Shakespeare; Director, Michael Kahn; Scenery, Karl Eigsti; Costumes, Jane Greenwood; Lighting, John Gleason; Music Composed and Directed by Conrad Susa; Duels Staged by Christopher Tanner; Executive Producer, Joseph Verner Reed; Managing Producer, Berenice Weiler; Production Assistant, Bill Capobianco.

CAST

Roderigo	John Tillinger
Iago	Lee Richardson
Brabantio	Josef Sommer
Othello	Moses Gunn
Cassio	Peter Thompson
Duke of Venice	Wyman Pendleton
First Senator	Bernard Frawley
Lodovico	Danny Davis
Second Senator	Ken Parker
Senators	Tom Tarpey, Robert Blumenfeld
First Messenger	Gary Poe
Second Messenger	Paul Corum
Desdemona	Roberta Maxwell
Montano	James Cromwell
First Cypriot Soldier	Tim Riley
Second Cypriot Soldier	John Ventantonio
Third Cypriot Soldier	Josef Warik
Emilia	Jan Miner
Bianca	Maureen Anderman

OFFICERS, ATTENDANTS, CYPRIOTS: Eugene Brezany, Patricia Callahan, Gary Copeland, Jack Heifner, Ron Lohse, Edwin McDonough, Lizbeth Mackay, William Schory, Mark Niedzialkowski, Joseph Remmes, Cabot Ogden, Mary Ellen Ray, Ralph Redpath, Paul Shutt, Garland Wright, Mary Wright.

UNDERSTUDIES: Iago, Josef Sommer; Cassio, John Ventantonio; Emilia, Mary Ellen Ray; Roderigo, Josef Warik; Brabantio, Bernard Frawley; Duke, Ken Parker; Lodovico, Paul Corum; Senators, Tom Tarpey; Messengers, Ron Lohse; Soldiers, Tim Riley, Garland Wright.

A Tragedy presented in two acts.

General Manager: Berenice Weiler
Press: Reginald Denenholz, Ellen Levene
Stage Managers: Lo Hardin, Nikos Kafkalis

* Closed Sept. 26, 1971 after limited engagement of 16 performances.

Moses Gunn, Roberta Maxwell Above: Lee Richardson, Jan Miner Right: Peter Thompson, Maureen Anderman

Martha Swope Photos

JOHN GOLDEN THEATRE

Opened Thursday, September 24, 1970.*
Joseph I. and Johnna Levine in association with
Hy Saporta present:

BOB AND RAY--THE TWO AND ONLY

Material created and written by Bob Elliott and Ray
Goulding; Director, Joseph Hardy; Scenery, William
Ritman; Lighting, Thomas Skelton; Associate Producer,
Ben Gerard; Production Assistant, Iris Merlis; Techni-
cian, Jack Cassidy; Slides by Visual Environments.

CAST

Bob Elliott
Ray Goulding

An entertainment in two acts.

General Manager; Grayson & Olim
Company Manager: Dorothy Olim
Press: Harvey B. Sabinson, Lee Solters, Leo Stern
Stage Managers: D. W. Koehler, Richard Thayer

* Closed Feb. 13, 1971 after 162 performances and 14
previews. Opened tour at Royal Alexandra, Toronto,
on March 8, and closed there March 20, 1971.

Ray Goulding, Bob Elliott, also above

10

ETHEL BARRYMORE THEATRE

Opened Monday, October 12, 1970.*
Donald Albery and Roger L. Stevens present:

CONDUCT UNBECOMING

By Barry England; Director, Val May; Designed by
Finlay James; Technical Director, Ian B. Albery; Associate Producer, Nobuko Morris; Production Supervisor,
Paul Morrison; Production Assistants, Doris Blum, William E. Becker.

CAST

Second Lt. Edward Millington	Jeremy Clyde
Second Lt. Arthur Drake	Paul Jones
Colonel Strang	Michael Barrington
Major Lionel Roach	Michael Bradshaw
Major Alastair Wimbourne, V.C.	Paul Harding
Lt.-Col. Dr. Maurice Pratt	Robert Hewitt
Capt. Rupert Harper	Donald Pickering
Lt. Richard Fothergill	Richard Lupino
Lt. Frank Hart	Richard Clarke
Second Lt. John Truly	Nicholas Hammond
Second Lt. Simon Boulton	Robert Murch
Second Lt. Edward Winters	Noel Craig
Second Lt. Frank Hutton	Edwin Owens
Major Domo Pradah Singh	Ronald Drake
Mess Head Waiter	Thomas Cover
Mrs. Marjorie Hasseltine	Elizabeth Shepherd
Mrs. Mem Strang	Sylvia O'Brien
Mrs. Bandanai	Madhur Jaffrey
Indian Servant Woman	Pandora Bronson Lupino
Ladies at the Ball	Vanya Franck, Pandora Bronson Lupino, Jean Hogan
Waiters	James Tripp, Dan Hamilton, James Leggi

UNDERSTUDIES: Millington, Rex Thompson; Drake,
Nicholas Hammond; Harper, Richard Clarke; Mrs. Hasseltine, Mrs. Strang, Vanya Franck; Wimbourne, Pradah,
Edwin Owens; Pratt, Howard Fischer; Roach, Ronald
Drake; Mrs. Bandanai, Pandora Bronson Lupino.

A Drama in three acts. The action takes place in India
in the ante-room to the Officers' Mess of a regiment in
the Indian Army in the late 1800's.

General Manager: Victor Samrock
Press: Harvey B. Sabinson, Lee Solters,
Ted Goldsmith
Stage Managers: Frederic deWilde, Howard Fischer,
James Leggi

* Closed Feb. 14, 1971 after 144 performances and 16
previews.

Zodiac Photos

Top Right: Elizabeth Shepherd, Jeremy Clyde, Paul Jones

Elizabeth Shepherd, Erik Howell, Donald Pickering, Paul Jones

Richard Lupino, Paul Harding, Paul Jones
Above: Michael Barrington, Paul Jones, Donald Pickering

11

Hal Linden, Timothy Jerome, Chris Sarandon,
Paul Hecht, David Garfield, Allan Gruet

LUNT-FONTANNE THEATRE
Opened Monday, October 19, 1970.*
Lester Osterman presents the Hillard Elkins
production of:

THE ROTHSCHILDS

Music, Jerry Bock; Lyrics, Sheldon Harnick; Book,
Sherman Yellen; Based on book by Frederic Morton;
Directed and Choreographed by Michael Kidd; Settings
and Costumes, John Bury; Lighting, Richard Pilbrow;
Orchestrations, Don Walker; Musical Direction and
Vocal Arrangements, Milton Greene; Dance Music
Arranged by Clay Fullum; Production Supervision,
Michael Thoma; Production Assistants, Theodore
Chapin, Nicolas Gill; Original Cast Album by Columbia
Records.

CAST

Prince William of Hesse	Keene Curtis
Guard	Roger Hamilton
Mayer Rothschild	Hal Linden
First Urchin	Michael Maitland
Second Urchin	Kim Michaels
Third Urchin	Robby Benson
Gutele (Mama) Rothschild	Leila Martin
First Vendor	Thomas Trelfa
Second Vendor	Kenneth Bridges
Third Vendor	Jon Peck
General	Paul Tracey
Budurus	Leo Leyden
First Banker	Elliott Savage
Second Banker	Carl Nicholas
Young Amshel Rothschild	Lee Franklin
Young Solomon Rothschild	Robby Benson
Young Nathan Rothschild	Michael Maitland
Young Jacob Rothschild	Mitchell Spera†1
Blum	Howard Honig
Mrs. Kaufman	Nina Dova
Mrs. Segal	Peggy Cooper
Peasant	Christopher Chadman
Amshel Rothschild	Timothy Jerome†2
Solomon Rothschild	David Garfield
Jacob Rothschild	Chris Sarandon†3
Nathan Rothschild	Paul Hecht†4
Kalman Rothschild	Allan Gruet
Joseph Fouche	Keene Curtis
Herries	Keene Curtis
Sceptic	Paul Tracey
Banker	Roger Hamilton
Hannah Cohen	Jill Clayburgh†5
Prince Metternich	Keene Curtis

MEMBERS OF THE COURT, THE GHETTO, ETC:
Rick Atwell, Steve Boockvor, Kenneth Bridges, Henry
Brunges, Chris Chadman, Peggy Cooper, Patrick Cum-
mings, Nina Dova, Vicki Frederick, Penny Guerard,
Roger Hamilton, Ann Hodges, Howard Honig, Del
Lewis, John Mineo, Carl Nicholas, Jon Peck, Ted Pejo-
vich, Denise Pence, Jean Richards, Elliott Savage,
Wilfred Schuman, Lani Sundsten, Paul Tracey, Thomas
Trelfa

UNDERSTUDIES: Mayer, Howard Honig; Nathan,
Chris Sarandon; Gutele, Nina Dova; Fouche, Herries,
Metternich, Roger Hamilton; Hannah, Jean Richards;
Budurus, Elliott Savage; Solomon, Amshel, Del Lewis;
Jacob, Ted Pejovich; Kalman, John Mineo; Young
Rothschilds, Kim Michels; Urchins, Lee Franklin

MUSICAL NUMBERS: "Pleasure and Privilege," "One
Room," "He Tossed a Coin," "Sons," "Everything,"
"Rothschild and Sons," "Allons," "Give England
Strength," "This Amazing London Town," "They Say,"
"I'm in Love! I'm in Love!," "In My Own Lifetime,"
"Have You Ever Seen a Prettier Little Congress?,"
"Stability," "Bonds"

A Musical in 2 acts and 18 scenes. The action takes
place between 1772 and 1818.

General Manager: Emanuel Azenberg
Company Manager: Edmonstone Thompson, Jr.
Press: Samuel J. Friedman, Rod Jacobsen,
Louise Weiner Ment
Stage Managers: Charles Gray, John Actman,
Mitch Dana

* Still playing May 31, 1971. "Tonys" were awarded Hal
Linden for Best Actor, and Keene Curtis for Best
Supporting Actor in a musical.

† Succeeded by: 1. Paris Themmen, 2. Sidney Ben-Ali, 3.
David Rounds, 4. Timothy Jerome, 5. Caroline McWilliams

Martha Swope Photos

**Top Left: Leila Martin, Hal Linden
Below: Michael Maitland, Robert Benson, Kim
Michaels, Hal Linden**

Keene Curtis and company
Above: (L) Hal Linden, Keene Curtis (R) Hal Linden
Top: (L) Paul Hecht, Jill Clayburgh (R) Keene Curtis

AMBASSADOR THEATRE

Opened Monday, October 26, 1970.*
Zev Bufman presents:

PAUL SILLS' STORY THEATRE

Adapted and Directed by Paul Sills; Setting and Projections, Michael Devine; Costumes, Stephanie Kline; Lighting, H.R. Poindexter; Music performed by The True Brethren; Presented with the help and cooperation of the Shubert Organization and Theatre Development Fund; Production Assistant, Gladys Simmons; Original Cast Album by Columbia Records.

CAST

Peter Bonerz †1	Valerie Harper†2
Hamid Hamilton Camp	Richard Libertini
Melinda Dillon	Paul Sand
Mary Frann	Richard Schaal 3

Alternates: Lewis Arquette, Molly McKasson

PART I: "The Little Peasant," "Bremen Town," "Venus and the Cat," "The Fisherman and His Wife," "Is He Fat," "Henny Penny"

PART II: "The Master Thief," "The Robber Bridegroom," "Two Crows," "The Golden Goose"

General Manager: Robert Kamlot
Press: John Springer Associates, Howard Haines
Stage Manager: Don Winton

* Closed July 3, 1971 after 270 performances and 14 previews. Paul Sand received "Tony" for Best Supporting Actor. On Thursday, Apr. 22, 1971 "Metamorphoses" opened to play alternating performances.

† Succeeded by: 1. Peter Boyle, MacIntyre Dixon, 2. Linda Lavin, Valerie Harper, 3. Charles Bartlett

Top Right: Paul Sand, Richard Libertini, Richard Schaal, Peter Bonerz

Paul Sand, Valerie Harper

Peter Bonerz, Mary Frann, Richard Schaal

AMBASSADOR THEATRE

Opened Thursday, April 22, 1971.*
Zev Bufman presents:

OVID'S
METAMORPHOSES

Adapted and Translated with Lyrics by Arnold Weinstein; Director, Paul Sills; Music Composed and Performed by The True Brethren; Settings, James Trittipo; Costumes, Noel Taylor; Lighting, H. R. Poindexter; Original Cast Album by Columbia Records.

CAST

Lewis Arquette	Valerie Harper
Regina Baff	Paula Kelly
Charles Bartlett	Richard Libertini
Hamid Hamilton Camp	Paul Sand
Melinda Dillon	Richard Schaal
MacIntyre Dixon	Avery Schreiber
Mary Frann	Penny White

PROGRAM

ACT I: Io, Vulcan and Venus and Mars, Peleus and Thetis, Procris and Cephalus, Callisto

ACT II: Picus and Canens, Pygmalion, Europa, Phaethon, Baucis and Philemon

General Manager: Robert Kamlot
Press: John Springer, Howard Haines
Stage Manager: Martin Gold

* Closed July 3, 1971 after 35 performances in repertory with "Story Theatre."

Top Left: Richard Schaal, Valerie Harper Left: Hamid Hamilton Camp, Paul Sand, Avery Schrieber, Charles Bartlett, Richard Schaal

Avery Schreiber surrounded by Paula Kelly, Penny White, Valerie Harper, Mary Frann, Regina Baff

Charles Bartlett, Paula Kelly

BELASCO THEATRE

Opened Tuesday, October 27, 1970.*
Sol Dickstein presents:

LIGHT, LIVELY AND YIDDISH

Adaptation, Ben Bonus; Text and Lyrics, A. Shulman, Wolf and Sylvia Younin; Music, Eli Rubinstein; Sets, Josef Ijaky; Costumes, Sylvia Friedlander; Musical Conductor, Renee Solomon; Additional Texts, M. Gershenson, Ch. N. Bialik, Ch. Cheffer, Mina Bern; Musical Staging and Choreography, Felix Fibich; Director, Mina Bern.

CAST

English Narrator.................................David Ellin
Zelde ....Mina Bern
Rag Seller ....Leon Liebgold
Dumpling Woman.............................Reizl Bozyk
Bagel Woman...................................Lili Liliana
Sosye the Peacemaker.......................Miriam Kressyn
Nokhem the Broker ....Seymour Rexite
Kvas Seller ....David Carey
Gitele...Diane Cypkin
Hershele of Ostropolie......................Ben Bonus
Kalmen..Leon Liebgold
Innkeeper ....Reizl Bozyk

DANCERS: Marcia Brooks, Helen Butleroff, Jack Dyville, Harry Endicott, Robyn Kessler, Tony Masullo, Maggie Masullo, Eileen McCabe, Joseph Tripolino

MUSICAL NUMBERS: "A Fair," "Yiddish," "It's Hard to Be a Jewish Woman," "Nobody Told Me This," "Ten O'Clock," "Prayer to God," "Where Is Justice," "A Joyful Song," "Light, Lively and Yiddish," "Girl Friends," "The Song of My Generation," "Israel," "Shoe Shine Boy," "A Letter," "The Day Will Come."

A Musical in 2 acts and 15 scenes. The action takes place in the shtetl, New York City, and Israel.

General Manager: Lawrence Rothman
Press: Max Eisen, Sol Dickstein, Milly Schoenbaum
Stage Manager: Bernard Sauer

* Closed Jan. 10, 1971 after 87 performances and 8 previews.

16

Reisl Bozyk, Ben Bonus Above: Reisl Bozyk, Leon Liebgold, Lili Liliana, Ben Bozyk, Mina Bern, Seymour Rexite, Miriam Kressyn

BROOKS ATKINSON THEATRE

Opened Thursday, October 29, 1970.*
James Nederlander, George M. Steinbrenner III,
by arrangement with Michael Codron present:

NOT NOW, DARLING

By Ray Cooney, John Chapman; Director, George
Abbott; Designed by Lloyd Burlingame; Associate Pro-
ducers, Sheldon B. Guren, Edward Ginsberg; Furs,
Monsieur Leon; Hairstylist, Pierre Hambur; Production
Supervisor, Ben Janney.

CAST

Miss Whittington	Marilyn Hengst
Arnold Crouch	Norman Wisdom
Miss Tipdale	Joan Bassie
Mrs. Fencham	Jean Cameron
Gilbert Bodley	Rex Garner
Harry McMichael	Ed Zimmermann
Janie McMichael	Roni Dengel
Mr. Fencham	Claude Horton
Sue Lawson	Ardyth Kaiser
Maude Bodley	M'el Dowd
Mr. Lawson	Curt Dawson

UNDERSTUDIES: Bodley, Fencham, Crouch, McMi-
chael, Lawson, Hugh Alexander; Miss Tipdale, Mrs.
Fencham, Maude, Elizabeth Owens; Sue, Miss Whitting-
ton, Pamela Gruen

A Comedy in two acts. The action takes place at the
present time in the fourth floor salon of Bodley, Bodley,
and Crouch, an exclusive London firm of furriers.

Press: Sol Jacobson, Lewis Harmon
Stage Managers: Ben Janney, Hugh Alexander,
Pamela Gruen

* Closed Sunday, Nov. 15, 1970. (21 performances)

Zodiac Photos

**Ardyth Kaiser, Ed Zimmermann Top Right: Roni
Dengel, Norman Wisdom**

Norman Wisdom, Roni Dengel, Rex Garner, Joan
Bassie Above: M'el Dowd, Rex Garner, Norman Wisdom

"Orlando Furioso"
Also Above and Top

Martha Swope Photos

BILLY ROSE THEATRE

Opened Tuesday, November 3, 1970.*
Jacob Jacobs presents:

THE PRESIDENT'S DAUGHTER

Book, H. Kalmanov; Music, Murray Rumshinsky;
Direction and Lyrics, Jacob Jacobs; Choreography,
Henrietta Jacobson; Musical Director, Murray Rumshinsky.

CAST

Frances	Michele Burke
Esther	Sarah Gingold
Yanek	Jack Rechtzeit
Minke	Diana Goldberg
Freidel	Chayele Rosenthal
Nathan	Jacob Jacobs
Sam Golden	George Guidall
Reb Yosel	Jaime Lewin
Bertha	Thelma Mintz
Miriam	Rachela Relis

MUSICAL NUMBERS: "Women's Liberation," "The
President's Daughter," "I Have What You Want," "A
Lesson in Yiddish," "Everything Is Possible in Life,"
"Welcome, Mr. Golden," "Stiochket," "Without a
Mother," "Love at Golden Years," "If Only I Could Be
a Kid Again," "An Old Man Shouldn't Be Born," "We
Two," "What More Do I Need?," "What Would You
Do?"

A Yiddish-American Musical Comedy in two acts. The
action takes place at the present time in Sam Golden's
Flatbush home.

General Manager: Joseph R. Burstin
Company Manager: Rose Goldstein
Press: William Mercur
Stage Manager: Mordecai Yachson

* Closed Jan. 2, 1971 afte   rformances and 4
previews. (No pictures available)

BUBBLE THEATRE

Opened Thursday, November 5, 1970.*
Dick Feldman and Joseph Wishy in association
with Doyle Dane Bernbach present:

ORLANDO FURIOSO

Based on poem by Ludovico Ariosto; Adapted by
Eduardo Sanguineti; Director, Luca Ronconi; Producer,
Paolo Radaelli; A Production of Teatro Libero di Roma;
Lighting Consultant, Imero Fiorentino; Scenery, Uberto
Bertacca; Costumes, Elena Mannini; Presented in cooperation with the office of Mayor John V. Lindsay and the
Parks Recreational and Cultural Affairs Administration.

CAST

Astolfo	Antonio Fattorini
Orlando	Massimo Foschi
Rinaldo	Sergio Nicolai
Angelica	Paola Tanziani
Sacripante	Carlo Montagna
Ferrau	Cesare Gelli
Bradamante	Anna Nogara
Ruggiero	Luigi Diberti
Olimpia	Adriana Asti
Melissa	Pina Cei
Atlante	Enrico Ostermann
Pinabello	Enzo Robutti
Alcina	Barbara Valmorin
Isabella	Paola Gassmann
Marfisa	Maria Grazia Grassini
Zerbino	Giorgio Favretto
Gabrina	Liu Bosiso
Doralice	Elettra Bisetti
Dardinello	Paolo Bonetti
Bireno	Marco Berneck

and Nino Bignamini, Gaetano Campisi, Francesco
Censi, Marina Coffa, Vittorio De Bisogno, Spiros
Focas, Veronica Lazar, Giorgio Maich, Pino Manzari,
Marzio Margine, Loredana Martinez, Luigi Masironi,
Michelangelo Masironi, Gino Milli, Daniela Nobili,
Michele Placido, Giancarlo Prati, Armando Pugliese,
Aldo Puglisi, Anna Teresa Rossini, Benedetto
Simonelli, Gabriele Tozzi

"Theatre in the Surround" presented in 12 scenes
without intermission in Italian.

General Manager: Norman Kean
Press: Lee Solters, Harvey B. Sabinson,
Marilynn LeVine
Stage Manager: Gianni DeBenedictis

* Closed Sunday, Nov. 29, 1970. (29 performances)

HELEN HAYES THEATRE

Opened Monday, November 9, 1970.*
Leonard Sillman presents:

HAY FEVER

By Noel Coward; Director, Arvin Brown; Setting and Lighting, Ben Edwards; Costumes, Jane Greenwood; Associate Producers, Zenon R. Mocarski, Inc., Brandon Maggart, James Catusi; Production Assistant, Catherine Corley; Hairstylist, Ronald DeMann.

CAST

Sorel Bliss	Roberta Maxwell
Simon Bliss	Sam Waterston
Clara	Sudie Bond
Judith Bliss	Shirley Booth
David Bliss	John Williams
Sandy Tyrell	John Tillinger
Myra Arundel	Marian Mercer
Richard Greatham	Michael McGuire
Jackie Coryton	Carole Shelley

UNDERSTUDIES: Judith, Myra, Clara, Carol Teitel; Jackie, Sorel, Kendall March; David, Richard, Richard Woods; Simon, Sandy, Joseph Hindy

A Comedy in three acts. The action takes place in the Bliss country home at Cookham, England in June.

General Manager: Norman Maibaum
Press: Howard Atlee, David Roggensack, Irene Gandy
Stage Managers: Mortimer Halpern, Dean McIlnay

* Closed Nov. 28, 1970 after 24 performances.

Original production opened Oct. 5, 1925 at the Maxine Elliott with Laura Hope Crews for 49 performances. Revived Dec. 29, 1931 at the Avon with Constance Collier for 95 performances.

Martha Swope Photos

Michael McGuire, Marian Mercer, John Tillinger, Shirley Booth, Sam Waterston, Roberta Maxwell, John Williams, Carole Shelley Top Left: Shirley Booth

Michael Karm, Tricia O'Neil, Danny Kaye
Above: Walter Willison, Danny Kaye

Danny Kaye, Harry Goz, Madeline Kahn
Above: Danny Kaye, Harry Goz, Joan Copeland

Opened Tuesday, November 10, 1970.*
Richard Rodgers presents:

TWO BY TWO

Music, Richard Rodgers; Lyrics, Martin Charnin; Book, Peter Stone; Based on play "The Flowering Peach" by Clifford Odets; Conceived and Directed by Joe Layton; Scenery, David Hays; Costumes, Fred Voelpel; Lighting, John Gleason; Musical Direction, Jay Blackton; Orchestrations, Eddie Sauter; Dance and Vocal Arrangements, Trude Rittman; Technical Adviser, Mitch Miller; Associate Conductor, Robert Stanley; Production Supervisor, Jerome Whyte; Projections Designed by Cris Alexander; Hairstylist, Ronald DeMann; Original Cast Album by Columbia Records.

CAST

Noah	Danny Kaye†
Esther	Joan Copeland
Japheth	Walter Willison
Shem	Harry Goz
Leah	Marilyn Cooper
Ham	Michael Karm
Rachel	Tricia O'Neil
Goldie	Madeline Kahn

STANDBYS: Noah, Harry Goz; Ham, Japheth, Jess Richards; Shem, Stephen Pearlman; Esther, Leah, Janet McCall; Goldie, Rachel, Caryl Jeanne Tenney.

MUSICAL NUMBERS: "Why Me?," "Put Him Away," "The Gitka's Song," "Something, Somewhere," "You Have Got to Have a Rudder on the Ark," "Something Doesn't Happen," "An Old Man, "Ninety Again!," "Two by Two," "I Do Not Know a Day I Did not Love You," "When It Dries," "You," "The Golden Ram," "Poppa Knows Best," "As Far as I'm Concerned," "Hey, Girlie," "The Covenant."

A Musical in two acts. The action takes place before, during and after the Flood, in and around Noah's home, on the ark, and atop Mt. Ararat.

General Manager: Morris Jacobs
Company Manager: Maurice Winters
Press: Frank Goodman, Les Schecter
Stage Managers: Harry Young, Phil King, Jess Richards

* Still playing May 31, 1971.

† Harry Goz after Mr. Kaye's accident from Feb. 5-17, 1971 when Mr. Kaye returned with wheel chair and crutches.

Zodiac Photos

Marilyn Cooper, Harry Goz, Michael Karm

**Tricia O'Neil, Danny Kaye, Walter Willison
Above: Danny Kaye**

21

LONGACRE THEATRE
Opened Sunday, November 15, 1970.*
Konrad Matthaei presents:

LES BLANCS

By Lorraine Hansberry; Final text adapted by Robert Nemiroff; Director, John Berry; Scenery, Peter Larkin; Costumes, Jane Greenwood; Lighting, Neil Peter Jampolis; Ritual, Louis Johnson; Sound, Jack Shearing; Script Associate, Charlotte Zaltzberg; General Adviser, Abel Enklewitz; Staff Associate, Stephanie Bass; African Language Consultant, Josiah Ade Ilori.

CAST

Warrior	Charles Moore
Witch Doctor	Joan Derby
Drummers	Ladji Camara, Charles Payne
Dr. Marta Gotterling	Marie Andrews
First African	Dennis Tate
Second African	George Fairley
African Child	Gregory Beyer
Peter	Clebert Ford
Charlie Morris	Cameron Mitchell
Third African	William Ware
Dr. Willy Dekoven	Humbert Allen Astredo
Major George Rice	Ralph Purdom
First Soldier	Garry Mitchell
Second Soldier	Gwyllum Evans
Madame Neilsen	Lili Darvas
Eric	Harold Scott
Tshembe Matoseh	James Earl Jones
Abioseh Matoseh	Earle Hyman

UNDERSTUDIES: Tshembe, Earle Hyman; Morris, Rice, Garry Mitchell; Abioseh, Clebert Ford; Dekoven, Gwyllum Evans; Eric, Dennis Tate; Peter, George Fairley; Africans, Charles Briggs; Drummers, Butch Jackson.

A Drama presented without intermission. The action is set in and about a Mission compound and the Matoseh hut in Africa. The time is yesterday, today, tomorrow — but not very long after that.

General Manager: Paul B. Berkowsky
Company Manager: Edward A. Blatt
Press: Max Eisen, Warren Pincus, Milly Schoenbaum
Stage Managers: Martin Gold, Charles Briggs

* Closed Dec. 19, 1970 after 40 performances and 30 previews.

Earle Hyman, James Earl Jones, Harold Scott
Above: Cameron Mitchell, James Earl Jones
Right: Lili Darvas

MUSIC BOX

Opened Thursday, November 12, 1970.*

Helen Bonfils, Morton Gottlieb, Michael White present:

SLEUTH

By Anthony Shaffer; Director, Clifford Williams; Designed by Carl Toms; Lighting, William Ritman; Production Assistant, E. J. Oshins.

CAST

Andrew Wyke ....Anthony Quayle
Milo Tindle ....Keith Baxter
Inspector Doppler ....Philip Farrar
Detective Sgt. Tarrant ....Harold K. Newman
Police Constable Higgs..................................Roger Purnell

STANDBYS: Andrew, Michael Allinson; Milo, Victor Arnold; Doppler, Henry Raymond; Tarrant, Higgs, John Stephen.

A Mystery Drama in two acts. The action takes place at the present time in Andrew Ayke's country home in Wiltshire, England.

General Manager: Ben Rosenberg
Company Manager: Martin Cohen
Press: Dorothy Ross, Herb Striesfield
Stage Managers: Warren Crane, John Stephen,

Henry Raymond

* Still playing May 31, 1971. Winner of 1971 "Tony" Award for Best Play.

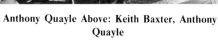

Anthony Quayle Above: Keith Baxter, Anthony Quayle

Anthony Quayle, Keith Baxter (also above)

MOROSCO THEATRE
Opened Tuesday, November 17, 1970.*
Alexander H. Cohen presents the Royal Court
Theatre Production of:

HOME

By David Storey; Director, Lindsay Anderson; Designed by Jocelyn Herbert; Lighting, Jules Fisher; Music, Alan Price; Associate Producer, Clinton Wilder; Production Associates, Hildy Parks, Roy A. Somlyo; Production Supervisor, Jerry Adler; Production Assistants, Joan Barnett, Dorothy Krantz; Staff Assistant, Robert Frissell.

CAST

Harry ....John Gielgud
Jack ....Ralph Richardson
Marjorie ....Dandy Nichols†
Kathleen...Mona Washbourne
Alfred ....Graham Weston

STANDBYS:Kathleen, Stellar Bennett; Marjorie, Lucy Landau; Alfred, Andrew Johns

A Drama in two acts. The action takes place before and after lunch.

Company Manager: Seymour Herscher
Press: James D. Proctor, Richard Hummler
Stage Manager: Robert L. Borod

* Closed Feb. 20, 1971 after a limited engagement of 110 performances and 6 previews.

† Succeeded by Jessica Tandy

Recipient of New York Drama Critics Circle Award as Best Play of 1970-71.

Zodiac Photos

Mona Washbourne, Dandy Nichols
Top Left: John Gielgud, Mona Washbourne

Jessica Tandy, Ralph Richardson, Mona
Washbourne, John Gielgud, also top with Graham Weston

PLYMOUTH THEATRE

Opened Sunday, December 13, 1970.*
Saint-Subber presents:

THE GINGERBREAD LADY

By Neil Simon; Director, Robert Moore; Setting, David Hays; Costumes, Frank Thompson; Lighting, Martin Aronstein; Hairstyle, Phyllis Sagnelli; Produced by Nancy Enterprises and Footlight Productions, Inc.

CAST

Jimmy Perry	Michael Lombard
Manuel	Alex Colon
Toby Landau	Betsy von Furstenberg
Evy Meara	Maureen Stapleton
Polly Meara	Ayn Ruymen
Lou Tanner	Charles Siebert

STANDBYS: Evy, Toby, Jan Farrand; Jimmy, Ken Kimmins; Lou, Don Billett; Polly, Eda Zahl; Manuel, Hector Troy.

A Comedy-Drama in three acts. The action takes place at the present time in a New York brownstone apartment in the West Seventies.

General Manager: C. Edwin Knill
Company Manager: James Turner
Press: Harvey B. Sabinson, Lee Solters, Cheryl Sue Dolby, Edie Kean
Stage Managers: Tom Porter, George Rondo

* Closed May 29, 1971 after 193 performances. Maureen Stapleton received "Tony" for Best Actress.

Ayn Ruymen, Maureen Stapleton Top Right: Michael Lombard, Maureen Stapleton

Betsy von Furstenberg, Ayn Ruymen, Maureen Stapleton, Michael Lombard Above: Maureen Stapleton, Charles Siebert

HELEN HAYES THEATRE

Opened Friday, December 18, 1970.*
Jeff Britton in association with Sagittarius
Productions, Inc. presents:

THE ME NOBODY KNOWS

Music, Gary William Friedman; Lyrics, Will Holt;
Adapted by Robert H. Livingston, Herb Schapiro; Based
on book of same name, edited by Stephen M. Joseph;
Original Idea, Herb Schapiro; Director, Robert H. Liv-
ingston; Musical Numbers Staged by Patricia Birch;
Scenery and Lighting; Clarke Dunham; Costumes, Patri-
cia Quinn Stuart; Media Design and Photography, Stan
Goldberg and Mopsy; Additional Lyrics, Herb Schapiro;
Arrangements and Orchestrations, Gary William Fried-
man; Musical Director, Edward Strauss; Assistant to
Producer, Erlinda Zetlin; Associate to Producer, Sidney
Annis; Original Cast Album by Atlantic Records.

CAST

Rhoda	Melanie Henderson
Lillian	Laura Michaels
Carlos	Jose Fernandez
Lillie Mae	Irene Cara
Benjamin	Douglas Grant
Catherine	Beverly Ann Bremers†
Melba	Jerri Dean
Lloyd	Northern J. Calloway
Donald	Paul Mace
Clorox	Carl Thoma
William	Kevin Lindsay
Nell	Hattie Winston

UNDERSTUDIES: Roy Bailey, Lenny Bari, Edloe,
Giancarlo Esposito, Elaine Petricoff

MUSICAL NUMBERS: "Dream Babies," "Light Sings,"
"This World," "Numbers," "What Happens to Life,"
"Take Hold the Crutch," "Flying Milk and Runaway
Plates," "I Love What the Girls Have," "How I Feel,"
"If I Had a Million Dollars," "Fugue for Four Girls,"
"Rejoice," "Sounds," "The Tree," "Robert, Alvin, Wen-
dell and Jo Jo," "Jail-Life Walk," "Something Beauti-
ful," "Black," "The Horse," "Let Me Come In," "War
Babies"

A Musical in two acts. The action takes place at the
present time in New York's ghetto.

General Managers: Malcolm Allen, Jose Vega
Press: Samuel J. Friedman, Louise Ment
Stage Managers: Martha Knight, Jason Travis,
G. Dean

* Still playing May 31, 1971. Opened Off-Broadway at
the Orpheum on May 18, 1970 and was closed by
Equity strike on Nov. 15, 1970. For original production, see THEATRE WORLD, Vol. 26.

† Succeeded by Julienne Clukowski for two weeks

Hattie Winston, Carl Thoma

**Beverly Ann Bremers, Jose Fernandez
Top: Douglas Grant, Northern Calloway**

Eleanor Calbes, Kenneth Nelson, Ron Husmann
Above: Eleanor Calbes (L)

MAJESTIC THEATRE
Opened Monday, December 28, 1970.*
Herman Levin presents:

LOVELY LADIES, KIND GENTLEMEN

Book, John Patrick; Music and Lyrics, Stan Freeman, Franklin Underwood; Based on Vern J. Sneider's novel "The Teahouse of the August Moon" and the play by John Patrick; Director, Lawrence Kasha; Dances and Musical Numbers Staged by Marc Breaux; Scenic Production, Oliver Smith; Costumes, Freddy Wittop; Lighting, Thomas Skelton; Musical Direction and Choral Arrangements, Theodore Saidenberg; Orchestrations, Philip J. Lang; Dance Arrangements, Al Mello; Associate Choreographer, Gary Menteer; Associate Producer, Angus Equities, Inc. Hair Stylist, Jack Mei Ling; Makeup, Bob O'Bradovich.

CAST

Sakini	Kenneth Nelson
Missionary	David Steele
Col. Wainwright Purdy III	David Burns
Sgt. Gregovich	Lou Wills
Capt. Fisby	Ron Husmann
Old Lady	Sachi Shimizu
Daughter	Tisa Chang
Children	June Angela, Gene Profanato, Dana Shimizu
Lady Astor	Herself
Ancient Man	Sab Shimono
Mr. Seiko	Alvin Lum
Miss Higa Jiga	Lori Chinn
Mr. Oshira	David Thomas
Mr. Hokaida	Big Lee
Lotus Blossom	Eleanor Calbes
Mr. Keora	Sab Shimono
Capt. McLean	Remak Ramsay
Logan	David Steele
Miller	Jim Weston
O'Malley	Stephen Bolster
Cabot	Stuart Craig Wood
Stock	James B. Spann
Lipshitz	Kirk Norman
Swenson	James Hobson
Cardone	Dennis Roth
Mancini	Richard Nieves
Colombo	Charlie J. Rodriguez

OKINAWANS AND AMERICANS: Barbara Coggin, Catherine Dando, Joan Nelson, Sumiko, Tisa Chang, Lori Chinn, Christi Curtis, Marjory Edson, Rosalie King, Sylvia Nolan, Jo Ann Ogawa, Sachi Shimizu, Susan Sigrist, Stephen Bolster, James Hobson, Alvin Lum, Richard Nieves, Kirk Norman, Charlie J. Rodriguez, Dennis Roth, Sab Shimono, James B. Spann, David Steele, Jim Weston, Stuart Craig Wood, Henry Boyer, Paul Charles, Charlies Goeddertz, J.J. Jepson, Tim Ramirez, Steven Ross, Joe Milan, Ken Urmston

UNDERSTUDIES: Sakini, J. J. Jepson; Fishby, Stephen Bolster; Purdy, David Thomas; Lotus, Sumiko; McLean, Jim Weston; Gregovich, James B. Spann; Oshira, Sab Shimono; Hokaida, Alvin Lum

MUSICAL NUMBERS: "With a Snap of My Finger," "Right Hand Man," "Find Your Own Cricket," "One Side of World," "Geisha," "You Say--They Say," "This Time," "Simple Word," "Garden Guaracha," "If It's Good Enough for Lady Astor," "Chaya," "Call Me Back," "Lovely Ladies, Kind Gentlemen," "You've Broken a Fine Woman's Heart," "One More for the Last One."

A Musical Comedy in two acts. The action takes place on the island of Okinawa during a few months in the year 1946.

General Manager: Max Allentuck
Company Manager: Joseph M. Grossman
Press: Martin Shwartz
Stage Managers: Phil Friedman, Richard Hughes, Robert Corpora, Jim Weston

* Closed Jan. 9, 1971 after 19 performances and 3 previews.

Zodiac Photos

Top Left: David Burns, Ron Husmann

MARK HELLINGER THEATRE

Opened Friday, January 15, 1971.*
Ken Gaston and Leonard Goldberg in
association with Henry Stern present:

ARI

Book and Lyrics, Leon Uris; Based on his novel
"Exodus"; Music, Walt Smith; Director, Lucia Victor;
Choreography, Talley Beatty; Scenery, Robert Ran-
dolph; Costumes, Sara Brook; Lighting, Nananne
Porcher; Vocal Arrangmeents and Musical Direction,
Stanley Lebowsky; Orchestrations, Philip J. Lang;
Dance and Incidental Music Arranged by Peter Howard;
Additional Music, William Fisher; Associate Producers,
Ronald Reckseit, Lisa Lipsky; Hairstylist, Ray Iagnacco;
Assistant to Producers, Skip Nederlander; Production
Assistant, Jack Damios.

CAST

Joab	Joseph Della Sorte
Zev	Mark Zeller
David	Martin Ross
Mandria	C. K. Alexander
General Sutherland	Jack Gwillim
Major Caldwell	Jamie Ross
Ari Ben Canaan	David Cryer
Mark Parker	Norwood Smith
Kitty Fremont	Constance Towers
Dov	John Savage
Karen	Jacqueline Mayro
Benjy	Roger Morgan
Armeteau	Alexander Orfaly
His Friend	Edward Becker
Captain Henley	Casper Roos

CHILDREN: Tracey Eman, Kelley Boa, Mona Daleo,
Toni Lund, Lynn Reynolds, Timmy Ousey, Todd Jones,
Johnny Welch, Tony Dean

DANCERS: Bryant Baker, Bjarne Buchtrup, Ron Cro-
foot, Richard Dodd, Pi Douglass, Richard Maxon, Ronn
Steinman, Carol Estey, Reggie Israel, Karen L. Jablons,
Joanna Mendl, Gayle Pines, Deborah Strauss

SINGERS: Edward Becker, Ted Bloecher, Bennett Hill,
Henry Lawrence, Art Mathews, Caspter Roos, D. Brian
Wallach, Bonnie Marcus, Patricia Noal, Susan Schevers,
Suzanne Horn

UNDERSTUDIES: Kitty, Rita Gardner; Ari, Norwood
Smith; Karen, Patricia Noal; Benjy, Timmy Ousey; Dov,
Ronn Steinman; Armeteau, Henry Lawrence; Suther-
land, Casper Roos; Caldwell, Henley, Art Mathews;
Dinsmore, Ted Bloecher; Timmy, Tony, Todd Jones

MUSICAL NUMBERS: "Children's Lament,"
"Yerushaliam," "The Saga of Haganah," "Give Me One
Good Reason," "Dov's Nightmare," "Karen's Lullaby,"
"Aphrodite," "My Galilee," "The Lord Helps Those
Who Help Themselves," "Alphabet Song," "My Broth-
er's Keeper," "The Exodus," "He'll Never Be Mine,"
"One Flag," "I See What I Choose to See," "Hora-
Galilee," "Ari's Promise."

A Musical in two acts and 18 scenes. The action takes
place on the island of Cyprus in 1947.

General Manager: Victor Samrock
Company Manager: James Awe
Press: David Lipsky
Stage Managers: Wade Miller, Jack Timmers,
Dorothy Hanning, Didi Francis

* Closed Jan. 30, 1971 after 19 performances and 12
previews.

Zodiac Photos

Top Right: David Cryer, Constance Towers

John Savage, Jacqueline Mayro

Susan Watson, Roger Rathburn

FORTY-SIXTH STREET THEATRE
Opened Tuesday, January 19, 1971.*
Pyxidium Ltd. presents:

NO, NO, NANETTE

Book, Otto Harbach, Frank Mandel; Music, Vincent Youmans; Lyrics, Irving Caesar, Otto Harbach; Adapted and Directed by Burt Shevelove; Dances and Musical Numbers Staged by Donald Saddler; Designed by Raoul Pene du Bois; Lighting, Jules Fisher; Musical Direction and Vocal Arrangements, Buster Davis; Orchestrations, Ralph Burns; Dance Music Arranged and Incidental Music Composed by Luther Henderson; Colston and Clements at Twin Pianos; Production Manager, May Muth; Tap Supervisors, Mary Ann Niles, Ted Cappy; Sound, Jack Shearing; Coiffures, Vidal Sassoon, Bruce Steier; Assistant Choreographer, Mary Ann Niles; Assistant to Producers, Steve Beckler; Beach Ball Instructor, Ernestine Mercer; Entire Production Supervised by Busby Berkeley; Recorded by Columbia Records.

CAST

Pauline	Patsy Kelly
Lucille Early	Helen Gallagher
Sue Smith	Ruby Keller
Jimmy Smith	Jack Gilford
Billy Early	Bobby Van
Tom Trainor	Roger Rathburn
Nanette	Susan Watson
Flora Latham	K. C. Townsend†
Betty Brown	Loni Zoe Ackerman
Winnie Winslow	Pat Lysinger

NANETTE'S FRIENDS: Bob Becker, John Beecher, Joretta Bohannon, Roger Braun, Marcia Brushingham, Kenneth Carr, Jennie Chandler, Kathy Conry, Christine Cox, Kevin Daly, Ed Dixon, Ellen Elias, Mercedes Ellington, Jon Engstrom, Marian Haraldson, Gregg Harlan, Jamies Haskins, Gwen Hillier, Sayra Hummel, Scott Hunter, Dottie Lester, Cheryl Locke, Joanne Lotsko, Mary Ann Niles, Kate O'Brady, Sue Ohman, Jill Owens, Ken Ploss, John Roach, Linda Rose, Ron Schwinn, Sonja Stuart, Monica Tiller, Pat Trott, Phyllis Wallach.

STANDBYS AND UNDERSTUDIES: Sue, Betty Wragge; Jimmy, Ted Tiller; Pauline, Dorothy Claire; Billy, Roger Braun; Lucille, Pat Lysinger; Nanette, Kathy Conry; Tom, Kenneth Carr; Betty, Linda Rose; Flora, Dottie Lester; Winnie, Gwen Hillier

MUSICAL NUMBERS: "Too Many Rings Around Rosie," "I've Confessed to the Breeze," "Call of the Sea," "I Want to Be Happy," "No, No, Nanette," "Peach on the Beach," "Tea for Two," "You Can Dance with Any Girl," "Telephone Girlie," "Where-Has-My-Hubby-Gone Blues," "Waiting for You," "Take a Little One-Step," Finale.

A Musical Comedy in 3 acts. The action takes place on a weekend in early summer of 1925 in Jimmy's New York home, and Chickadee Cottage in Atlantic City.

General Management: Gatchell & Neufeld
Company Manager: James Mennen
Press: Merle Debuskey, M. J. Boyer, Faith Geer
Stage Manager: Robert Schear, John H. Lowe III

* Still playing May 31, 1971. Original production opened Sept. 16, 1925 and ran for 321 performances with Eleanor Dawn, Louise Groody, Charles Winninger, and Wellington Cross.

"Tony" Awards went to Helen Gallagher for best actress in a musical, and Patsy Kelly for best supporting actress in a musical, Raoul Pene du Bois for best costumes, and Donald Saddler for best choreography.

†Succeeded by Sandra O'Neill

Top Left: Helen Gallagher
Below: Ruby Keeler (C)

Ruby Keeler, Bobby Van
Above: Jack Gilford Ruby Keeler, Patsy Kelly, Bobby Van

BILLY ROSE THEATRE

Opened Wednesday, January 20, 1971.*
David Merrick Arts Foundation presents The
Royal Shakespeare Company in the Stratford-
upon-Avon production of:

A MIDSUMMER NIGHT'S DREAM

By William Shakespeare; Director, Peter Brook; Sets
and Costumes, Sally Jacobs; Music, Richard Peaslee;
Lighting, Lloyd Burlingame; Production Supervisor,
Samuel Liff.

CAST

Theseus/Oberon	Alan Howard
Hippolyta/Titania	Sara Kestelman
Philostrate/Puck	John Kane
Egeus/Quince	Philip Locke
Bottom	David Waller
Flute	Glynne Lewis
Starveling	Philip Manikum
Snout	Patrick Stewart
Snug	Barry Stanton
Hermia	Mary Rutherford
Lysander	Terence Taplin
Helena	Frances De La Tour
Demetrius	Ben Kingsley
Cobweb	Hugh Keays Byrne
Moth	Ralph Cotterill
Peaseblossom	Celia Quicke
Mustardseed	John York
Percussion	Tony McVey, Robin Weatherall
Guitar	Martin Best

A Comedy presented in two parts

General Manager: Jack Schlissel
Company Manager: Vincent McKnight
Press: Lee Solters, Harvey B. Sabinson, Leo Stern,
Edie Kean
Stage Managers: Roger Howells, Roger Gregory,
Lawrence Burns, Julian Beech, John Watts

* Closed March 13, 1971 after a limited engagement of
62 performances and 2 previews. Re-opened Mar. 16,
1971 at Brooklyn Academy of Music for 16 additional
performances, closing to tour on Mar. 27, 1971.

David Farrell Photos

**Top Right: Sara Kestelman, Alan Howard Below:
Ralph Cotterill, Celia Quicke, Sara Kestelman,
Hugh Keays Byrne, John York**

**Ralph Cotterill, John York, Celia Quicke,
Sara Kestelman**

**Alan Howard, Sara Kestelman, David Waller,
John Kane**

BROADHURST THEATRE
Opened Saturday, January 30, 1971.*
David Merrick presents:

FOUR ON A GARDEN

Adapted by Abe Burrows; Director, Abe Burrows; Scenic Production, Oliver Smith; Costumes, William McHone; Lighting, Martin Aronstein; Produced in association with Beresford Productions Ltd., and Charles Lowe Productions, Inc.; Wigs, Vidal Sassoon.

CAST

Act I: House of Dunkelmayer
TV Repairman............................George S. Irving
Maid......................................Mary Hamill
Mrs. Dunkelmayer ....Carol Channing
Max.......................................Sid Caesar
Delivery Man............................Tom Lee Jones

Act II: Betty
Real Estate Agent ....George S. Irving
Jessica..................................Christine Lavren
Bob.......................................Sid Caesar
Betty.....................................Carol Channing

Act III: Toreador
Painter...................................Sid Caesar
Irene......................................Carol Channing
Joel.......................................Tom Lee Jones

Act IV: The Swingers
Mr. Lewis................................Sid Caesar
Mrs. Wexel ....Carol Channing
Understudies: Lee Ames, Carolyn Lagerfelt

A Comedy performed without intermission. The action takes place at the present time in a four-room cooperative brownstone apartment in Manhattan.

General Manager: Jack Schlissel
Company Manager: Richard Highley
Press: Harvey B. Sabinson, Lee Solters,
Sandra Manley, Edie Kean
Stage Managers: Jeff Chambers, Lee Ames,
Carolyn Lagerfelt

* Closed March 20, 1971 after 57 performances and 47 previews.

Martha Swope Photos

**Sid Caesar, Carol Channing, also top left and above
with Tom Lee Jones**

33

Brian Bedford, Joan Van Ark
Left: George Pentecost, Brian Bedford

LYCEUM THEATRE

Opened Tuesday, February 16, 1971.*
Phoenix Theatre (T. Edward Hambleton,
Managing Director) presents:

THE SCHOOL FOR WIVES

By Moliere; New verse translation by Richard Wilbur;
Director, Stephen Porter; Scenery and Lighting, James
Tilton; Costumes, Nancy Potts; Music, Conrad Susa;
Hair Styles, Steve Atha; Technicians, Ralph Beebe,
Robert T. Prouse.

CAST

Crysalde	Paul Ballantyne†1
Arnolphe	Brian Bedford
Alain	James Greene
Georgette	Peggy Pope
Agnes	Joan Van Ark†2
Horace	David Dukes
Notary	George Pentecost
Enrique	Mario Siletti
Oronte	Gordon Gould

UNDERSTUDIES: Arnolphe, George Pentecost; Agnes,
Georgette, Brooke Harrow; Horace, Enrique, Oronte,
Notary, Anthony Manionis; Crysalde, Gordon Gould;
Alain, Mario Siletti.

A Comedy presented in two parts. The action takes
place on a street in front of Arnolphe's house.

General Manager: Marilyn S. Miller
Assistant General Manager: Gintare Sileika
Assistant Manager: June Renfrow
Press: Sol Jacobson, Lewis Harmon, Ruth D. Smuckler
Stage Managers: Bob Beard, Anthony Manionis

* Closed May 29, 1971 after 120 performances and 5
previews. Brian Bedford received "Tony" for Best
Actor.

† Succeeded by: 1. Stephen Joyce, Stephen D. Newman,
2. Maria Tucci.

**David Dukes, Brian Bedford, Peggy Pope, James
Greene, Joan Van Ark Above: James Greene,
Brian Bedford, Peggy Pope**

Van Williams Photos

BELASCO THEATRE

Opened Thursday, February 25, 1971.*
Hillard Elkins in association with Michael White, Gordon Crowe and George Platt present:

OH! CALCUTTA!

Devised by Kenneth Tynan; Contributors: Samuel Beckett, Jules Feiffer, Dan Greenburg, John Lennon, Jacques Levy, Leonard Melfi, David Newman and Robert Benton, Sam Shepard, Clovis Trouille, Kenneth Tynan, Sherman Yellen; Music and Lyrics, The Open Window: Robert Dennis, Peter Schickele, Stanley Walden; Choreography, Margo Sappington; Scenery, James Tilton; Lighting, David F. Segal; Costumes, Fred Voelpel; Projected Media Designs, Gardner Compton, Emile Ardolino; Still Photography, Michael Childers; Musical Director, Norman Bergen; Production Supervisor, Michael Thoma; Production Associate, Bill Liberman; An E.P.I.C. Production; Conceived and Directed by Jacques Levy.

CAST

Mel Auston	William Knight
Raina Barrett	Mitchell McGuire
Ray Edelstein	Pamela Pilkenton
Samantha Harper	Gary Rethmeier
Patricia Hawkins	Nancy Tribush†

Standby: Maureen Byrnes

PROGRAM

ACT I: "Taking off the Robe," "Dick and Jane," "Suite for Five Letters," "Will Answer All Sincere Replies," "Paintings of Clovis Trouille," "Jack and Jill," "Delicious Indignities," "Was It Good for You Too?"

ACT II: "Much Too Soon," "One on One," "Rock Garden," "Four in Hand," "Coming Together, Going Together."

General Manager: Edmonstone F. Thompson, Jr.
Press: Samuel J. Friedman, Louise Weiner Ment, Shirley Herz
Stage Managers: Greg Taylor, Janet Beroza

* Still playing May 31, 1971. Opened off Broadway at the Eden Theatre on Tuesday, June 17, 1969 and played there until its move to Broadway.

† Succeeded by Cindy Howard. Ed Phillips and Jack Shearer were also added to the cast.

Henry Grossman Photos

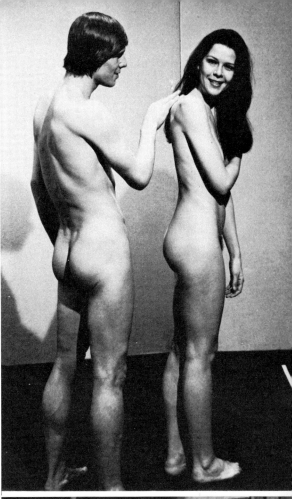

Jack Shearer, Pamela Pilkenton

Eddie Phillips, Mitchell Maguire
Above: Gary Rethmeier, Samantha Harper

MOROSCO THEATRE

Opened Thursday, February 25, 1971.*
James B. McKenzie, Spofford J. Beadle, Seth L. Schapiro, Kenneth Waissman, Maxine Fox present:

AND MISS REARDON DRINKS A LITTLE

By Paul Zindel; Director, Melvin Bernhardt; Scenery, Fred Voelpel; Lighting, Martin Aronstein; Costumes, Sara Brook; Hairstylist, Ray Iagnocco; Produced in association with Gordon Crowe; Assistant to Producers, Linda Ford; Staff Associate, Judi McAllister.

CAST

Catherine Reardon	Estelle Parsons
Mrs. Pentrano	Virginia Payne
Delivery Boy	Paul Lieber
Ceil Adams	Nancy Marchand
Anna Reardon	Julie Harris
Fleur Stein	Rae Allen
Bob Stein	Bill Macy

A Drama in three acts. The action takes place at the present time in the apartment of Catherine and Anna Reardon.

General Manager: Ralph Roseman
Press: Harvey B. Sabinson, Lee Solters, Sandra Manley, Edie Kean
Stage Manager: James Haire

* Closed May 29, 1971 after 108 performances and 3 previews. Rae Allen received "Tony" for Best Supporting Actress.

Bert Andrews Photos

Top Left: Julie Harris, Nancy Marchand Below: Paul Lieber, Estelle Parsons, Virginia Payne

Julie Harris, Nancy Marchand, Bill Macy, Rae Allen

Estelle Parsons

Julie Harris, Rae Allen, Bill Macy
Above: Estelle Parsons, Julie Harris, Nancy Marchand

BROOKS ATKINSON THEATRE

Opened Wednesday, March 10, 1971.*
Elliot Martin, James Nederlander and George M.
Steinbrenner III, by arrangement with John Gale
present:

ABELARD AND HELOISE

By Ronald Millar; Inspired by "Peter Abelard" by
Helen Waddell, and the letters of Heloise and Abelard;
Director, Robin Phillips; Designed by Christopher Mor-
ley; Costumes, Daphne Dare; Lighting, H. R. Poindex-
ter; As presented at The Ahmanson Theatre, The Music
Center, Los Angeles.

CAST

Peter Abelard	Keith Michell
Heloise	Diana Rigg
Alain	Dirk Benedict
Gerard	Ron Hale
Philippe	Barney McFadden
Bernard	John Tremaine
Robert de Montboissier	Peter Coffield
Guilbert	Robert H. Rovin
Gilies de Vannes	Ronald Radd
Jehan	Christopher Pennock
Fulbert	Barnard Hughes
Belle Alys	Barbara Lester
Abbess of Argenteuil	Jacqueline Brookes
Sister Laura	Barbara Lester
Sister Godric	Beulah Garrick
Sister Constance	Jennifer Moore
Mariella	Samantha Doane
Gisela	Nora Coppola
Alberic of Rheims	Byron Webster
Denise	DeAnn Mears
Hugh	Kelly Fitzpatrick

STANDBYS AND UNDERSTUDIES: Heloise, DeAnn
Mears; Abelard, Barney McFadden; Robert, Dirk Bene-
dict; Fulbert, Kelly Fitzpatrick; Gilles, Byron Webster;
Godric, Barbara Lester; Alys, Samantha Doane; Guil-
bert, Robert, John Tremaine; Denise, Heloise, Jennifer
Moore; Hugh, Alberic, Fulbert, Ron Hale; Abelard,
Hugh, Robert, Christopher Pennock

A Drama in two acts. The play is set in the first half of
the Twelfth Century in France.

General Manager: Al Goldin
Press: Mary Bryant, Stanley F. Kaminsky, Sadie Stein
Stage Managers: Norman A. Grogan, Dom Salinaro

* Closed Apr. 24, 1971 after 53 performances and 6
previews.

**Keith Michell, Diana Rigg Top Right: Ronald
Radd, Diana Rigg**

**Peter Coffield, Keith Michell
Above: Diana Rigg, Jacqueline Brookes**

ETHEL BARRYMORE THEATRE
Opened Monday, March 15, 1971.*
David Merrick in association with Byron
Goldman, and Michael Codron in association
with the Royal Court Theatre presents:

THE PHILANTHROPIST

By Christopher Hampton; Director, Robert Kidd;
Designed by John Gunter; Costumes, Sara Brook; Lighting, Lloyd Burlingame; Associate Producer, Samuel Liff;
Staff Associates, Sylvia Schwartz, John Bonanni, Elizabeth Kaye.

CAST

Philip	Alec McCowen
Donald	Ed Zimmermann
John	Paul Corum
Celia	Jane Asher
Braham	Victor Spinetti
Araminta	Penelope Wilton
Liz	Carolyn Lagerfelt

A Comedy in two acts. The action takes place in an
English university town in the near future.

General Manager: Jack Schlissel
Press: Harvey B. Sabinson, Lee Solters, Leo Stern,
Edie Kean
Stage Managers: Mitchell Erickson, Carolyn Lagerfelt

* Closed May 15, 1971 after 64 performances and 5
previews.

Alec McCowen Above: Alec
McCowen, Jane Asher

JOHN GOLDEN THEATRE
Opened Tuesday, March 16, 1971.*
Joseph Kipness and Lawrence Kasha present:

FATHER'S DAY

By Oliver Hailey; Director, Donald Moffat; Scenery and Lighting, Jo Mielziner; Costumes, Ann Roth; Production Associate, Phyllis Dukore.

CAST

Louise	Brenda Vaccaro
Estelle	Jennifer Salt
Marian	Marian Seldes
Harold	Ken Kercheval
Richard	Donald Moffat
Tom	Biff McGuire

STANDBYS AND UNDERSTUDIES: Louise, Marian, Rue McClanahan; Tom, Richard, Michael Prince; Estelle, Garn Stephens; Harold, Gene Tyburn

A Comedy in two acts. The action takes place in Manhattan on Father's Day of 1971.

General Manager: Philip Adler
Company Manager: Joseph M. Grossman
Press: Bill Doll & Co., Dick Williams,
Virginia Holden, Susan L. Schulman
Stage Managers: Phil Friedman, Gene Tyburn

* Closed March 16, 1971 after 1 performance and 16 previews.

Bill Pierce Photos

Biff McGuire, Brenda Vaccaro Above: Brenda
Vaccaro, Jennifer Salt, Marian Seldes

MARTIN BECK THEATRE
Opened Saturday, March 27, 1971.*
Theatre 1971 (Richard Barr, Charles Woodward,
Edward Albee) presents:

ALL OVER

By Edward Albee; Director, John Gielgud; Setting
and Costumes, Rouben Ter-Arutunian; Lighting, Richard Nelson; Assistant to Producers, Jack Custer; Production Assistant, Drew Kalter.

CAST

The Wife	Jessica Tandy
The Daughter	Madeleine Sherwood
The Mistress	Colleen Dewhurst
The Doctor	Neil Fitzgerald
The Son	James Ray
The Best Friend	George Voskovec
The Nurse	Betty Field
Newspapermen	John Gerstad, Charles Kindl, Allen Williams

STANDBYS: Mistress, Daughter, Frances Sternhagen;
Wife, Nurse, Carolyn Coates; Friend, Doctor, Wyman
Pendleton; Son, John Gerstad.

A Drama in two acts. The action takes place at the
present time.

General Manager: Michael Kasdan
Company Manager: Oscar Abraham
Press: Betty Lee Hunt, Harriett Trachtenberg,
Maria Pucci, Henry Luhrman
Stage Managers: Bruce A. Hoover, Charles Kindl

* Closed May 1, 1970 after 40 performances and 14
previews.

Martha Swope Photos

**Left: George Voskovec, Jessica Tandy,
Colleen Dewhurst**

Madeleine Sherwood

Jessica Tandy, Betty Field

**Kurt Peterson, Virginia Sandifur, Harvey Evans,
Marti Rolph Above: John McMartin
Top: "Loveland" showgirls**

WINTER GARDEN
Opened Sunday, April 4, 1971.*
Harold Prince in association with Ruth Mitchell
presents:

FOLLIES

Book, James Goldman; Music and Lyrics, Stephen
Sondheim; Directors, Harold Prince, Michael Bennett;
Choreography, Michael Bennett; Scenic Production,
Boris Aronson; Costumes, Florence Klotz; Lighting,
Tharon Musser; Musical Direction, Harold Hastings;
Orchestrations, Jonathan Tunick; Dance Music Arrange-
ments, John Berkman; Production Supervisor, Ruth
Mitchell; Associate Choreographer, Bob Avian; Produc-
tion Assistant, Ted Chapin; Hairstylist, Joe Tubens;
Make-up, Ted Azar; Original Cast Album by Capitol
Records.

CAST

Major-Domo	Dick Latessa
Sally Durant Plummer	Dorothy Collins
Young Sally	Marti Rolph
Christine Crane	Ethel Barrymore Colt
Willy Wheeler	Fred Kelly
Stella Deems	Mary McCarty
Max Deems	John J. Martin
Heidi Schiller	Justine Johnston
Chauffeur	John Grigas
Meredith Lane	Sheila Smith
Chet Richards	Peter Walker
Roscoe	Michael Bartlett
Deedee West	Helon Blount
Sandra Donovan	Sonja Levkova
Hattie Walker	Ethel Shutta
Young Hattie	Mary Jane Houdina
Emily Whitman	Marcie Stringer
Theodore Whitman	Charles Welch
Vincent	Victor Griffin
Vanessa	Jayne Turner
Young Vincent	Michael Misita
Young Vanessa	Graciela Daniele
Solange LaFitte	Fifi D'Orsay
Carlotta Campion	Yvonne De Carlo
Phyllis Rogers Stone	Alexis Smith
Benjamin Stone	John McMartin
Young Phyllis	Virginia Sandifur
Young Benjamin	Kurt Peterson
Buddy Plummer	Gene Nelson
Young Buddy	Harvey Evans
Dimitri Weismann	Arnold Moss
Kevin	Ralph Nelson
Young Heidi	Victoria Mallory

PARTY MUSICIANS: Taft Jordan, Aaron Bell, Charles
Spies, Robert Curtis

SHOWGIRLS: Suzanne Briggs, Trudy Carson, Kathie
Dalton, Ursula Maschmeyer, Linda Perkins, Margot
Travers

SINGERS AND DANCERS: Graciela Daniele, Mary
Jane Houdina, Rita O'Connor, Julie Pars, Suzanne
Rogers, Roy Barry, Steve Boockvor, Michael Misita,
Joseph Nelson, Ralph Nelson, Ken Urmston, Donald
Weissmuller.

STANDBYS AND UNDERSTUDIES: Phyllis, Carlotta,
Solange, Sheila Smith; Dimitri, Edwin Steffe; Buddy,
Dick Latessa; Sally, Heidi, Ethel Barrymore Colt; Benja-
min, Peter Walker; Christine, Hattie, Stella, Helon
Blount; Theodore, Major-domo, Fred Kelly; Vincent,
Donald Weissmuller; Vanessa, Sonja Levkova

MUSICAL NUMBERS: "Beautiful Girls," "Don't Look
at Me," "Waiting for the Girls Upstairs," "Rain on the
Roof," "Ah, Paris!," "Broadway Baby," "The Road You
Didn't Take," "Bolero d'Amour," "In Buddy's Eyes,"
"Who's That Woman?," "I'm Still Here," "Too Many
Mornings," "The Right Girl," "One More Kiss," "Could
I Leave You?," "Loveland," "You're Gonna Love To-
morrow," "Love Will See Us Through," "The God-Why-
Don't-You-Love-Me Blues," "Losing My Mind," "The
Story of Lucy and Jessie," "Live, Laugh, Love."

A Musical presented without intermission. The action
takes place at the present time on the stage of the
Weimann Theatre in New York.

General Manager: Carl Fisher
Press: Mary Bryant, Stanley F. Kaminsky, Sadie Stein
Stage Managers: Fritz Holt, George Martin,
John Grigas, Donald Weissmuller

* Still playing May 31, 1971. Recipient of New York
Drama Critics Circle Award as Best Musical of 1970-
71.

Martha Swope Photos

Sheila Smith, Ethel Barrymore Colt, Alexis Smith, Dorothy Collins, Helon Blount, Yvonne DeCarlo
Top: (L) Ursula Maschmeyer, Justine Johnston, John Grigas (R) Gene Nelson

ROYALE THEATRE

Opened Monday, March 29, 1971.*
Michael Myerberg, Peter Bridge and Eddie
Kulukundis, in association with Lawrence Shubert
Lawrence present:

HOW THE OTHER HALF LOVES

By Alan Ayckbourn; Director, Gene Saks; Setting,
David Mitchell; Costumes, Winn Morton; Lighting,
Peggy Clark; Production Executive, Tom Erhardt.

CAST

Fiona Foster	Bernice Massi
Teresa Phillips	Sandy Dennis
Frank Foster	Phil Silvers
Bob Phillips	Richard Mulligan
William Detweiler	Tom Aldredge
Mary Detweiler	Jeanne Hepple

Standby: Monica Moran

A Comedy in 2 acts and 4 scenes. The action takes
place at the present time in the living rooms of the
Fosters and the Phillipses.

General Manager: G. Warren McClane
Press: Harvey B. Sabinson, Lee Solters, Leo Stern,
Edie Kean
Stage Managers: Mortimer Halpern, Wayne Carson

* Closed June 26, 1971 after 104 performances and 8
previews.

Sandy Dennis, Jeanne Hepple
Top Right: Phil Silvers, Bernice Massi

BROADHURST THEATRE

Opened Thursday, April 15, 1971.*
Arthur Whitelaw in association with Seth Harrison presents:

70, GIRLS, 70

Book, Fred Ebb, Norman L. Martin; Based on play "Breath of Spring" by Peter Coke; Adaptation, Joe Masteroff; Music, John Kander; Lyrics, Fred Ebb; Director, Paul Aaron; Dances and Musical Numbers Staged by Onna White; Sets and Lighting, Robert Randolph; Costumes, Jane Greenwood; Musical Direction and Vocal Arrangements, Oscar Kosarin; Orchestrations, Don Walker; Dance Music, Dorothea Freitag; Associate Choreographer, Martin Allen; Hair Stylist, Joe Tubens; Entire Production Supervised by Stanley Prager; Original Cast Album by Columbia Records; Furs, Ben Kahn; Procuction Assistant, Tim Cope.

CAST

Thomas Anderson, Tommy Breslin, Hans Conried, Robert G. Dare, Sally DeMay, Joey Faye, Dorothea Freitag, Ruth Gillette, Lloyd Harris, Lillian Hayman, Henrietta Jacobson, Gil Lamb, Lucie Lancaster, Marjorie Leach, Abby Lewis, Steve Mills, Mildred Natwick, Naomi Price, Lillian Roth, Goldye Shaw, Beau Tilden, Bobbi Tremain, Jay Velie, Coley Worth

STANDBYS: Karen Gustafson, Nancy Andrews

MUSICAL NUMBERS: "Old Folks," "Home," "Broadway, My Street," "The Caper," "Coffee in a Cardboard Cup," "You and I, Love," "Do We?," "Hit It, Lorraine," "See the Light," "Boom Ditty Boom," "Believe," "Go Visit," "70, Girls, 70," "The Elephant Song," "Yes."

A Musical in 2 acts and 18 scenes with prologue. The action takes place at the present time in New York City.

General Manager: Marvin A. Krauss
Company Manager: David Wyler
Press: Max Eisen, Warren Pincus, Milly Schoenbaum
Stage Managers: Edwin P. Aldridge, Victor Straus, John Johann

* Closed May 15, 1971 after 35 performances and 9 previews.

Top: (L) Henrietta Jacobson, Tommy Breslin
(R) Gil Lamb, Mildred Natwick, Hans Conried

Jay Velie, Coley Worth, Lillian Roth, Thomas Anderson, Joey Faye Above: Coley Worth, Lucie Lancaster, Mildred Natwick, Joey Faye

LONGACRE THEATRE

Opened Saturday, April 24, 1971.*
Sandy Farber and Stanley Barnett in association
with Nate Friedman present:

FRANK MERRIWELL
(or Honor Challenged)

Book, Skip Redwine, Larry Frank, Heywood Gould;
Music and Lyrics, Skip Redwine, Larry Frank; Directed
and Choreographed by Neal Kenyon; Scenery, Tom
John; Costumes, Frank Thompson; Lighting John Gleason; Orchestrations, Arnold Goland; Musical Director,
Vocal Arrangements, Jack Lee; Conductor, Dance Arrangements, Jack Holmes; Associate Producer, Aaron
Ziegelman; Assistant Choreographer, Bonnie Ano; Production Coordinator, Don Eckstein.

CAST

Clyde	J. J. Jepson
Ned	Larry Ross
Hugh	Walter Bobbie
Belinda Belle Snodd	Neva Small
Snella Jean	Lori Cesar
Una Marie	Ellie Smith
Prof. Burrage	Thomas Ruisinger
Mrs. Snodd	Liz Sheridan
Esther Carmichael	Jennifer Williams
Bart Hodge	Peter Shawn
Tad Jones	Gary Keith Steven
Frank Merriwell	Larry Ellis
Inza Burrage	Linda Donovan
Manuel	Bill Hinnant

MUSICAL NUMBERS: "There's No School Like Our
School," "Howdy, Mr. Sunshine," "Prim and Proper,"
"Inza," "Look for the Happiness Ahead," "I'd Be Crazy
to Be Crazy over You," "Now It's Fall," "The Fallin'-
out-of-love Rag," "Frank, Frank, Frank" "In Real Life,"
"The Broadway of My Heart," "Winter's Here," "The
Pure in Heart," "Don't Turn His Picture to the Wall,"
"Manuel Your Friend," Finale.

A Musical in 2 acts and 12 scenes.

General Manager: Elias Goldin
Company Manager: Barry Hoffman
Press: Seymour Krawitz, Martin Shwartz,
Patricia McLean Krawitz
Stage Managers: Don Lamb, James Bernardi

* Closed April 24, 1971 after 1 performance and 7
previews.

Linda Donovan, Larry Ellis

Zodiac Photos

BILLY ROSE THEATRE

Opened Wednesday, May 5, 1971.*
David Black presents:

EARL OF RUSTON

Book and Lyrics, C. C. Courtney, Ragan Courtney; Music, Peter Link; Played by Goatleg; Director, C. C. Courtney; Designed by Neil Peter Jampolis; Production Manager, Martin Herzer; Production Assistant, Lilli Afan.

CAST

Earl	C. C. Courtney and Ragan Courtney
Leda Pearl Crump	Jean Waldo Beck
Herself	Leecy R. Woods Moore
Sheriff/Bass Guitar	Leon Medica
Mr. Turner/Lead Guitar	Bootsie Normand
Rev. Reynolds/Rhythm Guitar	Chip McDonald
Doctor/Drums	Bobby Thomas
Ernestine	Lynda Lawley
Mary Lee Woods	Bonnie Guidry
Pianist	John Bergeron

Standby: Terry Mace

MUSICAL NUMBERS: "Just Your Old Friend," "Earl Is Crazy," "Guitar Song," "Easy to Be Lonely," "Standing," "Der Blues," "Probably," "Mama, Earl Done Ate the Tooth Paste Again," "Silvers Theme," "Mama, Mama, Mama," "I've Been Sent Back to the First Grade," "The Revival," "My Name Is Leda Pearl," "Insane Poontang," "You Still Love Me," "Earl Was Ahead."

A Country Rocker Musical presented without intermission. The action takes place in Ruston, La.

General Manager: Jose Vega
Company Manager: R. Tyler Gatchell, Jr.
Press: Betty Lee Hunt, Henry Luhrman, Harriett Trachtenberg, Maria Pucci
Stage Managers: Alvarez Kelly, Errol Courtney

* Closed May 8, 1971 after 5 performances.

Zodiac Photos

Leecy R. Woods Moore, Ragan Courtney

Ragan Courtney, C.C. Courtney
Above: C. C. Courtney, Jean Waldo Beck

47

SCRATCH

By Archibald MacLeish; Suggested by Stephen Vincent Benet's short story "The Devil and Daniel Webster"; Director, Peter H. Hunt; Scenery, John Conklin; Costumes, Patricia Zipprodt; Lighting, Feder; Hairstyles, Ernest Adler; Makeup, Joseph Cranzano; Audio Design, Gary Harris.

CAST

Jabez Stone	Will Mackenzie
Daniel Webster	Patrick Magee
Scratch	Will Geer
Forbes	Daniel Keyes
Mrs. Forbes	Mary Loane
Susan	Joanne Nail
Porter Wright	Rex Robbins
Seth Peterson	Roy Poole
Judge Hathorne	Thomas Barbour

FARM HANDS AND JURY: Robert Baines, Philip Carling, Dominic Chianese, John Coe, William Francis, Walter Gorney, Richard Hamilton, Peter Harris, Dino Laudicina, Garnett Smith

UNDERSTUDIES: Jabez, Rex Robbins; Seth, Daniel Keyes; Forbes, Richard Hamilton; Mrs. Forbes, Joanne Nail; Judge, Walter Gorney; Wright, Robert Baines; Jury, Peter Blaxill.

A Play in four scenes with one intermission. The action takes place at Daniel Webster's farmhouse in Marshfield, Mass., and at Jabez Stone's farm in Cross-Corners, New Hampshire, in July of 1850.

General Managers: Joseph Harris, Ira Bernstein
Press: Harvey B. Sabinson, Lee Solters,
Cheryl Sue Dolby. Edie Kean
Stage Managers: Mark Healy, Lola Shumlin

* Closed May 8, 1971 after 4 performances and 4 previews.

Will Mackenzie, Will Geer, Patrick Magee

**Roy Poole, Patrick Magee
Above: Will Geer, Patrick Magee**

BROOKS ATKINSON THEATRE

Opened Wednesday, May 26, 1971.*
Jules Fisher, Marvin Worth, Michael Butler
present:

LENNY

By Julian Barry; Based on life and words of Lenny
Bruce; Music and Direction, Tom O'Horgan; Scenery,
Robin Wagner; Costumes, Randy Barcelo; Lighting,
Jules Fisher; Executive Producer, Ivor David Balding,
Production Assistants, Robyn Watson, Richard Pinter.

CAST

Lenny Bruce	Cliff Gorman
Judges, Sherman Hart, General, Vampire Priest, Plainclothesman, Mr. Wollenstein, Photographer	Joe Silver
Sally, Gypsy, Phone Operator	Erica Yohn
Rusty	Jane House
Arty, Igor, Hitler, Southern Gentleman, Photographer	Johnny Armen
Juan, Primitive Drummer, Cop	Marker Bloomst
Trumpet, Nod Out	Vaughn DeForest
Mema, Stripper, Lucille, R. C. Lady, Matron, Southern Lady	Jeannette Ertelt
Bass, Life Reporter, Cop	Ernie Furtado
Trombone, Nod Out	John Gordon
Ernie, Interviewer	Paul Lieber
Piano, Lawyer, Eichman	Warren Meyers
Saxophone, Clarinet, Flute, Nod Out	Ron Odrich
Girl in Wheel Chair	Jody Oliver
Stripper, Singer, Mrs. Hart, Secretary, Girl with I.D. Card	Melody Santangelo
Drums, Cop	Adam Smith
Clubowner, Father, Ike, Judge, D.A., Photographer	Robert Weil
Cop, Witchdoctor, Waiter, Bishop	James Wigfall

UNDERSTUDIES: Lenny, Johnny Armen; Mr. Silver,
Robert Weil; Misses Yohn and Santangelo, Jeannette
Ertelt; Misses House and Ertelt, Melody Santangelo;
Mr. Armen, Paul Lieber; Mr. Weil, Mr. Wigfall, Warren
Meyers; Messrs. Lieber, DeForest, Futado, Gordon,
Odrich, Smith, Marker Bloomst; Mr. Bloomst, Galen
McKinley

A Play in two acts. The action takes place between
1951 and 1966.

General Manager: James Walsh
Production Manager: Richard Seanga
Press: Gifford/Wallace
Stage Managers: Galen McKinley, Marker Bloomst

* Still playing May 31, 1971.

Martha Swope Photos

**Top: Melody Santangelo, Jane House,
Jeannette Ertelt**

**Cliff Gorman Above: Cliff Gorman,
Joe Silver (top), Johnny Armen**

IMPERIAL THEATRE

Opened Tuesday, September 22, 1964.*
(Moved Feb. 27, 1967 to Majestic; Dec. 14, 1970
to Broadway Theatre)
Harold Prince presents:

FIDDLER ON THE ROOF

Book, Joseph Stein; Based on Sholom Aleichem's
stories; Music, Jerry Bock; Lyrics, Sheldon Harnick;
Director-Choreographer, Jerome Robbins; Settings,
Boris Aronson; Costumes, Patricia Zipprodt; Lighting,
Jean Rosenthal; Orchestrations, Don Walker; Musical
Direction, Vocal Arrangements, Milton Greene; Dance
Music Arrangements, Betty Walberg; Hairstylist, D.
Rusty Bonaccorso; Original Cast Album by RCA Victor
Records.

CAST

Tevye	Paul Lipson†1
Golde	Peg Murray†2

Their daughters:

Tzeitel	Judith Smiley†3
Hodel	Adrienne Barbeau†4
Chava	Peggy Longo†5
Shprintze	Faye Menken†6
Bielke	Leslie Silvia†7
Yente	Florence Stanley
Motel	Peter Marklin
Perchik	Richard Morse†8
Mordcha	Zvee Scooler†9
Lazar Wolf	Boris Aplon
Rabbi	Sol Frieder
Mendel	James McDonald
Avram	Jerry Jarrett
Nachum	Reuben Schafer
Grandma Tzeitel	Anna Perez†10
Fruma-Sarah	Harriet Slaughter
Constable	Joseph Sullivan
Fyedka	John-Michael Savaige†11
Shandel	Elaine Kussack†12
The Fiddler	Ken LeRoy†13

VILLAGERS: Bagel Man, Dan Tylor; Streetsweeper,
Glen McClaskey; Fishmonger, Lorenzo Bianco; Seltzer
Man, Ben Gillespie; Surcha, Maralyn Nell; Woodsman,
Tony Gardell; Potseller, Victor Pieran; Grocer, Ross
Gifford; Baker, Peter DeNicola; Knifeseller, John Bar-
tholomew; Fredel, Gretchen Evans; Bluma, Lee Arthur;
Berille, Christine Jacobs; Mirala, Charlet Oberley; Sima,
Jill Harmon; Rivka, Ann Tell; Cobbler, Del Franklin;
Anya, Faye Menken; Hatmaker, Roger Briant; Vladimir,
Bill Bugh; Sasha, Fred Weiss.

UNDERSTUDIES: Tevye, Jerry Jarrett; Golde, Yente,
Laura Stuart; Tzeitel, Gretchen Evans; Hodel, Christine
Jacobs; Chava, Jill Harmon; Shprintze, Bielke, Faye
Menken; Perchik, John Bartholomew; Motel, James
McDonald; Fyedka, Fred Weiss; Rabbi, Reuben
Schafer; Nachum, Dan Tylor; Constable, Ross Gifford;
Mendel, Peter DeNicola; Lazar, Jerry Jarrett; Avram,
Reuben Schafer; Grandma, Lee Arthur; Fruma, Gret-
chen Evans; Shandel, Charlet Oberley; Fiddler, Roger
Briant; Mordcha, Tony Gardell

MUSICAL NUMBERS: "Tradition," "Matchmaker,
Matchmaker," "If I Were a Rich Man," "Sabbath
Prayer," "To Life," "Miracle of Miracles," "The Tailor,"
"Sunrise, Sunset," "Bottle Dance," "Wedding Dance,"
"Now I Have Everything," "Do You Love Me?," "I Just
Heard," "Far from the Home I Love," "Anatevka,"
Epilogue.

A Musical in two acts. The action takes place in
Anatevka, a village in Russia, in 1905 on the eve of the
revolutionary period.

General Manager: Carl Fisher
Company Manager: Warren O'Hara
Press: Sol Jacobson, Lewis Harmon
Stage Managers: Ruth Mitchell, Jay Jacobson,
Paul Waigner, David Wolf

* Still playing May 31, 1971. Winner of 1966 "Tony" for
Best Musical, NY Drama Critics Circle Citation. For
original production, see THEATRE WORLD, Vol. 21.

† Succeeded by: 1. Jerry Jarrett during vacation, 2. Mimi
Randolph for vacation, 3. Mimi Turque, 4. Susan
Hufford, 5. Peggy Atkinson, 6. Leslie Silvia, 7. Pamela
Greene, 8. Michael Zaslow, 9. Fyv Finkel for vacation,
10. Faye Menken, 11. Don Lawrence, Michael Petro,
12. Laura Stuart, 13. Marc Scott

Zodiac Photos

**Peg Murray, Peggy Atkinson, Paul Lipson, Susan
Hufford, Mimi Turque Above: Paul Lipson, Boris
Aplon Top: Paul Lipson, Peg Murray**

ANTA WASHINGTON SQUARE THEATRE

Opened Monday, November 22, 1965.*
(Moved to Martin Beck, March 19, 1968; to Eden, March 2, 1971; to Mark Hellinger, May 25, 1971)
Albert W. Selden and Hal James present:

MAN OF LA MANCHA

Book, Dale Wasserman; Music, Mitch Leigh; Lyrics, Joe Darion; Book and Musical Staging, Albert Marre; Choreography, Jack Cole; Settings and Lighting, Howard Bay; Costumes, Howard Bay, Patton Campbell; Musical Direction, R. Bennett Benetsky; Dance Arrangements, Neil Warner; Musical Arrangements, Music Makers; Hairstylist, Charles LoPresto; Technical Adviser, John Higgins; Production Assistant, Dwight Frye; Original Cast Album by Kapp Records.

CAST

Don Quixote (Cervantes)	Charles West†1
(matinees, Jack Dabdoub)	
Aldonza	Gaylea Byrne†2
(matinees, Emily Yancy†3)	
Innkeeper	Ray Middleton
Padre	Robert Rounseville
Dr. Carrasco	Timothy Jerome†4
Antonia	Dianne Barton
Barber	Leo Bloom
Pedro	Carmine Caridi†5
Anselmo	Wilson Robey
Housekeeper	Eleanore Knapp†6
Jose	Bert Michaels†7
Juan	John Aristides†8
Paco	Bill Stanton
Tenorio	Robert Rayow†12
Sancho	Titos Vandis†9
Maria	Rita Metzger†10
Dancing Horses	Bill Stanton, Bert Michaels†7
Horses	Leo Bloom, Carmine Caridi†5
Fermina	Marcia O'Brien†11
Captain of Inquisition	Renato Cibelli
Guitarist	Stephen Sahlein
Guards	Ray Dash, Angelo Nazzo, Jeff Killion, James Leverett

UNDERSTUDIES: Quixote, Innkeeper, Jack Dabdoub; Quixote, Carrasco, Renato Cibelli; Sancho, Eddie Roll, Wilson Robey; Aldonza, Dell Brownlee, Violet Santangelo; Innkeeper, Shev Rodgers, Renato Cibelli; Padre, Ralph Farnworth, Wilson Robey; Carrasco, Alfred Leberfeld; Barber, Eddie Roll, Alfred Leberfeld; Antonia, Fermina, Rosemary Harvey; Pedro, Jeff Killion; Maria, Violet Santangelo; Housekeeper, Louise Armstrong; Captain, Ray Dash; Swing Dancer, John Gorrin.

MUSICAL NUMBERS: "Man of LaMancha," "It's All the Same," "Dulcinea," "I'm Only Thinking of Him," "I Really Like Him," "What Does He Want of Me," "Little Bird," "Barber's Song," "Golden Helmet," "To Each His Dulcinea," "The Quest," "The Combat," "The Dubbing," "The Abduction," "Moorish Dance," "Aldonza," "Knight of the Mirrors," "A Little Gossip," "The Psalm."

A Musical Play suggested by the life and works of Miguel de Cervantes, and performed without intermission. All the characters are imprisoned in a dungeon in Seville at the end of the 16th Century. The entire action takes place there, and in various other places in the imagination of Cervantes.

Company Manager: Gino Giglio
Press: Merle Debuskey, Faith Geer
Stage Managers: James S. Gelb, Michael Turque, Al Leberfeld

* Closed June 26, 1971 after 2329 performances and 12 previews. Winner of 1966 "Tony" and NY Drama Critics Citation for Best Musical. For original production, see THEATRE WORLD, Vol. 22.

† Succeeded by: 1. Gideon Singer, David Atkinson, 2. Emily Yancy, 3. Dell Brownlee, 4. Ian Sullivan, 5. Shev Rodgers, 6. Rita Metzger, 7. Hector Mercado, 8. Robert Rayow, 9. Rudy Tronto, Edmond Varrato 10. Louise Armstrong, 11. Violet Santangelo, 12. Don Bonnell

Zodiac Photos

Eleanore Knapp, Robert Rounseville, Dianne Barton Above: David Atkinson Top: Emily Yancy, Gideon Singer, Rudy Tronto

51

**Guy Thomas, Lorrie Davis, Debbie Offner, Larry
Marshall, Singer Williams**

BILTMORE THEATRE
Opened Monday, April 19, 1968.*
Michael Butler presents:

HAIR

Book and Lyrics, Gerome Ragni, James Rado; Music,
Galt McDermot; Executive Producer, Bertrand Castelli;
Director, Tom O'Horgan; Assistant Director, Dan Sullivan; Dance Director, Julie Arenal; Musical Director,
Galt McDermot; Costumes, Nancy Potts; Scenery,
Robin Wagner; Lighting Jules Fisher; Hairstylist, Wig
City; Sound, Abe Jacob; Original Cast Album by RCA-
Victor Records.

CAST

Claude	Allan Nicholls†1
Berger	Oatis Stephens†2
Woof	Robin McNamara†3
Hud	Larry Marshall
Sheila	Victoria Medlin†4
Jeanie	Sally Eaton
Dionne	Joan Johnson†5
Crissy	Lillian Wong†6
Mother	Sally Eaton, Jonathan Kramer†7
	Obie Bray†8
Father	Rick Granat+9
	Debbie Offner+10, Larry Marshall†11
Principal	Rick Granat+12
	Debbie Offner+13, Larry Marshall†14
Tourist Couple	Jonathan Kramer†15, John Aman†9
Waitress	Debbie Offner†10
Young Recruit	Jonathan Kramer†11
General Grant	Rick Granat†8
Abraham Lincoln	Lorrie Davis†10
Sergeant	Obie Bray†16
Parents	Debbie Offner†17, Rick Granat†9

THE TRIBE: Zenobia Conkerite, Robbie Ferguson,
George Garcia, Gloria Goldman, Nat Grant, Delores
Hall, Fluffer Hirsch, Ursuline Kairson, Clifford Lipson,
Bobby London, Mary Mendum, Valerie Williams, Kathrynann Wright

UNDERSTUDIES: Berger, George Garcia, Larry Marshall; Hud, Nat Grant, Robalee Barnes; Claude, Allan
Braunstein; Woof, Fluffer Hirsch; Jeanie, Angie Ortega,
Valerie Williams; Crissy, Dale Soules; Sheila, Ursuline
Kairson, Gloria Goldman

MUSICIANS: Margaret Harris, Charlie Brown, Alan
Fontaine, Jimmy Lewis, Zane Paul, Donald Leight,
Eddy Williams, Warren Chaisson, Idris Muhammad

MUSICAL NUMBERS: "Aquarius," "Donna," "Hashish," "Sodomy," "Colored Spade," "Manchester," "Ain't
Got No," "Dead End," "I Believe in Love," "Air,"
"Initials," "I Got Life," "Going Down," "Hair," "My
Conviction," "Easy to Be Hard," "Don't Put It Down,"
"Frank Mills," "Be-In," "Where Do I Go," "Electric
Blues," "Black Boys," "White Boys," "Walking in
Space," "Abie Baby," "Three-Five–Zero-Zero," "What
a Piece of Work Is Man," "Good Morning Starshine,"
"The Bed," "The Flesh Failures," "Let the Sun Shine
In"

The American Tribal-Love Rock Musical in two acts.

Company Manager: William Orton
Press: Gifford/Wallace, Tom Trenkle
Stage Managers: Joe Donovan, Ronald Schaeffer

* Still playing May 31, 1971. For original NY production, see THEATRE WORLD, Vol. 24.

† Succeeded by: 1. Robin McNamara, 2. Steven Curry,
3. Alan Braunstein, 4. Marta Heflin, 5. Delores Hall, 6.
Shelley Plimpton, 7. Nat Grant, 8. Charles O. Lynch,
9. Clifford Lipson, 10. Valerie Williams, 11. Fluffer
Hirsch, 12. George Garcia, 13. Angie Ortega, 14.
Bobby Ferguson, 15. Bryan Spencer, 16. Robalee
Barnes, 17. Kathrynann Wright

Martha Swope Photos

**Top Left: Larry Marshall, Robin McNamara,
Allan Nicholls, Victoria Medlin, Oatis Stephens**

Jenny O'Hara, Norman Shelly, Anthony Roberts
Above: James Congdon, Jenny O'Hara

SAM S. SHUBERT THEATRE

Opened Sunday, December 1, 1968.*
David Merrick presents:

PROMISES, PROMISES

Book, Neil Simon; Based on Screenplay "The Apartment" by Billy Wilder, I. A. L. Diamond; Music Burt Bacharach; Lyrics, Hal David; Director, Robert Moore; Musical Numbers Staged by Michael Bennett; Settings, Robin Wagner; Costumes, Donald Brooks; Lighting, Martin Aronstein; Musical Direction, Dance Arrangements, Harold Wheeler; Orchestrations, Jonathan Tunick; Associate Producer, Samuel Liff; Assisstant Choreographer, Bob Avian; Hairstylist, Joe Tubens; Musical Director, Arthur Azenzer; Staff Associates, Sylvia Schwartz, John Bonanni, Linda Bate, Elizabeth Kaye; Original Cast Album by United Artists Records.

CAST

Chuck Baxter	Jerry Orbach†1
J. D. Sheldrake	Edward Winter†2
Fran Kubelik	Jill O'Hara†3
Bartender Eddie	Dick Sabol
Mr. Dobitch	Paul Reed
Sylvia Gilhooley	Adrienne Angel
Mr. Kirkeby	Ronn Carroll
Mr. Eichelberger	Henry Sutton
Vivien Della Hoya	Baayork Lee
Dr. Dreyfuss	Norman Shelly
Jesse Vanderhof	Dick O'Neill
Dentist's Nurse	Carolyn Kirsch†4
Company Nurse	Carole Bishop†5
Company Doctor	Joe Nelson†6
Peggy Olson	Millie Slavin
Lum Ding Hostess	Barbara Monte-Britton
Waiter	Gene Cooper
Madison Square Garden Attendant	Frank Pietri
Dining Room Hostess	Betsy Haug†7
Miss Polansky	Julane Stites†8
Miss Wong	Barbara Monte-Britton
Bartender Eugene	Frank Pietri
Marge MacDougall	Pam Zarit†9
Clancy's Employees	Eileen Casey, Carol Hanzel, Peggy Haug
Helen Sheldrake	Kay Oslin†10
Karl Kubelik	Dick Sabol
New Young Executive	Frank Newell
Interns and Dates	Barbara Alston, Carol Hanzel, Bob Fitch, John Medeiros
Orchestra Voices	Rei Golenor, Bettye McCormick, Ilona Simon, Ilene Graff

CLANCY'S LOUNGE PATRONS: Eileen Taylor, Jacki Garland, Pam Blair, Dick Korthaze, John Medeiros, Scott Pearson, Sandra West, Oscar Antony

UNDERSTUDIES: Fran, Ilene Graff; Dobitch, Dick O'Neill; Vanderhof, Henry Sutton; Eichelberger, Ronn Carroll; Kirkeby, Dick Korthaze; Peggy, Carol Hanzel; Marge, Rei Golenor; Vivien, Barbara Monte-Britton; Karl, Frank Pietri; Sylvia, Carol Hanzel; Swing Dancers, Debra Lyman, Andy Bew

MUSICAL NUMBERS: "Half as Big as Life," "Upstairs," "You'll Think of Someone," "Our Little Secret," "She Likes Basketball," "Knowing When to Leave," "Where Can You Take a Girl," "Wanting Things," "Turkey Lurkey Time," "A Fact Can Be a Beautiful Thing," "Whoever You Are," "A Young Pretty Girl Like You," "I'll Never Fall in Love Again," "Promises, Promises."

A Musical in 2 acts and 14 scenes. The action takes place at the present time in New York.

General Manager: Jack Schlissel
Press: Harvey B. Sabinson, Lee Solters, Marilynn LeVine
Stage Managers: Charles Blackwell, Henry Velez, Robert St. Clair

* Still playing May 31, 1971. For original production see THEATRE WORLD, Vol. 25.

† Succeeded by: 1. Anthony Roberts, 2. James Congdon, 3. Jenny O'Hara, 4. Sandra West, 5. Eileen Taylor, 6. Andy Bew, 7. Peggy Haug, 8. Barbara Alston, 9. Mary Louise Wilson, 10. Marylou Sirinek

Martha Swope Photos

**Top Left: Mary Louise Wilson, Anthony Roberts
Below: Dick O'Neill, Henry Sutton, Anthony
Roberts, Ronn Carroll, Paul Reed**

FORTY-SIXTH STREET THEATRE
Opened Sunday, March 16, 1969.*
(Moved Apr. 26, 1971 to Majestic)
Stuart Ostrow presents:

1776

Book, Peter Stone; Based on conception by Sherman Edwards; Music and Lyrics, Sherman Edwards; Scenery and Lighting, Jo Mielziner; Costumes, Patricia Zipprodt; Musical Direction, Peter Howard; Orchestrations, Eddie Sauter; Director, Peter Hunt; Musical Numbers Staged by Onna White; Dance Music Arrangements, Peter Howard; Vocal Arrangements, Elise Bretton; Hairstylist, Ernest Adler; Assistant to Producer, Judy Korman; Original Cast Album by Columbia Records.

CAST

John Hancock, President of the Continental Congress	Charles Cioffi†1
Dr. Josiah Bartlett, N. H	Paul-David Richards
John Adams, Mass.	William Daniels†2
Stephen Hopkins, R. I.	Roy Poole†3
Roger Sherman, Conn.	David Vosburgh
Lewis Morris, N.Y.	Ronald Kross†4
Robert Livingston, N.Y.	Henry LeClair
Rev. Jonathan Witherspoon, N.J.	Charles Rule†5
Benjamin Franklin, Pa.	Howard DaSilva
John Dickinson, Pa.	Paul Hecht†6
James Wilson, Pa.	Emory Bass
Caesar Rodney, Dela.	Robert Gaus
Col. Thomas McKean, Dela.	Bruce MacKay
George Read, Dela.	Duane Bodin
Samuel Chase, Md.	Philip Polito†7
Richard Henry Lee, Va	Ronald Holgate†8
Thomas Jefferson, Va	Peter Lombard†9
Joseph Hewes, N.C.	William Stenson
Edward Rutledge, S.C.	John Cullum
Dr. Lyman Hall, Ga.	Edmund Lyndeck†10
Charles Thomson, Secretary	Ralston Hill
Andrew McNair, Custodian	William Duell
A Leather Apron	B. J. Slater
Courier	Scott Jarvis
Abigail Adams	Virginia Vestoff
Martha Jefferson	Mary Bracken Phillips†11

UNDERSTUDIES: Franklin, Bruce MacKay; Dickinson, James Noble; Rutledge, Paul-David Richards; Hancock, McKean, Charles Rule; Thomson, Edmund Lyndeck; Courier, B. J. Slater,; Abigail, Martha, Chris Callan; Jefferson, Lee, Evan Thompson; Hall, Stanley Simmonds; Rodney, David Vosburgh; Wilson, Hopkins, Ronald Kross; McNair, Duane Bodin; Adams, Paul-David Richards; Franklin, Charles Rule; General Understudies, Arthur Anderson, Evan Thompson.

MUSICAL NUMBERS: "Sit Down, John," "Piddle, Twiddle and Resolve," "Till Then," "The Lees of Virginia," "But, Mr. Adams," "Yours, Yours, Yours," "He Plays the Violin," "Cool, Cool, Considerate Men," "Momma Look Sharp," "The Egg," "Molasses to Rum," "Is Anybody There?"

A Musical Play in 7 scenes, presented with one intermission. The action takes place in May, June, and July of 1776 in a single setting representing the Chamber and Anteroom of the Continental Congress in Philadelphia, and certain reaches of John Adams' mind.

General Managers: Joseph Harris, Ira Bernstein
Press: Harvey B. Sabinson, Lee Solters, Sandra Manley
Stage Managers: Peter Stern, Lee Murray, Herman Magidson

* Still playing May 31, 1971. Winner of 1969 "Tony" and NY Drama Critics Circle Awards. For original production see THEATRE WORLD, Vol. 25.

† Succeeded by: 1. Roy Cooper, James Noble, 2. John Cunningham, 3. Edmund Lyndeck, 4. Stanley Simmonds, 5. Philip Polito, 6. David Ford, 7. Charles Rule, 8. Gary Oakes, 9, Brian Foley, 10. Ronald Kross, 11. Betty Buckley, Pamela Hall

Martha Swope Photos

Top Left: John Cullum, John Cunningham, Brian Foley, Howard DaSilva

Brian Foley, Howard DaSilva, John Cunningham

BOOTH THEATRE

Opened Tuesday, October 21, 1969.*
Arthur Whitelaw, Max J. Brown, Byron Goldman present:

BUTTERFLIES ARE FREE

By Leonard Gershe; Director, Milton Katselas; Set, Richard Seger; Costumes, Robert Mackintosh; Lighting, Jules Fisher; Associate Producer, Ruth Bailey; Hairstylist, Joe Tubens; Title Song, Steve Schwartz.

CAST

Don Baker	Keir Dullea†1
Jill Tanner	Blythe Danner†2
Mrs. Baker	Eileen Heckart†3
Ralph Austin	Michael Glaser

STANDBYS: Don, Ralph, Richard Backus; Jill, Karen Grassle; Mrs. Baker, Patricia Wheel

A Comedy in 2 acts and 2 scenes. The action takes place at the present time in Don Baker's apartment on East llth Street in New York.

General Manager: Marvin A. Krauss
Company Manager: David Wyler
Press: Max Eisen, Warren Pincus, Milly Schoenbaum
Stage Managers: Elizabeth Caldwell, Preston Fischer

* Still playing May 31, 1971. Blythe Danner won "Tony" Award for Best Supporting Actress. For original production, see THEATRE WORLD, Vol. 26.

† Succeeded by: 1. Kipp Osborne, 2. Kathleen Miller, 3. Rosemary Murphy, 4. Tom Fucello, Robert Anthony, Richard Fasciano

Top Left: Keir Dullea, Eileen Heckart, Blythe Danner Below: Rosemary Murphy, Kathleen Miller

Kipp Osborne, Kathleen Miller

Kipp Osborne

EUGENE O'NEILL THEATRE
Opened Sunday, December 28, 1969.*
Saint-Subber presents:

LAST OF THE RED HOT LOVERS

By Neil Simon; Director, Robert Moore; Scenic Production, Oliver Smith; Costumes, Donald Brooks; Lighting, Peggy Clark; Hairstylist, Joe Tubens, Michael Chianese; Production Supervisor, Tom Porter.

CAST

Barney Cashman	James Coco†1
Elaine Navazio	Linda Lavin†2
Bobbie Michele	Marcia Rodd†3
Jeanette Fisher	Doris Roberts

STANDBYS: Barney, Tom Lacy; Elaine, Rita Gardner; Bobbi, Carol Richards; Jeanette, Stella Longo

A Comedy in 3 acts. The action takes place at the present time in an apartment in the East 30's in Manhattan.

General Manager: C. Edwin Knill
Company Manager: James Turner
Press: Harvey B. Sabinson, Lee Solters, Cheryl Sue Dolby
Stage Managers: James Bernardi, Philip Cusack

* Still playing May 31, 1971. For original production, see THEATRE WORLD, Vol. 26.

† Succeeded by: 1. A. Larry Haines for vacation, Dom DeLuise, 2. Rita Moreno, Cathryn Damon, 3. Barbara Sharma, Carol Richards

James Coco, Doris Roberts Above: James Coco, Barbara Sharma (R) Rita Moreno, James Coco

Opened Sunday, March 15, 1970.*
(Moved to Winter Garden Dec. 15, 1970; to
ANTA Mar. 15, 1971)
Philip Rose presents:

PURLIE

Book, Ossie Davis, Philip Rose, Peter Udell; Based on
Play "Purlie Victorious" by Ossie Davis; Music, Gary
Geld; Lyrics, Peter Udell; Director, Philip Rose; Chore-
ographer, Louis Johnson; Scenery, Ben Edwards; Light-
ing, Thomas Skelton; Costumes, Ann Roth; Hairstylist,
Ernest Adler; Orchestrations-Choral Arrangements,
Garry Sherman, Luther Henderson; Musical Supervisor,
Garry Sherman; Musical Conductor, Joyce Brown;
Dance Music Arranged by Luther Henderson; Original
Cast Album by AMPEX Records.

CAST

Purlie	Cleavon Little
Church Soloist	Linda Hopkins
Lutiebelle	Melba Moore†1
Missy	Novella Nelson†2
Gitlow	Sherman Hensley
Charlie	C. David Colson
Idella	Helen Martin
Ol' Cap'n	John Heffernan

DANCERS: Loretta Abbott, Hope Clarke, Pattie Harris,
Lavinia Hamilton, Arlene Rolant, Ella Thompson,
Myrna White, Morris Donaldson, George Faison, Al
Perryman, Michael Peters, William Taylor, Andy Torres

SINGERS: Carolyn Byrd, Vera Moore, Denise Elliott,
Synthia Jackson, Mildred Lane, Alyce Webb, Mildred
Pratcher, Peter Colly, Milt Grayson, Ray Pollard, Tony
Middleton, Ted Ross

UNDERSTUDIES: Purlie, Morgan Freeman; Lutiebelle;
Synthia Jackson; Gitlow, Ted Ross; Cap'n, Charlie, Curt
Williams; Swing Dancer, Ted Goodridge; Missy, Idella,
Alyce Webb

MUSICAL NUMBERS: "Walk Him up the Stairs,"
"New Fangled Preacher Man," "Skinnin' a Cat,"
"Purlie," "The Harder They Fall," "Charlie's Songs,"
"Big Fish, Little Fish," "I Got Love," "Great White
Father," "Down Home," "First Thing Monday Mornin',"
"He Can Do It," "The World Is Comin' to a Start,"
"Walk Him up the Stairs."

A Musical in 2 acts and 6 scenes, with prologue and
epilogue. The action takes place in South Georgia not
too long ago.

General Manager: Helen Stern Richards
Press: Merle Debuskey, Faith Geer
Stage Managers: Leonard Auerbach, Jerry Laws,
Bert Wood

* Still playing May 31, 1971. For original production, see
THEATRE WORLD, Vol. 26.

† Succeeded by: 1. Patti Jo, 2. Carol Jean Lewis

Zodiac Photos

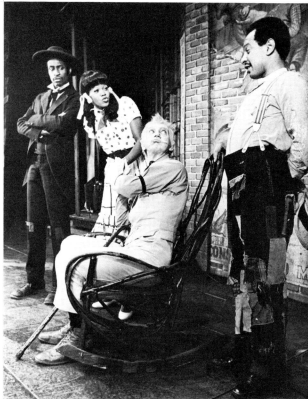

**Sherman Hemsley, Carol Jean Lewis, Patti Jo,
Cleavon Little Top Right: Cleavon Little, Patti Jo**

**Cleavon Little, Patti Jo, John Heffernan,
Sherman Hemsley**

PALACE THEATRE

Opened Monday, March 30, 1970.*
Joseph Kipness and Lawrence Kasha in association with Nederlander Productions and George M. Steinbrenner III present:

APPLAUSE

Book, Betty Comden, Adolph Green; Based on film "All About Eve" and original short story by Mary Orr; Music, Charles Strouse; Lyrics, Lee Adams; Director-Choreographer, Ron Field; Scenery, Robert Randolph; Costumes, Ray Aghanyan; Lighting, Tharon Musser; Musical Direction-Vocal Arrangements, Donald Pippin; Orchestrations, Philip J. Lang; Dance and Incidental Music Arranged by Mel Marvin; Production Associate, Phyllis Dukore; Directorial Assistant, Otto Pirchner; Choreographic Assistant, Tom Rolla; Hairstylist, Joe Tubens; Original Cast album by ABC Records.

CAST

Tony Announcer	John Anania
Tony Host	Alan King
Margo Channing	Lauren Bacall
Eve Harrington	Penny Fuller
Howard Benedict	Robert Mandan
Bert	Tom Urich
Buzz Richards	Brandon Maggart
Bill Sampson	Len Cariou†1
Duane Fox	Lee Roy Reams
Karen Richards	Ann Williams†2
Bartender	Jerry Wyatt
Peter	John Anania
Bob	Howard Kahl†3
Piano Player	Orrin Reiley
Stan Harding	Ray Becker
Danny	Bill Allsbrook
Bonnie	Bonnie Franklin
Carol	Carol Petri
Joey	Mike Misita†4
TV Director	Orrin Reiley
Autograph Seeker	Carol Petri
Musicians	Gene Kelton, Nat Horne, David Anderson

SINGERS: Patti Davis, Peggy Hagan, Gail Nelson, Jeannette Seibert, Merrill Leighton, John Herbert, Orrin Reiley, Jerry Wyatt

DANCERS: Renee Baughman, Joan Bell, Debi Carpenter, Patti D'Beck, Bonnie Walker, Marybeth Kurdock, Carol Petri, Bill Allsbrook, David Anderson, Wayne Boyd, John Cashman, Nikolas Dante, Gene Foote, Gene Kelton, Nat Horne, Christopher Chadman, Ed Nolfi, Sammy Williams

UNDERSTUDIES: Eve, Patti Davis; Bill, Tom Urich; Howard, John Anania; Buzz, Ray Becker; Karen, Peggy Hagan; Duane, Gene Foote; Bonnie, Carol Petri; Bert, Stan, Jerry Wyatt; Peter, Lanier Davis

MUSICAL NUMBERS: "Backstage Babble," "Think How It's Gonna Be," "But Alive," "The Best Night of My Life," "Who's That Girl?," "Applause," "Hurry Back," "Fasten Your Seat Belts," "Welcome to the Theatre," "Inner Thoughts," "Good Friends," "She's No Longer a Gypsy," "One of a Kind," "One Halloween," "Something Greater," Finale.

A Musical in 2 acts and 16 scenes. The action takes place at the present time in and around New York City.

General Manager: Philip Adler
Company Manager: S. M. Handelsman
Press: Bill Doll & Co., Cindy Reagan, Dick Williams, Virginia Holden, Susan L. Schulman
Stage Managers: Terence Little, Donald Christy, Lanier Davis, John Herbert

* Still playing May 31, 1971. Winner of "Tony" Awards for Best Musical, Best Director, Best Choreographer, Best Actress in a Musical (Miss Bacall). For original production, see THEATRE WORLD, Vol. 26.

† Succeeded by: 1. Keith Charles, 2. Gwyda DonHowe, 3. John Herbert, 4. Christopher Chadman, Gene Foote for Mr. Reams' vacation, Patti Davis for Miss Fuller's vacation, Carol Petri for Miss Franklin's, Renee Baughman for Miss Petri.

Top Left: Bonnie Franklin Below: Brandon Maggart, Ann Williams, Lauren Bacall

**Lauren Bacall, Lee Roy Reams, Sammy Williams
Above: Penny Fuller, Len Cariou**

Penny Fuller Above: Lee Roy Reams, Bonnie Franklin

Lauren Bacall, and above with Len Cariou

ALVIN THEATRE

Opened Sunday, April 26, 1970.*
Harold Prince in association with Ruth Mitchell
presents:

COMPANY

Music and Lyrics, Stephen Sondheim; Book, George
Furth; Director, Harold Prince; Sets and Projections,
Boris Aronson; Costumes, D. D. Ryan; Lighting, Robert
Ornbo; Musical Director, Harold Hastings; Orchestra-
tions, Jonathan Tunick; Dance Music Arrangements,
Wally Harper; Musical Numbers Staged by Michael
Bennett; Production Supervisor, Ruth Mitchell; Associ-
ate Choreographer, Bob Avian; Hairstylists, Robert
Vega, Mr. Vincent; Original Cast Album by Columbia
Records.

CAST

Robert	Larry Kert
Sarah	Barbara Barrie
Harry	Charles Kimbrough[1]
Susan	Merle Louise[2]
Peter	John Cunningham[3]
Jenny	Teri Ralston[4]
David	George Coe[5]
Amy	Beth Howland[6]
Paul	Steve Elmore
Joanne	Elaine Stritch[7]
Larry	Charles Braswell[8]
Marta	Pamela Myers
Kathy	Donna McKechnie
April	Susan Browning

VOCAL MINORITY: Cathy Corkill, Carol Gelfand,
Marilyn Saunders, Dona D. Vaughn

UNDERSTUDIES: Robert, Kenneth Cory; Joanne,
Sandra Deel; David, Paul, Robert Carle; Harry, Larry,
Bob Roman; Kathy, Priscilla Lopez; Amy, Sarah, Audre
Johnston; April, Jenny, Charlotte Frazier; Marta, Mar-
ilyn Saunders

MUSICAL NUMBERS: "Company," "The Little Things
You Do Together," "Sorry-Grateful," "You Could Drive
a Person Crazy," "Have I Got a Girl for You," "Some-
one Is Waiting," "Another Hundred People," "Getting
Married Today," "Side by Side by Side," "What Would
We Do Without You?," "Poor Baby," "Tick Tock,"
"Barcelona," "The Ladies Who Lunch," "Being Alive."

A Musical Comedy in two acts. The action takes place
at the present time in New York City.

General Manager: Carl Fisher
Company Manager: John Caruso
Press: Mary Bryant, Stanley F. Kaminsky, Sadie Stein
Stage Managers: Ben Strobach, Bob Burland

* Still playing May 31, 1971. Winner of 1971 "Tony"
Award for Best Musical. For original production, see
THEATRE WORLD, Vol. 26.

† Succeeded by: 1. Charles Braswell, 2. Alice Cannon,
Charlotte Frazier, 3. Kenneth Cory, 4. Jane Johnstone,
5. Lee Goodman, 6. Marian Hailey, 7. Jane Russell, 8.
Stanley Grover

Zodiac Photos

**Top Right: Charles Braswell, Elaine Stritch
Below: Barbara Barrie, Larry Kert, Kenneth
Kimmins**

George Wallace, Larry Kert, Jane A. Johnston

Marian Hailey Above: Larry Kert, Stanley
Grover, Jane Russell

Annie McGreevey, Susan Browning, Brenda
Thomson Above: Susan Browning, Larry Kert

BROADWAY PRODUCTIONS FROM OTHER SEASONS THAT CLOSED DURING THIS SEASON

Title	Opened	Closed	Performed
Hello, Dolly!	Jan. 16, 1964	Dec. 27, 1970	2844
Plaza Suite	Feb. 14, 1968	Oct. 3, 1970	1097
Forty Carats	Dec. 26, 1968	Nov. 7, 1970	780
Child's Play	Feb. 17, 1970	Dec. 12, 1970	343
Coco	Dec. 18, 1969	Oct. 3, 1970	333
Borstal Boy	Mar. 31, 1970	Aug. 1, 1970	143
The Boy Friend	Apr. 14, 1970	July 18, 1970	119

OFF-BROADWAY
PRODUCTIONS

GARRICK THEATRE

Began previews Wednesday, April 22, 1970.*
Ken Gaston and Leonard Goldberg present:

CIRCLE IN THE WATER

By Gerry Raad; Adapted and Directed by Jerry
Douglas; Design and Lighting, Leo Meyer; Production
Assistant, Brian Richmond.

CAST

Cadet Lt. Frank Ramsey	Laurence Manning
Cadet Lt. Clifford Blake	Michael Petro
Cadet Lt. Scott Coleman	Ted Wuerffel
Cadet Pvt. Mark Windon	Dean Tait
Cadet Sgt. Dirk Van Steed	Martin Kove
Elsie McBride	Davay Holland
Cadet Lt. Gregg Chandler	Calvin Culver

A Melodrama in 2 acts. The action takes place at the
present time at a ski lodge in northern Michigan at end
term of Creighton Military Academy.

General Manager Don Slaton
Press: Samuel Lurie
Stage Managers: Schorling Schneider, James DiAngelo

* Closed June 28, 1970 after 85 previews only.

Van Williams Photos

Right: Calvin Culver, Larry Manning

**Above: Martin Kove, Michael Petro, Calvin
Culver**

**Sydney Walker, Robert Brink, Maxine Herman,
Roy R. Scheider**

CHERRY LANE THEATRE

Opened Monday June 1, 1970*
Don Parker in association with Stanley J. Hatoff
presents:

THE NUNS

By Eduardo Manet; Adapted by Don Parker and Paul
Verdier; Director, Paul Verdier; Sets, Peter Harvey;
Costumes, Rita Riggs; Lighting, F. Mitchell Dana;
Production Associate, Sandra Berke; Assistant to the
Producers, Walter Stratton; Production Assistants, Diane
Singer, Dean Tulipane.

CAST

Mother Superior	Thayer David
Sister Angela	Roy R. Scheider
Sister Inez	Robert Brink
The Senora	Maxine Herman

A Parable in two acts. The action takes place in Haiti
at the time of the revolution of the slaves.

General Managers: George Thorn, Leonard A. Mulhern
Company Manager: Gary Fifield
Press: Betty Lee Hunt Associates, Henry Luhrman,
Ellen Levene, Harriett Trachtenberg
Stage Manager: Elissa Lane

* Closed June 1, 1970 after 1 performance.

Zodiac Photo

THEATRE DE LYS

Opened Wednesday June 3, 1970.*
Bruce W. Paltrow and Mitchell Fink by special arrangement with Lucille Lortel Productions, Inc. present:

WHISPERS ON THE WIND

Book and Lyrics, John B. Kuntz; Music, Lor Crane; Director, Burt Brinckerhoff; Scenery and Lighting, David F. Segal; Costumes, Joseph G. Aulisi; Musical Director, Jack Holmes; Orchestrations and Musical Supervision, Arthur Rubinstein; Musical Consultant, Wally Harper; Technical Director, John Beven; Production Assistant, Judy Binus.

CAST

Narrator .... David Cryer
First Woman .... Nancy Dussault
First Man .... Patrick Fox
Second Man .... R. G. Brown
Second Woman .... Mary Louise Wilson

MUSICAL NUMBERS: "Whispers on the Wind," "Welcome Little One," "Midwestern Summer," "Why and Because," "Children's Games," "Miss Cadwallader," "Upstairs-Downstairs," "Strawberries," "Is There a City?," "Carmen Viscenzo," "Neighbors," "Apples & Raisins," "Things Are Going Nicely," "It Won't Be Long," "Prove I'm Really Here," Finale.

A Musical in two acts.

General Manager: Paul B. Berkowsky
Company Manager: Bob MacDonald
Press: Max Eisen, Warren Pincus, Milly Schoenbaum
Stage Managers: Iris O'Connor, Robert Nigro

* Closed Wednesday, June 10, 1970 after 9 performances and 13 previews.

**Right: Nancy Dussault, David Cryer
Above: R.G. Brown, Nancy Dussault, David Cryer, Patrick Fox, Mary Louise Wilson**

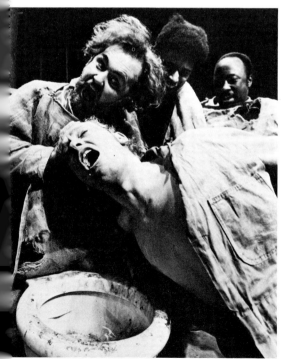

Randolph Dobbs, Rick Cluchey, Robert Poole, Ernie Allen

PLAYHOUSE THEATRE

Opened Thursday, June 18, 1970.*
David Carroll presents the Barbwire Theatre Production of:

THE CAGE

By Rick Cluchey; Director, Kenneth Kitch; Setting and Lighting, Jonathan Stuart.

CAST

Hatchet .... Rick Cluchey
Al .... Robert Poole
Doc .... Ernie Allen
Jive .... Randolph Dobbs
Guard Captain .... Henry Everhart
Guard Lieutenant .... Gene Ackley

A Drama in one act, followed by a question and answer period.

Press: Robert Ganshaw
Production Manager: Jonathan Stuart

* Closed June 28, 1970 after 14 performances. Reopened July 7, 1970 at Actors Playhouse, and closed there Nov. 15, 1970.

Lee Owens-Patrick Owens Photos

CIRCLE THEATRE

Opened Thursday, June 11, 1970.*
The World Cultural Center of the Council for International Recreation, Culture, and Lifelong Education (Dr. Harry H. Lerner, Executive Director) presents the Circle Theatre Company in repertory in:

THE THREE SISTERS

By Anton Chekhov; Director, Marshall W. Mason; Set, Ronald Radice; Lighting, Toby Mailman, Steve Askinazy; Visual Effects, Communicados; Technical Director, Lance Taylor, Jr.; Managing Director, Rob Thirkield; Artistic Director, Marshall W. Mason; Administrative Director, Tanya B. Thirkield; Executive Producer, Beverly Landau.

CAST

(Traditional Production)

Olga Sergeyevna Prozorov ....Jane Lowry
Irina Sergeyevna Prozorov ....Suzanne Pred
Marya Sergeyevna Prozorov ....Stephanie Gordon
Anfisa ....Dawn Gray
Baron Nikolai Lvovich Tusenbach.......Roddy O'Connor
Vassily Vassilyevich Solyony..........................Lee DeRoss
Ivan Romanovich Chebutykin ....Robert Frink
Ferapont ....Rob Thirkield
A Maid ....Patricia Carey
Alexander Ignatyevich Vershinin.................David Stekol
Andrey Sergeyevich Prozorov ....Antony Tenuta
Fyodor Ilych Kulygin ....Burke Pearson
Natalya Ivanovna ....Tanya Berezin
Alexei Petrovich Fedotik ....Michael Fesenmeier
Vladimir Karlovich Rode..........................Joseph DeJohn
A Lieutenant...Ronald Radice
A Maid ....Conchata Ferrell

A Drama in four acts. The action takes place on the Prozorov's estate between 1896 and 1900.

Opened Friday, June 12, 1970.*

(Experimental Production)

Olga...Sharon Ann Madden
Irina...Beth Bowden
Masha...Marina Stefan
Tusenbach ....David Starkweather
Chebutykin...Rob Thirkield
Solyony ....Matthew Silverman
Anfisa ....Berrilla Kerr
Ferapont ....Michael Fesenmeier
Vershinin......................................Joseph Campbell Butler
Andrey...Bob Shields
Kulygin ....Steve DeFleuter
Natasha ....Alice Tweedie
Fedotik ....Lance Taylor, Jr.
Rode...Frank Meyer
Maid ....Conchata Ferrell

Presented in two acts. The time is now and here.

* Closed July 3, 1970 after a limited engagement of 20 performances in repertory.

Malcolm E. Barker Photos

Top Left: Stephanie Gordon, Jane Lowry, Suzanne Pred

Experimental "Three Sisters"

CIRCLE IN THE SQUARE
Opened Monday June 22, 1970.*
Theodore Mann, Paul Libin in association with
John Berry presents:

BOESMAN AND LENA

By Athol Fugard; Director, John Berry; Set, Karl
Eigsti; Lighting, David F. Segal; Costumes, Margie
Goldsmith; Production Manager, Charles Hamilton;
Production Assistant, Penelope H. Parkhurst.

CAST

Boesman ....James Earl Jones†1
Lena ....Ruby Dee
Old African..................................Zakes Mokae†2

A Drama in 1 act. The action takes place in the mud
flats of the river Swartkaps, South Africa.

Press: Merle Debuskey, M. J. Boyer, Faith Geer
Stage Manager: Jan Moerel

* Closed Jan. 24, 1971 after 205 performances.

† Succeeded by: 1. Zakes Mokae, 2. Paul Benjamin

Zodiac Photos

Zakes Mokae, James Earl Jones, Ruby Dee

ASTOR PLACE THEATRE

Opened Saturday June 27, 1970.*
Jeff Barry Enterprises, Inc. / Ellen Stewart-Bruce
Mailman in association with The Theatre Of The
Eye Repertory Company 1970 present:

THE DIRTIEST SHOW IN TOWN

By Tom Eyen; Director, Tom Eyen; Set, T. E. Mason;
Lighting, Steve Whitson; Costumes, Victor Bijou; Music,
Jeff Barry.

CAST

Blonde...Madeleine le Roux
Brunette..Jennifer Mitchell
Jet Black ....Sommer Sally
Redhead...Elsa Tresko
Jonathan...........................Paul Matthew Eckhart
Cyril ....Jeffrey Herman
Lawrence..Bradford Riley
Blonde Bird Watcher................................Robert Schrock
Second Sergeant..Arthur Morey
Jiffy Mover ....R A. Dow†1
Stoned Angel...Ellen Gurin

A Documentary of the destructive effects of air, water,
and mind pollution in New York City.

General Manager Albert Poland
Press: Saul Richman, Peggy Mitchell
Stage Manager: Bonnie Gable

* Still playing May 31, 1971.

† Succeeded by Mark Russel

Entire Company Top Right: R.A. Dow, Madeleine le Roux

TRUCK AND WAREHOUSE THEATRE

Opened Tuesday, June 30, 1970.*
Ivor David Balding presents:

STEAMBATH

By Bruce Jay Friedman; Director, Anthony Perkins;
Scenery, David Mitchell; Lighting, Jules Fisher; Costumes, Joseph G. Aulisi; Special Visual Effects, Marvin
Torffield; Choreographer, Grover Dale; Associate Producer, Richard Scanga; A 54th Street Landlord Company, Inc. Production.

CAST

Old Timer	Conrad Bain
Tandy	Anthony Perkins†
Bieberman	Marvin Lichterman
Young Man	Jere Admire
Young Man	Teno Pollick
Gottlieb	Gabor Morea
Meredith	Annie Rachel
Broker	Mitchell Jason
Attendant	Hector Elizondo
Longshoreman	Jack Knight
Young Girl	Eileen Dietz
Flanders	Alfred Hinckley

A Comedy in two acts. The action takes place at the
present time in a steambath.

General Manager: William Craver
Press: Shirley Herz, Mary Thomas
Stage Managers: Robert Pitman, Alfred Hinckley

* Closed Oct. 18, 1970 after 127 performances.

† Played in previews by Dick Shawn, Rip Torn, Charles
Grodin.

Ted Yaple Photos

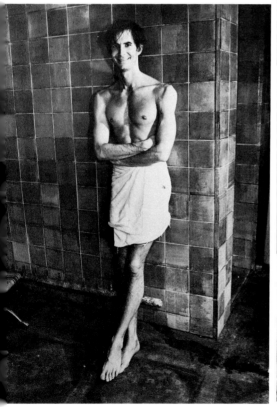

**Anthony Perkins Top Right: Hector Elizondo,
Mitchell Jason, Anthony Perkins, Conrad Bain**

**Anthony Perkins, Eileen Dietz
Above: Hector Elizondo**

JONES BEACH THEATRE
Opened Wednesday, July 1, 1970.*
Guy Lombardo presents:

THE SOUND OF MUSIC

Music, Richard Rodgers; Lyrics, Oscar Hammerstein 2nd; Book, Howard Lindsay, Russel Crouse; Suggested by "The Trapp Family Singers" by Maria Augusta Trapp; Director, John Fearnley; Scenery, Peter Wolf; Costumes, Winn Morton; Lighting, Peggy Clark; Orchestrations, Robert Russell Bennett; Choral Arrangements, Trudi Rittman; Choreography, Vincent Alexander; Musical Direction, Oscar Kosarin; Entire Production under Supervision of Arnold Spector.

CAST

Maria Rainer	Constance Towers
Sister Berthe	Rosalind Hupp
Sister Margaretta	Joan Caplan
Mother Abbess	Beatrice Krebs
Sister Sophia	Lorna Dallas
Capt. Georg von Trapp	John Michael King
Franz	Jim Oyster
Frau Schmidt	Helen Noyes

Children of Capt. von Trapp:

Liesl	Lee Wilson
Friedrich	Shawn McGill
Louisa	Doreen Miller
Brigitta	Dawn Johnson
Kurt	Richard Arnold Beattie
Marta	Phyllis Sposta
Gretl	Barbara Ann Beattie
Rolf Gruber	Vincent Alexander
Elsa Schraeder	Nancy Eaton
Ursula	Jocelyn McKay
Max Detweiler	Christopher Hewett
Herr Zeller	Larry Swansen
Frau Zeller	Donna Klimoska
Baron Elberfeld	Lee Cass
Baroness Elberfeld	Leonore Lanzillotti
A Postulant	Sandi Sanders
Admiral von Schreiber	Jay Velie

NEIGHBORS, NUNS, SOLDIERS, ETC: Linda Andrews, Jeanette Branin, Lynn East, Doris Galiber, Donna Klimoska, Sherry Lambert, Leonore Lanzillotti, Jocelyn McKay, Donna Monroe, Marilyn Murphy, Christine Owen, Mary Ann Rydzeski, Sandi Sanders, Jeannie Shea, Dixie Stewart, Rex Bennetts, Peter Clark, Peter Costanza, Peter Flores, Lloyd Harris, Jeff Kahn, Robert Montell.

UNDERSTUDIES: Maria, Lorna Dallas; Captain, Max, Lee Case; Abbess, Rosalind Hupp; Elsa, Donna Monroe; Berthe, Leonore Lanzillotti; Sophia, Jeanne Shea; Margaretta, Jeanette Brainin; Liesl, Sherry Lambert; Rolf, Rex Bennetts; Frau Schmidt, Marilyn Murphy; Franz, Peter Flores; Elberfeld, Peter Costanza; Schreiber, Lloyd Harris; Zeller, Peter Clark; von Trapp girls, Janine Mathews, Christine Owens; Friedrich, Paul Dwyer; Kurt, Charles Beattie.

MUSICAL NUMBERS: "Praeludium," "The Sound of Music," "Maria," "My Favorite Things," "Do Re Mi," "You Are Sixteen," "Lonely Goatherd," "How Can Love Survive?," "Laendler Waltz," "So Long, Farewell," "Climb Every Mountain," "No Way to Stop It," "Something Good," "Processional," "Edelweiss," Finale.

A Musical in 2 acts. The action takes place in Austria in 1938, in and near Nonnberg Abbey, and the von Trapp Villa.

Company Manager: Martin Cohen
Press: Saul Richman, Peggy Mitchell
Stage Managers: Mortimer Halpern, William Krot, Lloyd Harris

* Closed Sunday, Sept. 6, 1970.

Barry Kramer Photos

Top Left: Constance Towers, John Michael King

Lee Wilson, Vincent Alexander

SHERIDAN SQUARE PLAYHOUSE
Opened Tuesday, July 21, 1970.*
Kermit Bloomgarden and Arthur Cantor present
Tokyo Kid Brothers in:

GOLDEN BAT

Book and Lyrics, Yutaka Higashi; Music, Itsuro Shimoda; Director, Yutaka Higashi; English Language Coach, Becky Davis; Set, Kenkichi Sato; Lighting and Special Effects, Barry Arnold; Costumes, Kiyoko Chiba; Musical Director, Itsuro Shimoda; Musical Arrangements, Yoko Shimoda; Interpreter, Kazuko Ashima.

CAST

Yukiko Kobayashi	Yasunori Saito
Kyoichi Nagakura	Jun Arakawa
Reiko Nagai	Setsuko Nakagawa
Shoichi Saito	Noboru Mine
Sakae Kato	Kenkichi Sato
Sansho Shinsui	Yoshie Matsuno

MUSICAL NUMBERS: Introduction, "America, America," "Goeika," "Ba-Ba-Ba," "Home," "I Like Girls," "Western Movies," "Soliloquy," "North-Northwest," "American Rock," "Rock, Crane's Town," "I Like," "Love, Love, Love," "Dare No Tame," "Mawari Toro," "Hana Wa," "Namu Amida Butsu," "Medeta," "Okage!," "Hana, Yuki, Kaze."

A Japanese Rock Celebration without intermission.

General Manager: Joseph Beruh
Company Manager: Jewel Howard
Press: Tom Sergott, Jay Smith

* Closed Nov. 29, 1970 after 152 performances.

Arthur Cantor Photos

PUERTO RICAN TRAVELING THEATRE

Opened Monday, August 10, 1970.*
Urban Action Task Force with The Parks,
Recreation and Cultural Affairs Administration of
Mayor John V. Lindsay (August Heckscher,
Administrator; Dore Schary, Commissioner)
presents:

THE GOLDEN STREETS

By Piri Thomas; Producer-Director, Miriam Colon;
Set, Joan Braden; Costumes, Maria Ferreira; Sound,
Richard Logothetis; Visuals, John Braden; Project Co-
ordinator, Allen Davis III: Technical Director, Bob
Anderson

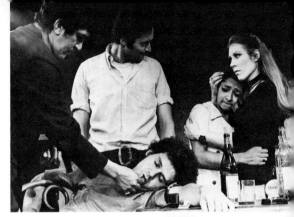

CAST

Luis Perez	Robert Burgos
Anibal	Reinaldo Arana
Raul Perez	Alex Colon
Susana Perez	Carmen Maya
Mariano Perez	Art Vasil
Myrna	Maria De Landa
Chino	Shelly Desai
Child	Christopher Medina
Cathy Donalds	Kathleen Scarlett
Priest	Tomy Vargas
Young Girl	Kitty-Alice Snead
Young Man	Jeffrey Grimes

A Drama in 2 acts and 10 scenes. The action takes
place at the present time in Spanish Harlem (El Barrio)
in New York City.

Company Manager: Gilberto Zaldivar
Press: Marian Graham
Stage Managers: Bob Volin, Kitty-Alice Snead

* Closed Aug. 30, 1970 after 17 performances in New
York City's parks. Spring tour opened Tuesday, Apr.
6, 1971 and closed May 29, 1971 after 45 performances,
with Chico Martinez as Raul, Gloria Irizarry as Su-
sana, Ellen O'Mara as the Young Girl, and Luis Avalo
as the Young Man.

Bert Andrews Photos

**Right Center: Kathleen Scarlett, Chico Martinez
Top: Tomy Vargas, Robert Burgos, Alex Colon,
Maria De Landa, Kathleen Scarlett in 'The
Golden Streets'**

**Carlos Cestero and company in performance of
'El Maleficio de la Mariposa'**

PUERTO RICAN TRAVELING THEATRE

Opened Friday, August 14, 1970.*
The New York State Council on the Arts in
association with the New York City Parks
Department presents:

EL MALEFICIO DE LA MARIPOSA

By Federico Garcia Lorca; Producer, Miriam Colon;
Director, Norberto Kerner; Choreography, Jay Norman;
Set, John Braden; Costumes, Maria Ferreira; Assistant
to the Director, Raul Moncada; Project Coordinator,
Alan Davis III; Administrator, Gilberto Zaldivar.

CAST

Narrador	Carlos Cestero
Dona Curiana	Iraida Polanco
Curianita Nigromantica	Miriam Cruz
Curianita Silvia	Laura Figueroa
Curianito El Nene	Edwin Marcial or Fernando Lugo
Nina 1	Elena Cole
Nina 2	Floria Martinez
Alacranito El Corta Mimbres	Alonso Parra
Mariposa	Graciela Daniele
Campesino 2	Fernando Lugo or Edwin Marcial
Campesino 3	Raul Moncada
Dona Orgullos	Zulema Atala
Curianita Santa	Laura Figueroa
Campesina 1	Zulema Atala
Campesina 4	Gloria Martinez
Campesina 5	Elena Cole
Gusano 1	Fernando Lugo or Edward Marcial
Gusano2	Walter Rodriguez

Press: Marian Graham
Technical Director: Bob Anderson

* Closed in Central Park on August 30, 1970 after
limited engagement of 9 performances in city parks.

GRAMERCY ARTS THEATRE

Opened Tuesday, September 1, 1970.*
Henry P. Testa presents:

THE EMERALD SLIPPERS

Written and Directed by Jose Alcarez; Scenery, Leo
K. Cohen; Lighting, Louis Rios; Costumes, Sandra
Takahashi; Choreography, Tony Anton

CAST

Blossom Flower ....Inez Yvette Perez
Magic Mirror ....Donald J. Scotti
Truth Box ....Frederick Tuso
Liar Box...Alfred Lozito
Foo Young Kow ....Paul Kaniuk
Prince Won Ton ....Rob Sadang
Princess Consume....................................Nessa Lynn Segal
Lo Ming ....Tony Anton
Emperor ....Glen Peters
Chow Mein ....Bruno Flego
Ming Yon ....Alfred Lozito
Butterfly...Maria Sanchez
Dancers.............................Juanita Lento, Maria Sanchez
People of Char Chu Ding ....Peter Vitiello, Exavier
Frejomiel

A Fantasy in 2 acts and 6 scenes. The action takes
place in the land of Char Chu Ding.

General Manager: Leo K. Cohen
Press: Betty Lee Hunt, Henry Luhrman,
Harriett Trachtenberg
Stage Manager: William Bowen

* Closed Sept. 7, 1970 after 10 performances.

Sheldon Ramsdell Photos

**Right: Nessa Lynn Segal, Rob Sadang Top: Inez
Perez, Tony Anton**

Roger Morden, Martha Greenhouse

JAN HUS THEATRE

Opened Tuesday, September 22, 1970.*
Winters/Rosen Productions in association with
Elliott Taubenslag presents:

THREE BY FERLINGHETTI

By Lawrence Ferlinghetti; Director, William E. Hunt;
Sets, Sandi Marks; Lighting, Ray McCutcheon; Costumes, Deborah Foster; Sound, Hamilton O'Hara; Production Manager, Virginia Friedman; Technical Director, Victor Doria

CAST

Martha Greenhouse
Roger Morden
Charles Gregory

PROGRAM: "Three Thousand Red Ants," "The Alliga-
tion," "The Victims of Amnesia"

Press: Sol Jacobson, Lewis Harmon,
Stanley F. Kaminsky

* Closed Sept. 27, 1970 after 8 performances and 8
previews.

PLAZA 9 MUSIC HALL

Opened Tuesday, September 22, 1970.*
Jordan Hott and Jack Millstein present:

DAMES AT SEA

Book and Lyrics, George Haimsohn and Robin Miller; Music, Jim Wise; Directed and Choreographed by Neal Kenyon; Sets and Costumes, Peter Harvey; Lighting, Chenault Spence; Musical Director, Richard Demone; Assistant Choreographer, Bonnie Ano; Associate Producer, Robert S. Mankin; Production Manager, Don Lamb; Piano Interludes, Baldwin Bergersen; Original Cast Album by Columbia Records; Conductor-Pianist, Richard DeMone.

CAST

Mona Kent	Janie Sell
Joan	Carol Morley
Henessey	Raymond Thorne
Ruby	Leland Palmer
Dick	Kurt Peterson
Lucky	Voight Kempson
Captain	Raymond Thorne

Standbys: Walter Bobbie, Charlotte Frazier

MUSICAL NUMBERS: "Wall Street," "It's You," "Broadway Baby," "That Mister Man of Mine," "Choo-Choo Honeymoon," "The Sailor of My Dreams," "Good Times Are Here to Stay," "Dames at Sea," "The Beguine," "Raining in My Heart," "There's Something About You," "The Echo Waltz," "Star Tar," "Let's Have a Simple Wedding"

A Musical in two acts. The action takes place in the early 1930's.

Press: Saul Richman, Peggy Mitchell

* Closed Jan. 31, 1971 after 170 performances.

Kenn Duncan Photos

Top Right: Carol Morley, Leland Palmer, Janie Sell Below: Janie Sell

Raymond Thorne, Voight Kempson, Kurt Peterson

Kurt Peterson, Leland Palmer

72

BOUWERIE LANE THEATRE

Opened previews Tuesday, September 29, 1970.*
Mendo Productions presents:

THE EVIL THAT MEN DO

By Ed Jacobs: Director, Loren Andrews; Settings, Larry Reehling; Lighting, John Tedesco; Hairstylist, Raffaele.

CAST

Roy ....R. J. Brooks†1
Diane ....Cathy Boyd
Joel...John Hoffmeister†2
Dennis..Bill Moher†3
Beau..Ron Mangravite†4
Parish ....Douglas Travis†5
Understudy: Dennis Edenfield

A Play in 2 acts and 7 scenes. The action takes place at the present time on Fire Island on a summer Thursday.

Press: Betty Lee Hunt, Henry Luhrman,
Harriett Trachtenberg
Stage Manager: Dennis Moore

* Closed Nov. 1, 1970 after 40 previews only.

† Succeeded by: 1. Fred Barry, 2. Alan Castner, 3. Dennis Edenfield, 4. Eddie Rambeau, 5. Michael D. Moore

"The Evil that Men Do"

CHERRY LANE THEATRE

Opened Friday, October 2, 1970.*
James Clifford Productions presents:

CHILDREN IN THE RAIN

By Dennis McIntyre; Director, Frank R. Giordano; Assistant Director/Designer, Patrick Donovan.

CAST

Twigs......................................Elizabeth Harryman
Max..Lane Smith
Gibbs ....Frank R. Giordano
Understudy: Tracy Brooks Swope

A Play without intermission. The action takes place at the present time in an abandoned theatre in New York City.

Press: Sol Jacobson, Lewis Harmon,
Stanley F. Kaminsky
Stage Manager: John Van Domlin

* Closed Oct. 2, 1970 after 1 performance.

George Shivone Photo

Elizabeth Harryman, Jock O'Neill, Frank R. Giordano

EDISON THEATRE

Opened Monday, October 5, 1970.*
Preston Fischer and Norman Kean by arrangement with Marc Princi Ltd. present:

OPIUM

Translated and adapted for the stage by Roc Brynner from Jean Cocteau's "Opium, Journal of a Cure"; Conceived and Directed by Ranald Graham; Scenery, Roger Cheveley; Lighting, Lloyd Burlingame; Costumes, Mr. Fish; Hairstylist, John DeConey.

CAST

ROC BRYNNER

A Drama in two acts, showing the first stage of the cure as the patient is slowly weaned from the drug, and the second stage when he is withdrawn completely.

General Manager: Janet Spencer
Press: Lee Solters, Harvey B. Sabinson,
Marilynn LeVine
Stage Manager: R. Derek Swire

* Closed Oct. 10, 1970 after 7 performances.

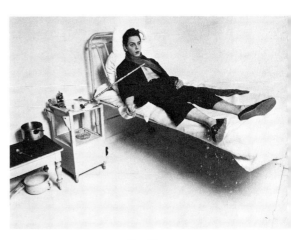

Roc Brynner

THEATRE DE LYS

Opened Wednesday, October 7, 1970.*
Lester M. Goldsmith presents:

HAPPY BIRTHDAY, WANDA JUNE

By Kurt Vonnegut, Jr.; Director, Michael J. Kane; Settings, Ed Wittstein; Lighting, David F. Segal; Costumes, Joseph G. Aulisi; Sound, Gary Harris; Associate Producer, Walter Rosen Scholz; Presented by special arrangement with Lucille Lortel Productions; Technical Director, John Beven.

CAST

Penelope Ryan	Marsha Mason
Looseleaf Harper	William Hickey
Paul Ryan	Steven Paul
Dr. Norbert Woodly	Keith Charles
Herb Shuttle	Nicolas Coster
Harold Ryan	Kevin McCarthy
Wanda June	Ariane Munker
Siegfried von Konigswald	Louis Turenne
Mildred	Pamela Saunders

UNDERSTUDIES: Harold, Louis Turenne; Paul, Jeffrey Edmund; Wanda June, Ellen Dano; Penelope, Mildred, Dianne Wiest; Woodly, Herb, Siegfried, Harper, Jess Osuna

A Comedy in two acts. The action takes place in the Ryan apartment in a large city at the present time.

General Manager: Paul B. Berkowsky
Company Manager: Bill Schwartz
Press: Ben Washer
Stage Manager: Paul John Austin

* Closed by Actors Equity strike on Nov. 15, 1970 after 47 performances. Re-opened at Edison Theatre on Tuesday, Dec. 22, 1970 and closed there March 14, 1971 after 96 performances, making a total of 143.

Bert Andrews Photos

Left: Kevin McCarthy, Steven Paul Top: Kevin McCarthy, Keith Charles

Marsha Mason, Kevin McCarthy

William Hickey, Keith Charles, Kevin McCarthy

LUCRETIA BORI THEATRE
Opened Monday, October 5, 1970.*
The Spanish Institute presents:

A MEDIA LUZ LOS TRES

B120(The Three of Us in Dim Light)

By Miguel Mihura; Director, Rene Buch; Set, Bob Troie; Lighting, Ray McCutcheon

CAST

The Woman..Luz Castanos
The Man..Jean-Paul Delgado
The Friend ...,..Esteban Chalbaud

A Comedy in three acts with epilogue.

Press: Marian Graham

* Closed Oct. 11, 1970 after limited engagement of 6 performances. Re-opened at Greenwich Mews Theatre Sunday, Oct. 25, 1970 for 17 additional performances, closing Nov. 15, 1970.

Top Left: Jean-Paul Delgado, Luz Castanos, Esteban Chalbaud in 'A Media Luz Los Tres'

Above: Saskia Noordhoek Hegt, Tom Costello, Angela Pietropinto, Gerry Bamman, Lary Pine (kneeling), Jerry Mayer

THE EXTENSION THEATRE
Opened Thursday, October 8, 1970.*
Lyn Austin and Oliver Smith present an N.Y.U.S.O.A. Theatre Company Manhattan Project in:

ALICE IN WONDERLAND

Adapted by The Manhattan Project Company from writings of Lewis Carroll; Director, Andre Gregory; Designers, Eugene Lee, Franne Newman; Translator, Kenneth Cavander.

CAST

Gerry Bamman
Tom Costello
Saskia Noordhock Hegt
Cecil MacKinnon
Jerry Mayer
Angela Pietropinto
Larry Pine

Press: Alan Eichler
Stage Manager: John P. Holms

* Closed May 2, 1971 after 122 performances on weekends only.

John Veltri Photos

Tom Costello, Angela Pietropinto

ELLEN STEWART THEATRE

Opened Wednesday, October 14, 1970.*
Cheryl Crawford in association with Mary W.
John presents:

COLETTE

Adapted by Elinor Jones: Based on "Earthly Paradise," the collection of Colette's autobiographical writings by Robert Phelps; Director, Gerald Freedman; Scenery, David Mitchell; Costumes, Theoni V. Aldredge; Lighting, Roger Morgan; Lyrics, Tom Jones; Music, Harvey Schmidt; Technical Director, Ralph Maffongelli; Hairstylist, Randy Coronato.

CAST

Colette	Fenella Fielding
Sido	Ruth Nelson
Willy	Albert Stratton
The Captain, Max, George Wague, Reporter	Erik Rhodes
Daniele, Polaire, Ida, Amalia, Marguerite, Reporter	Janet Dowd
Leo, Jacques, Pierre, Jean, Henri de Jouvenel, Maurice	Michael Goodwin
Pianist	Elman Anderson

UNDERSTUDIES: Misses Fielding and Nelson, Janet Dowd; Messrs. Rhodes and Stratton, Ray Stewart; Mr. Goodwin, Peter Coffield

A Play in two acts. The action takes place in France between 1873 and 1954.

General Manager: Paul B. Berkowsky
Company Manager: Bill Schwartz
Press: David Powers
Stage Managers: Gail Bell, Peter Coffield

* Closed Oct. 18, 1970 after 7 performances and 9 previews. For original production with Zoe Caldwell, see THEATRE WORLD, Vol. 26.

Martha Swope Photos

Right: Janet Dowd, Fenella Fielding Top: Ruth Nelson, Erik Rhodes, Fenella Fielding

Harry Eno, Jenny O'Hara   *Howard Photos*

PLAYERS THEATRE

Opened Thursday, October 15, 1970.*
John J. Nestor in association with Wolf William Moss presents:

MY HOUSE IS YOUR HOUSE

By Lee Loeb and Sam Ross; Director, William Tregoe; Scenery and Lighting, Robert Engstrom; Costumes, Leila Larmon.

CAST

Delivery Man	Don Bishop
Lucy Tyler	Jenny O'Hara
Ray Prentiss	Don Fellows
Ben Tyler	Frank Moon
Harry Fenton	Milo Boulton
Charlene	Anita Stewart
Vicky	Jan McElhaney
Sidney Lindquist	Harry Eno
Mrs. Randall	June Graham

A Comedy in 3 acts. The action takes place in a city in Massachusetts in July of 1927.

Manager: J. J. Nestor
Press: David Lipsky, Lisa Lipsky
Stage Managers: Elissa Lane, Iris Spielberg

* Closed Oct. 15, 1970 after 1 performance.

Zodiac Photos

FIRST MORAVIAN CHURCH

Opened Thursday, October 15, 1970.*
The Foundation for Classic Theatre and
Academy in association with the First Moravian
Church of New York presents The Classic
Theatre Workshop Company in repertory in:

THE TROJAN WOMEN

By Euripides; Adapted by Edith Hamilton; Director,
Sala Staw; Choreography, Valentina Litvinoff; Score,
David Earnest; Sets and Lights, Kent Cottam; Tapes,
Ted Mornell; Sound, George Jacobs

CAST

Poseidon ....Raymond Stato
Athena...Susanne Gilbert
Hecuba ....Sala Staw
Women.................Winifred Chester, Dawn Powell,
   Zahra Kader, Fran Leslie, Grace Paynter,
   Elizabeth Howard, Joan Maniscalco, Susann
      Metcalf, Leslie Ann Kurtz
Talthybius ....Richard Bennett
Soldiers................................Earl Thompson, Ray Jennette
Cassandra...................................Katherine Rao
Solo Dancer.............................Valentina Litvinoff
Dancers ....Lise Eger, Wendy Gross, Susan Metcalf,
      Zahra Kader
Andromache........................Flavia Bartholomew
Astyanax ....E. Sturdivant
Menelaus..R. Sebastian Russ
Helen of Troy............................Rachel Yossiffon

Opened Friday, October 16, 1970.*

BRITANNICUS

By Racine; Henderson-Landis translation.

CAST

Albina...Lonni Merrill
Agrippina ....Sala Staw
Burrus ....Raymond Stato
Narcissus ....Philip Hanson
Britannicus...Hill Stinson
Nero...Larry Martin
Junia...Katherine Rao
Guards ....Ray Jennette, Earl Thompson

STANDBYS for both plays: Judith Morley Levitan, Earl
Thompson, Ray Jennette, Kent Cottam

Press: Paul Boston
Stage Managers: Richard Bennett, Kent Cottam,
    Earl Thompson

* Closed Nov. 8, 1970 after limited engagement of 7
performances and 5 previews for each production.

Leonard Speier Photos

Catherine Rae, Winifred Chester, Sala Staw,
Grayce Paynter, Joan Maniscalco in "Trojan
Women" Below: Hill Stinson, Elisabeth Howard
in "Britannicus"

**Denise Lor, Evelyn Kingsley, Moti Giladi, Sarah
Rubine**

BARBIZON PLAZA THEATRE

Opened Monday, October 19, 1970.*
Henry Colgran and Arthur V. Briskin present:

TO BE OR NOT TO BE....
What Kind of a Question Is That?

Written by H. Ritterman and Zvi Reisel; Music by Eli
Rubinstein; Lyrics, Max Meszel; Staged by Marvin
Gordon; Musical Director, Eli Rubinstein; Art Consul-
tant, Ami Shamir; Lighting, Sally Small; Production
Coordinator, Larry Whiteley.

CAST

James Brochu   Denise Lor
Moti Giladi   Sarah Rubine
Shmulik Goldstein   Yoel Sharr
Evelyn Kingsley   Mark Stuart

An American-Israeli Topical Musical Revue in two
acts.

General Manager: Marvin A. Krauss
Press: Max Eisen
Stage Manager: Patricia Smisko

* Closed Nov. 15, 1970 after 32 performances.

HUNTER COLLEGE PLAYHOUSE

Opened Monday, October 19, 1970.*
Hunter College Concert Bureau and Sherman
Pitluck present:

BALUSTRADE THEATRE
OF PRAGUE

Directors, Vladimir Vodicka and Ladislav Fialka

CAST

Ladislav Fialka

Ludmila Kovarova	Josef Fajta
Zdenka Kratochvilova	Jiri Kaftan
Lucie Hoffmeisterova	Ivan Lukes
Olga Przygrodska	Rudolf Papezik
Bozena Vechetova	Richard Weber

PROGRAM

"Button, Button," "Nine Etudes," "Theme and Variations"

Press: Bernard Gurtman, Irving Jones

* Closed Oct. 24, 1970 after limited engagement of 6
performances to tour U. S.

Ladislav Fialka

PLAYHOUSE THEATRE

Opened Tuesday, October 20, 1970.*
Roy N. Nevans and Albert J. Schiff present:

GANDHI

By Gurney Campbell; Director, Jose Quintero; Designed by Ming Cho Lee; Costumes, Jane Greenwood; Lighting, Roger Morgan.

CAST

The Antagonist	David Selby
Sarojini (Mrs. Naidu)	Estelle Omens
Mahadev	Leroy Lessane
Mohandas K. Gandhi	Jack MacGowran
Kasturbai Gandhi	Betty Miller
Station Master	Lawrence Stern
Passenger	Jack Axelrod
Convict	Tom Coble
Dala	Rik Colitti
Judge	Thomas B. Markus
Kallenbach	Martin Meyers
Man with Knife	Shelly Desai
Woman	Donna Pizzi
Sergeant Major	Thomas B. Markus
Venerable Old Man	Jack Axelrod
Patel	Louis Guss
Mirabehn (Madeline Slade)	Dina Paisner
Dewan	Martin Meyers
Maharajah	Rik Colitti
Father Nehru	Lawrence Stern
Jinnah Sahib	Jack Axelrod
Jawaharlal Nehru	Vic Mohica
Webb Miller	Tom Coble
Man with Bloody Face	Kenneth Marsolais
Sobbing Woman	Cathryn Roskam
Convict Cook	Rik Colitti
Sushila (Dr. Nayyan)	Donna Pizzi
Viceroy	Thomas B. Markus
Chief Inspector	Kenneth Marsolais
Manu	Cathryn Roskam
Metab	Shelly Desai
Hindu Youth	Frank Liu
The Maulvi	Joseph C. Davies
Messenger	Leroy Lessane

A Drama in 2 acts and 30 scenes.

General Management: Grayson & Olim
Press: Bill Doll & Co., Midori Lederer
Stage Managers: Iris O'Conner, Kenneth Marsolais

* Closed Oct. 20, 1970 after 1 performance.

Bert Andrews Photos

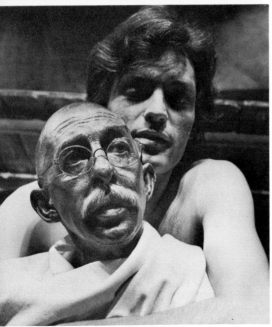

David Selby, Jack MacGowran

NEW YORK THEATRE ENSEMBLE

Opened Friday, October 23, 1970.*

The New York Theatre Ensemble presents:

LYSISTRATA

A Free Adaptation of Aristophanes' play by Darrel deChaby; Director, Bill Accles; Settings, Robert Wacker; Costumes, Paula Dianne Meade; Lighting, Oswald Daljord; Graphics, Fran Marsh.

CAST

Lysistrata	Ingrid Sonnichsen
Calonice	Fran Marsh
Myrinne	Susan Marshall
Lampito	Julia Randall
Ismenia	Ellen Roth
Cora	Claudia Wilkins
Strymodorus	Ronald Silver
Laches	Jeffrey Cohen
Drakes	Larry Blauvert
Philurgus	William Greisel
Magistrate	Brian Hartigan
Kinesias	Jeff Druce
Spartan Herald	Rory Gerstle
Spartan Ambassador	Al Stephans
Lycon	Al Stephans

A Comedy presented without intermission. The action takes place in Ancient Greece in 455 B.C.

Stage Manager: Bill Capobianco

* Closed Nov. 21, 1970 after a limited engagement of 16 performances.

Michael Campione Photo

Ronald Silver, Fran Marsh, Ellen Roth, Jeff Cohen

THEATRE FOUR

Opened Sunday, October 25, 1970.*

John Bowab and Charles Celian present:

SENSATIONS

Concept and Lyrics, Paul Zakrzewski; Music, Wally Harper; Suggested by Shakespeare's "Romeo and Juliet"; Director, Jerry Dodge; Designed by William and Jean Eckart; Costumes, Jeanne Button; Musical Direction, Jack Lee; Lighting, Beverly Emmons; Orchestrations, Bill Brohn; Production Assistant, Edward Eller; Technical Consultant, Chuck Vincent; Sculpture by Girv Milligan.

CAST

Lady Capulet	Paulette Attie
The Friar	Arthur Bartow
Juliet	Judy Gibson
Lord Montague	Joe Masiell
Tybalt	Ron Martin
Lord Capulet	James Ray
Lady Montague	Marie Santell
Romeo	John Savage
Mercutio	Bruce Scott

Understudies: Michael Vita, Ron Martin

MUSICAL NUMBERS: "Lonely Children," "Sensations," "Good Little Boy," "The Beginning," "What Kind of Parents," "Power," "Up and Down," "Friar's Tune," "Oh, My Age," "Outracing Light," "War Is Good Business," "The Kill," "Lying Here," "Middle Class Revolution," "I'll Stay, I'll Go," "Queen Mab," "I Cannot Wait," "Sounds," "No Place for Me," "Morning Sun," "In Nomine Dei," Finale.

General Management: Grayson & Olim
Company Manager: Richard Grayson
Press: Saul Richman, Peggy Mitchell
Stage Manager: Barbara Wood

* Closed Nov. 8, 1970 after 16 performances.

Barry Kramer Photos

Marie Santell, John Savage, Joe Masiell
Above: John Savage, Judy Gibson

CHERRY LANE THEATRE
Opened Tuesday, October 27, 1970.*
W. Randolph Galvin presents:

THE IMMACULATE MISCONCEPTION

By W. Randolph Galvin; Director, William E. Kinzer; Settings, Kinzer and Galvin; Costumes, Mary Lou Harvey; Lighting, Lee Goldman.

CAST

Mr. Mueller...Frank Borgman
Gloria Mueller...Mary McGregor
Dr. Zaharako..William Kelsey
Addie..Gwenn Mitchell
Bob Crouley ....John Swearingen
Jack ....Tony Thomas
Mr. Beeler...Herb Buck
Mr. Snagsby & Heavenly Voice..................James Glenn

A Comedy in 2 acts and 14 scenes. The action takes place at the present time somewhere in mid-America.

General Manager: Malcolm Allen
Company Manager: Paul Bosten
Press: Betty Lee Hunt, Henry Luhrman,
Harriett Trachtenberg
Stage Manager: Michael Burke

* Closed Oct. 30, 1970 after 4 performances.

Zodiac Photos

Left: Frank Borgman Above: William Kelsey, Mary McGregor, Gwen Mitchell, John Swearingen

MARTINIQUE THEATRE
Opened Wednesday, October 28, 1970.*
Michael Harvey presents:

SCORE

Written and Directed by Jerry Douglas; Setting, T. E. Mason; Lighting, Candace Kling; Music Consultant, William R. Cox.

CAST

Elvira...Claire Wilbur
Jack..Michael Beirne
Betsy ....Lynn Swann
Eddie..Ben Wilson†
Mike ....Sylvester E. Stallone

A Play in 2 acts and 5 scenes. The action takes place at the present time in an apartment in Queens.

General Manager: Fred Walker
Press: Alan Eichler, Stanley F. Kaminsky
Stage Manager: Mark Healy

* Closed Nov. 15, 1970 after 23 performances.

† Succeeded by Eddie Rambeau

Jerry Kean Photo

Michael Beirne, Claire Wilbur, Lynn Swan, Ben Wilson

ALICE TULLY HALL
Opened Tuesday, November 3, 1970.*
S. Hurok presents:

EMLYN WILLIAMS
as
Charles Dickens

A Solo performance of scenes from the famous novels and stories by Charles Dickens, including "Our Mutual Friend," "Christmas Stories," "Dombey and Son," "The Battle of Life," "Little Dorrit," "A Tale of Two Cities," and "The Uncommercial Traveller."

Production Supervisor: Robert Crawley
Press: Martin Feinstein, Gertrude Smith

* Closed Nov. 8, 1970 after a limited engagement of 5 performances to tour.

Left: Emlyn Williams

PROMENADE THEATRE
Opened Sunday, November 8, 1970.*
Harvey and Clara Klingeman present:

A DREAM OUT OF TIME

By Irv Bauer; Director, Paul Aaron; Scenery and Lighting, David F. Segal; Costumes, Joseph G. Aulisi; Dance Movement, Kathryn Posin; Original Music, Kirk Nurock; Sound, Maury Benkoil; Technician, Michael O'Rand.

CAST

Mike	James J. Sloyan
Laura	Patsy Sabline
Hanna	Clara Heller
Aaron	Sam Levene†1
Morris	Philip Bruns†2
Cybil	Zina Jasper
Blanche	Ruth Manning
Josh	Gary Tigerman
Raymond	John Towey

A Play in three acts. The action takes place in reality and dreams at the present time.

General Manager: Jose Vega
Company Manager: Sherman Gross
Press: Max Eisen, Warren Pincus, Milly Schoenbaum
Stage Managers: Martin Herzer, David Taylor

* Closed Jan. 24, 1971 after 48 performances.

† Succeeded by: 1. Alvin Kupperman, Philip Bruns, 2. Louis Guss

Zina Jasper, James J. Sloyan Above: Sam Levene, Ruth Manning, Clara Heller

81

VILLAGE ARENA THEATRE

Opened Sunday, November 8, 1970.*
(Moved June 1, 1971 to Martinique Theatre)
Edith O'Hara and Albert Poland present The
Plowright Players in:

TOUCH

Book by Kenn Long in collaboration with Amy Saltz;
Kenn Long, Jim Crozier; Lyrics, Kenn Long; Director,
Amy Saltz; Musical Direction, David J. Rodman, Jim
Crozier; Sets, Robert U. Taylor, Robert Alexander
Kates; Lighting, Charles Lewis, Barry Arnold; Original
Cast Album by Ampex Records.

CAST

Awol	Norman Jacob
Guiness	Barbara Ellis
Wyan	Kenn Long
Melissa	Phyllis Gibbs
Roland	Gerard S. Doff†1
Mark	Peter J. Mitchell†2
Patti	Susan Rosenblum
Susan April	Ava Rosenblum
Alex	Dwight Jayne

TOWNSPEOPLE: Eileen Gottermeyer, David J. Stoud-
nour, Jackie Shaw, Gary Graham, Judy Baldwin, Patti
Ruben

MUSICAL NUMBERS: "Declaration," "Windchild,"
"City Song," "Sitting in the Park," "I Don't Care,"
"Goodbyes," "Come to the Road," "Reaching, Touch-
ing," "Quiet Country," "Guiness, Woman," "Susan's
Song," "Maxine!," "Tripping," "Garden Song," "Watch-
ing," "Hasseltown," "Confrontation Song," "Alphagene-
sis"

A Country-Rock Musical in two acts.

General Manager: Albert Poland
Press: Saul Richman, Robert Ganshaw
Stage Manager: David Stoudner

* Still playing May 31, 1971.

† Succeeded by: 1. Michael Price, 2. J. M. Jonas

Scene from 'Touch'

STAIRWAY THEATRE

Opened Wednesday, November 18, 1970.*
Jeff Britton presents:

THE CASTRO COMPLEX

By Mel Arrighi; Director, James Burrows; Scenery,
Kert Lundell; Lighting, Roger Morgan; Costumes, John
J. Whitmore; Associate Producer, Sidney Annis; Assist-
ant to Producers, Erlinda Zetlin; Technical Adviser,
Lowell Sherman.

CAST

Betsy Kress	Marian Hailey
Hadley Marcus	Terry Kiser
Paco Montoya	Raul Julia

Understudies: Norman Parker, Ruth Alda

A Comedy in two acts. The action takes place in Betsy
Kress' apartment at the present time.

General Manager: Jeff Britton
Company Manager: Lynda M. Patrie
Press: David Powers
Stage Manager: Gail Hubbard

* Closed Nov. 22, 1970 after 7 performances.

Martha Swope Photos

**Terry Kiser, Marian Hailey Right Center: Marian
Hailey, Raul Julia**

GREENWICH MEWS THEATRE

Opened Thursday, November, 19, 1970.*
Greenwich Mews Spanish Theatre presents
English and Spanish productions of:

THREE SPANISH PLAYS

English versions by Luz Castanos, Carlos Solorzano,
Rene Buch; Sets, Bob Troie, Zita Gomez de Kanelba;
Costumes, Barbara Naomi Cohen, Bob Troie; Lighting,
Ray McCutcheon; Choreography, Marcelino Rosado

CAST

"La Difunta" (The Dead Wife)
by Miguel de Unamuno; Director, Luz Castanos
Freddy...Jean Paul Delgado
                               or Emilio Rodriguez
Ramona...Maria Dolores
Mark...Esteban Chalbaud
                               or Pablo De La Torre
Grace ....Barbara Elliott
                               or Lolina Gutierrez
"Cruce de Vias" (The Railroad Crossing)
by Carlos Solorzano; Director, Luz Castanos
Switchman...Jean Paul Delgado
                               or Joe Vega
Young Man..Esteban Chalbaud
Woman...Gay Darlene Bidart
Train.....................Marcelino Rosado, Idalia Diaz, Jason
                               Jennings, Maria Dolores
"Las Pericas" (The Parrots)
                by Nicolas Dorr; Director, Rene Buch
Rosita...Shelly Pearson
Panchita ....Miriam Cruz
Felina..Florencia Moncada
Serafina...Barbara Elliott
                               or Milagros Horrego

Understudy: Isabel Segovia

Press: Marian Graham

* Closed Dec. 20, 1970 after 26 performances in Spanish
  and English.

Bert Andrews Photo

**Top Right: Miriam Cruz, Milagros Horrego,
Shelly Pearson in 'The Parrots'**

**Ray Edelstein, Raymond Singer, Irene Bunde
Right Center: John Beal**

EDISON THEATRE

Opened Monday, November 23, 1970.*
William F. DeSeta presents:

THE CANDYAPPLE

By John Grissmer; Director, Stuart Bishop; Sets and
Lighting, David R. Ballou; Costumes, Sara Brook; Production Assistant, Susan Walker.

CAST

Foster Fine...Raymond Singer
Frank McGrath...Ray Edelstein
Jim Ferndock...Noel Conlon
Joanie Klinger...Irene Bunde
Connie Antonelli...Joy Garrett
Larry McGrath.....................................Arlen Dean Snyder
Tom McGrath...John Beal
                Understudy: Edward Lally

A Comedy in 2 acts and 3 scenes. The action takes
place at the present time in the apartment of Foster Fine
and Frank McGrath in Cincinnati----plus an assortment
of phone booths.

Company Managers: Gatchell & Neufeld
Press: Bill Doll, Virginia Holden
Stage Manager: Robert Burgos

* Closed Nov. 23, 1970 after 1 performance.

Bert Andrews Photos

83

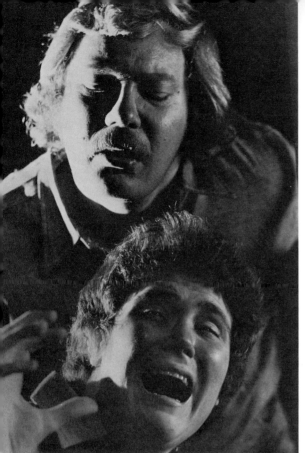

THIRTEENTH STREET THEATRE
Opened Friday, November 27, 1970.*
The Thirteenth Street Theatre presents:

THE LAST PAD

By William Inge; Director, Jack Doroshow, Set, Clyde Wachsberger; Executive Assistant, and Artistic Coordinator, Connie Lewis; Lighting, Tony Davis, Michael Ysebaert.

CAST

Jess	Tim Lewis
Archie	Warren Pincus
Luke	Jack Kiernan
Guard	Rick Petrucelli
Chaplain	Burt Grosselfinger
Mona	Lydia Simmons
Jess's Father	William Robertson
Second Guard	Eugene Baxter
Joe Ruselli	Gil Pacheco
Barber	Bill Rothmel
Mortician	Leonard Nagel

A Drama in two acts. The action takes place at the present time on Death Row of a state penitentiary in the Midwest.

Press: Max Eisen, Warren Pincus
Stage Managers: Tony Davis, Michael Ysebaert

* Closed Dec. 13, 1970 after a limited engagement of 6 performances.

Left: Warren Pincus (top), Tim Lewis

NEW YORK CITY CENTER
Opened Saturday, November 28, 1970.*
City Center of Music and Drama (Norman Singer, General Director) presents:

MOON WALK

Book, Betty Jean Lifton; Music and Lyrics Written and Performed by The Open Window; Staged by Hal Wicke; Visuals by Group II; Costumes and Props, Jack McGroder; Choreography, Anne Wilson; Production Supervised by Chuck Eisler; Production Assistant, James Hazel.

CAST

Jimmy	Tommy Breslin
Granny	Annie Abbott
Buddy	Ronald Dennis
Linda	Ann Hodapp
Moonblowfoofoo	James Barbosa
Moonbeam	Roberta Rodin
Moonosaur	Ralph Santinelli
Moonmoth	Annie Abbott
Galaxy	Jerry DiGiacoma
Old Woman of the Universe	Annie Abbott

DANCERS: Lindsay Ann Crouse, Jim Gates, David Gleaton, Stephanie Satie, Paul Wittenborn

MUSICAL NUMBERS: "Ready to Go," "Moon Walk," "Moonblowfoofoo," "Sea of Tranquility," "Millions of Envelopes," "Making the Moonmoth Laugh," "Grand Tour of the Planets," "On Moonrock Mountain," "Moonrock Candy Freak-Out," "Love Song to a Monster," "Earth Fall," Finale.

Press: Gifford/Wallace, Tom Trenkle
Stage Manager: A. Robert Altschuler

* Closed Dec. 6, 1970 after limited engagement of 8 performances. (No photos available)

Warren Pincus, Jack Kiernan

BIJOU THEATRE
Opened Thursday, December 10, 1970.*
Sweet Alice Ltd. presents:

FOREPLAY

By Robert M. Lane; Director, Nicholas Rock; Setting and Lighting, Leo B. Meyer; Production Assistant, Chris Cunningham.

CAST

Walter ....Donn Whyte
Neil ....Sam Stoneburner
Alice ....Tara Tyson
Rich ....Alan Castner

A Drama in two acts and four scenes. The action takes place at the present time in a Central Park West apartment somewhere in the 80's.

General Management: Gatchell & Neufeld
Press: Betty Lee Hunt, Henry Luhrman,
Harriet Trachtenberg
Stage Manager: Clint Jakeman

* Clsoed Jan. 10, 1971 after 38 performances.

Martha Swope Photos

Tara Tyson Right: Sam Stoneburner,
Alan Castner

WEST SIDE YMCA
Opened Saturday, December 12, 1970.*
Hunter College Playwrights presents:

MISBEGOTTEN ANGELS

Three one-act plays by Stanley Taikeff; Director, Barbara Schoenfeld; Set and Lighting, Joe Kaminsky; Lighting Director, Ray Crawley; Producer, Aaron Weingarten.

CAST

"Solo Recital"
Mother..Frances Peter
Father..Donald Keyes
Walter..Ben Wingate

"The Afflictions of Marlene"
Mother...Jeanmarie Evans
Father ....John Tarrant
Marlene ....Winnie Benjamin

Intermission
"Into That Good Night"
Agnes ....Frances Peter
Albert..Alex Wolfson
George ....Elek Hartman
Grace..Muriel Mason
Mother..Josephine Harris
Cathy...Carol Williard

Press: Patricia Molino
Stage Manager: Myles Conrad

* Closed Dec. 20, 1970 after limited engagement of 5 performances. (No photos available)

"Misbegotten Angels"

Russell Schwartz Photo

85

Chris Phelan (L), Marc Reymont (R)

"Commune"

**Judith Martin, Pilar Garcia
in "Hot Feet"**

McALPIN ROOFTOP THEATRE
Opened Thursday, December 17, 1970.*
Lester Productions presents:

OCCULTISM IN THE 70'S

Executive Producer, Ed Lester; Producer, Marc Reymont; Director, Chris Phelan; Light and Sound, Bruce Edwards; Technician, David Myles; Graphics, Elaine Summers; Costumes, Rosenna Richardson.

CAST

Marc Reymont
Chris Phelan
Nan Wilton
Lyle Pearsons
Ruth Kamens
Mychelle Smiley
Understudies: Ruth Reachel, Victor Germaine

A multi-media experience of lights, sound, music, scents, demonstrations and explanations designed to explore and enlighten the shadowy world of the occult.

Press: Wilma Ross, Darylan Stratton
Stage Managers: John Garner, Vincent Germaine

* Closed Dec. 27, 1970 and re-opened Dec. 29, 1970 at the Fortune Theatre.

THE PERFORMING GARAGE
Opened Thursday, December 17, 1970.*
The Performance Group presents:

COMMUNE

Text compiled and arranged from various sources and Group improvisations; Director, Richard Schechner; Associate Director, Paul Epstein; Environmentalist, Jerry Rojo; Technical Director, Jerry Powell; Dramaturg, Lado Kralj; Administrative Director, Catherine Farinon; Assistant Environmentalist, Robert Adzema; Construction, Frank Davis.

CAST

David Angel	Stephen Borst
Lara	Patricia Bower
Mischa	Mik Cribben
Jayson	Jayme Daniel
Susan Belinda Moonshine	Patric Epstein
Spalding	Spalding Gray
Fearless Jim	James Griffiths
Big Time Clementine	Joan MacIntosh
Bruce	Bruce White

A vision of what has gone on in America during the last 400 years, about living and working together, the quest for El Dorado.

Press: Catherine Farinon
Stage Manager: Elizabeth LeCompte

* Closed June 6, 1971 after 107 performances and 20 previews.

HUNTER COLLEGE PLAYHOUSE
Opened Saturday, December 19, 1970.*
Hunter College presents The Paper Bag Players
(Judith Martin, Director) in:

HOT FEET

Created, Designed, and Directed by Judith Martin; Original Music by Donald Ashwander; Assistant Director, Irving Burton; Administrator, Judith Liss.

CAST

Irving Burton	Janet MacKenzie
Pilar Garcia	Douglas Richardson
Douglas Ashwander at Harpsichord	

Stage Manager: Adam Perl

* Closed Dec. 23, 1970 after limited engagement of 10 performances. Repeated on March 6, 1971 in the Forum Theater at Lincoln Center.

A PLACE WITHOUT DOORS

By Marguerite Duras; Translated from the French by Barbara Bray; Director, Brian Murray; Set, John Conklin; Lighting, Ronald Wallace; Executive Producer, Eugene V. Wolsk.

CAST

The Questioner	Alvin Epstein
Pierre Lannes	Richard A. Dysart
Claire Lannes	Mildred Dunnock

A Drama in two acts. The action takes place in France in 1966.

Press: Betty Lee Hunt, Henry Luhrman,
Harriett Trachtenberg
Stage Manager: Mitch Erickson

* Closed January 16, 1971 after 30 performances.

Martha Swope Photos

Mildred Dunnock, Richard A. Dysart, Alvin Epstein

Left: Mildred Dunnock, Alvin Epstein

HUNTER COLLEGE PLAYHOUSE

Opened Saturday, December 26, 1970.*
The Hunter College Concert Bureau presents the Oxford and Cambridge Shakespeare Company in:

HAMLET

By William Shakespeare; Director, Jonathan Miller; Designed by Bernard Culshaw; Lighting, David Hersey; Fight Direction, William Hobbs; Assistant Director, Nicholas Arnold; Makeup, Barbara Naomi Cohen; Technical Director, Thomas Price; Stage Technicians, Joseph Londin, Leonard Suib.

CAST

Claudius	Jonathan James-Moore
Hamlet	Hugh Thomas
Polonius	Mike Baker
Horatio	James Harris
Laertes	Keith Kirby
Rosencrantz	Charles Sturridge
Guildenstern	Gal Hawkesworth
Osric	John Madden
Priest	James Barraclough
Marcellus	Adrian Webster
Barnado	Richard Willey
Reynaldo	Stephen Wright
Ghost	Andrew Hilton
Grave-digger	Mike Baker
Fortinbras	Andrew Hilton
Gertrude	Christabel Gairdner
Ophelia	Claire Howard
Player King	Andrew Hilton
Player Queen	James Barraclough
Lucianus	Adrian Webster
Lords	Richard Willey, Stephen Wright
Ladies	Gaynor Arnold, Sue Urwin

A Tragedy presented in two parts. The action takes place in Elsinore Castle.

Company Manager: David Frost
Press: Pearl Sotone, Montgomery Byers
Stage Managers: Jeremy Dain, Christine Barton, Sue Urwin

* Closed Sunday, Dec. 27, 1970 after limited engagement of 3 performances.

Hugh Thomas

David Ware Photo

ACTORS PLAYHOUSE

Opened Wednesday, December 30, 1970.*
Howard Otway, Susan Richardson, Lawrence
Goossen present:

ONE NIGHT STANDS OF A NOISY PASSENGER

By Shelley Winters; Director, Patricia Carmichael;
Scenery, Peter Harvey;Costumes, Joseph G. Aulisi;
Lighting, Roger Morgan; Hairstylist, Joe Tubens,; Pro-
duction Assistants, Lawrence Eichler, Suzanne Egan.

CAST

"The Noisy Passenger"
New York City, Feb. 14, 1940 at 1 A.M.
Young Man ....Richard Lynch
Young Girl ....Sally Kirkland

"Un Passage"
Paris, April 1953 at 4 A. M.
Girl ....Elizabeth Franz
Man ....Sam Schacht

"Last Stand"
Hollywood, Now, just before dawn
Woman.....................................Diane Ladd
Boy.....................................Robert DeNiro

Press: Alan Eichler, Stanley F. Kaminsky
Stage Manager: Barbara Tuttle

* Closed Jan. 3, 1971 after 7 performances.

Martha Swope Photo

Right: Diane Ladd, Robert DeNiro Above: Sally Kirkland, Richard Lynch

Adrienne Barbeau, Tod Miller, Stan Wiest

GATE THEATRE

Opened Sunday, January 3, 1971.*
Robert L. Steele presents:

STAG MOVIE

Book and Lyrics, David Newburge; Music, Jacques
Urbont; Director, Bernard Barrow; Dances and Musical
Staging, Doug Rogers, Scenery and Lighting, David
Chapman; Costumes, David Toser; Music Direction and
Arrangements, Jacques Urbont; Music Supervision, Len
Berg; Associate Producer, Charles Prentiss; Produced in
association with Erani Corp.; Production Assistant,
Jimmy Cuomo; Technical Director, Howard Vischinsky;
Associate Set Designer, Dianne Chapman.

CAST

Mike Rosenthal ....Hy Anzell
Marty Strauss.....................................Stan Wiest
Tanya Taranovna ....Renata Mannhardt
Tommy Tucker.....................................Tod Miller
Rip Cord ....Brad Sullivan†1
Cookie Kovac ....Adrienne Barbeau
Arthur Jensen ....Moose Matthews
Cop ....Josip Elic
Maid.....................................Shirl Bernheim†2
Understudy: Robert Barry

MUSICAL NUMBERS: "Stag Movie," "Looking at the
Sun," "I Want More Out of Life than This," " "Grocery
Boy," "Splendor in the Grass," "It's So Good," "Get in
Line," "Try a Trio," "Get Your Rocks off Rock," "We
Came Together," "Bows,"

A Musical Comedy presented without intermission.
The action takes place at the present time in a motel
room near Kennedy Airport.

General Manager: David Lawlor
Press: Sol Jacobson, Lewis Harmon
Stage Manager: Howard Smith

* Closed Mar. 21, 1971 after 89 performances.

† Succeeded by: 1. Gene GeBauer, 2. Sylvia Gassell

Zodiac Photo

MERCER-O'CASEY THEATRE

Opened Monday, January 4, 1971.*
(Moved April 27, 1971 to Soho Theatre)
Cora Gay Carr and Jerry Schlossberg present:

MACBETH

By William Shakespeare; Production Conceived and
Directed by Dino DeFilippi; Lighting, Richard Nelson;
Setting and Costumes, David Chapman.

CAST

Macbeth	David H. Leary†1
First Witch	Anne Ashcraft†2
Third Witch	David Aaron†4
Duncan	Peter Murphy
Malcolm	Dalton Cathey
Lennox	Devin Scott
Ross	David Snell
Fleance	Tony Battelle
Banquo	Rob Evan Collins†5
Macduff	Richard Greene
Lady Macbeth	Lyn Milgrim†6
Gentlewoman	Sheila Coonan†7
Porter	Peter Murphy
Macbeth's Servant	Jared Davis
Lady Macduff	Gwen Saska†8
Macduff's Son	David Aaron†9
Doctor	Peter Murphy

,A Tragedy presented in two parts.

Press: Michael Alpert
Stage Manager Robert Vandergriff

* Closed May 9, 1971 after 132 performances and 24
previews.

† Succeeded by: 1. Anthony Passantino during Mr.
Leary's illness. 2. Gwendolyn Brown, 3. Anne
Ashcraft, 4. Kay Tornborgh, 5. Anthony Passantino, 6.
Jane Gregory, 7. Anne Ashcraft, 8. Gwendolyn Brown,
9, Dawn Akins.

Carl Samrock Photo

"Soon"

RITZ THEATRE

Opened Tuesday, January 12, 1971.*
Bruce W. Stark and Sagittarius Productions Inc.
present:

SOON

Adaption, Martin Duberman; Based on story by
Joseph Martinez Kookoolis, Scott Fagan, Robert Green-
wald; Music, Joseph M. Kookoolis, Scott Fagan; Lyrics,
Scott Fagan; Scenery, Kert Lundell; Lighting, Jules
Fisher; Costumes, David Chapman; Orchestrations,
Howard Wyeth, Jon Huston; Musical Direction, Louis
St. Louis; Vocal Arrangements, Louis St. Louis, Jacque-
line Penn; Choreography, Fred Benjamin; Audio De-
sign, Jack Shearing; Production Assistants, Dyanne
Hochman, Eileen Dietz; Wigs by Wig City.

CAST

Kelly	Barry Bostwick
Annie	Marta Heflin
Wilson Wilson	Dennis Belline
Michael	Richard Gere
Neil	Joseph Campbell Butler
Henry	Peter Allen
Groupies:	
Hope	Marion Ramsey
Faith	Leata Galloway
Charity	Vicki Sue Robinson
Rita	Pamela Pentony
Sharon	Nell Carter
Jimmy	Singer Williams
Bobby	Michael Jason
Phil	John C. Nelson
Mr. Par	Del Hinkley
Elsworth Median	Angus Cairns
Gran Statisto	Larry Spinelli
Al Ti Telson	Paul Eichel
Songwriter	Tony Middleton
Psychedelic Necktie	Pendleton Brown
Messenger Boy	John C. Nelson
Mail Room Boy	Singer Williams
Delivery Boy	Michael Jason
Secretaries	Pamela Pentony, Leata Galloway, Marion Ramsey

PITSHIT: Tim Case, Sonny Coppola, Richard Apuzzo,
Adam Ippolito, Louis St. Louis.

UNDERSTUDIES: Kelly, Michael, Michael Jason; Neil,
Wilson, Necktie, John C. Nelson; Par, Elsworth, Gran,
Telson, Pendleton Brown

MUSICAL NUMBERS: "Let the World Begin Again,"
"In Your Hands," "I See the Light/Gentle Sighs,"
"Everybody's Running," "Henry Is Where It's At,"
"Music, Music," "Glad To Konw Ya," "Rita Cheeta,"
"Henry's Dream Theme," "To Touch the Sky," "Every-
body's Running," "Marketing," "Sweet Henry Loves
You," "One More Time," "Straight," "Wait," "Faces,
Names, Places," "Annie's Things," "Doing the High,"
"Soon," "Country Store Living," "What's Gonna Hap-
pen to Me," "On the Charts," "Molecules," "So Much
that I Know," "Child of Sympathy," "Frustration," "It
Won't Be Long."

A Rock Opera in 2 acts and 10 scenes.

General Manager: James E. Walsh
Press: Seymour Krawitz, Patricia McLean Krawitz,
Bruce Silke
Stage Managers: Alan Hall, Mary Porter Hall,
Del Hinkley

* Closed Jan. 13, 1971 after 3 performances and 21
previews.

Lyn Milgrim, David H. Leary

Zodiac Photo

89

PLAYHOUSE THEATRE

Opened Wednesday, January 13, 1971.*
Hillard Elkins presents:

A DOLL'S HOUSE

By Henrik Ibsen; New Adaptation by Christopher
Hampton: Based on translation by Helene Gregoire;
Director, Patrick Garland; Sets, Costumes,, Lighting,
John Bury; Production Supervisor, Michael Thoma;
Associated Producer, George Platt.

CAST

Torvald Helmer	Donald Madden
Nora	Claire Bloom
Dr. Rank	Roy Shuman
Mrs. Kristine Linde	Patricia Elliott
Nils Krogstad	Robert Geringer
Anne-Marie	Kate Wilkinson
Helene	Eda Reiss Merin†
Helmer children	Michael Calvet, Jill Grafflin

STANDBYS AND UNDERSTUDIES: Nora, Diane
Kagan; Torvald, Gil Rogers,; Mrs. Linde, Anne-Marie,
Helene, Dorothy Lyman; Dr. Rank, Gil Rogers; Krog-
stad, Simm Landres

A Drama in three acts. The action takes place during
Christmas in the Helmer's flat.

General Managers: Bill Liberman, Edmonstone F.
Thompson, Jr.
Press: Samuel J. Friedman, Shirley Herz
Stage Managers: Simm Landres, Susan Walker

* Closed June 26, 1971 after 111 performances and 15
previews in repertory with "Hedda Gabler."

† Succeeded by Camilla Ashland

Henry Grossman Photos

Left: Donald Madden, Claire Bloom

Donald Madden, Patricia Elliott, Claire Bloom

Robert Gerringer, Patricia Elliott

Claire Bloom

PLAYHOUSE THEATRE

Opened Wednesday, February 17, 1971.*
Hillard Elkins presents:

HEDDA GABLER

By Henrik Ibsen; New Adaptation by Christopher
Hampton; Director, Patrick Garland; Sets, Costumes,
Lighting, John Bury; Production Supervisor, Michael
Thoma; Associate Producer, George Platt; Dance Con-
sultant, Patrick Cummings.

CAST

Aunt Julia	Kate Wilkinson
Berte	Eda Reiss Merin†
George Tesman	Roy Shulman
Hedda Gabler	Claire Bloom
Mrs. Elvsted	Diane Kagan
Judge Brack	Robert Gerringer
Eilert Lovborg	Donald Madden

STANDBYS AND UNDERSTUDIES: Hedda, Patricia
Elliott; Lovbor, Simm Landres; Tesman, Judge, Gil
Rogers; Aunt, Berte, Mrs. Elvsted, Dorothy Lyman

A Drama presented in two acts and four scenes. The
action takes place in Tesman's villa in the fashionable
quarter of town.

General Managers: Bill Liberman,
Edmonstone F. Thompson, Jr.
Press: Samuel J. Friedman, Shirley Herz

* Closed June 26, 1971 after 26 performances in repertory with "A Doll's House."

† Succeeded by Camilla Ashland

Henry Grossman Photos

**Donald Madden, Claire Bloom Above: Roy
Shulman, Donald Madden, Claire Bloom, Robert
Gerringer**

Judith Anderson as Hamlet

CARNEGIE HALL

Opened Thursday, January 14, 1971.*
Paul Gregory in association with The American
Conservatory Theatre, and by arrangement with
The Carnegie Hall Corporation, presents:

HAMLET

By William Shakespeare; Director, William Ball; Scenery and Costumes, Robert Fletcher; Lighting, Jules Fisher; Associate Director, Eugene Barcone; Sound, Parker Young; Production Assistant, Mary O'Hanlon.

CAST

Prince Hamlet	Judith Anderson
King Claudius	Laurence Hugo
Polonius	Don McHenry
Queen Gertrude	Ludi Claire
Laertes	Philip Kerr
Ophelia	Jeanne Bartlett
Marcellus	Leon Charles
Rosencrantz	Rick Poe
Guildenstern	Robert Ground
Horatio	Stephen D. Newman
Ghost of King Hamlet	Laurence Hugo
Player Queen	Ruth Hunt
Player Murderer	Charles Dillon

A Tragedy presented in two parts. The action takes place in the Castle at Elsinore.

Company Manager: Irving Sudrow
Press: Karl Bernstein, Ann Mulhall
Stage Manager: Kenneth Julian

* Repeated on Jan. 15, 1971 for a limited engagement of 2 performances.

LIBRARY & MUSEUM OF THE PERFORMING ARTS

Opened Thursday, January 14, 1971.*
The Library and Museum of The Performing Arts at Lincoln Center presents:

TALLULAH, A MEMORY

Created by Eugenia Rawls; Designed by Antoni N. Sadlak, Jr., Costume, Jo Ellen LaRue; Sculpture, Lillian Greneker; Production Assistant, Anne Marie Borger.

CAST

EUGENIA RAWLS

* Repeated for three additional performances on Jan. 15, Apr. 22 and 23, 1971.

MERCURY THEATRE

Opened Sunday, January 17, 1971.*
Tony Capodilupo and John Fink present:

THE SHRINKING BRIDE

By Jonathan Levy; Music, William Bolcom; Lyrics, Jonathan Levy; Scenery, T. E. Mason; Costumes, Joseph G. Aulisi; Lighting, Molly Friedel; Production Assistant, Penny duPont; Directed and Staged by Marvin Gordon.

CAST

Delano Ounce	Jake Dengel
D. Norman Cates	Jack Somack
Nat	Sully Boyar
Vinnie	Frank Nastasi
Allison Cates Fisch	Louisa Flaningam
Richie	Danny DeVito
Jeanine Cates	Diane Simkin
Julius Katz	Joe Silver
Michael Fisch	John Pleshette
Sir Anthony Baer	Donald Symington

A Comedy with songs in three acts. The action takes place at the present time in Tantamount Hall, the Cates estate on the upper Hudson River, and on its grounds.

General Manager: William Craver
Company Manager: Harry Chittenden
Press: Michael Alpert, Shirley Herz, Dennis Helfend
Stage Managers: Kate M. Pollock, Vincent Cangiano

* Closed Jan. 17, 1971 after one performance.

Jack Somack, Jake Dengel

GARRICK THEATRE

Opened Sunday, January 17, 1971.*
Garrick Productions and Artists International
Management present:

EARTHLIGHT

Created by Allan Mann and The Earthlight Ensemble; Music Written and Performed by Pure Love & Pleasure; Sound, Stan Goldstein; Lighting, Jim Gaine; Settings, Ron Tannis; Additional Choreography, Peggy Chiereska; Production Assistant, Holland Williams

ENSEMBLE

Wendy Blakely, Sheila Rachel Cohen, Ellyn Diskin, Doug Fowley, Joseph D'Esposito, Tylar Gustafson, Don Marino, Eva Nicholson, Lew Prudenti, Barbara Pieters, Rick Pieters, Jane Richardson, Greg Stone, Richard Williams

PURE LOVE & PLEASURE; John Allair, Bob Bohann, Jaque Furman, Rob Moitoza, David McAnally, Peggye May (This group was succeeded by Shaker: Chuck DeFranics, Melinda Wayne, Drew Salperto, Bob Sheehan, Leo Adamian)

A Play with music presented without intermission.

General Managers: Frederick R. Walker, Mike Rivelle
Company Manager: Jill Rosner
Press: Leslie Coven, Saul Richman, Peggy Mitchell

* Closed March 21, 1971 after 56 performances.

Earthlight Ensemble

HENRY STREET PLAYHOUSE

Opened Tuesday, January 26, 1971.*
Henry Street Settlement's New Federal Theatre
(Woodie King, Jr., Dick Williams, Directors)
presents:

IN NEW ENGLAND WINTER

By Ed Bullins; Director, Dick Williams; Scenery, Pedro Lujan; Lighting, Buddy; Production Assistants, August Laguer, Hasafa As Salam; Costumes, Edna Watson.

CAST

1960:
Cliff Dawson ....Mel Winkler
Steve Benson ....Norman Bush
Chuckie ....Tony Major
Bummie ....J. Herbert Kerr, Jr.
1955:
Liz...Gloria Edwards
Oscar ....Darryl W. Lee
Carrie ....Donna O. Black
Crook...Garrett Morris

Presented in seven scenes and prologue without intermission.

General Manager: Adna Karns
Press: Howard Atlee, David Roggensack, Irene Gandy
Stage Manager: Harry Grier

* Closed Feb. 7, 1971 after 24 performances.

Bert Andrews Photo

CARNEGIE HALL

Opened Wednesday, January 20, 1971.*
Michael E. Fesco presents:

IT'S LYNNE CARTER

Special Material, Fred Ebb, John Kander, Bob Lees, Dickson Hughes, Franklyn Underwood, Lynne Carter; Musical Arrangements and Orchestrations, Ted Simons; Conductor, Dickson Hughes; Wardrobe and Costumes, Mr. Bruno of New York; Wigs, Bob Kelly; Feather Works, Larry Sittenberg; Hair Styles, George Shetla; Lighting, Paul Sullivan; Additional Staging, Jim Hoskins.

CAST

LYNNE CARTER

ACT I: "Gorgeous," "Disney for Adults," "A Freak-out in Feathers," "I Didn't Raise My Girl to Be a Bunny," "The Torch Song," "The Star Spot."

ACT II: "Famous Dietrich Medley," "Shaking My Can in Front of Carnegie Hall," "Bette Davis," "Miss Pearl Bailey," "The Final Curtain."

Press: Betty Lee Hunt, Henry Luhrman, Harriett Trachtenberg

* Presented for one performance only.

Left: Lynne Carter as Bette Davis

Tony Major, Mel Winkler, Norman Bush, J. Herbert Kerr, Jr.

SHERIDAN SQUARE PLAYHOUSE

Opened Wednesday, February 3, 1971.*
Edgar Lansbury, Mark Wright, Joseph Beruh in
association with Stuart Duncan and H. B. Lutz
present:

WAITING FOR GODOT

By Samuel Beckett; Director, Alan Schneider; De-
signed by William Ritman; Costumes, Brooks-Van Horn;
Wigs, Bob Kelly; Produced in association with Alanjean
Productions.

CAST

Estragon "Gogo"	Paul B. Price†1
Vladimir "Didi"	Henderson Forsythe†2
Lucky	Anthony Holland†3
Pozzo	Edward Winter†4
A Boy	David Jay

A Comedy in two acts. The action takes place along a
country road.

General Manager: Joseph Beruh
Press: Max Eisen, Warren Pincus, Jeanne Merrick
Stage Managers: Gigi Cascio, Dan Stone

* Still playing May 31, 1971.

† Succeeded by: 1. Oliver Clark, Warren Pincus, 2.
Warren Pincus during illness, Jordan Charney for 2
weeks, David Byrd, Tom Ewell, 3. Tom Rosqui, Dan
Stone 4. Larry Bryggman, Ed Bordo.

Alan B. Tepper Photos

**Right: Paul B. Price, Henderson Forsythe,
Anthony Holland, Edward Winter**

**Henderson Forsythe, Edward Winter,
Paul B. Price**

**David Jay, Joey Faye, Tom Ewell, Larry
Bryggman, Tom Rosqui**

WEST SIDE YMCA

Opened Saturday, February 6, 1971.*
Hunter College Playwrights present:

THE WHIP LADY

By David Zlochower; Director, Robert Saidenberg;
Set and Lighting, Joe Kaminsky; Technical Director,
Ray Crawley; Producer, Aaron Weingarten.

CAST

Moish	Jay M. Jonas
Gloria	Eileen Rubin
Sydney	Verona Barnes
Cop	Roy E. Brocksmith
Girl	Sheila Coren
Feinberg	Frederic Cook
Whip Lady	Pat O'Toole

Press: Patricia Molino
Stage Manager: Stuart Baker

* Closed Feb. 14, 1971 after limited engagement of 4
performances.

"Whip Lady"

PLAZA 9-MUSIC HALL

Opened Sunday, February 7, 1971.*
Plaza 9-Music Hall presents Second City's:

COOLER NEAR THE LAKE

Producer-Director, Bernard Sahlins; Associate Producer, Joyce Sloane; Music, Fred Kaz; Choreography, Mel Spinney; Set, Lighting, and Stanby, Sandy Martin; Piano Interludes, Baldwin Bergersen.

CAST

David Blum
Jim Fisher
Roberta Maguire
Judy Morgan
Brian Doyle-Murray
Joseph O'Flaherty
Dan Ziskie

A Revue in two acts.

Press: Saul Richman, Peggy Mitchell
Stage Manager: Sandy Martin

* Closed Feb., 28, 1971 after 25 performances.

**Judy Morgan, Joseph O'Flaherty, Brian Doyle-Murray
Right Center: Dan Ziskie, Joseph O'Flaherty,
Brian Doyle-Murray, Roberta Maguire, David Blue,
Judy Morgan, Jim Fisher**

GOOD SHEPHERD-FAITH CHURCH

Opened Sunday, February 7, 1971.*
Phoenix Theatre (T. Edward Hambleton,
Managing Director) and Leland Hayward
present:

THE TRIAL OF THE CATONSVILLE NINE

By Daniel Berrigan; Director, Gordon Davidson;
Setting, Peter Wexler, Costumes, Albert Wolsky; Light-
ing, Tharon Musser; Text for New York production by
Saul Levitt; Technical Director, Neil Louison; Staff
Assistants, Doris Ginsberg, Lucie Goidell.

CAST

Daniel Berrigan	Ed Flanders†1
Philip Berrigan	Michael Kane
David Darst	Leon Russom
John Hogan	Barton Heyman
Thomas Lewis	Sam Waterston
Marjorie Melville	Gwen Arner
Thomas Melville	Joe Ponazecki
George Mische	Richard Jordan†2
Mary Moylan	Nancy Malone†3
Defense	David Spielberg
Judge	William Schallert†4
Witness	Mary Jackson
Prosecution	Davis Roberts
Marshals	Peter Gorwin, James O'Connell, Harry Spillman

UNDERSTUDIES: Daniel, Prosecution, Defense, Jake
Dengel; Philip, John, Judge, Thomas, Arlen Snyder;
Mary, Marjorie, Witness, Ronnie Claire Edwards;
George, Thomas, David, Peter Gorwin

A Play presented without intermission.

General Manager: Marilyn S. Miller
Press: Sol Jacobson, Lewis Harmon, Ruth D. Smuckler
Stage Managers: Daniel Freudenberger, Bethe Ward

* Still playing May 31, 1971. Moved to Broadway's
Lyceum Theatre on Monday, June 7, 1971.

† Succeeded by: 1. Colgate Salsbury, 2. Michael Moriarty, 3. Ronnie Claire Edwards, 4. Mason Adams

Van Williams Photos

Leon Russom, San Waterston, Gwen Arner, Richard Jordan, Joe Ponazecki, Michael Kane, Ed Flanders, Barton Heyman, Nancy Malone Top Left: Michael Kane

ACTORS PLAYHOUSE

Opened Monday, February 8, 1971.*
Robert Weinstein in association with Trendsetter Enterprises Ltd. presents:

ISTANBOUL

By Rochelle Owens; Director, Robert Weinstein,; Set, Robert U. Taylor; Lighting, John Dodd; Costumes, Mylo Quam; Music Composed and Performed by George Mgrdichian; Additional Music and Sound, David Walker; Movement Consultant, Louis Johnson; Production Assistant, Karen de Francis.

CAST

Godfrigh	Conard Fowkes
Baldwin	Peter Carew
Leo	Joseph Hunter
Zoe	Marilyn Sokol
Mary	Sarina C. Grant
Alice	Gayla Osbourne
Gertrude	Irene Cooper
St. Mary of Egypt	Despo

A Play in five scenes without intermission. The action takes place in Constantinople in the 15th Century.

General Management: Albert Poland
Press: Saul Richman, Peggy Mitchell
Stage Manager: Jon Froscher

* Closed Feb. 14, 1971 after 8 performances and 13 previews.

Joseph Hunter, Despo
Right: Conard Fowkes, Sarina C. Grant

TOWN HALL

Opened Saturday, February 13, 1971.*
Performing Arts Repertory Theatre Foundation and New York University's Town Hall present:

YOUNG ABE LINCOLN

Book, Richard N. Bernstein, John Allen; Music, Victor Ziskin; Lyrics, Joan Javits; Special Dialogue and Lyrics, Arnold Sundgaard; Director, Jay Harnick; Designed by Fred Voelpel; Musical Director, Walter Mitchell Cree.

CAST

Abe	Robert Larsen
Ann Rutledge	Ann Hodapp
Minnie	Liz O'Neal
Judge Bowling Green	Frank Groseclose
Jack Armstrong	Herbert Duval
John McNeil	Alan Easterby
Josh	James Rivers
Bill Berry	John Remme
Ninian Edwards	Bailey Davis

MUSICAL NUMBERS: "Same Old Me," "Cheer Up," "You Can Dance," "Someone You Know," "Frog," "Clarey Grove," "Don't Point Them Guns," "Drill, "Run Injuns," "Welcome Home," "Vote for Lincoln," "Frontier Politics."

A Musical in 2 acts and 7 scenes.

* Presented for one performance only.

Robert Larsen

TRUCK & WAREHOUSE THEATRE
Opened Wednesday, February 10, 1971.
Warren Lyons and Betty Ann Besch present:

THE HOUSE OF BLUE LEAVES

By John Guare; Director, Mel Shapiro; Setting, Karl Eigsti; Costumes, Jane Greenwood; Lighting, John Tedesco; Original Songs, John Guare; Production Assistants, Carl Hunt, J. Kevin Hanlon, Tom Flynn.

CAST

Artie Shaughnessy	Harold Gould†1
Ronnie Shaughnessy	William Atherton†2
Bunny Flingus	Anne Meara
Bananas Shaughnessy	Katherine Helmond
Corrina Stroller	Margaret Linn
Head Nun	Rita Karen
Second Nun	Kay Michaels
Little Nun	Alix Elias†3
M. P.	Thomas F. Flynn
The White Man	Carl Hunt
Billy Einhorn	Frank Converse†4

UNDERSTUDIES: Ronnie, Carl Hunt; Bunny, Margaret Linn; Bananas, Kay Michaels; Nuns; Christie Virtue

A Comedy in three acts and a prologue, presented with one intermission. The action takes place in the El Dorado Bar and Grill, and in an apartment in Sunnyside, Queens, N. Y., on Oct. 4, 1965.

General Manager: William Craver
Company Manager: Harry Chittenden
Press: Merle Debuskey, Faith Greer
Stage Managers: Charles Briggs, Carl Hunt

* Still playing May 31, 1971. Recipient of New York Drama Critics Circle Award as Best American Play of 1970-71.

† Succeeded by: 1. Lee Allen for 2 weeks, Ralph Meeker, 2. Glenn Walken, 3. Georgia Engel, 4. Jeremiah Sullivan, Jered Mickey

Martha Swope Photos

William Atherton, Tom Flynn, Anne Meara, Katherine Helmond, Harold Gould, Carl Hunt, Frank Converse, Margaret Linn (on floor), Rita Karin, Alix Elias, Kay Michaels
Top Left: Katherine Helmond, Harold Gould

Katherine Helmond, Peggy Pope, Ralph Meeker
Above: Ralph Meeker, John Glover, Katherine
Helmond

Katherine Helmond, Peggy Pope

THEATRE DE LYS

Opened Monday, February 15, 1971.*
The New Comedy Theatre (Jerry Schlossberg,
James Hammerstein, Israel Horovitz, Albert
Poland) present:

ACROBATS and LINE

By Israel Horovitz; Director, James Hammerstein;
Designed by Neil Peter Jampolis; Additional Staging by
Grover Dale; Production Consultants, Jerry Cutler En-
terprises; Technical Director, Jack Magnifico; Production
Assistants, Jeffrey Cohen, Marvin Horowitz, Jane
Schlossberg; Presented by special arrangement with
Lucille Lortel Productions Inc.

CAST

"Acrobats'
Man ....Danny duVal
Edna...Trina duVal

"Line"
Fleming ....John Randolph
Stephen..Richard Dreyfuss
Molly...Ann Wedgeworth
Dolan...John Cazale
Arnall ....Barnard Hughes

Both plays take place at the present time.

General Managers: Leonard A. Mulhern,
George W. Thorne
Press: Samuel J. Friedman, Louise Weiner Ment
Stage Manager: Robert Vandergriff

* Closed March 14, 1971 after 31 performances.

Steve Schapiro Photo

**Danny and Trina duVal, Barnard Hughes, John
Randolph, John Cazale, Ann Wedgeworth, Richard Dreyfuss**

PROMENADE THEATRE

Opened Thursday, February 18, 1971.*
Jay H. Fuchs with Stuart Duncan presents:

DO IT AGAIN!

Conceived and Directed by Bert Convy; Musical
Supervision, William Cox; Lighting, Roger Morgan;
Scenic Consultant, Barry Arnold; Production Coordina-
tor, Gail Bell; Assistant to Producers, Lee Ackerman;
Production Assistant, Wendie Owen.

CAST

Margaret Whiting

Clifton Davis   Susan Long
Robin Benson   Marion Ramsey

A George Gershwin Musicade presented in two acts.

General Manager: Joseph Beruh
Company Manager: Al Isaac
Press: Marvin Kohn

* Closed Feb. 28, 1971 after 14 performances.

Alan B. Tepper Photo

PROVINCETOWN PLAYHOUSE

Opened Thursday, February 18, 1971.*
Jules and Gila Zalon present:

THINGS THAT ALMOST HAPPEN

By Claude McNeal; Directed by Mr. McNeal; Sce-
nery, Tim Wilson; Lighting, Paul T. Holland; Set, Anton
Hok; Production Assistant, Robert Johnston; Costumes,
Minerva Farrell.

CAST

"Morton: The Patient"
Morton...Richard Lynch
Doctor...Sam Coppola
Nurse...Karen Rosenblatt

"The Courtship of Kevin and Roxanne"
Kevin ....Patrick McDermott
Roxanne...Karen Rosenblatt
Cop...Sam Coppola

"Dominic's Lover"
(Based on Browning's "Porphyria's Lover")
Dominic...Sam Coppola
Eleanor..Karen Rosenblatt
Jerry ....Patrick McDermott

General Managers: Barry Hoffman, Sol Posnack
Company Manager: Paul T. Holland
Press: Howard Atlee, David Roggensack, Irene Gandy
Stage Manager: Robert W. Perkins

* Closed Feb. 21, 1971 after 5 performances.

Bert Andrews Photo

**Margaret Whiting, Clifton Davis Left Center:
Sam Coppola, Karen Rosenblatt, Patrick
McDermot**

GREENWICH MEWS THEATRE

Opened Thursday, February 25, 1971.*
Greenwich Mews Spanish Theatre (Gilberto Zaldivar, Producer) presents:

YERMA

By Federico Garcia Lorca; English version, James Graham-Lujan, Richard L. O'Connell; Director, Rene Buch; Scenery and Costumes, Bob Troie; Lighting, Ray McCutcheon; Choreography, Graciela Daniele; Musical Direction, Juan Viccini; English Speech Coach, Elaine Eldridge.

CAST

Yerma ....Luz Castanos†
Juan ....Norberto Kerner
Maria ....Miriam Cruz
Victor ....Nino Roger or Rafael Triana
Old Pagan Woman ..Lolina Gutierrez or Gail Kellstrom
Young Girl ....Magaly Raffo or Janice Dean
Second Young Girl.......................Isabel Segovia
Dolores ....Conchita Vargas
Boy ....Marcelino Rosado
Female Figure.......................Elisa Vietta
Male Figure ....Carlos Sawage or James H. Poulliot
Sisters-in-law..............Susan Seltzer, Alicia Kaplan, Lina Centeno, Milagros Horrego
Laundresses..............Lina Centeno, Alicia Kaplan, Linda Monteiro, Magaly Raffo, Milagros Horrego, Elisa Vietta, Susan Seltzer
Men ..Pedro Fernandez, Enrique Puebla, Orlando Morfi, Esteban Chalbaud, Jean Rosado, Jean-Paul Delgado, Larry Ramos

A Drama presented without intermission.

Press: Marian Graham

* Closed May 30, 1971 after 69 performances, alternately in Spanish and English.

† Succeeded by Ketti Melonas

Avery Willard Photo

ANDERSON THEATRE

Opened Sunday, February 28, 1971.*
Haila Stoddard, Neal DuBrock present:

THE SURVIVAL OF ST. JOAN

Book and Lyrics, James Lineberger; Music, Hank and Gary Ruffin; Performed by Smoke Rise; Setting and Costumes, Peter Harvey; Musical Supervisor, Stephen Schwartz; Lighting, Thomas Skelton; Conceived and Directed by Chuck Gnys.

CAST

Friar, Accuser ....F. Murray Abraham
Child, Villager ....Willie Rock
Jailer, Philippe ....Lenny Baker
Bishop, Soldier....................Ronald Bishop
Shepherd ....Richard Bright
Joan...............................Gretchen Corbett
Witch, Whore, Nun ....Elizabeth Eis
Monk, Soldier......................Bill Braden
Mother, Whore.....................Judith Granite
Monk, Penitent ....Peter Lazer
Shepherd's son, Leper....................Anthony Marciona
Whore, Nun, Mother...........................Patricia O'Connell
Whore, Leper, Penitent................Janet Sarno
Friar, Abbot, Executioner..............Tom Sawyer
Scribe, Hunter, Man....................Matthew Tobin
Standby: Steve Reinhardt

A Medieval Rock Opera in 19 scenes performed without intermission.

General Manager: Norman E. Rothstein
Company Manager James Walsh
Press: Betty Lee Hunt, Henry Luhrman, Harriett Trachtenberg, Maria Pucci
Stage Managers: Sean Gillespie, Lynne Prather

* Closed March 14, 1971 after 17 performances.

Martha Swope Photo

Luz Castanos, Miriam Cruz in "Yerma"

BROOKLYN ACADEMY OF MUSIC

Opened Thursday, February 25, 1971.*
The Brooklyn Academy of Music and the Byrd Hoffman Foundation present:

DEAFMAN GLANCE

Written and Directed by Robert M. Wilson; Set, Fred Kolouch; Costumes, Margaret S. Hall; Lighting, Johnny Dodd; Sound and Music Coordination, Igor Demjen; Adviser, Cindy Lubar.

CAST

Raymond Andrews
and 85 members of the Byrd Hoffman School of Byrds.

Press: Debbie Steinfirst, Tom Kerrigan
Stage Managers: Ellie Wittman, Melvin Andringa

* Repeated on Friday, March 5, 1971. (No photos available)

Mathew Tobin, Ronald Bishop, Gretchen Corbett

CABARET THEATRE

Opened Tuesday, March 2, 1971.*
Cabaret Theatre at Noon presents:

MEEOW!!

Adapted by A. Devon; From Lewis Carroll; Director, MacIntyre Dixon; Production Co-ordinator, Howard Girven; Managing Director, Donna Seigfried; Production Assistants, Ellen Stoltz, Mary Ann Linde, Dorothy Allerheiligen.

CAST

Carpenter	Jay Bonnell
Walrus	MacIntyre Dixon
March Hare	Howard Girven
Dormouse	Bolen High
Alice	Saundra MacDonald
Queen	Rose Roffman
Pianist	Ellen Wright

A Mad Musical Meringue presented without intermission.

* Closed April 2, 1971 after 48 performances.

Mary Bracken Phillips, Ron Husmann

Back: Jay Bonnell, Howard Girven, MacIntyre Dixon, Rose Roffman Front: Ellen Wright, Bolen High, Saundra MacDonald

CENTRAL PRESBYTERIAN CHURCH

Opened Wednesday, March 17, 1971.*
Robert Teuscher and the Religion and Arts Committee of Central Church present:

MURDER IN THE CATHEDRAL

By T. S. Eliot; Director, Robert Teuscher; Lighting, Sandy Reading; Designed by Clyde Spooner.

CAST

Archbishop Thomas Becket	Jonathan Frid
Messenger	Marji Yablon
Attendants	Bernard Cooper, Clyde Spooner
Priests	Len Auclair, Bob Demato, David Smith
Tempters/Knights	Frederick Spreyer, Jr., Philip Fisher, James Hummert, Mark Dempsey
Women of Canterbury	Becky Reading, Jean Baur, Maggi Francis, Lenore Harris, Eileen McComb, Marji Yablon

A Poetic Drama in two parts.

Press: Cathy Beal, Debora Brown
Stage Manager: Mary Schreiber

* Closed March 27, 1971 after limited engagement of 8 performances.

Carmian Reading Photo

THEATRE FOUR

Opened Friday, March 5, 1971.*
Jean Merie-Lee presents:

LOOK WHERE I'M AT!

Adapted by James Leasor from Thorne Smith's novel "Rain in the Doorway"; Music, Jordan Ramin; Lyrics, Frank H. Stanton, Murray Semos; Director, Choreographer, Wakefield Poole; Sets and Lighting, Robert Guerra; Orchestrations and Dance Arrangements, Wally Harper; Musical Director, Jack Lee; Costumes, Rosemarie Heyer; Associate Choreographer, Frank DeSal; Conductors, Mack Schlefer, Production Coordinator, Mary Hope Condon; Production Assitant, Maureen Baker.

CAST

Hector	Ron Husmann
Horrid	Martin Ross
Satin	Mary Bracken Phillips
Larkin	Arthur Bartow
Gloria	Sherri Spillane

SINGERS AND DANCERS: Yveline Baudez, Lonnie Burr, Denny Martin Flinn, Eileen Shannon, Eleanor Smith, Jennifer Williams

MUSICAL NUMBERS: "Change of Scene," "What a Day for a Wonderful Day," "Animals," "What Are You Running From, Mister?," "Partners," "Who Does She Think She Is?," "Look Where I'm At!," "Never, Never Leave Me," "Money Isn't Everything, But," "Party Scene," "Company of Men," "The Me I Want to Be," "Little Sparrow," "Euphoria."

A Musical Comedy in 2 acts and 18 scenes.

General Manager: William Craver
Company Manager: Barry Hoffman
Press: Bill Doll & Co.
Stage Managers: Richard Thayer, Jeanne Beauvais, Larry Steckman

* Closed Mar. 5, 1971 after 1 performance.

Jonathan Frid

BIJOU THEATRE

Opened Tuesday, March 9, 1971.*
Robert Shelley presents:

A DAY IN THE LIFE OF JUST ABOUT EVERYONE

Music and Lyrics, Earl Wilson, Jr.; Director, Tom Panko; Additional Dialogue, Michael Sawyer; Costumes, Miles White; Scenery and Lighting, Andrew Greenhut; Musical Director, Bill Cunningham; Orchestrations and Vocal Arrnagements, Don Pippin; Art Director and Visuals, Terry Santry; Associate Producers, Lawrence Simon, Midge LaGuardia; Producers' Assistant, Esther Flaster.

CAST

Smitty	Earl Wilson, Jr.
Penny	June Gable
Friends and Acquaintances	Daniel Fortus, Dickie Evans, DeMarest Grey, Bennett Kinsey
Understudy: Howard Feuer	

MUSICAL NUMBERS: "If I Could Live My Life Again," "The View from My Window," "A Brief Dissertation on the Relevancy of a Liberal Education in a Contemporary Society," "Fare Thee Well," "A Waltz for Two Balloons," "Safe," "When I Was a Child," "Give Us This Day," "Goin' Home," "Out of Town," "Merrill, Lynch, Pierce, Fenner and Clyde," "Everybody Loves a Single Girl," "Two Grown-up People at Play," "What Do I Do Now," "Got to Be a Woman Now," "He's Beginning to Look a Lot Like Me," "A Woman Is Just a Female," "Faces without Names," "Paper Tiger," "The People in the Street," "Visiting Hours," "The Man I Could Have Been," "Isn't that What Makes Life Worthwhile," "If I Could Live My Life Again."

A Musical in 26 scenes without intermission. The action takes place any time and any place.

General Manager: Paul Vroom
Company Manager: Bill Dean
Press: David Lipsky, Lisa Lipsky, Joel Dein

* Closed Mar. 14, 1971 after 7 performances.

Bert Andrews Photo

Front: Bennett Kinsey, Earl Wilson, Jr.,
DeMarest Grey, Back: Dickie Evans, June Gable,
Daniel Fortus

ST. PHILIP'S COMMUNITY THEATRE

Opened Wednesday, March 17, 1971.*
The Al Fann Theatrical Ensemble (Albert L. Fann, Director) and St. Philip's Community Service Council present:

KING HEROIN

Written and Directed by Al Fann; Technical Director, Druth McClure; Costumes and Set, Al Fann; Choreographer, Vernee Watson; Sound Technician, William Pelt; Administrative Assistant, Barbara Fann.

CAST

Bessie	Barbara Fann
Doctor, Bartender	Victor Mims
Mrs. Johnson, Barfly	Marilyn Thomas
Court Clerk, Lucky	Joe Johnson or Adam Wade
First Child	Melanie Fann
Second Child	Tracy Fann
Shelley	Shelley Fann
Mark	Alfred Little
Candy, Nurse	Candy Mobley
Benny the Cat	Tim Pelt
Crap Shooter, Gary	Gary Harris
Sylvester, Weasel	Duke Sparks
Mable, Nurse's Aide	Vernee Watson
Lt. Henrix, Voice of King Heroin	Al Fann
Secretary, Booster, Social Worker	Susan Singleton
Second Woman, Mrs. Grey	Nathylin Flowers
Reeta Johnson	Reeta White
Adam, Murphy, Hustler	Adam Wade
James "Mad Daddy" McDonald	William Pelt
Socialite	LaVern Fields

A Drama in 2 acts and 19 scenes. The action takes place at the present time.

Press: Robert Ganshaw
Stage Managers: Tim Pelt, Adam Wade, Victor Mims

* Closed Apr. 11, 1971 after 28 performances to tour public schools.

Ed Bailey Photo

Richard Hunter, Tim Pelt, Al Fann

MERCER-HANSBERRY THEATRE

Opened Tuesday, March 23, 1971.*
Sankowich/Golyn Productions presents:

ONE FLEW OVER THE CUCKOO'S NEST

By Dale Wasserman; From the novel by Ken Kesey; Director, Lee D. Sandowich; Designed by Neil Peter Jampolis; Producer, Rudi Golyn; Production Supervisor, Harvey Medlinsky; Music, James Barnett, John Blakeley; Costumes, Teddi Kern; Recordings, Gary Harris; Sound, Dan Dugan.

CAST

Chief Bromden	William Burns
Aide Williams	William Paterson, Jr.
Aide Washington	John Henry Redwood
Nurse Ratched	Janet Ward
Nurse Flinn	Eve Packer
Dale Harding	James J. Sloyan
Billy Bibbitt	Lawrie Driscoll
Charles Atkins Cheswick III	William Duff-Griffin
Frank Scanlon	Jon Richards
Anthony Martini	Danny DeVito
Ruckly	Joseph Napoli
Randle Patrick McMurphy	William Devane
Dr. Spivey	Jack Aaron
Aide Turkle	Jeffrey Miller
Candy	Louie Piday
Technician	Kelly Monaghan
Sandy	Sydney Adreani

VOICES: John Garber, Doug Armand, Joseph Napoli, Danny Rich, Marc Nelsen, Teddi Kern, James Barnett, John Blakeley, Lee D. Sankowich

UNDERSTUDIES: McMurphy, James J. Sloyan; Ratched, Louis Piday; Harding, Jack Aaron; Patients and Staff, Steve Keitz, Kelly Monaghan

A Drama in two acts. The action takes place at the present time in a ward in a state mental hospital.

General Manager: William Craver
Press: Seymour Krawitz, Patricia McLean Krawitz, Bruce Silke
Stage Managers: Daniel Hild, Harry Chittenden

* Still playing May 31, 1971.

Zodiac Photos

Janet Ward, John Redwood, William Devane, William Burns Top Left: William Devane, Janet Ward, and also below with inmates

David Holliday, Bernadette Peters in
'Nevertheless They Laugh'

THE LAMBS CLUB
Opened Wednesday, March 24, 1971.*
The Lambs Club presents:

NEVERTHELESS THEY LAUGH

Book and Lyrics, LaRue Watts; Based on "He Who Gets Slapped" by Leonid Andreyev; Music, Richard Lescsak; Director-Choreographer, Tod Jackson; Set, Mark Ivancic; Costumes, Peter Joseph; Lighting, Beverly Emmons; Conductor, William R. Cox; Orchestrations, Vocal Arrangements, Dance and Incidental Music, Richard Lescsak; Technical Director, Dean Crane; Producers, Arthur Benjamin, Harry Endicott, Tod Jackson.

CAST

He	David Holliday
Consuelo	Bernadette Peters
Zinida	Marilyn Child
Jackson	Bill Starr
Jezebel	Lu Leonard
Papa Briquet	Michael Byrne
Mancini	Dick Korthaze
Bezano	Craig Yates
Baron Regnard	Charles Caron
A Gentleman	Gordon Fearing
Ernestine	Terry Nicholson
Dodo	J. J. Coyle
Helene	Diane Ball
Sylvette	Anne Piacentini
Hugo	Dennis Edenfield
Roustabout Clowns	Robert Middleton, Peter Loffredo, Allayne Johnson

MUSICAL NUMBERS: "You Must Forget," "The Clown," "No One Will Know," "Can You Love," "The Baron," "Believe," "Nevertheless, They Laugh," "One Simple Song," "I Don't Understand It," "Consuelo," "More Than You," "Freaks," "Soliloquy," "Once and For All," "More than Me," "Everything Fine," "I Charmed the Wine," "You Must Forget."

A Musical in two acts. The action takes place with a European circus prior to the turn of the century.

Press: Barbara Schwei
Stage Managers: Igors Gavon, Robert Middleton

* Closed Mar. 28, 1971 after a limited engagement of 5 performances.

Jason Photo

CARNEGIE HALL
Opened Wednesday, March 24, 1971.*
Pacific World Artists Inc. presents:

NOH-KYOGEN

The National Theatres of Japan, supported by the Foreign Ministry, K.B.S., and the Asahi Shimbun; Lecturer, Prof. Kensuke Tamai of Kyoritsu University in Tokyo.

COMPANY

NOH: Michio Sakurama, Kintaro Sakuama, Yoshimi Moriya, Nobutaka Komparu, Tatsuyuki Seo, Yasuaki Komparu, Mitsuhiro Hondo, Keisuke Suzuki, Iichiro Hase, Yasutoshi Moriya, Kogen Kazuyama, Katsumi Izumi, Kan Hoshio, Kazuya Kudo
KYOGEN: Manzo Nomura, Mannojio Nomura, Mansaku Nomura, Matasaburo Nomura, Mannosuku Nomura

REPERTOIRE

NOH: Boshibari, Futari Daimyo, Shido Hogaku, Futari Bakama
KYOGEN: Funabenkei (Benkei in the Boat), Aoi No Ue (The Lady Aoi), Sumidagawa (The Curlew River)

Press: Ann Mulhall
Stage Manager: Kakigahara

* Closed Mar. 26, 1971 after limited engagement of three performances to tour.

Noh company in performance

GRAMERCY ARTS THEATRE
Opened Wednesday, March 24, 1971.*
(Moved April 28, 1971 to Mercer-Shaw Arena)
Manon Enterprises Ltd. and Propositions Inc.
present:

THE PROPOSITION

Conceived and Directed by Allan Albert; Designed by
Allan Albert and Clint Helvey; Musical Director and
Pianist, Danny Troob; Bass, Gualberto Pillich.

CAST

Paul Kreppel   Jane Curtin
Josh Mostel   Munson Hicks
Karen Welles   Judy Kahan

An Improvisational Musical Revue in two parts.

General Manager: Cynthia Parker
Press: Harvey B. Sabinson, Lee Solters,
Sandra Manley

* Still playing May 31, 1971.

William L. Smith Photos

Below: Josh Mostel, Jane Curtin, also Top Right
with Paul Kreppel, Judy Kahan, Munson Hicks

THEATRE DE LYS
Opened Wednesday, March 31, 1971.*
Woodie King Associates (Russell Price-Ida Epps,
Co-Producers; National Center for Afro-American
Artists) present:

BEHOLD! COMETH THE VANDERKELLANS

By William Wellington Mackey; Director, Edmund
Cambridge; Scenery, George Corrin; Costumes, Audrey
Smaltz; Lighting, Roger Morgan; Sound, Gary Harris;
Associate Producer, William Wellington Mackey; Pre-
sented by Special Arrangement with Lucille Lortel
Productions, Inc.: Production Assistant, Horacena Tay-
lor.

CAST

Dr. Vanderkellan..Graham Brown
Mrs. Vanderkellan......................................Frances Foster
Desiree Vanderkellan ....Roxie Roker
Gregory Vanderkellan ....Carl Byrd
Luiz Vanderkellan ....Robert Christian

A Drama in 3 acts. The action takes place at Holden
University, a leading Southern School, on the Saturday
before Easter in 1960.

General Manager: Paul B. Berkowsky
Company Manager: Beldon Raspberry
Press: Howard Atlee, David Roggensack, Irene Gandy
Stage Manager: Steven Holmes

* Closed Apr. 18, 1971 after 23 performances.

PLAYERS THEATRE
Opened Tuesday, March 30, 1971.* Donald
Goldman presents:

THE RED WHITE AND BLACK

Book and Lyrics, Eric Bentley; Music, Trad Brug;
Production Conceived by John Dillon; Director, Eric
Bentley; Musical Arrangements and Direction, Brad
Burg; Setting, Mil Mikeulewicz; Lighting, Robert Eng-
strom; Costumes, Margaret Tobin

CAST

Pamela Adams   Philip Patterson
Sofia Andoniadis   Marilyn Sokol
Antonio Azito   Bill Sweeney
Rob Farkas   The History of Russia

"A Musical Roll Call" (political revue) presented
without intermission.

Stage Manager: Rick Rotante

* Closed March 30, 1971 after one performance.

**Frances Foster, Graham Brown (seated), Carl
Byrd, Roxie Roker, Robert Christian**

THEATRE 80 ST. MARKS
Opened Thursday, April 1, 1971.*
The A & A Project presents:

LIFE IN BED

By Joseph Renard; Director, Lea Hopkins; Scenery, Jay Kotcher; Lighting, Bruce Peyton; Entire Production under Artistic Supervision of Nyla Lyon.

CAST

Terry Cash	Jerry Rodgers
Linda, Francine, Welfare Worker	Nancy Rhoades
Iceman, Mr. Greene, Telephone Man	Bill Cola-Pinto
Mother	Patricia John†
Marvin	Garry Restifo

A Comedy in two acts. The action takes place at the present time in a slum apartment on Manhattan's lower East Side.

Press: Alan Eichler
Stage Manager: Peggy Gilbride

* Closed June 6, 1971 after 79 performances.

† Succeeded by Sandra Bertrand

Carl Samrock Photo

Nancy Rhoades, Jerry Rodgers in 'Life in Bed'

EDISON THEATRE
Opened Sunday, April 11, 1971.*
Timothy Gray and Robert Fletcher in association with Midge LaGuardia present:

JOHNNY JOHNSON

Book and Lyrics, Paul Green; Music, Kurt Weill; Director, Jose Quintero; Choreography, Bertram Ross; Scenery, Peter Harvey; Costumes, Robert Fletcher; Lighting, Roger Morgan; Orchestrations, Kurt Weill; Musical Direction, Joseph Klein; Assistant to Producers, Anne Kendall

CAST

Ralph Williams

James Billings	Nadine Lewis
Alice Cannon	Bob Lydiard
Norman Chase	Paul Michael
June Helmers	Gordon Minard
Clay Johns	Alexander Orfaly
Charlotte Jones	Norman Riggins
Christopher Klein	Wayne Sherwood

MUSICAL NUMBERS: "Over in Europe," "Democracy's Call," "Up Chickamauga Hill," "Johnny's Melody," "Aggie's Song," "Oh Heart of Love," "Farewell, Goodbye," "Sergeant's Chant," "Valentine's Tango," "You're in the Army Now," "Johnny's Oath," "Song of the Goddess," "Song of the Wounded Frenchmen," "Tea Song," "Cowboy Song," "Johnny's Dream," "Song of the Guns," "Music of the Stricken Redeemer," "Army Song," "Mon Ami, My Friend," "Allied High Command," "Laughing Generals," "The Battle," "Prayer: In Times of War and Tumults," "No Man's Land," "Psychiatry Song," "Hymn to Peace," "Johnny Johnson's Song," "How Sweetly Friendship Binds," Finale.

A Musical in 2 acts and 14 scenes. The action takes place in 1917, and some years later, in America and France.

General Manager: Norman Maibaum
Company Manager: John J. Miller
Press: Howard Atlee, David Roggensack, Irene Gandy
Stage Manager: Jamie Howard

* Closed Apr. 11, 1971 after one performance and 10 previews.

Bert Andrews Photo

ACTORS PLAYHOUSE
Opened Monday, April 5, 1971.*
Rene Enriquez and Jack Marshall present:

THE OLATHE RESPONSE

By Jack Marshall; Director, Rene Enriquez; Designed by Jim Hardy; Costumes, Alexis Blassini; Special Music Composed by Joe Cain; Hairstylist, Joe Pignatore.

CAST

Federico	Joe Santos
Angela	Ann Whiteside
Christopher	Peter Burnell

A Drama in two acts. The action takes place at the present time.

General Manager: Thesing/Ralston Enterprises
Press: Betty Lee Hunt, Henry Luhrman, Harriett Trachtenberg, Maria Pucci
Stage Manager: James J. Thesing

* Closed Apr. 11, 1971 after 6 performances.

Martha Swope Photo

Left Center: Joe Sanos, Peter Burnell, Ann Whiteside

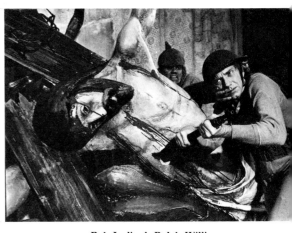

Bob Lydiard, Ralph Williams

107

CRICKET PLAYHOUSE

Opened Monday, April 12, 1971.*
Slade Brown presents Charles Strouse's:

SIX

Director, Peter Coe; Assistant, Denny Flinn; Designed by Richard Nelson; Musical Director, Wally Harper; Associate, Rod Derefinko; Film Effects, Charles M. Atlas

CAST

Johanna Albrecht   Gail Nelson
Lee Beery   Gilbert Price
Alvin Ing   Hal Watters
Understudies: Barbara Hoffman, John Bayliss

MUSICAL NUMBERS: "What Is There to Sing About?," "The Garden," "Love Song," "Six," "Coming Attractions," "The Invisible Man," "The Critic," "Trip," "The Beginning," "The Dream"

A Musical without intermission.

General Manager: David Lawlor
Press: Samuel J. Friedman, Shirley Herz
Stage Manager: Curtiss Sayblack

* Closed Apr. 18, 1971 after 8 performances.

Henry Grossman Photos

Alvin Ing, Lee Beery, Johanna Albrecht, Gilbert
Price, Gail Nelson, Hal Watters
in "Six"

ALL SOULS UNITARIAN CHURCH

Opened Friday, April 16, 1971.*
All Souls Players present:

GOLDILOCKS

Book, Walter and Jean Kerr; Music, Leroy Anderson; Lyrics, Joan Ford, Walter and Jean Kerr; Directed and Choreographed by Jeffery K. Neill; Musical Director, Wendell Kindberg; Settings, Jimmy Cuomo; Costumes, Sydney Brooks; Lighting, George Turski; Produced by Dorothy Harris, Walter Landa, Mary McCartney.

CAST

Maggie Harris	Sandy Sprung
Clown	Randy Wilson
George Randolph Brown	John York
Max Grady	Ed Penn
Lois	Barbara Coggin
Pete	Jon Harris
Andy	Randy Wilson
Harvey	Arthur Silber
Sam	Tran William Rhodes
J. C	Joel Greenhouse
Bessie	Eileen Ronaldes
Bear	Douglas Clark

ENSEMBLE: Ginny Riagini, Douglas Clark, Dorie DonVito, Edwin A. Folts, Don Hinde, Neil Howard, Barbara Jones, Lila Koven, Judy Lee, Don Madison, Michele Mazur, Caroline Mode, Barbara Mungyer, Martha Robinson, Trudy Smith, Ron Talbert

MUSICAL NUMBERS: "Lazy Moon," "Give the Little Lady," "Save a Kiss," "Little Girls Should Be Seen," "Indian Sequence," "No One'll Ever Love You," "Who's Been Sitting in My Chair," "There Never Was a Woman," "The Pussyfoot," "Pirate Sequence," "Are We Feeling Any Better," "Lady in Waiting," "Silent Movie Ballet," "The Beast in You," "Shall I Take My Heart and Go," "I Can't Be in Love," "Bad Companions," "Guess Who," "I Never Know When," "Two Years in the Making," "Heart of Stone," "

A Musical in 2 acts and 11 scenes. The action takes place in 1913.

Stage Managers: Mary McCartney, Dee Riffle

* Closed April 24, 1971 after a limited engagement of 8 performances on weekends only.

(No photos available)

Gilbert Price, Gail Nelson
in "Six"

BARBIZON-PLAZA THEATRE

Opened Wednesday, April 14, 1971.*
Le Treteau de Paris (Jean de Rigault, Executive Producer) by special arrangement with Seff Associates Ltd. presents:

L'AMANTE ANGLAISE

By Marguerite Duras; Director, Claude Regy; Announcement recorded by Francois Perier; Managing Director, Jacques Courtines; General Administrator, Yves Berthiau.

CAST

Claire Lannes	Madeleine Renaud
Pierre Lannes	Claude Dauphin
L'interrogateur	Michael Lonsdale

A Drama in two parts presented without intermission. The action takes place in France in 1966.

Company Manager: Robert Fishko
Press: Arthur Cantor
Stage Managers: Francis Charles, Henry Abbott

* Closed April 24, 1971 after limited engagement of 15 performances. An English translation entitled "A Place without Doors" was presented Dec. 22, 1970 at the Stairway Theatre for 30 performances with Mildred Dunnock, Richard A. Dysart, and Alvin Epstein.

Michael Lonsdale, Madeleine Renaud, Claude Dauphin

MARTINIQUE THEATRE

Opened Tuesday, April 20, 1971.*
Ramsey, Formaad and Stitt present:

KISS NOW

Book and Lyrics, Maxine Klein; Music, William S. Fischer; Conceived and Directed by Maxine Klein; Choreography, Sandar Caprin; Vocal Arrangements and Musical Direction, Herbert Kaplan; Orchestrations, Bill Brohn; Lighting and Set, Richard Devin; Costumes, Nancy Adzima; Assistant to Producers, Barbara Wood; Production Assistants, Naneen Boyce, James, R. Pollock, Frederick P. Reinhart

CAST

Lloyd Bremseth	Irving A. Lee
Sandra Caprin	Susan McAneny
Nancy Denning	Lyle Pearsons
Louise Hoven	Eddie Silas

MUSICAL NUMBERS: "This City Is a Kisser," "Travelin' Man," "The June Taylor," "Too Tired to Love," "Try the Sky," "Death Dance," "No Touch Mine," "Strawberry Day," "Touch Kiss," "Rodeo," "French Thing Tango," "Kabuki Rock," "Kiss Now."

A Musical presented without intermission.

General Managers: Grayson & Olim
Company Manager: Derek Mali
Press: Howard Atlee, David Roggensack, Irene Gandy
Stage Managers: Peter Von Mayrhauser, Alberto Torres

* Closed Apr. 23, 1971 after 3 performances.

Martha Holmes Photo

Susan McAneny, Lyle Pearsons, Nancy Denning, Lloyd Bremseth

PROMENADE THEATRE

Opened Wednesday, April 21, 1971.*
Edgar Lansbury/Jay H. Fuchs/Stuart Duncan/
Joseph Beruh present:

LONG DAY'S JOURNEY INTO NIGHT

By Eugene O'Neill; Director, Arvin Brown; Setting,
Elmon Webb, Virginia Dancy; Costumes, Whitney Blausen; Lighting, Ronald Wallace; Production Assistant,
Julia Fremon.

CAST

James Tyrone	Robert Ryan
Mary Cavan Tyrone	Geraldine Fitzgerald
James Tyrone, Jr.	Stacy Keach
Edmund Tyrone	James Naughton
Cathleen	Paddy Croft

A Drama in 4 acts and 5 scenes. The action takes
place in August of 1912 in the living room of the
Tyrones' summer home.

General Manager: Joseph Beruh
Company Manager: Al Isaac
Press: Max Eisen, Warren Pincus, Milly Schoenbaum
Stage Manager: Gail Bell

* Still playing May 31, 1971. The following appeared at
matinees: John Beal, Carol Teitel, David Gantry, Dan
Hamilton, Paddy Croft.

**Left: Stacy Keach, Robert Ryan, James
Naughton, Geraldine Fitzgerald**

Robert Ryan, Geraldine Fitzgerald

James Naughton, Geraldine Fitzgerald

Carol Teitel, John Beal, Dan Hamilton, Donald Gantry Above: Robert Ryan, Stacy Keach

Dan Hamilton, John Beal Above: Robert Ryan, Geraldine Fitzgerald

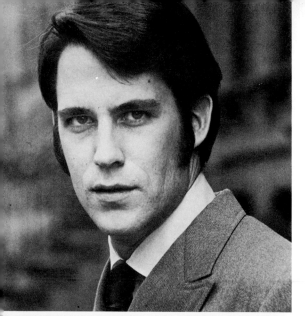

THEATRE FOUR

Opened Monday, April 26, 1971.*
Wyler Productions and Bob McDevitt present:

THE BALLAD OF JOHNNY POT

Book and Lyrics, Carolyn Richter; Music, Clinton Ballard; Director, Joshua Shelley; Choreography, Jay Norman; Scenery and Lighting, Lloyd Burlingame; Costumes, Alvin Colt; Musical Direction and Dance Arrangements, Harrison Fisher; Music performed by Bandana; Orshestrations, William Goldstein; Production Assistant, Keith Drummond; Musical Supervisor, Mel Rodnan.

CAST

Leroy	Leroy Lessane
Sara	Betty Buckley
Johnny Pot	John Bennett Perry†
Sandra	Sandra Thornton
Watson	Colin Garrey
Nancy Dalton	Nancy Dalton
Tony	Tony Stevens
Sharron	Sharron Miller
Bob	Robert Berdeen
David	David Eric
Garwood Heever	Ben Bryant
Marshal	Peter Jason
Desiree	Barbara Brownell
Preacher	Robert Berdeen
H. L.	Jim Weston
The Fugitive	Tony Stevens
Happy Man	David Eric
White Cloud	Leroy Lessane
The Hayseed	Tony Stevens

UNDERSTUDIES: Watson, Robert Berdeen; Heever, H.L., Marshal, David Eric; Johnny, Peter Jason; Desiree; Sharron Miller; Sarah, Sandra Thornton

MUSICAL NUMBERS: "The Ballad of Johnny Pot," "Johnny's Creed," "Hard Hat Stetsons," "The Letter," "Discarded Blues," "Whaddaya Say Kid," "Crazy," "Head Down the Road," "A Carol," "Lonely Is the Life," "What About Me," "Have Some Pot," "Scared," "How Wonderful It Is," "Like It," "Dance of Distraction," "Saskatchewan," "Little Sparrows," "Find My Way Alone."

A Musical in two acts. The action takes place in the early 1970's in the United States of America as it was then.

General Managers: Norman Kean, Janet Spencer
Press: Betty Lee Hunt, Henry Luhrman,
Harriett Trachtenberg, Maria Pucci
Stage Managers: Paul W. Stetz, Tom Gardner

* Closed May 9, 1971 after 16 performances.

† David Carradine in previews.

Zodiac Photos

Barbara Brownell, Betty Buckley Above: John Bennett Perry

RITZ THEATRE

Opened Wednesday, April 28, 1971.*
Leo Kerz, Allan Pepper and Stanley Snadowsky present:

DANCE OF DEATH

By August Strindberg; Adapted by Paul Avila Mayer; Director, Alfred Ryder; Setting and Lighting, Leo Kerz; Costumes, Marjorie Slaiman; Technical Director, James Hamilton; Produced in association with Portales Productions.

CAST

Edgar	Rip Torn
Alice	Viveca Lindfors
Kurt	Michael Strong
Lieutenant	Robert O'Herron

A Drama in 3 acts and 7 scenes. The action takes place inside a fortress on an island off the coast of Sweden at the turn of the century.

Company Manager: Lawrence Rothman
Press: David Lipsky, Joel Dein
Stage Managers: William Dodds, Robert O'Herron

* Closed May 1, 1971 after 5 performances and 6 previews.

Rip Torn, Viveca Lindfors

Zodiac Photo

Loretta Fury, Kathryn Grody, Martin
Shakar, Richard Dreyfuss, Henry Calvert

McALPIN ROOFTOP THEATRE
Opened Monday, May 3, 1971.*
Haap Productions Company presents:

AND WHOSE LITTLE BOY ARE YOU?

By Rod Parker; Director, Sherwood Arthur; Settings and Costumes, Charles Rosen; Lighting, Robert Guerra; Production Assistant, Robert Johnston.

CAST

Skippy Hilliard ....Richard Dreyfuss
Colonel..Will Hussung
News Commentator.................................Stratton Walling
Skippy (as a boy) ....Paul Morrison
Harry Hilliard...Henry Calvert
Mary Ellen Hilliard ....Loretta Fury
Helen Kurowski...Kathryn Grody
Anna Kurowski..Loretta Fury
Mr. Singer..Marty Greene
Father Dominic Petrocelli ....Martin Shakar
Cardinal O'Connor......................................Grant Code
Bishop Follett..Philip Huston
Rabbi Weidman ....Rudolph Weiss
Doctor..Stratton Walling

A Comedy in 3 acts and 5 scenes. The action takes place at the present time somewhere in Asia, and in the Kurowski apartment.

General Managers: Norman Maibaum, John Miller
Company Manager: Jerry Livengood
Press: Seymour Krawitz, Martin Shwartz,
Patricia McLean Krawitz
Stage Managers: Robert W. Perkins, Martin Shakar

* Closed May 3, 1971 after one performance.

Zodiac Photos

ORPHEUM THEATRE
Opened Monday, May 17, 1971.*
The Orpheum Group presents:

THE WANDERERS

From the stories of Eudora Welty; Director, Robert Maitland; Choreographer, Cleo Quitman; Costumes, Richard Hardt.

CAST

Mabel Mercer, Marian Mercer, Jacque Lynn Colton, Ray Aranha, Maria Caretti, Judith Charney, Lorrie Davis, Rich DeRusso, Judith Evans, Gil Frazier, Jamie Beth Goldstein, Louanne Gardner, Richard Hardt, By-ian Johnson, Mimi McCauliff, Tom Pemberton, Cleo Quitman, Bruce Robinson, Sandra Roll, Donald Ray Shannon, Nedda Sindin, Clark Stooky, Mimi Torchin, Dolores Vanison, A. J. Walker

PROGRAM

"The Wanderers," "The Purple Hat," "Petrified Man," "Lily Daw and the Three Ladies," "Asphodel"

Company Manager: Pat Carney
Press: Saul Richman
Stage Manager: Edward Strum

*Closed May 31, 1971 after limited engagement of 3 performances on Mondays only.

Mabel Mercer   Marian Mercer

CHERRY LANE THEATRE

Opened Monday, May 17, 1971.*
Edgar Lansbury, Stuart Duncan, Joseph Beruh
present:

GODSPELL

Conceived and Directed by John-Michael Tebelak;
Based on the Gospel According to St. Matthew; Music
and New Lyrics, Stephen Schwartz; Lighting, Lowell B.
Achziger; Costumes, Susan Tzu; Associate Producer,
Charles Haid; Musical Arrangement and Direction,
Stephen Schwartz.

CAST

Lamar Alford	Sonia Manzano
Peggy Gordon	Gilmer McCormick
David Haskell	Jeffrey Mylett
Joanne Jonas	Stephen Nathan
Robin Lamont	Herb Simon

ORCHESTRA: Steve Reinhardt, Jesse Cutler, Richard
Labonti, Ricky Shutter

MUSICAL NUMBERS: "Tower of Babble," "Prepare
Ye the Way of the Lord," "Save the People," "Day by
Day," "Learn Your Lessons Well," "Bless the Lord,"
"All for the Best," "All Good Gifts," "Light of the
World," "Turn Back, O Man," "Alas for You," "By My
Side," "We Beseech Thee," "On The Willows," Finale.

A Musical in 2 acts and 16 scenes.

Company Manager Al Isaac
Press: Gifford/Wallace
Stage Manager: Nina Faso

* Still playing May 31, 1971.

entire company of "Godspell"
Stephen Nathan (C)

BIJOU THEATRE

Opened Tuesday, May 18, 1971.*
Joel W. Schenker presents:

THE HOMECOMING

By Harold Pinter; Director, Jerry Adler; Scenery and
Lighting, Dahl Delu; Production Assistant, Alisa Jill
Adler.

CAST

Max	Eric Berry
Lenny	Tony Tanner
Sam	Norman Barrs
Joey	Danny Sewell
Teddy	Lawrence Keith
Ruth	Janice Rule†

UNDERSTUDY: Jack Davidson

A Drama in two acts. The action takes place at the
present time in an old house in the north of London.

General Managers: Robert S. Fishko, John A. Prescott
Press: Sol Jacobson, Lewis Harmon, Ruth D. Smuckler
Stage Manager: David Taylor

* Closed June 12, 1971 after 34 performances and 9
previews.

† Succeeded by Gretchen Oehler

Zodiac Photo

Tony Tanner, Danny Sewell, Norman Barrs
114 Front: Eric Berry, Lawrence Keith, Janice Rule

GATE THEATRE

Opened Monday, May 24, 1971.*
Lou-Na–Poseidon Ltd. by arrangement with
Robert L. Steele presents:

ANY RESEMBLANCE TO PERSONS LIVING OR DEAD

By Elliott Caplin; Director, Loukas Skipitaris; Music,
Saul Honigman; Scenery, Donald Padgett; Costumes,
David Toser; Lighting, Richard Nelson; Sound, Port-
O-Vox.

CAST

Lars	Marc Alaimo
Betulla	Joanne Dusseau
Mrs. Frodo	Ruth Warrick
Anastasia	Ruth Warrick
Polly	Joanne Dusseau
Ulysses	John Call
Prof. Applegate	Matthew Tobin
Briefcase Man	Frank Feda
First Man	Fred Morsell
Second Man	Charles Hudson
General Flinch	Ted Thurston
African	Fred Morsell
Attendant	Charles Hudson
Dr. Harkness	Joanne Dusseau

A Comedy in seven scenes.

General Manager: David Lawlor
Press: Robert Ganshaw
Stage Managers: Smith Lawrence, Curt Sayblack

* Closed May 30, 1971 after 9 performances.

Ed Flournoy Photo

Ruth Warrick, Marc Alaimo

FORTUNE THEATRE

Opened Tuesday, May 25, 1971.*
Robert Weinstein in association with Two Arts
Playhouse present The Actors' Group production
of:

WOYZECK

By Georg Buchner; Translated by Henry J. Schmidt;
Additional adaptation by Richard Reich; Director, Rob-
ert Weinstein; Designed by Bob Olson; Costumes,
Daniel Michaelson; Lighting, Jon Brittain; Assistant to
Director, Deborah Pees.

CAST

Andrews	Kenneth W. Lowry
Woyzeck	Curt Karibalis
Drum Major	Michael Joseph
Marie	Julienne Marshall
Katey	Dorin McGough
Clown	James Greiner
Old Man	Robert Rodriguez
Strongman	Pat Montes
Barker	Richard Jacobs
Monkey	Tracy Yu
Ballerina	Jeanne Cramer
Children	Edward Cramer, Dennis Lieberson
Horse	Kenneth W. Lowry
Sergeant	Peter St. Mu
Captain	David Raphael
Doctor	Richard Jacobs
First Apprentice	James Greiner
Second Apprentice	Peter St. Mu
Third Apprentice	Pat Montes
The Jew	David Raphael
Karl	Robert Rodriguez
Innkeeper	Pat Montes
Clerk	James Greiner

A Drama presented without intermission. The action
takes place in the early 19th Century in Germany.

General Manager: Fred Walker
Press: Saul Richman, Paul Eade
Stage Manager: Robert O'Rourke

* Closed May 29, 1971 after 6 performances.

Kenneth V. Lowry, Juliene Marshall,
Curt Karibalis

SULLIVAN STREET PLAYHOUSE
Opened Tuesday, May 3, 1960.*
Lore Noto presents:

THE FANTASTICKS

Book and Lyrics, Tom Jones; Suggested by Edmond Rostand's play "Les Romantiques"; Music, Harvey Schmidt; Director, Word Baker; Musical Direction and Arrangements, Julian Stein; Designed by Ed Wittstein; Associate Producers, Sheldon Baron, Dorothy Olim, Robert Alan Gold; Original Cast Album by MGM Records.

CAST

The Narrator	Michael Tartel
The Girl	Carolyn Mignini†1
The Boy	Michael Glenn-Smith†2
The Boy's Father	Charles Welch†3
The Girl's Father	John J. Martin†4
The Actor	Ron Prather†5
The Man Who Dies	Bill McIntyre
The Mute	Les Shenkel†6
At the piano	William F. McDaniel
At the harp	Sally Foster

STANDBYS: Joe Bellomo, Annie Kaye, Geoffrey Taylor

MUSICAL NUMBERS: "Try to Remember," "Much More," "Metaphor," "Never Say No," "It Depends on What You Know," "Soon It's Gonna Rain," "Rape Ballet," "Happy Ending," "This Plum Is Too Ripe," "I Can See It," "Plant a Radish," "Round and Round," "They Were You."

A Musical in two acts.

General Manager: Bob MacDonald
Press: Harvey B. Sabinson, Cheryl Sue Dolby
Stage Managers: Geoffrey Brown, Edward Garrabrandt, Robert Crest

* Still playing May 31, 1971. For original production, see THEATRE WORLD, Vol. 16.

† Succeeded by: 1. Virginia Gregory, 2. Jimmy Dodge, Geoffrey Taylor, 3. Donald Babcock, 4. David Vaughan, 5. Justin Gray, 6. Robert Crest.

Van Williams Photos

Bill McIntyre, Jimmy Dodge, Robert Crest (top), Virginia Gregory, Justin Gray

Jimmy Dodge, Robert Crest, Virginia Gregory, Michael Tartel

VILLAGE GATE

Opened Monday, January 22, 1968.*
3W Productions Inc. presents:

JACQUES BREL IS ALIVE AND WELL AND LIVING IN PARIS

Production Conception, English Lyrics, Additional Material, Eric Blau, Mort Shuman; Based on Brel's Lyrics and Commentary; All Dialogue Adapted from works of Jacques Brel; Director, Moni Yakim, Music Arranged and Conducted by Wolfgang Knittel; Musical Direction, Mort Shuman; Consultant, Nat Shapiro; Scenery, Henry E. Scott III; Costumes, Ilka Suarez; Vocal Direction, Lillian Strongin; Lighting, James Nisbet Clark; Production Supervised by Eric Blau; Assistant Conductor, Bertha Melnik; Production Assistant, Jerry Lee.

Henrietta Valor

Jack Blackton

CAST

† Elly Stone	Shawn Elliot
Mort Shuman	Alice Whitefield

MUSICAL NUMBERS: "Marathon," "Alone," "Madeleine," "I Loved," "Mathilde," "Bachelor's Dance," "Timid Frieda," "My Death," "Girls and Dogs," "Jackie," "The Statue," "Desperate Ones," "Sons of.," "Amsterdam," "The Bulls," "Old Folks," "Marieke," "Brussels," "Fannette," "Funeral Tango," "The Middle Class," " "You're not Alone," "Next," "Carousel," "If We only Have Love."

A Musical Entertainment in two acts.

General Manager: Lily Turner
Press: Ivan Black
Stage Managers: James Nisbet Clark, Philip Price

* Still playing May 31, 1971. For original production, see THEATRE WORLD, Vol. 24.

† During the season, the following appeared in this production: Rita Gardner, Betty Rhodes, J. T. Cromwell, John C. Attle, Michael Vita, Robert Guillaume, Joe Masiell, Howard Ross, Barbara Gutterman, Elinor Ellsworth, Henrietta Valor, Joy Franz, George Ball, Fran Uditsky, Jack Blackton

Robert Guillaume

Amanda Bruce

George Ball

Betty Rhodes

MERCER-O'CASEY THEATRE

Opened Tuesday, April 7, 1970.*
(Moved Aug. 11, 1970 to New Theatre)
Orin Lehman presents:

THE EFFECT OF GAMMA RAYS ON MAN-IN-THE-MOON MARIGOLDS

By Paul Zindel; Director, Melvin Bernhardt; Music and Sound, James Reichert; Settings, Fred Voelpel; Lighting, Martin Aronstein; Costumes, Sara Brook; Associate Producer, Julie Hughes; Production Assistant, Peggy Cohen.

CAST

Tillie	Pamela Payton-Wright†1
Beatrice	Sada Thompson†2
Ruth	Amy Levitt†3
Nanny	Judith Lowry†4
Janice Vickery	Swoosie Kurtz†5

STANDBYS: Tillie, Marlena Lustik; Beatrice, Mary Hara, Erica Yohn; Ruth, Jennifer Harmon; Nanny, Ann Ives; Janice, Jennifer Harmon

A Drama in two acts. The action takes place at the present time in the home of Beatrice.

General Manager: Norman E. Rothstein
Company Manager: Patricia Carney
Press: David Powers, Alan Eichler, Seymour Krawitz
Stage Manager: Bud Coffey

* Still playing May 31, 1971. Winner of 1971 Pulitzer Prize, 1970 NY Drama Critics Circle Citation. For original production, see THEATRE WORLD, Vol. 26.

† Succeeded by: 1. Swoosie Kurtz, 2. Cathryn Damon, Carolyn Coates, 3. Swoosie Kurtz, Jennifer Harmon, 4. Ann Ives during vacation, 5. Marlena Lustik

Bert Andrews Photos

Sada Thompson, Amy Levitt, Pamela Payton-Wright
Above: Sada Thompson, Judith Lowry

Jennifer Harmon, Judith Lowry, Cathryn Damon, Swoosie Kurtz

Cathryn Damon (also above), Judith Lowry

Jennifer Harmon, Carolyn Coates (also above)

ANTA MATINEE SERIES
Lucille Lortel, Artistic Director
Fifteenth Season

Earle Hyman   **Teresa Wright**

THEATRE DE LYS

Monday, October 26, and Tuesday Matinee, October 27, 1970.

A PASSAGE TO E. M. FORSTER

Arranged by William Roerick and Thomas Coley from the writings of the novelist; Staged by William Roerick; Stage Manager, Bob MacDonald; Presented in two parts.

CAST

Peggy Wood	Teresa Wright
William Roerick	Thomas Coley
Robert Dryden	

Gail Mansfield   **Brenda Spigner**

Monday, November 16, and Tuesday Matinee, November 17, 1970.

THE PERFECT MATCH

Written and Directed by William Derringer; Lighting, Harry Pinkerton; Stage Manager, Bob MacDonald.

CAST

Shirley...Gail Mansfield
Bernie ....Tom Bade

SLOW MEMORIES

By Barry Litvack; Directed by Joseph Cali; Stage Manager, Bob MacDonald.

CAST

Martin...Jordan Charney
Susan..Cynthia Harris
Mother ....Jane Hoffman
Marylou...Esther Koslow

Virginia Downing   **Tom Bade**

Monday, December 7, and Tuesday Matinee, December 8, 1970.

THE LIFE AND TIMES OF J. WALTER SMINTHEUS

By Edgar White; Director, Alice Spivak; Lighting, Harry Pinkerton; Stage Manager, Bob MacDonald; Presented in two acts.

CAST

J. Walter Smintheus ....Earle Hyman
Edward ....Cain Richards
Robert..Walter Jones
Joyce..Brenda Spigner
Dr. Comma..Robert Guillaume
Margie ....Yvonne Southerland
Waiter..David Green
Bob...Peter Giuliano
Karl...Robert Guillaume
Angela..Zaida Coles
Manager...Jud Davis
Paul..Bob Stoneman

Monday, January 25, and Tuesday Matinee, January 26, 1971.

HERITAGE

Written and Directed by P. J. Barry; Costumes, Steven Askinazy; Stage Manager, Peter D. Greene; Guitar, Diane Mennella; An American folk tale about the Lincoln women in two acts.

CAST

Narrator 1, Tom Lincoln...................Alan Sklar
Lucy Hanks ....Elaine Jenkins
Various Women...................................Virginia Downing
Bachelor, Narrator 2, James
  Rutledge, Stephen A. Douglas.................Donald Buka
Henry Sparrow, Minister, Narrator 3,
  Ninian Edwards, John Wilkes Booth......Clinton Dunn
Nancy Hanks ....Joan Penn
Sarah Bush Johnston ....Marguerite McNeil
Ann Rutledge ....Nanci Addison
Mary Todd..Geraldine Teagarden

General Manager: Paul B. Berkowsky
Series Coordinator: Ken Richards
Press: Saul Richman

THE BLACKFRIARS'GUILD
Rev. Thomas F. Carey, Moderator
Thirtieth Season

BLACKFRIARS' THEATRE
Opened Tuesday, October 13, 1970.*
The Blackfriars' Guild presents:

TRANSFIGURATION

By Brendan Larnen; Director, Walter Cool; Settings and Lighting, T. Fabian; Costumes, J. Bormann; Assistant to Director, Ellis Nassour.

CAST

Morris	Edward Klein or Robert A. Guinan
Kate	Nancy McHugh or Alice O'Keefe
Bennet	Jack Rose or Richard Nettum
Dr. James	Robb McIntire or James Fisher
Clare	Patricia Power or Pat Maniccia

A Mystery-Drama in three acts. The action takes place in Morris Hapner's apartment office in New York City, in the vicinity of 3 P.M. on June 25, 1970.

Press: Michael Joseph, M. Martin
Stage Managers: James Bormann, Richard Dunham

* Closed Sunday, Nov. 22, 1970 after 41 performances.

Jack Rose, Edward Klein, Patricia Power,
Robb McIntire

Ted Legere, Paul Messink, Doc Slevin Right
Center: Ted Legere, Paul Messink, Doc Slevin,
Mary Ann Strossner, Harold Biegelson

BLACKFRIARS' THEATRE
Opened Thursday, February 25, 1971.*
The Blackfriars' Guild (Rev. Thomas F. Carey, Moderator) presents:

AND THE DEVIL MAKES FIVE

By Walter Cool; Directed by Mr. Cool; Setting and Lighting, Allen Edward Klein; Costumes, R. Charles, M. Martin.

CAST

Rose Tracey	Mary Ann Strossner or Pat Maniccia
David Tracey	Ted Legere or Richard Pohlers
Father Thomas Joyce	Paul Messink or E. W. Kane
Dr. Michael Spenser	Harold Biegelson or Robert Charles
The Devil	Doc Slevin

A Mystery Drama in 3 acts and 5 scenes. The action takes place in the corner of the living room of a large deserted house in the burned-out, torn-down, abandoned Inner City of a large metropolis in the U.S. in 1990.

Press: Emily Cowan
Stage Managers: Maureen Martin, Richard Dunham

* Closed Apr. 4, 1971 after a limited engagement of 39 performances.

Norman Gitler Photos

121

AMERICAN PLACE THEATRE

Wynn Handman, Director   Michael Tolan, Associate Director

Seventh Season

ST. CLEMENT'S CHURCH

Opened Monday, November 2, 1970.*
The American Place Theatre presents:

SUNDAY DINNER

By Joyce Carol Oates; Director, Curt Dempster; Scenery, Kert Lundell; Costumes, Willa Kim; Lighting, Roger Morgan; Music, Kirk Nurock; Production Assistant, Judy Metskas; Technical Director, Bill Ostrowski.

CAST

Estella	Jacqueline Brookes
Mary	Lois Smith
Jake	Brooks Morton
Jack	Jerome Dempsey
Leroy	Martin Shakar
Census Taker	Patrick McVey

UNDERSTUDIES: Estella, Mary, Ruth Livingston; Jake, Jack, Census Taker, Don Plumley; Leroy, James Evans Nichols

A Drama presented without intermission. The action takes place in a family home in our time.

Press: Howard Atlee, David Roggensack, Irene Gandy
Stage Managers: David Sell, Grania Hoskins

* Closed Nov. 28, 1970 after 49 performances.

Martha Holmes Photo

Martin Shakar, Lois Smith, Brooks Morton, Jerome Dempsey, Jacqueline Brookes, Patrick McVey (seated)

AMERICAN PLACE THEATRE

Opened Monday, December 21, 1970.*
The American Place Theatre presents:

THE CARPENTERS

By Steven Tesich; Director, Eugene Lesser; Scenery, Kert Lundell; Costumes, Jeanne Button; Lighting, William Mintzer; Sound, James Reichert; Production Assistant, Jacqueline Grant; Technical Director, Richard Emerson.

CAST

Father	Vincent Gardenia
Mother	Alice Drummond
Waldo	Jon Korkes
Sissy	Laura Esterman
Mark	Glenn Walken

UNDERSTUDIES: Father, Edmund Williams; Mother, Sissy, Barbara Tarbuck

A Drama presented without intermission. The action takes place at the present time.

Press: Howard Atlee, David Roggensack
Stage Managers: Peter B. Mumford, Grania Hoskins

* Closed Jan. 16, 1971 after 49 performances.

Martha Holmes Photos

Jon Korkes, Alice Drummond, Vincent Gardenia
Above: Glenn Walken, Vincent Gardenia

ST. CLEMENT'S CHURCH

Opened Wednesday, March 17, 1971.*
The American Place Theatre (Wynn Handman,
Director) presents:

PINKVILLE

By George Tabori; Diréctor, Martin Fried; Music
Composed and Directed by Stanley Walden; Designed
by Wolfgang Roth; Costumes, Ruth Morley; Movement,
Anna Sokolow; Electronic Music, Jacob Druckman;
Technical Director, Richard Emerson; Production Assist-
ant, Steve Samuels.

CAST

Jerry the Naz	Michael Douglas
The Honeychild	Milton Earl Forrest
Consequently Joe	Raul Julia
The Jock	Bob Lesser
Two Ton Tessie (Sergeant)	James Tolkan
Suck Ass (Henchman)	Art Evans
Acting Jack (Henchman)	Constantine Katsanos
The Captain	Lane Smith
Papasan	Dimo Condos
The Girl	Barbara Tai Sing

Understudies: Lou Courtney, Jim Quinn

A Drama presented without intermission.

Press: Howard Atlee, David Roggensack, Irene Gandy
Stage Managers: Peter B. Mumford, Kenneth Cox

* Closed Apr. 3, 1971 after 42 performances.

Martha Holmes Photo

**from back: Art Evans, Constantine Katsanos,
James Tolkan, Michael Douglas, Lane Smith**

AMERICAN PLACE THEATRE

Opened Thursday, April 29, 1971.*
The American Place Theatre (Wynn Handman,
Director) presents:

BOG BAY BEAST BAIT

By Sam Shepard; Director, Tony Barsha; Scenery,
Dick Emerson; Lighting, Johnny Dodd; Costumes, Patricia McGourty; Technical Director, Richard Emerson

CAST

Ghost Girl	Yolande Bavan
Slim	Beeson Carroll
Shadow	James Hall
Maria	Antonia Rey
Preacher	Robert Glaudini
Gris Gris	O-Lan Johnson-Shepard

Understudies: Michael Brody, Yolande Bavan

Presented without intermission

Press: Howard Atlee, David Roggensack
Stage Manager: Grania Hoskins

* Closed June 5, 1971 after 32 performances.

Martha Holmes Photo

**James Hall, Antonia Rey, O-Lan Johnson-
Shepard**

CHELSEA THEATER CENTER OF BROOKLYN

Robert Kalfin, Artistic Director;
Michael David, Executive Director

BROOKLYN ACADEMY OF MUSIC

Opened Tuesday, October 20, 1970.*
The Chelsea Theater Center of Brooklyn
presents:

SAVED

By Edward Bond; Director, Alan Schneider; Designed by Eugene Lee, Franne Newman; Lighting, Roger Morgan; Production Manager, Burl Hash; Technical Assistant, Dorothea Albert; Sound, Patricia Jones

CAST

Pam	Dorrie Kavanaugh
Len	James Woods
Fred	Kevin Conway
Pete	Stefan Hartman
Barry	Donald Warfield
Mike	Richard Cox
Colin	Tom Leopold
Mary	Margaret Braidwood
Harry	Donald Ewert†
Liz	Lynn Ann Leveridge

Understudies: Veronica Castang, Ed Bordo

A Drama in two acts. The action takes place in South London at the present time.

Press: Ron Christopher
Stage Manager: David Eidenberg

* Closed Nov. 8, 1970 after a limited engagement of 21 performances. Re-opened Friday, Nov. 13, 1970 at the Cherry Lane Theatre

† Succeeded by Norman Barrs

Alan B. Tepper Photo

James Woods, Margaret Braidwood
in "Saved"

Tom Leopold, Stefan Hartman, Don Warfield,
Richard Cox in "Saved"

BROOKLYN ACADEMY OF MUSIC

Opened Friday, December 11, 1970.*
The Chelsea Theater Center of Brooklyn
presents:

TAROT

Conceived by The Rubber Duck; Composed by Tom Constanten; Directors, The Rubber Duck, Robert Kalfin; Designed by Stephen Hendrickson; Lighting, John Dodd, Burl Hash; Production Manager, Burl Hash; Production Assistant, F. Patrick Flynn; Choreographic Assistant, Cynthia Briggs.

CAST

Edward Barton, Yolande Bavan, Cassia Besson, Cynthia Briggs, Maxine Herman, Susan Kornzweig, John Kuhner, Deatra Lambert, Gloria Maddox, Renos Mandis, John Proctor Parriot, Sandra Peabody, Frederick Rivera, Rubber Duck, Trish Sandberg

The Rubber Band: Jim Byers, Tom Constanten, Paul Dresher, Art Fayer, Gary Hirsh, Wes Steele, Jerry Garcia

A Musical in two parts.

Press: Ron Christopher
Stage Manager: Judi Fisher

* Closed Dec. 20, 1970 after a limited engagement of 13 performances. Re-opened at Circle in the Square on Thursday, March 4, 1971 and closed there Apr. 4, 1971 after 45 performances.

BROOKLYN ACADEMY OF MUSIC

Opened Tuesday, February 23, 2971.*
The Chelsea Theater Center of Brooklyn (Robert Kalfin, Artistic Director; Michael David, Executive Director) presents:

AC/DC

By Heathcote Williams; Director, John Hirsch; Designed by John Scheffler; Lighting, Burl Hash; Video by Video Free America; Costumes, James Crawford; Production Assistants, Harris Riordan, Laurel Gross.

CAST

Gary	James Cromwell
Melody	Jillian Lindig
Sadie	Susan Batson
Maurice	Edward Zang
Perowne	Stefan Gierasch
Pixie Bosanquet	Margaret Braidwood

Standbys: Joan Harris, Robert Einenkel

A Play in two acts. The action takes place at the present time in London.

Press: Ron Christopher, Monica Frakes
Stage Manager: Judi Fisher

* Closed March 14, 1971 after a limited engagement of 28 performances.

Alan B. Tepper Photos

Right: James Cromwell, Jillian Lindig, Edward Zang
Above: Edward Zang, Stefan Gierasch
in "AC/DC"

**Maxine Herman, Rubber Duck, Gloria Maddox
in "Tarot"**

BROOKLYN ACADEMY OF MUSIC

Opened Tuesday, April 27, 1971.*
The Chelsea Theater Center of Brooklyn (Robert Kalfin, Artistic Director; Michael David, Executive Director) presents a Brown Bag Project:

PETER HANDKE/TWO PLAYS

By Peter Handke; Translated by Michael Roloff; Director, Wieland Schulz-Keil; Designed by Bill Carpenter; Masks, Ulrich Niemeyer; Lighting, Burl Hash, Barbara Becker; Sound, Greg Macosko.

CAST

"My Foot My Tutor"

Warden	Martin Newman
Ward	Mark Lonow

"Self-Accusation"
with Veronica Castang and Robert Einenkel

Stage Manager: Greg Macosko
Press: Ron Christopher, Monica Frakes

* Closed May 8, 1971 after limited engagement of 7 performances.

(No photos available)

125

THE CUBICULO
Philip Meister, Artistic Director Elaine Sulka, Managing Director

THE CUBICULO
Opened Thursday, July 2, 1970.*
The Cubiculo presents:

ORESTES

Adapted by Gregory Rozakis from Euripides' play; Director, Ron Link; Music, Mark Shangold; Lyrics, Andrew Amic-Angelo; Lighting, Philip Cohen; Set, F. P. Cuneo.

CAST

Orestes	Gregory Rozakis
Electra	Linda Eskenas
Narrator/Hermes	Andrew Amic-Angelo
Hermione	Ellyn Meade
Satyr/Dionysus	Jay Bonnell
Helen	Marcia Loring
Menelaus	Renos Mandis
Phrygian Slave	Tom Yourk
Tyndareus	Dennis Helfend
Pylades	Moti Baharav
Apollo	Earle Edgerton

The action is laid in no specific time or place to give the play its full measure of universality.

Stage Manager: Frank Moss

* Closed Wednesday, July 8, 1970 after 13 performances.

Patrick LaBanca Photo

Renos Mandis, Gregory Rozakis in "Orestes"

THE CUBICULO
Opened Wednesday, July 22, 1970.*
The Cubiculo presents the American Premiere of:

THE PICKWICKIANS AT MANOR FARM

From "The Pickwick Papers" of Charles Dickens; Music by Edwin Carr; Choreography by Geraldine Stephenson; Director, Sandy Black; Lighting, William Lambert.

CAST

BRIAN D. BARNES

A One-Man Show presented in two parts with a prologue and epilogue.

CAST

Closed July 25, 1970 after limited engagement of 5 performances to tour U.S.

Michael J. Barrett Photo

**Brian D. Barnes
in "The Pickwickians"**

THE CUBICULO
Opened Thursday, October 22, 1970.*
The Cubiculo presents:

INFIDELITY ITALIAN STYLE

By Mario Fratti; Director, Maurice Edwards; Producer, Nicholas John Stathis; Sets, Rick Cuneo; Costumes, M. Aileen Clark; Sound, George Prideaux; Lighting, William Lambert; Technical Assistant, James Kearns

CAST

"Waiting"

The Girl	Patricia Elliott
The Servant	Rob Testut
The Friend	Elizabeth Jones
The Seducer	Frank Biancamano
The Girl's Father	Chris Gampel
The Maid	Nancilou Moretti
The Milkman	Charles Faranda

The action takes place today in a Venetian house.

"The Doorbell"

First Man	Frank Biancamano
Second Man	Joe Hunter
Old Woman	June Whitaker
Sailor	Herb Streicher
Wife	Elaine Sulka
Husband	Chris Gampel

The action takes place today in a Venetian brothel

"The Academy"

Afro	Ray Cole
Fortunato	Rob Testut
Benito	Herb Streicher
Donato	Charles Faranda
Corso	Joe Hunter
Elio	Frank Biancamano
Signora	Patricia Elliott
Professor	Chris Gampel

The action takes place today in a Venetian academy

* Closed Oct. 31, 1970 after limited engagement of 8 performances.

THE CUBICULO

Opened Thursday, December 3, 1970.*

The Cubiculo presents:

SUNDECK

By Leon Wittack; Director, Philip Meister; Set, Clyde Wachsberger; Lighting, William Lambert; Music and Sound, George Prideaux; Stage Manager, James O'Leary

CAST

Alma	Marion Herrod
Bob	Michael Stoddard
A Man	Norman Matlock

A Play in 2 acts and 5 scenes. The action takes place at the present time on a sundeck.

* Closed Dec. 15, 1970 after limited engagement of 9 performances.

Marion Herrod, Michael Stoddard in "Sundeck"

THE CUBICULO

Opened Monday, December 28, 1970.*

The Cubiculo presents:

THE HOLE IN THE SKY

By Douglas Nichols; Original Music, John-Charles Miller; Choreography, Saeko Ichinohe; Costumes, Joyce Marcel; Lighting, William Lambert; Sound, Marie McKim; Staged by Maurice Edwards

CAST

First Councilor	Albert Verdesca
Second Councilor	Phillip Filiato
Third Councilor	J. Richard Beneville
Fourth Councilor	Roy Callaway
Little Fly-Big Fly	Herb Streicher
Thunderbird	Phyllis Rice
Turquoise Girl	Barbara Fiorello or Katherine Rao

EAGLES: Sheila Byrd, J. Richard Beneville, Kathy Joyce, Roy Gallaway, Dalienne Major, Phillip Filiato, Yung Yung Tsuai, Albert Verdesca

* Repeated Dec. 29, 30, 1970 for limited engagement of 3 performances.

Tadashi Endo Photo

Phyllis Rice, Herb Streicher in "Hole in the Sky"

THE CUBICULO

Opened Thursday, February 4, 1971.*

The Cubiculo presents:

THE SWEETSHOPPE MYRIAM and KLARA

By Ivan Klima; Adapted by Ruth Willard; Director, Pirie MacDonald; Sets, Victor di Napoli; Lighting, Frank Moss; Stage Managers, Maggie Carrington, Chris Moore.

CAST

"The Sweetshoppe Myriam"

Manager	Dalton Dearborn
Old Lady	Elizabeth Donnelly
Young Man	Jerry Zaks
Pastry Chef	Dean Buck
Peter	Ross Bickell
Julie	Ann Sachs
Young Man in Black	Lloyd Bremseth
Girl in Veil	Sandy Caprin
Mushroom Picker	Layne Stone
First Policeman	Richmond Hoxie
Second Policeman	David Pursley
Prosecutor	Jack Axelrod
Councilman	Nick Savian

"Klara"

Klara	Jacqueline Coslow
Gentleman **Friend**	Theodore Sorel
A Man	Lloyd Bremseth

* Closed Feb. 14, 1971 after limited engagement of 10 performances.

(No photos available)

Chris Gampel, Frank Biancamano in "Infidelity Italian Style"

127

EQUITY LIBRARY THEATRE PRODUCTIONS
George Wojtasik, Managing Director
Twenty-eighth Season

MASTER THEATRE
Opened Thursday, October 15, 1970.*
Equity Library Theatre presents:

BEN BAGLEY'S SHOESTRING REVUES

Based on revues by Ben Bagley; Directed and Choreographed by Miriam Fond; Musical Direction, Bob Waxman; Special Dances Choreographed by Bick Goss; Sets, Rita H. Weissmann; Lighting, Gwen Jo Hamill; Costumes, Sydney Lee Brooks; Assistant Musical Director, John R. Williams; Technical Director, F. Dan Olderman; At the pianos, Bob Waxman, John R.Williams.

CAST

Jay Bonnel	Ann Hodapp
Susan Campbell	Bill LaVallee
Richard Caine	Susan Lehman
George Cavey	Jane Robertson
Douglas Fisher	Sandy Sprung
Lucy Lee Flippin	Lou Vitacco

MUSICAL NUMBERS: "Man's Inhumanity to Man," "Queen of Spain," "Garbage," "The Trouble with Miss Manderson," "Good Little Girls," "Coffee," "Someone Is Sending Me Flowers," "Pretty Miss Brown," "Couldn't Be Happier," "Lest We Forget," "Three Loves," "Medea in Disney Land," "On a Shoestring," "Sweet Belinda," "Art of Mime," "Auf Wiedersehen," "Game of Dance," "Group Analysis," "Family Trouble," "Cream and Punishment," "The Rochelle Hudson Tango," "Laddie," "Two Way Play," "Time to Say Goodnight."

A Musical Revue in two acts.

Press: Sol Jacobson, Lewis Harmon
Stage Manager: Joe Lane

* Closed Nov. 1, 1970 after 22 performances.

LIBRARY & MUSEUM OF PERFORMING ARTS
Opened Monday, October 19, 1970.*
Equity Library Theatre presents:

A MUSICAL TIMEPIECE

By Alan Foster Friedman; Director, Allen R. Belknap; Setting and Lighting, David Jenkins; Production Assistants, Barbara Herzog, Rose Graziano; Stage Manger, Charles Anzalone.

CAST

Jeanne	Jeanne Allen
George	George Lee Andrews
Tom	Thomas Ingram
Ellen	Ellen Wells

An all music-musical about four people who search, find, touch, trust, love, enjoy---then then lose each other.

* Closed Oct. 21, 1970 after limited engagement of 3 performances. (No photos available)

LIBRARY & MUSEUM OF PERFORMING ARTS
Opened Monday, December 7, 1970,*
Equity Library Theatre presents:

SMALLER THAN LIFE

By Dorothy Vann and Jim Evering; Director, Leland Ball; Presented in two parts.

CAST

Dorothy Vann
Jim Evering

* Closed Dec. 9, 1970 after limited engagement of 3 performances. (No photos available)

Jay Bonnell, Douglas Fisher, George Cavey
in "Shoestring Revues"

Madeleine Berger, Irwin Pearl, Fay Sappington
in "Johnny No-Trump"

MASTER THEATRE
Opened Thursday, November 12, 1970.*
Equity Library Theatre presents:

JOHNNY NO-TRUMP

By Mary Mercier; Director, Chuck Vicent; Set, Frad Sammut; Lighting, Barry-Robert Molitch; Costumes, Bill Blackwell.

CAST

Florence Edwards	Jean Barker
Mrs. Franklin	Madeleine Berger
Bettina	Bernadette Jones
Johnny Edwards	Irwin Pearl
Nanna	Fay Sappington
Alexander Edwards	Mark Shapiro
Harry Armstrong	Joel Wolfe

A Comedy-Drama in two acts. The action takes place in the Armstrong's Long Island home at the present time.

Press: Sol Jacobson, Lewis Harmon
Stage Manager: James Curtan

* Closed Nov. 22, 1970 after a limited engagement of 14 performances.

MASTER THEATRE

Opened Thursday, December 3, 1970.*
Equity Library Theatre presents:

GREENWILLOW

Music and Lyrics, Frank Loesser; Book, Lesser Samuels and Frank Loesser; Based on novel by B. J. Chute; Director, Clinton Atkinson; Musical Director, Norman Dean; Choreography, Deborah Jowitt; Scenery, William Puzo; Lighting, Rick Miller; Costumes, Betsey Potter; Pianist, John Williams

CAST

Jabez Briggs..Matthew Atkinson
Mr. Preebs..James Brochu
Jeremiah..Robert Brooks
Gramma Briggs ....Mary Jo Catlett
Martha Briggs...................................Carolyn Chrisman
Clara Clegg..Joan B. Duffin
Gideon Briggs..John Fennessy
Rev. Birdsong.......................................Bernard Frawley
Abigail...Dorothy Hershkowitz
Will...Dennis Higgins
Rev. Lapp...John High
Dorrie...Laurie Hutchinson
Mr. Pringle...Bruce Israel
Thomas Clegg..................................Robert Lanchester
Enoch...Mark Mathews
Andrew..Jim May
Mrs. Hasty...Barbara Meyer
Emma..Jean Nuchtern
Maidy...Anne O'Donnell
Amos...Ed Penn
Mrs. Lunny...Anne Piacontini
Mr. Jones...James Rilley
Sheby Briggs..Ivy Siegler
Nell...Sherry Lee Snider
Sarah..Dolores Vanison
Micah Briggs and Young Gideon ....Martin Whelan

MUSICAL NUMBERS: "A Day Borrowed from Heaven, "Dorrie's Wish," "The Music of Home," "Gideon Briggs, I Love You," "The Autumn Courting," "The Call to Wander," "Summertime Love,"Walking Away Whistling," "The Sermon," "Could've Been a Ring," "Halloweve," "Never Will I Marry," "Greenwillow Christmas," "Faraway Boy," "Clang Dang the Bell," "What a Blessing," "He Died Good," "The Spring Courting," "The Call."

A Musical in two acts. The action takes place during four seasons in and about Greenwillow.

Press: Sol Jacobson, Lewis Harmon
Stage Managers: Susan Robinson, Charles Anzalone

* Closed Dec. 20, 1970 after 22 performances.

LIBRARY & MUSEUM OF THE PERFORMING ARTS

Opened Monday, February 1, 1971.*
Equity Library Theatre presents:

SKYE

Book and Lyrics, Avery Corman, Dan Rustin; Music, Ben Finn; Director, James Curtan; Setting, Donald Padgett; Musical Director, Wendell Kindberg; Lighting, Allison Anthorne; Technical Director, Larry Clinton.

CAST

Prince Mosgood...Jay Kirsch
Donald MacCutcheon ....Andrew Amic–Angelo
MacDuff...James Brochu
King Peingowan ....Larry Whiteley
Queen Talbot..Betty Lynn
Princess Angeline..Sue Long
Uncle Bayswater......................................Larry Clinton

MUSICAL NUMBERS: "The Isle of Skye," "And More," "The Story that History Won't Tell," "Ring, Ring the Bell," "Raise up the Flagon," "The Faerie Piper," "I'll Never Move a Mountain," "Cross Your Finger," "Showmanship," "Bridal Bouquet," "Underneath a Dragon Moon," "Someone Else Will Know," "The Wedding," "Only One Shadow," Finale.

A Musical Fairy Tale in two acts.

Press: Sol Jacobson, Lewis Harmon
Stage Managers: Anthony J. Limoli, Frannie Kleinfeld

* Performed Feb. 2 & 3 for a limited engagement of 3 performances.

(No photos available)

Carolyn Chrisman, Ed Penn, John High, Mary Jo Catlett, Martin Whelan, Ivy Siegler in "Greenwillow"

MASTER THEATRE

Opened Thursday, January 14, 1971,*
Equity Library Theatre (George Wojtasik, Managing Director) presents:

PRESENT LAUGHTER

By Noel Coward; Director, Raphael Kelly; Sets, Bennet Averyt; Lighting, Bennett Taber; Assistant Technical Director, Linda Jessup; Techinical Director, Dan Olderman.

CAST

Daphne Stillington ....Pamela Blafer
Miss Erickson...Ann Freeman
Fred..Montgomery Davis
Monica Reed...Lois DeBanzie
Garry Essendine...Colin Hamilton
Liz Essendine..Mae Marmy
Roland Maule...Don Bozick
Morris Dixon ....William McLuckey
Hugo Lyppiatt.....................................William H. Boesen
Joanna Lyppiatt................................Patricia McGregor
Lady Salburn...Tamara Daniel

A Comedy in three acts, and four scenes. The action takes place at the present time in Garry Essendine's studio in London.

Press: Sol Jacobson, Lewis Harmon
Stage Managers: Scott C. Chase, Rose Graziano, Maggie Goodenow

* Closed Jan. 24, 1971 after limited engagement of 14 performances.

Gene R. Coleman Photos

Mae Marmy, Tamara Daniel, William McLuckey,
William H. Boesen, Pamela Blafer, Don Bozick,
Colin Hamilton in "Present Laughter"

LIBRARY & MUSEUM OF THE PERFORMING ARTS

Opened Monday, March 1, 1971.*
Equity Library Theatre presents:

SHOE STORE

By Shirley Rhodes; Director, Joe Silver; Wardrobe, Alyce Gilbert; Hair Stylist, John Michel

CAST

Salesman...Harvey Keitel
Doreen...Chevi Colton
Vi..Sandra Harrison

The action takes place at the present time in a shoe store at 6:55 P.M.

Press: Sol Jacobson, Lewis Harmon
Stage Managers: William E. Briggs, Sally Burke, Victoria Harrison

* Performed for limited engagement of 3 performances only Mar. 2 & 3, 1971 (No photos available)

**Marian Levittan, Marta Brennan, James B. Spann,
Osa Danam, Roberta Rodin, Bette Glenn,
Raymond Cox, C.E. Jennifer Stock, Paula Hostetter,
Genette Lane in "Ruddigore"**

MASTER THEATRE

Opened Thursday, February 4, 1971.*
Equity Library Theatre presents:

HELOISE

By James Forsyth; Director, S. Darrell Calvin; Scenery and Costumes, Thomas Pritchard, Jim Swann; Lighting, Ken Billington; Composer, Maurice Ehrlich; Music Director, Marjorie Brewster; Technical Director, Dan Olderman.

CAST

The Singer ....James LaFerla
Supiro ....Stephan Weyte
Hugo ....Ric Mancini
Heloise ....Liesha Gullison
Fulbert ....Philip Hanson
Alberic ....Michael Diamond
Theo ....Christopher Murphy
Abelard ....Lindsay Moller
Abbess ....Sydney Ford
Soloist ....Paul Sebastian
Friar ....Robert Marshall

NUNS, MONKS, TOWNSPEOPLE: Claire Abbey, John Battiloro, Rosalind Breslow, Betty Friar, Robert Marshall, Tom Claypool, John Mitchell, Joann Myers, Dale Olson, Susan Schlansky, Paul Sebastian

A Drama in three acts. The action takes place in Paris in 1118, 1116, and 1126.

Press: Sol Jacobson, Lewis Harmon
Stage Managers: Patrick Conlon, John Battiloro

* Closed Feb. 14, 1971 after limited engagement of 14 performances.

Gene R. Coleman Photos

Top Left: Lindsay Moller, Liesha Gullison, Christopher Murphy (standing) in "Heloise"

MASTER THEATRE

Opened Thursday, March 4, 1971.*
The Equity Library Theatre presents:

RUDDIGORE

By Gilbert and Sullivan; Director, Lewis Pierce; Musical Director, Carl Sebok; Choreographer, Joan Ashlyn; Scenery, Richard Traubner; Lighting, Cammie Caroline Lavine; Costumes, Patricia Sheridan, Mark Mathews; Assistant Musical Director-Pianist, John R. Williams.

CAST

Robin, Richard Dauntless ....Steve Anthony
Bridesmaid ....Marta Brennan
Richard Dauntless, Ghost ....Raymond Cox
Ruth ....Osa Danam
Bridesmaid ....Donna Forbes
Old Adam Goodheart ....Barry Ford
Richard Dauntless, Ghost ....Jon Garrison
Rose Maybud ....Bette Glenn
Bridesmaid..Paula Hostetter
Zorah ....Genette Lane
Bridesmaid ....Marian Levittan
Sir Roderic Murgatroyd ....Richard Malone
Mad Margaret...Linda Mays
Dancer, Mad Margaret................................Joanna Mendl
Ghost ....Fred Randall
Sir Despard Murgatroyd.............................Ronnie Newman
Bridesmaid..Robert Rodin
Ghost ....Guy Rossitto
Dame Hannah...Suzan Sidney
Robin Oakapple, Sir Ruthven Murgatroyd.....Jim Spann
Bridesmaid..C.E. Jennifer Stock
Rose Maybud ....Marianne Tatum
Ghost, A.S.M...David Villaire
Old Adam Goodheart, Ghost.................Carl Von Conta
Ghost ....Byron Wright

Press: Sol Jacobson, Lewis Harmon, Ruth D.Smuckler
Stage Manager: Arnold Aronson, David Villaire

* Closed Mar. 21, 1971 after limited engagement of 22 performances.

MASTER THEATRE

Opened Thursday, April 1, 1971.*
Equity Library Theatre presents the New York
premiere of:

FALSE CONFESSIONS

By Pierre de Marivaux; Director, Kent Paul; Scenery,
Donald Padgett; Costumes, Christina Weppner; Light-
ing, Atlee Stephan 3rd; English Version, W. S. Merwin;
Production Adviser, Colette Nivelle.

CAST

Marton	Marjorie Lynne Feiner
DuBois	John Fitzgibbon
The Comte	Steven Gilborn
Harlequin	Frederick Keeler
Jeweler's Son	Ryan Listman
M. Remy	Ralph Nilson
Madame Argante	Ann Boothby Ross
Dorante	Michael Stoddard
Araminte	Kate Webster
Young Jeweler	Ian Wilder

A Comedy in three acts. The action takes place in
Araminte's house in Paris on a Spring day in the 1730's.

Press: Sol Jacobson, Lewis Harmon
Stage Managers: Ian Wilder, Iris Helfand

* Closed Apr. 11, 1971 after a limited engagement of 14
performances.

Gene R. Coleman Photos

**Top Right: Marjorie Lynne Feiner, Ralph Nilson,
Michael Stoddard in "False Confessions"**

MASTER THEATRE

Opened Thursday, April 29, 1971.*
Equity Library Theatre presents:

NOW IS THE TIME FOR ALL GOOD MEN

Book and Lyrics, Gretchen Cryer; Music, Nancy Ford;
Director, Ronald Roston; Musical Director, John R.
Williams; Sets, Steven Askinazy; Costumes, Meryl Levy;
Lighting, Michael Hopper; At the piano, John R. Wil-
liams; Percussionist, Don Marcone; Technical Director,
Dan Olderman.

CAST

Miss Togney	Avril Gentles
Bill Miller	Bill Abrams
Jasper Wilkins	Bernie Passeltiner
Betty Brown	Geraldine Baker
Ramona	Valerie Beaman
Tommy	Edmund Gaynes
Eugenie Seldin	Bonnie Hinson
Herbert Heller	Vincent Duke Milana
Albert McKinley	William Countryman
Mike Butler	John Hamilton
Esther Mason	Marcia O'Brien
Sarah Larkin	Judy Knaiz

MUSICAL NUMBERS: "We Shall Meet in the Great
Hereafter," "Keep 'Em Busy, Keep 'Em Quiet," "What's
in the Air," "Tea in the Rain," "What's a Guy Like You
Doin' in a Place Like This?," "Halloween Hayride,"
"Katydid," "See Everything New," "All Alone," "He
Could Show Me," "Washed Away," "Stuck-up," "My
Holiday," "Down through History," "It Was Good
Enough for Grandpa," "A Simple Life," "A Star on the
Monument," "Rain Your Love on Me," "There's Goin'
to Be a Wedding."

A Musical in two acts. The action takes place at the
present time in Bloomdale, Ind., population 973.

Company Manager: Cammie Caroline Lavine
Press: Sol Jacobson, Lewis Harmon
Stage Managers: Scott C. Chase, Maggie Goodenow

* Closed May 16, 1971 after limited engagement of 14
performances and 2 previews.

**Right Center: Edmund Gaynes, Avril Gentles,
Valerie Beaman (seated) in "Now Is The
Time. . ."**

LIBRARY & MUSEUM OF PERFORMING ARTS

Opened Monday, May 24, 1971.*
Equity Library Theatre presents:

THE PSYCHIATRISTS

By Ed Rombola; Director, Ian Wilder; Sound Effects,
Joe Bly; Stage Manager, Cammie Caroline Lavine.

CAST

Part I: As Virtuously Given

Mac?	Victor Raider-Wexler
Joe?	Bernie Passeltiner

Part II: Project of Affection

Bill	Richard Fancy
Janice	Diana Ellis

* Closed May 26, 1971 after limited engagement of 3
performances. (No photos available)

REPERTORY THEATER OF LINCOLN CENTER
Jules Irving, Director   Robert Symonds, Associate Director

VIVIAN BEAUMONT THEATER
Opened Thursday, November 5, 1970.*
The Repertory Theater of Lincoln Center
presents:

THE GOOD WOMAN OF SETZUAN

By Bertolt Brecht; Translated by Ralph Manheim;
Director, Robert Symonds; Settings, Douglas W.
Schmidt; Lighting, John Gleason; Costumes, Carrie
Fishbein Robbins; Music, Herbert Pilhofer; Songs, Her-
bert Pilhofer, John Lewin; Assistant Director, Peter
Nyberg; Production Assistants, Karen Roston, Molly
Harris, Jo Sennet; Hairstylist, Jim Sullivan.

CAST

Wang	Lou Gilbert
First God	Philip Bosco
Second God	Sydney Walker
Third God	Ray Fry
Gentlemen	Jack Harrold, Luis Avalos
Shen Teh	Colleen Dewhurst
Mrs. Shin	Elizabeth Wilson
Husband	Maury Cooper
Wife	Eda Reiss Merin
Nephew	Robert Phalen
Unemployed Man	Robert Levine
Lin To	Michael Levin
Brother	Dan Sullivan
Sister-in-law	Elizabeth Huddle
Mrs. Mi Tzu	Frances Foster
Boy	Kenneth H. Maxwell
Grandfather	Herbert Foster
Niece	Tandy Cronyn
Policeman	Joseph Mascolo
Carpet Dealer's Wife	Anne Ives
Yang Sun	David Birney
Old Prostitute	Florence Tarlow
Mr. Shu Fu	Stephen Elliott
Carpet Dealer	Eugene R. Wood
Mrs. Yang	Priscilla Pointer
Waiter	Luis Avalos
Priest	Jack Harrold
Townspeople	James Cook, Susan Sharkey
Children	Toby Obayashi, Rebecca Symonds, Rico Williams

UNDERSTUDIES: Shen Teh, Elizabeth Huddle;
Wange, Luis Avalos; Gods, Michael Levin, Herbert
Foster; Mrs. Shin, Mrs. Yang, Florence Tarlow; Hus-
band, Lin To, Robert Levine; Wife, Niece, Prostitute,
Susan Sharkey; Mrs. Tzu, Tandy Cronyn; Nephew,
Grandfather, Priest, James Cook; Yang Sun, Robert
Phalen; Shu Fu, Maury Cooper; Waiter, Peter Nyberg

A Fable presented in two acts. The action takes place
in the capital of Setzuan, a half-Europeanized city.

Press: Susan Bloch, William Schelble
Stage Managers: Barbara-Mae Phillips, Paul Bengston,
Patrick Horrigan

* Closed Dec. 13, 1970 after 46 performances and 13
previews.

Martha Swope Photos

Top Right: Lou Gilbert, David Birney, Colleen
Dewhurst, standing front row: Elizabeth Wilson,
Stephen Elliott, Priscilla Pointer, back row:
Philip Bosco, Sydney Walker, Ray Fry Below:
Stephen Elliott, Elizabeth Wilson, David Birney,
Colleen Dewhurst

Colleen Dewhurst, David Birney, Priscilla Pointer

VIVIAN BEAUMONT THEATER

Opened Thursday, January 7, 1971.*
The Repertory Theatre of Lincoln Center under
the direction of Jules Irving presents:

THE PLAYBOY OF THE WESTERN WORLD

By John Millington Synge; Director, John Hirsch;
Settings and Costumes, Douglas W. Schmidt; Lighting,
John Gleason; Music, John Duffy, based on traditional
Irish folk songs; Assistant Director, Tim Ward; Hairstyl-
ist, Jim Sullivan.

CAST

Pegeen Mike	Martha Henry
Shawn Keogh	James Blendick
Michael James Flaherty	Sydney Walker
Philly Cullen	Ray Fry†
Jimmy Farrell	Philip Bosco
Christy Mahon	David Birney
Widow Quin	Frances Sternhagen
Honor Blake	Tandy Cronyn
Susan Brady	Susan Sharkey
Sara Tansey	Elizabeth Huddle
Old Mahon	Stephen Elliott
Bellman	Herbert Foster
Townspeople	James Cook, Maury Cooper, Peter Nyberg, Dan Sullivan

UNDERSTUDIES: Christy, James Cook; Pegeen,
Tandy Cronyn; Widow, Elizabeth Huddle; Michael, Old
Mahon, Maury Cooper; Shawn, Philly, Herbert Foster;
Jimmy, Dan Sullivan

A Comedy in three acts. The action takes place near a
village, on a wild coast of Mayo, in autumn.

Press: Susan Bloch, William Schelble, Sedgwick Clark
Stage Managers: Frank Bayer, Patrick Horrigan

* Closed Feb. 21, 1971 after a limited engagement of 52
performances and 13 previews.

† Succeeded by Herbert Foster

Martha Swope Photos

**Top Right: Martha Henry, David Birney, Stephen
Elliott Below: Maury Cooper, Herbert Foster,
Peter Nyberg, Ray Fry, David Birney, Sydney
Walker, Martha Henry**

**David Birney, Elizabeth Huddle, Martha Henry,
Susan Sharkey, Tandy Cronyn**

Philip Bosco, Frances Sternhagen, Stephen Elliott

133

FORUM THEATER

Opened Friday, February 5, 1971.*
The Repertory Theater of Lincoln Center presents:

THE BIRTHDAY PARTY

By Harold Pinter; Director, Jules Irving; Setting, Marsha Louis Eck; Lighting, John Gleason; Costumes, Joseph G. Aulisi; Assistant Director, Tim Ward; Hairstylist, Jim Sullivan; Production Assistant, Sandi Gaertner.

CAST

Petey	Ray Fry
Meg	Betty Field
Stanley	Robert Phalen
Lulu	Lee Lawson
Goldberg	Robert Symonds
McCann	John Harkins

UNDERSTUDIES: Meg, Lulu, Barbara Tarbuck; Stanley, Dan Sullivan; Petey, Maury Cooper; Goldberg, McCann, Macon McCalman

A Drama in three acts presented with one intermission. The action takes place in the living room of a house in an English seaside town during the summer.

Opened Tuesday, February 9, 1971.*

LANDSCAPE and SILENCE

By Harold Pinter; Director, Jules Irving; Settings, Douglas W. Schmidt; Lighting, John Gleason.

CAST

"Silence"

Ellen	Barbara Tarbuck
Rumsey	Robert Symonds
Bates	Robert Phalen

"Landscape"

Duff	Robert Symonds
Beth	Betty Field

UNDERSTUDIES: Beth, Barbara Tarbuck; Duff, Ray Fry; Ellen, Lee Lawson; Rumsey, Ray Fry; Bates, Dan Sullivan

Press: Susan Bloch, William Schelble
Stage Managers: Barbara-Mae Phillips, Paul Bengston

* "Birthday Party" closed Mar. 14, 1971 after 39 performances and 6 previews. "Landscape/Silence" closed after 6 performances of limited engagement in repertory with "Birthday Party."

Martha Swope Photos

Left: Robert Phelan, Betty Field, Ray Fry Above: Betty Field, Ray Fry, John Harkins, Lee Lawson, Robert Symonds

Robert Symonds, Betty Field in "Landscape"

Robert Phalen, Barbara Tarbuck, Robert Symonds in "Silence"

Stephen Elliott, Philip Bosco

VIVIAN BEAUMONT THEATER

Opened Thursday, March 11, 1971.*
The Repertory Theater of Lincoln Center (Jules Irving, Director) presents:

AN ENEMY OF THE PEOPLE

Arthur Miller's Adaptation of Henrik Ibsen's play; Director, Jules Irving; Setting, Douglas W. Schmidt; Costumes, Carrie Fishbein Robbins; Lighting, John Gleason; Assistant Director, Dan Sullivan; Production Assistants, Bennet Averyt, Jo Sennet; Hairstylist, Jim Sullivan.

CAST

Morten Kiil	Sydney Walker
Billing	James Blendick
Mrs. Stockmann	Barbara Cason
Peter Stockmann	Philip Bosco
Hovstad	David Birney
Dr. Stockmann	Stephen Elliott
Morten	Michael Meyers or Timmy Ousey
Ejlif	Michael Meyers or Barry Symonds
Captain Horster	Don Plumley
Petra	Tandy Cronyn
Aslaksen	Conrad Bain
The Drunk	Macon McCalman

TOWNSPEOPLE: Esther Benson, Robert Benson, Joseph Boley, Richard Bowler, James Cook, Blaine Cordner, Ronald Frazier, Robert Levine, David Little, Michael Miller, Susan Sharkey, George Van Den Houten

UNDERSTUDIES: Doctor, Macon McCalman; Peter, George Van Den Houten; Mrs. Stockman, Esther Benson; Hovstad, David Little; Ikkl, Richard Bowler; Petra, Susan Sharkey; Aslaksen, Drunk, Robert Benson; Horster, Michael Miller; Billing, James Cook.

A Tragedy in 3 acts and 5 scenes. The action takes place in a Norwegian town in the past.

Press: Susan Bloch, William Schelbe, Sedgwick Clark
Stage Managers: Barbara-Mae Phillips, Patrick Horrigan

* Closed Apr. 25, 1971 after limited engagement of 54 performances and 12 previews.

Martha Swope Photos

Top Right: Conrad Bain, James Blendick, Stephen Elliott, David Birney, Philip Bosco

Barbara Cason, Stephen Elliott, Tandy Cronyn
Above: Don Plumley, Elliott, Cason, James Blendick, David Birney, Cronyn

FORUM THEATER

Opened Thursday, March 25, 1971.*
The Repertory Theater of Lincoln Center
presents:

SCENES FROM AMERICAN LIFE

By A. R. Gurney, Jr.; Director, Dan Sullivan; Settings
and Lighting, John Scheffler; Costumes, James Berton
Harris; Hairstylist, Jim Sullivan; Production Assistants,
Sarah Nash Gates, Jo Sennet.

CAST

James Broderick	Lee Lawson
Herbert Foster	Priscilla Pointer
Martha Henry	Robert Symonds
Elizabeth Huddle	Christopher Walken

Pianist: David Frishberg

A play in two acts.

Press: Susan Bloch, William Schelble
Stage Managers: Paul Bengston, Jean-Daniel Noland

* Closed Apr. 18, 1971 after 30 performances and 6
previews.

Martha Swope Photos

Priscilla Pointer (center), and clockwise: Lee
Lawson, Robert Symonds, Elizabeth Huddle,
Christopher Walken, Herbert Foster, James
Broderick, Martha Henry Left Center: Robert
Symonds, Elizabeth Huddle, Priscilla Pointer,
Martha Henry in "Scenes from American Life"

THE FORUM THEATER

Opened Thursday, April 29, 1971.*
The Repertory Theater of Lincoln Center
presents:

PICTURES IN THE HALLWAY

Adapted from Sean O'Casey by Paul Shyre; Setting
and Costumes, Douglas W. Schmidt; Lighting, John
Gleason; Production Assistant, Micky Tekoah.

CAST

Narrator	Paul Shyre
Mrs. Casside	Aline MacMahon
John Casside	Stephen McHattie
Alice Boyd	Helena Carroll
Mr. Anthony	Michael McGuire
Uncle Tom	Dermot McNamara

UNDERSTUDIES: Misses MacMahon, Carroll, Rhoda
Gemignani; Messrs. McGuire, McNamara, Macon
McCalman; Mr. McHattie, Robert Phalen; Mr. Shyre,
Robert Benson.

A Reading in two parts. The action takes place in
Dublin during Sean O'Casey's boyhood.

Press: Susan Bloch, William Schelble
Stage Managers: Paul Bengston, Patrick Horrigan,
Robert Benson

* Closed May 15, 1971 after limited engagement of 20
performances and 6 previews.

Martha Swope Photo

Helena Carroll, Stephen McHattie, Aline
MacMahon, Paul Shyre, Michael McGuire,
Dermot McNamara

VIVIAN BEAUMONT THEATER

Opened Thursday, May 13, 1971.*
The Repertory Theater of Lincoln Center (Jules
Irving, Director) presents:

ANTIGONE

By Sophocles; English version by Dudley Fitts and
Robert Fitzgerald; Director, John Hirsch; Setting, Doug-
las W. Schmidt; Lighting, John Gleason; Costumes, Jane
Greenwood; Music, Lukas Foss; Assistant Director, Paul
Bengston; Production Assistant, Howard Lowell.

CAST

Messenger	John Harkins
Choragos	Charles Cioffi
Female Chorus Leader	Pauline Flanagan
Creon	Philip Bosco
Ismene	Tandy Cronyn
Antigone	Martha Henry
Sentry	James Blendick†
Haimon	David Birney
Teiresias	Sydney Walker
Boy	Timmy Ousey
Eurydice	Dimitra Arliss
Guards	Robert Legionaire, Frank T. Wells
Chorus	Diana Kirkwood, David Little, Myra Rubin, George Van Den Houten

A Tragedy presented in five scenes with prologue, and
without intermission.

Press: Susan Bloch, William Schelble
Stage Managers: Barbara-Mae Phillips, Jean-
Daniel Noland

* Closed June 20, 1971 after 46 performances and 12
previews.

† Succeeded by Ray Fray

Martha Swope Photo

**Philip Bosco, Martha Henry, David Birney
Above: Philip Bosco, Martha Henry in
"Antigone"**

THE FORUM THEATER

Opened Thursday, June 3, 1971.*
The Repertory Theater of Lincoln Center (Jules
Irving, Director) presents the American Premiere
of:

PLAY STRINDBERG

By Friedrich Durrenmatt; Translated by James
Kirkup; Director, Dan Sullivan; Setting, Douglas W.
Schmidt; Lighting, John Gleason; Costumes, James
Berton Harris; Musical Direction, Roland Gagnon;
Hairstylist, Jim Sullivan; Production Assistants, Fay
Kasmer, Joe Sennet.

CAST

Alice	Priscilla Pointer
Edgar	Robert Symonds†1
Kurt	Conrad Bain†
Stage Manager	Jean-Daniel Noland
Trumpet	Robert Harley†2
Tuba	Roger Ricci

UNDERSTUDIES: Rhoda Gemignani, Macon McCalman

A Comedy performed in 12 rounds with one intermission.

Press: Susan Bloch, William Schelble, Sedgwick Clark
Stage Managers: Patrick Horrigan, Macon McCalman,
Jean-Daniel Noland

* Closed July 3, 1971 after 36 performances and 6
previews.
† Succeeded by: 1. Ray Fry, 2. Howard Birnbaum

**Priscilla Pointer, Robert Symonds, Conrad Bain
in "Play Strindberg"**

THE NEGRO ENSEMBLE COMPANY
Douglas Turner Ward, Artistic Director   Robert Hooks, Executive Director
Frederick Garrett, Administrative Director
Fourth Season

Tonice Gwathney, Marilyn B. Coleman, Roxie
Roker in 'Ododo'

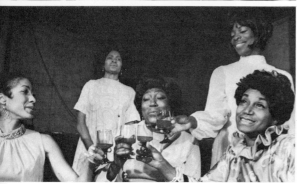

Anita Wilson, Frances Foster, Esther Rolle,
Roxie Roker, Clarice Taylor in 'Rosalee' Above:
William Jay, Adolph Caesar, Katherine McGrath,
Jeff David in 'Perry's Mission'

138

ST. MARKS PLAYHOUSE
Opened Tuesday, November 17, 1970.*
The Negro Ensemble Company presents:

ODODO
(Truth)

Written and Directed by Joseph A. Walker; Music and Musical Direction, Dorothy A. Dinroe; Choreography, Syvilla Fort, Joseph A. Walker; Sets, Edward Burbridge; Lighting, Ernest Baxter; Costumes, Dorothy A. Dinroe, Monica Myrie; Technical Director, Michael Wheeler

CAST

Ray Aranha	Jack Landon
Ethel Ayler	Garrett Morris
Marilyn B. Coleman	Roxie Roker
Deloris Gaskins	Garrett Saunders
Tonice Gwathney	Charles Weldon
Robert Jackson	Anita Wilson

MUSICIANS: Chuck Fowler, Eustis Guillemet, Dennis Heaven, Andre Strombert, Lawrence Thweat

A Musical in 2 acts and 14 scenes.

Company Manager: Gerald S. .Krone
Press: Howard Atlee, David Roggensack, Irene Gandy

* Closed Dec. 27, 1970 after 48 performances.

ST. MARKS PLAYHOUSE
Opened Thursday, January 21, 1971.*
The Negro Ensemble Company presents:

PERRY'S MISSION
and ROSALEE
PRITCHETT

Set, Edward Burbridge; Lighting, Ernest Baxter; Costumes, Monica Myrie; Wigs, Tovar Tresses, Charles Reuben; Technical Director, Michael Wheeler; Technical Advisor, Chuck Vincent; Sound Technician, Moses Boone, Jr.

CAST

"Perry's Mission"

By Clarence Young III; Director, Douglas Turner Ward

Lester "Bobo" Johnson	Adolph Caesar
Susie Collett	Katherine McGrath
Henry Jorden	Charles Weldon
Charles Stripling	William Jay
Bob Hinton	Jeff David
Boosie Taylor	Win Wilford
Pooky Fields	Charles Grant
A Black Man	David Downing
Jouba "Rockfist" Spinter	Arthur French
Bus Driver	Harold Triggs

The action takes place at the present time in a typical bar located in a Black Community in a medium-sized Mid-Western city.

"Rosalee Pritchett"
By Carlton and Barbara Molette; Director, Shauneille Perry

Rosalee Pritchett	Frances Foster
Doretha Ellen Sanders	Roxie Roker
Maybelle Johnson	Esther Rolle
Dolly Mae Anderson	Clarice Taylor
Robert Barron	Adolph Caesar
Augustin Lowe	Arthur French
Donald King	William Jay
Wilbur Wittmer	David Downing
Thelma Franklin	Anita Wilson

The action takes place at the present time during a riot in a Southern city.

Company Manager: Gerald S. Krone
Press: Howard Atlee, David Roggensack, Irene Gandy
Stage Manager: F. Rebecca Wragg

* Closed Feb. 21, 1971 after limited engagement of 48 performances.

Bert Andrews Photos

ST. MARKS PLAYHOUSE

Opened Sunday, March 14, 1971.*
The Negro Ensemble Company presents:

THE DREAM ON MONKEY MOUNTAIN

By Derek Walcott; Director, Michael A. Schultz;
Choreography, Mary Barnett; Set, Edward Burbridge;
Costumes, Lewis Brown; Lighting, Ernest Baxter,
Oyamo; Technical Director, Michael Wheeler.

CAST

Tigre	Lawrence Cook
Souris	Afolabi Ajayi
Corporal Lestrade	Ron O'Neal
Makak	Roscoe Lee Browne
The Apparition	Margret Spear
Moustique	Antonio Fargas
Basil	Robert Jackson
Market Wife	Esther Rolle
Market Inspector	David Downing

VILLAGE WOMEN, WIVES OF MAKAK: Esther Bailey, Charliese Drakeford, Freda Teresa Vanterpool, Anita Wilson, Alma Woolsey

VILLAGE MEN, WARRIORS; K. Lawrence Dunham, Laijba Durr, Noel Hall, Alexander O. Sallid

UNDERSTUDIES: Adolph Caesar, J. Herbert Kerr, Jr.

A Drama in 2 parts and 6 scenes with a prologue and epilogue. The action takes place on a West Indian island at the present time.

Company Manager: Gerald S. Krone
Press: Howard Atlee, David Roggensack, Irene Gandy
Stage Managers: Nate Barnett, F. Rebecca Wragg

* Closed Apr. 18, 1971 after a limited engagement of 40 performances.

Bert Andrews Photos

**Top Right: (C) Ron O'Neal, Roscoe Lee Browne
Below: Esther Rolle, Roscoe Lee Browne**

Graham Brown, Barbara Clarke in 'Ride a Black Horse'

ST. MARKS PLAYHOUSE

Opened Tuesday, May 25, 1971,*
The Negro Ensemble Company presents:

RIDE A BLACK HORSE

By John Scott; Director, Douglas Turner Ward; Set, Edward Burbridge; Costumes, Monica Myrie; Lighting, Ernest Baxter; Sound, Charles Vincent; Technical Director, Michael Wheeler.

CAST

Carl Blanks	Graham Brown
Bob	Madison Arnold
Edie	Marilyn Chris
Harold	Adolph Caesar
Max	William Countryman
Lloyd	Bill Cobbs
Faye	Esther Rolle
Junior Bonner	David Downing
Alfred	Charles Grant
Rudy	Charles Weldon
Sharon	Delores Gaskins
Sandy	Barbara Clarke
Harley	Jay Montgomery

A Drama in two acts. The action takes place in the mind of the city and in the city of the mind, now. . .before and after.

Company Manager: Gerald S. Krone
Press: Howard Atlee, David Roggensack, Irene Gandy
Stage Managers: David Hanigan, F. Rebecca Wragg

* Closed June 13, 1971 after 24 performances and 6 previews.

ESTELLE NEWMAN THEATER

Opened Sunday, October 4, 1970.*
New York Shakespeare Festival Public Theater
presents:

THE HAPPINESS CAGE

By Dennis J. Reardon; Director, Tom Aldredge;
Settings, Marjorie Kellogg; Costumes, Theoni V.
Aldredge; Lighting, Martin Aronstein; Music, Ronny
Cox; Associate Producer, Bernard Gersten; Production
Assistant, Vincent Liff; Assistant Director, Steven Shaw

CAST

Reese	Lewis J. Stadlen
Orderly	Charles Durning
Miles	Ronny Cox
Rhodes	James DeMarse
Dr. Freytag	Henderson Forsythe
General	Paul Sparer
Aide	George Loros
Visitors	John Benson, Walter DeLano, Alice Merton Benson
Nurse	Pamela Grey
Assistant	Jason Miller
Anna Ames	Bette Henritze
Press	Alice Merton Benson, John Benson, Walter DeLano, James DeMarse, Jason Miller

UNDERSTUDIES: Reese, Miles, Jason Miller; Freytag,
General, John Benson; Nurse, Anna, Hope Arthur

A Drama in 2 acts and 5 scenes. The action takes
place at the present time in a Veterans' Administration
hospital.

Press: Merle Debuskey, Faith Geer
Stage Manager: Jane Neufeld

* Closed Nov. 1, 1970 after 40 performances.

Zodiac Photos

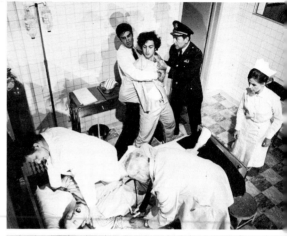

Right: Ronny Cox, Lewis J. Stadlen
**Above: (C) George Loros, Lewis J. Stadlen, Paul
Sparer**

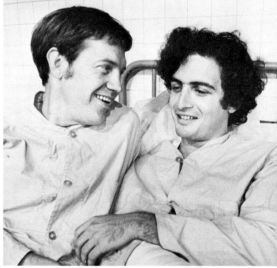

Jack MacGowran

PUBLIC/NEWMAN THEATER

Opened Thursday, November 19, 1970.*
New York Shakespeare Festival (Joseph Papp,
Producer) presents:

MacGOWRAN IN THE WORKS OF BECKETT

Text adapted by Jack MacGowran with the approval
and advice of Samuel Beckett; Setting, Ming Cho Lee;
Costume, Theoni V. Aldredge; Lighting, Martin Aronstein; Associate Producer, Bernard Gersten; Production
Manager, Andrew Mihok.

CAST

JACK MacGOWRAN

Program presented in two parts with selections from
"Embers," "Molloy," "Echo's Bones," "Cascando,"
"Waiting for Godot," "From an abandoned work,"
"Watt," "Words and Music," "Krapp's Last Tape,"
"Endgame," "The Unnamable," "Malone Dies."

General Manager: David Black
Press: Merle Debuskey, Faith Geer
Stage Manager: Andrew Mihok, Robert Kellogg

* Closed Jan. 24, 1971 after 61 performances.

140

Zodiac Photo

ANSPACHER THEATER

Opened Sunday, October 11, 1970.*
New York Shakespeare Festival (Joseph Papp, Producer) presents:

TRELAWNY OF THE "WELLS"

By Sir Arthur Wing Pinero; Director, Robert Ronan; Settings, David Mitchell; Costumes, Theoni V. Aldredge; Lighting, Martin Aronstein; Associate Producer, Bernard Gersten; Musical Supervision, John Morris; Production Assistants, Carl Pilo, Richard Vos.

CAST

Theatrical Folk:

James Telfer	Frederic Warriner
Augustus Colpoys	Geoff Garland
Ferdinand Gadd	Michael Wager
Tom Wrench	Robert Ronan
Mrs. Telfer	Elaine Eldridge
Avonia Bunn	Sasha von Scherler
Rose Trelawny of the Bagnigge-Wells Theatre	Nancy Dussault
Imogen Parrott	Valerie French
O'Dwyer	Gene Nye
Members of the Pantheon Theatre	Douglas Hayle, Arlene Nadel, Con Roche

Non-theatrical Folk:

Vice-Chancellor Sir William Gower	George Bartenieff
Arthur Gower	Dean Santoro
Clara de Foenix	Janet Kapral
Miss Trafalgar Gower	Esther Buffler
Captain de Foenix	Gene Nye
Mrs. Mossop	Jean Bruno
Mr. Ablett	Dan Durning
Charles	Grant Code
Sarah	Arlene Nadel

UNDERSTUDIES: Rose, Avonia, Arlene Nadel; Augustus, Tom, Douglas Hayle; Arthur, Ferdinand, O'Dwyer, Captain, Con Roche; Mrs. Telfer, Imogen, Trafalgar, Sarah, Tamara Daniel.

A Play in four acts presented with two intermissions. The action takes place in the early 1860's.

General Manager: David Black
Press: Merle Debuskey, Faith Geer
Stage Manager: Dean Compton

* Closed Nov. 16, 1970 by Actors Equity strike after 46 performances; re-opened Dec. 25, 1970 and closed Jan. 10, 1971 after a total of 67 performances.

Zodiac Photos

Robert Ronan, Valerie French

Robert Ronan, Sasha von Scherler
Above: Dean Santoro, Nancy Dussault

141

PUBLIC THEATER

Opened Sunday, February 14, 1971.*
The New York Shakespeare Festival (Joseph
Papp, Producer) presents:

SUBJECT TO FITS

A Response to Dostoyevsky's "The Idiot" by Robert
Montgomery; Director, A. J. Antoon; Setting, Leo Yoshimura; Costumes, Theoni V. Aldredge; Lighting, Ian
Calderon; Music, Robert Montgomery; Associate Producer, Bernard Gersten.

CAST

Prince Myshkin	Andy Robinson†1
Paryfon Rogozhin	Jason Miller†2
Lebedev	John Mahon
Madame Yepanchin	Jean David
Aglaya Yepanchin	Katharine Dunfee
Ganya Ivoglin	James DeMarse
General Ivoglin	Albert Quinton
Ippolit Ivoglin	Jim Borrelli
Natasha Fillipovna	Sharon Laughlin

MUSICIANS: Ken Guilmartin, Ruben Rivera, Todd
Roberto

A Play in two acts.

General Manager: David Black
Press: Merle Debuskey, Faith Geer
Stage Manager: Ken Glickfeld

* Closed May 30, 1971 after 127 performances.

† Succeeded by: 1. John Glover, 2. Walter McGinn

Zodiac Photos

**Right: Andy Robinson, Jason Miller Above:
James DeMarse, Sharon Laughlin, Andy
Robinson**

**Andy Robinson in box, surrounded by Sharon
Laughlin, Jason Miller, Katharine Dunfee**

Katharine Dunfee, John Glover

Opened Sunday, February 21, 1971.*
The New York Shakespeare Festival (Joseph
Papp, Producer) presents:

SLAG

By David Hare; Director, Roger Hendricks Simon;
Settings, Daisy Page Pickman; Costumes, Milo Morrow;
Lighting, Robert Kellogg; Associate Producer, Bernard
Gersten; Coordinator, Nancy Heller; Production Manager, Andrew Mihok.

CAST

Joanne..Roberta Maxwell
Elise...Margo Ann Berdeshevsky
Ann...Kathryn Walker
Brackenhurst Girls.......Gina Rose Horowitz, Rose Marie
Smith

A Play in six scenes with one intermission. The action
takes place at the present time in Brackenhurst, a
private school for girls.

Press: Merle Debuskey, Faith Geer
Stage Manager: John Beven

* Closed Mar. 21, 1971 after 32 performances.

PUBLIC/NEWMAN THEATER

Opened Monday, February 22, 1971.*
New York Shakespeare Festival Public Theater
(Joseph Papp, Producer) presents:

HERE ARE LADIES

Directed and Designed by Sean Kenny; Music, Sean
O'Riada; Associate Producer, Bernard Gersten.

CAST

SIOBHAN McKENNA

The Women of Joyce, Shaw, O'Casey, Yeats, Synge,
Stephens, and Beckett presented in two parts.

General Manager: David Black
Press: Merle Debuskey, Faith Geer
Stage Manager: Robert Kellogg

* Closed May 9, 1971 after 67 performances.

PUBLIC/MARTINSON THEATER

Opened Sunday, March 7, 1971.*
New York Shakespeare Festival Theater (Joseph
Papp, Producer) presents:

BLOOD

Text, Doug Dyer in collaboration with the Blood
company;Lyrics, Alex Ander, Mary Boylan, Christopher
Cox, Doug Dyer, Patrick Fox, Horald Griffiths, Avra
Petrides; Music, Alex Ander, David Cohen, Christopher
Cox, Margaret Dorn, Doug Dyer, Patrick Fox, Horald
Griffiths, Elizabeth Howard, Maggie Hyatt, Linda Swenson, Jim Turner, Tom Willis; Director, Doug Dyer;
Clothes, Theoni V. Aldredge; Lighting, Keith Nelson;
Movement, Cora Cohan; Musical Supervision, John
Morris; Musical Director, Patrick Fox; Associate Producer, Bernard Gersten.

COMPANY Alex Ander, Roberta Baum, Alexandra
Borrie, Mary Boylan, Christopher Cox, Margaret Dorn,
Doug Dyer, William Ellington, Patrick Fox, Horald
Griffiths, Elisabeth Howard, Maggie Hyatt, Madge Sinclair, Joyce Stanton, Jack Starkey, Linda Swenson, Jim
Turner

MUSICAL NUMBERS: Baby Rue, High Lonesome,
Hard Time War Time, Hear the Guns, Lullaby, Snake,
Cold Steel, Every Father, I had a Son, There You Go
Again, Father Father, Gas Can, Dance of Murder,
Nobody's Fault, I Dreamt about My Home, Madness
Murder, Whistles, I Woke Up Today, Prophesy, 4000
Years, Walk on Home, Heebie-Jeebie Furies, Don't Call
Us, Before You Knew I Loved You, Destruction,
Rhythms, Monkey in a Tree, Minute by Minute, Love
Game to Me, New Snow, Just a Little Bit, Hail to the
Blood

General Manager: David Black
Press: Merle Debuskey, Faith Geer
Stage Managers: Dean Compton, Jonathan Penzner

* Closed Mar. 21, 1971 after 39 performances.

Zodiac Photos

Kathryn Walker, Margo Ann Berdeshevsky,
Roberta Maxwell

Patrick Fox, Horald Griffiths, Alexandra Borrie
in "Blood" Above: Siobhan McKenna

PUBLIC/SOUTH HALL THEATER

Opened Wednesday, April 14, 1971.*
New York Shakespeare Festival Theater (Joseph
Papp, Producer) presents The Organic Theater
Company in:

CANDIDE

Adapted from Voltaire's novel of the same name;
Director, Stuart Gordon; Music and Musical Direction,
Jonathan Pearthree.

CAST

Amy Benesch	Carolyn Gordon
Simone Deely	Gerald Kirschbaum
Bob Engel	Cecil O'Neal

A Musical free adaptation of Voltaire's novel "Candide."

General Manager: David Black
Press: Merle Debuskey, Faith Geer

* Closed April 25, 1971 after limited engagement of 17
performances.

Bob Engel, Carolyn Gordon in "Candide"

PUBLIC THEATER/OTHER STAGE

Opened Sunday, April 18, 1971.*
New York Shakespeare Festival (Joseph Papp,
Producer) presents The Cornbread Players in:

UNDERGROUND

Director, Walter Jones; Setting, Leo Yoshimura; Costumes, Theoni V. Aldredge; Lighting, Ian Calderon;
Associate Producer, Bernard Gersten.

CAST

"The Life and Times of J. Walter Smintheus"
by Edgar White

J. Walter Smintheus	Dennis Tate
Hospital Orderly	Lennal Wainwright
Edward	Edward Seamon
Robert	Walter Jones
Joyce	Noorma Darden
Dr. Comma	John McCants Trotter
Margie	Robin Braxton
Bob Kaufman	John Gallagher
Paul	John Gallagher
Manager	Edward Seamon

"Jazznite" by Walter Jones

Leola	Robin Braxton
Dudder	Demond Wilson
Slick	Lennal Wainwright
Eligah	Sam Singleton
Baylock	Walter Cotton
Heavy	MacArthur Flack III
Barbara	Noorma Darden

General Manager: David Black
Press: Merle Debuskey, Faith Geer
Stage Managers: John Beven, Jenny Maybruck

* Closed May 16, 1971 after 38 performances.

Zodiac Photos

**Robin Braxton, John Gallagher, Dennis Tate in
"Life and Times. . ." Above: Robin Braxton,
Demond Wilson, Noorma Darden, Sam
Singleton in "Jazznite"**

NEWMAN THEATER

Opened Wednesday, May 19, 1971.*
The New York Shakespeare Festival Public
Theater (Joseph Papp, Producer) presents:

THE BASIC TRAINING OF PAVLO HUMMEL

By David Rabe; Director, Jeff Bleckner; Designed by
David Mitchell; Costumes, Theoni V. Aldredge; Light-
ing, Martin Aronstein; Associate Producer, Bernard
Gersten; Technical Adviser, Lennal Wainwright

CAST

Pavlo Hummel	William Atherton
Yen	Victoria Racimo
Ardell	Albert Hall
First Sergeant	Joe Fields
Capt. Saunders	Edward Cannan
Cpl. Ferrara	Anthony R. Charnota
Parker	Peter Cameron
Burns	Stephen Clarke
Ryan	John Walter Davis
Hall	Bob Delegall
Grennel	Tom Harris
Hinkle	Edward Herrmann
Kress	Earl Hindman
Pierce	Robert Lehman
Hendrix	D. Franklyn Lenthall
Mickey	Frederick Coffin
Mrs. Hummel	Sloane Shelton
Sgt. Brisbey	Lee Wallace
Cpl. Jones	Garrett Morris
Mama-san	Christal Kim
Sgt. Wall	John Benson
Parham	Bob Delegall
Linh	Hoshin Seki
Zung	Victoria Racimo
Farmer	Hoshin Seki

Understudy for Pavlo: Peter Cameron

A Drama in two acts. The action takes place in the
United States Army between 1965 and 1967.

Press: Merle Debuskey, Faith Geer, M. J. Boyer
Stage Managers: Dean Compton, David Eidenberg

* Still playing May 31, 1971.

Zodiac Photos

Frederick Coffin, William Atherton
Top Right: Joe Fields, William Atherton

Sloane Shelton, William Atherton Above: Albert
Hall, William Atherton, Victoria Racimo

ROUNDABOUT THEATRE

Gene Feist, Producing Director
Fifth Season

ROUNDABOUT THEATRE

Opened Sunday, October 18, 1970.*
The Roundabout Repertory Company presents:

HAMLET

By William Shakespeare; Director, Gene Feist; Original Score, Philip Campanella; Scenery, Holmes Easley; Costumes, Mimi Maxmen; Lighting, Loran Bruns; Technicians, Roger Cunningham, Arthur Rosen; Sword Play, Louis G. Trapani.

CAST

Hamlet	Art Burns
Gertrude	Philip Campanella
Claudius/Ghost	Sterling Jensen
Horatio/Player King	Bruce M. Kornbluth
Polonius/Gravedigger	Fred Stuthman
Ophelia	Louis G. Trapani
Laertes/Player Queen	Thomas McCann
Guildenstern/Marcellus	John Guerrasio
Rosencrantz/Francisco	Stephen Greenstein
Bernardo/Priest/Gonzago	Lyle Lorentz
Osric/Gentleman	Robert Marinaccio

A Tragedy presented in two acts.

Press: William Campbell
Stage Manager: Michael Fields

* Closed Nov. 29, 1970 after a limited engagement of 56 performances.

Sterling Jensen, Louis G. Trapani, Philip Campanella Above: Clockwise around Art Burns, Thomas McCann, John Guerrasio, Stephen Greenstein, Philip Campanella, Fred Stuthman, Bruce Kornbluth, Lyle Lorentz, Louis G. Trapani, Robert Marinaccio, Sterling Jensen in "Hamlet"

ROUNDABOUT THEATRE

Opened Friday, December 11, 1970.*
The Roundabout Repertory Company presents:

TUG OF WAR

By Alan Rossett; Director, William Campbell; Scenery, Michael Fields; Costumes, Mary Etta; Music, Philip Campanella; Lighting, Robert Murphy; Assistant Director, Louis G. Trapani; Technician, Lyle Lorentz.

CAST

Mopsy	Carole Martin
Peter	Philip Campanella
Liliane	Jacqueline Bertrand
Carol	Ann Sachs
Fred	Manuel Santiago
Robert	Jack Axelrod

A Drama in two acts. The action takes place at the present time in a country home during an afternoon and evening in summer.

Press: Michael Fried
Stage Manager: Michael Fields

Carole Martin, Ann Sachs, Jacqueline Bertrand in "Tug of War"

146

* Closed Jan. 3, 1971 after a limited engagement of 21 performances.

ROUNDABOUT THEATRE

Opened Wednesday, January 13, 1971.*
The Roundabout Repertory Company presents:

UNCLE VANYA

By Anton Chekhov; Director, Gene Feist; Scenery, Holmes Easley; Costumes, Mimi Maxmen; Lighting, Robert Murphy; Original Score, Philip Campanella; Assistant to Director, Louis G. Trapani; Technician, Lyle Lorentz.

CAST

Alexandre Serebryakov	Thayer David
Helena	Elizabeth Owens
Sonya	Julie Garfield
Marya Voynitsky	Ann Kingsley
Vanya	Sterling Jensen
Michael Astrov	Winston May
Telyegin	Fred Stuthman†
Marina	Joni Ruth White
A Laborer	Lyle Lorentz

Standby: Norman Lind

A Drama presented in two parts. The action takes place in the summer to fall of 1896 on a country estate in Russia.

Press: William Campbell, Max Eisen, Warren Pincus
Stage Manger: Michael Fields

* Closed Feb. 28, 1971 after 46 performances. Re-opened March 5, 1971 at the Cherry Lane Theatre, and closed there March 14, 1971 after 8 performances and 5 previews. Stuart Duncan, Jay H. Fuchs, and Joseph Beruh were co-producers.

† Succeeded by Arthur Ed Forman

Right: Thayer David, Elizabeth Owens
Above: Thayer David, Julie Garfield

ROUNDABOUT THEATRE

Opened Sunday, March 21, 1971.*
The Roundabout Repertory Company presents:

CHARLES ABBOTT & SON

By Lewis S. Salsburg; Director, Gene Feist; Scenery, Holmes Easley; Costumes, Gilson Sarmento; Lighting, Robert Murphy; Musical Supervision, Philip Campanella; Associate Director, Sterling Jensen; Producing Assistant, Ted Weiant.

CAST

Danny O'Boyle	Lyle J. Lorentz
Ann Honeywell	Alice Drummond
Charles Abbott	Fred Stuthman
Byron Abbott	Robert G. Murch
Eleanor Wagner	Nancy Reardon
Jacob Morris	Philip Campanella
Sylvia Abbott	Babette New
Mark Gilbert	Norman Lind

A Drama in 3 acts and 5 scenes. The action takes place during October 1928 in the offices of the furniture factory of Charles Abbott & Son.

Press: William Campbell
Stage Manager: Michael Fields

* Closed April 4, 1971 after limited engagement of 24 performances.

Paul J. Hoeffler Photo

Fred Stuthman, Robert G. Murch
in "Charles Abbott & Son"

147

ROUNDABOUT THEATRE

Opened Sunday, April 25, 1971.*
The Roundabout Repertory Company presents:

SHE STOOPS TO CONQUER

By Oliver Goldsmith; Director, Gene Feist; Original Score, Philip Campanella; Setting, Holmes Easley; Costumes, Mimi Maxmen; Lighting, Robert Murphy; Assistant Director, Paul Bennett; Technical Assistant, Steve Glagow.

CAST

Mrs. Hardcastle	Jane Connell
Miss Hardcastle	Nancy Reardon
Miss Neville	Arlene Nadel
Pimple	Judith Sullivan
Sir Charles Marlowe	Lyle J. Lorentz
Young Marlowe	Robert G.Murch
Hardcastle	Fred Stuthman
Hastings	Tom V. V. Tammi
Tony Lumpkin	Louis G. Trapani
Diggory	Philip Campanella
Roger	Roger Cunningham

A Comedy presented in two acts. The action takes place in and around the Hardcastle house outside of London on March 15, 1773.

Press: William Campbell
Stage Manager: Michael Fields

* Closed May 30, 1971 after limited engagement of 46 performances.

Paul H. Hoeffler Photos

Right: Jane Connell, Tom V. V. Tammi, Arlene Nadel, Louis G. Trapani Above: Jane Connell, Fred Stuthman

OFF BROADWAY PRODUCTIONS FROM OTHER SEASONS THAT CLOSED DURING THIS SEASON

Title	Opened	Closed	Performances
You're a Good Man, Charlie Brown	Mar. 7, 1967	Feb. 14, 1971	1597
Boys in the Band	Apr. 14, 1968	Sept. 6, 1970	1002
Adaptation/Next	Feb. 10, 1969	Oct. 18, 1970	707
No Place to Be Somebody	May 4, 1969	Oct. 18, 1970	576
The Last Sweet Days of Isaac	Jan. 26, 1970	May 2, 1971	485
The Concept	Aug. 21, 1969	June 28, 1970	268
What the Butler Saw	May 4, 1970	Nov. 15, 1970	224
Joy	Jan. 27, 1970	July 26, 1970	205
Colette	May 6, 1970	Aug. 2, 1970	101
Dark of the Moon	Apr. 3, 1970	June 14, 1970	86
Room Service	May 12, 1970	July 11, 1970	71
Mod Donna	May 3, 1970	June 7, 1970	56
Beggar on Horseback (LC)	May 14, 1970	June 28, 1970	54
The Lady from Maxim's	May 3, 1970	June 14, 1970	50
Awake and Sing	May 27, 1970	June 28, 1970	41
Slow Dance on the Killing Ground	May 13, 1970	June 14, 1970	36
The Pig Pen	May 20, 1970	June 6, 1970	35
Amphitryon (LC)	May 28, 1970	June 20, 1970	28
Chicago '70	May 25, 1970	June 14, 1970	24
The Open Theatre	May 30, 1970	June 14, 1970	18

NATIONAL TOURING COMPANIES

BUTTERFLIES ARE FREE

By Leonard Gershe; Director, Milton Katselas; Set,
Richard Seger; Costumes, Robert Mackintosh; Lighting,
Jules Fisher; Associate Producer, Ruth Bailey; Hairstylist, Joe Tubens; Presented by Arthur Whitelaw, Max J.
Brown, Byron Goldman. Opened Wednesday, May 20,
1970 at the Hartford in Los Angeles, and closed Oct. 24,
1970.

CAST

Don Baker	Wendell Burton
Jill Tanner	Ellen Endicott-Jones
Mrs. Baker	Eve Arden
Ralph Austin	William Tynan

UNDERSTUDIES: Mrs. Baker, Marijane Maricle; Don,
Ralph, Lloyd Kramer; Jill, Janice Lynde

A Comedy in 2 acts and 3 scenes. The action takes
place at the present time in Don Baker's apartment on
East 11th Street in Manhattan.

General Manager: Marvin A. Krauss
Company Manager: Archie Thomson
Press: Max Eisen, Maurice Turet
Stage Managers: Victor Straus, William Tynan,
Lloyd Kramer

For original New York production, see THEATRE
WORLD, Vol. 26.

Martha Swope Photos

**Wendell Burton, William Tynan, Ellen Endicott-Jones, Eve Arden
Top Right: Ellen Endicott-Jones, Wendell Burton, Eve Arden**

BUTTERFLIES ARE FREE

By Leonard Gershe; Director, Milton Katselas; Set, Richard Seger, Lighting, Jules Fisher; Costumes, Robert Mackintosh; Associate Producer, Ruth Bailey; Presented by Arthur Whitelaw, Max J. Brown, Byron Goldman. Opened Wednesday, July 22, 1970 at the Studebaker in Chicago, and closed May 1, 1971 at the Shubert in New Haven, Conn.

CAST

Don Baker	David Huffman
Jill Tanner	Kristina Callahan
Mrs. Baker	Gloria Swanson
Ralph Austin	Michael Shannon

UNDERSTUDIES: Mrs. Baker, Lynn Archer; Jill, Abby Kimbrough; Don, Michael Shannon, John Spencer

A Comedy in 2 acts and 3 scenes. The action takes place at the present time in Don Baker's apartment on East 11th Street in Manhattan.

General Manager: Marvin A. Krauss
Company Manager: Harold Kusell
Press: Max Eisen, Maurice Turet
Stage Managers: Don Fenwick, John Spencer, Michael Shannon

For original New York production, see THEATRE WORLD, Vol. 26.

Gloria Swanson, David Huffman

Gloria Swanson, Kristina Callahan, and above with David Huffman

COCO

Book and Lyrics, Alan Jay lerner; Music, Andre Previn; Director, Michael Benthall; Musical Numbers and Fashion Sequences Staged by Michael Bennett; Sets and Costumes, Cecil Beaton; Orchestration, Hershy Kay; Lighting, Thomas Shelton; Dance Music Continuity, Harold Wheeler; Music Direction, Robert Emmett Dolan; Associate Producer, Fred Hebert; Production Supervisor, Stone Widney; Hairstylist Joe Tubens; Film Sequences, Milton Olshin, Fred Lemoine; Produced by Frederick Brisson and Montfort Productions; Associate Choreographer, Bob Avian. Opened Monday, January 11, 1971 in the Public Music Hall, Cleveland, Ohio, and closed June 26, 1971 at the Chandler Pavilion in Los Angeles.

CAST

Coco	Katharine Hepburn
Louis Greff	George Rose
Pignol	Jeanne Arnold
Helene	Joan Shea
Sebastian Baye	Daniel Davis
Albert	Al DeSio
Docaton	Eve March
Georges	Don Chastain
Loublaye	Michael Amber
Marie	Candace Cooke
Jeanine	Susan Cartt
Claire	Denise Mauthe
Juliette	Pamela Serpe
Madelaine	Turid Olsen
Lucille	Diane Phillips
Colette	Annette Cardona
Simone	Charlene Ryan
Solange	Brenda Lynn
Mimi	Susan Sfreddo
Adrienne	Sandahl Bergman
Annette	Jane Karel
Noelle	Lana Shaw†
Dr. Petitjean	Richard Woods
Claude	James Oliver
Dwight Berkwit, Ohrbach's	Will B. Able
Eugene Bernstone, Saks	Ted Agress
Ronny Ginsborn, Bloomingdale's	Michael Dominico
Lapidus	Bill Biskup
Nadine	Gia DeSilva
Zizi	Graziella
Grand Duke Alexandrovitch	Bob Avian
Voice	Jack Dabdoub
Charles, Duke of Glenallen	Michael Allinson
Julian Lesage	Paul Dumont

SINGERS: Sean Allan, Michael Amber, Bill Biskup, Gia DeSilva, Brenda Lynn

DANCERS: Beverly Baker, Sandahl Bergman, Annette Cardona, Susan Cartt, Candace Cooke, Christine Cope, Nancy Dafgek, Jane Karel, Bonnie Lapka, Wendy Mansfield, Denise Mauthe, Kerry McGrath, Turid Olsen, Dianne Phillips, Louise Reichlin, Charlene Ryan, Patsy Sabline, Joana Serpe, Pamela Serpe, Susan Sfreddo, Freda Soiffer, Suzanne Walker, Mary Walling

UNDERSTUDIES: Coco, Jeanne Arnold; Gerff, Richard Woods, Georges, Michael Amber; Noelle, Candace Cooke; Sebastian, Will B. Able; Pignol, Joan Shea; Petitjean, Ted Agress; Berkwit, Rod Barry; Ginsborn, Bernston, Rosenberry, Albert, Danny Villa; Simone, Annette Cardona; Charles, Sean Allan; Julian, Bill Biskup; Docaton, Nadine, Graziella; Papa, James Oliver; Claude, Bill Biskup; Zizi, Sandahl Bergman

MUSICAL NUMBERS: Overture, "But That's the Way You Are," "The World Belongs to the Young," "Let's Go Home," "Mademoiselle Cliche de Paris," "On the Corner of the Rue Cambon," "The Money Rings Out Like Freedom," "A Brand New Dress," "A Woman Is How She Loves," "Gabrielle," "Coco," "The Preparation," Entr'acte, "Fiasco," "When Your Lover Says Goodbye," "Ohrbach's, Bloomingdale's, Best, & Saks," "Always Mademoiselle."

A Musical in 2 acts and 9 scenes. The action takes place in the Maison Chanel, Rue Cambon, Paris, either in the Salon, in the Apartment above, or in memory. It begins in late Fall of 1953 and ends late Spring of 1954.

General Manager: Ben Rosenberg
Company Manager: James Awe
Press: John L. Toohey
Stage Managers: Edward Preston, Michael Sinclair, Mark Krause

† Succeeded by: Gale Dixon

For original NY production, see THEATRE WORLD, Vol. 26.

Zodiac Photos

Jeanne Arnold, Daniel Davis, Katharine Hepburn, George Rose Above: Richard Woods, Katharine Hepburn Top: (C) Hepburn

COMPANY

Book, George Furth; Music and Lyrics, Stephen Sondheim; Sets and Projections, Boris Aronson; Costumes, D. D. Ryan; William H. Batchelder; Musical Direction, Jonathan Anderson; Orchestrations, Jonathan Tunick; Dance Music Arrangements, Wally Harper; Musical Numbers Staged by Michael Bennett; Director, Harold Prince; Presented by Harold Prince in association with Ruth Mitchell; Opened Thursday, May 20, 1971 in the Ahmanson Theatre, Los Angeles Music Center, and still playing May 31, 1971

CAST

Robert	George Chakiris
Sarah	Marti Stevens
Harry	Charles Braswell
Susan	Milly Ericson
Peter	Gary Krawford
Jenny	Teri Ralston
David	Lee Goodman
Amy	Beth Howland
Paul	Del Hinkley
Joanne	Elaine Stritch
Larry	Robert Goss
Marta	Pamela Myers
Kathy	Donna McKechnie
April	Bobbi Jordan
Vocal Minority	Barbara Broughton, Carolyn Kirsch, Mary Roche, Marilyn Saunders

UNDERSTUDIES: Joanne, Marti Stevens; Robert, Gary Krawford; Peter, Larry, Randall Robbins; Harry, David, Paul Edward Penn; Susan, Jenny, April, Preshy Marker; Marta, Marilyn Saunders; Kathy, Carolyn Kirsch; Sarah, Amy, Barbara Broughton

A Musical in two acts. The action takes place at the present time in NYC.

General Manager: Carl Fisher
Company Manager: G. Warren McClane
Press: Hal Wiener
Stage Managers: Ben Strobach, Bob Burland, Edward Penn

For original NY production, see THEATRE WORLD, Vol. 26

Rothschild Photos

Donna McKechnie, George Chakiris Above: George Chakiris, Robert Goss, Elaine Stritch

Beth Howland, Del Hinkley Top Left: Lee Goodman, George Chakiris, Teri Ralston

DEAR LOVE

By Jerome Kilty; Based on love letters of Robert
Browning and Elizabeth Barrett; Director, Burry Fredrik; Sets and Lighting, Robert Fletcher; Costumes,
John Boyt; Producer's Assistant, Geraldine Court; Presented by Weston Productions. Opened Thursday, September 17, 1970 at the Alley Theatre, Houston, Texas,
and closed January 16, 1971 at the Shubert in New
Haven.

CAST

The Actress, who becomes
  Elizabeth Barrett..............................Myrna Loy
The Actor, who becomes
  Robert Browning..........................Jerome Kilty

A Love Story in Two acts. The action takes place in
London in 1845 and 1846.

General Manager: Paul Vroom
Company Manager: Sam Pagliaro
Press: Fred Weterick
Stage Manager: Bruce Lovelady

Jerome Kilty, Myrna Loy (also above)

FIDDLER ON THE ROOF

Book, Joseph Stein; Based on Sholom Aleichem's stories; Music, Jerry Bock; Lyrics, Sheldon Harnick; Director-Choreographer, Jerome Robbins; Settings, Boris Aronson; Costumes, Patricia Zipprodt; Lighting, Jean Rosenthal; Vocal Arrangements, Milton Greene; Musical Direction, Philip Parnes; Dance Music Arrangements, Betty Walberg; Orchestrations, Don Walker; Hairstylist, D. Rusty Bonaccorso; Presented by Harold Prince in association with Theatre Now, Inc. Opened Aug. 4, 1968 at Dallas Music Hall, and still touring May 31, 1971.

CAST

Tevye	Bob Carroll†1
Golde	Fritzi Burr

Their Daughters:

Tzeitel	Doreen Dunn†2
Hodel	Marry Ann Chinn†3
Chava	Alexandra Stoddard†4
Shprintze	Laurie Scandurra
Bielke	Jacqueline Clark
Yente	Lila Teigh
Motel	Stacy McAdams
Perchik	Sidney Ben-Zali†5
Lazar Wolf	Ronald Coralian
Mordcha	Art Vestry
Rabbi	Sanford Seeger†6
Mendel	Michael Hardstark†7
Avran	Joel Fredrick
Grandma Tzeitel	Bess Meisler
Fruma-Sarah	Dede Washburn
Constable	Gerald E. McGonagill†8
Fyedka	Lewis Jacobson†9
Shandel	Nina Miller
The Fiddler	Stephen Wright†10
Bottle Dancers	Gary Dutton, Jay Grimes, Dan Cartagena†11, Charles Isen†12

VILLAGERS: Sheila Adams, Christopher Allen, Dan Cartagena, Larry Carter, Gary Dutton, Gladys Fredrick, Joel Fredrick, Jay Grimes, Michael Hardstark, Charles Isen, Lewis Jacobson, Melaine Lerner, Arnott Mader, Bess Meisler, Nina Miller, Wallace Munro, Brad Tyrrell, Art Vestry, Dede Washburn, Geri Wolcott, Stephen Wright

UNDERSTUDIES: Tevye, Ronald Coralian; Golde, Nina Miller, Lazar, Rabbi, Joel Fredrick; Hodel, Frumah, Melanie Lerner; Chava, Jacqueline Clark; Tzeitel, Dede Washburn; Perchik, Constable, Brad Tyrrell; Motel, Michael Hardstark; Yente, Bess Meisler; Fyedka, Larry Carter; Mordcha, Christopher Allen; Mendel, Stephen Wright; Bielke, Shprintze, Sheila Adams; Avram, Charles Isen; Fiddler, Dan Cartagena; Grandma, Geri Wolcott

Musical in two acts. The action takes place in 1905 in Anatevka, a village in Russia, on the eve of the revolutionary period.

General Manager: Carl Fisher
Company Manager: Donald Antonelli
Press: Dan Langan, Sol Jacobson, Lewis Harmon, Bernard Simon
Stage Managers: Ruth Mitchell, William Schill, T. Schuyler Smith, Wallace Munro, Michael Wuergler

† Succeeded by: 1. Harry Goz and Robert Merrill for one week each, 2. Helena Grenot, 3. Chris Andrea, 4. Adele Paige, 5. Keith Baker, 6. Maurice Brenner, 7. Stephen Wright, 8. Duane Morris, 9. Larry Carter, 10. Dan Cartegena, 11. Lee Delmer, 12. Derek Wolshonak, 13. David Thome, 14. Michael Wuergler

For original NY production, see THEATRE WORLD, Vol. 21

Zodiac Photos

Top Right: Mary Ann Chinn, Bob Carroll, Alexandra Stoddart, Doreen Dunn Below: Fritzi Burr, Lila Teigh

Fritzi Burr, Bob Carroll

FORTY CARATS

Adapted by Jay Allen from play by Pierre Barillet and Jean-Pierre Gredy; Director, Abe Burrows; Scenery, Will Steven Armstrong; Costumes, Sara Brook; Lighting, Martin Aronstein; Associate Producer, Samuel Liff; Presented by David Merrick; Opened Sept. 29, 1969 at Shubert Theatre, Cincinnati, and closed Mar. 13, 1971 at the Fisher in Detroit.

CAST

Ann Stanley	Barbara Rush
Peter Latham	Stephen Collins
Mrs. Adams	Doris Ingraham
Mrs. Margolin	Imogene Bliss
Billy Boylan	Scott McKay
Eddy Edwards	Gene Blakely
Maud Hayes	Audrey Christie
Trina Stanley	Sylvia Grand
Mrs. Latham	Eileen Letchworth
Mr. Latham	Art Barnett[1]
Pat	William Cox[2]

UNDERSTUDIES: Ann, Eileen Letchworth; Billy, Eddy, Latham, Ray Parker; Peter, Roger Baron; Maud, Mrs. Margolin, Mrs. Adams, Marcie Stringer; Trina, Fylys Burstein; Mrs. Latham, Doris Ingraham; Pat, Howard Burstein

A comedy in 2 acts. The action takes place at the present time in the apartment and office of Ann Stanley in NYC, after a prologue somewhere in the Greek islands.

General Manager: Jack Schlissel
Company Manager: James O'Neill
Press: Harvey B. Sabinson, Lee Solters, Gertrude Bromberg
Stage Managers: William Weaver, Howard Burstein, Roger Baron, Fylys Burstein

† Succeeded by: 1. Paul Larson, 2. Roger Baron

For original NY production, see THEATRE WORLD, Vol. 26.

Martha Swope Photos

Paul Larson, Eileen Letchworth Top Right:
Stephen Collins, Sylvia Grand, Barbara Rush,
Audrey Christie

Barbara Rush, Stephen Collins
Above: Scott McKay, Barbara Rush

FORTY CARATS

Adapted by Jay Allen from play by Pierre Barillet and Jean-Pierre Gredy; Director, Abe Burrows; Staged by Charles Maryan; Designed by Leo B. Meyer; Costumes, Sara Brook; Presented by Producing Managers Co.; Opened Monday, Nov. 9, 1970 in Oneida Auditorium, Oneida, N. Y., and closed Mar. 3, 1971 in Masonic Auditorium, Toledo, Ohio.

CAST

Ann Stanley	Barbara Britton
Peter Latham	Robert Dannenberg
Mrs. Adams	Judy Clegg
Mrs. Margolin	Barbara Stanton
Billy Boylan	Robert Darnell
Eddy Edwards	Hugh Reilly
Maud Hayes	Nancy Cushman
Trina Stanley	Tracy Brooks Swope
Mrs. Latham	Minette Hirsch
Mr. Latham	Ed Fuller
Pat	Phil Laurenson

UNDERSTUDIES: An, Mrs. Adams, Minette Hirsch; Peter, Mr. Latham, Phil Laurenson; Billy, Eddy, Ed Fuller; Maud, Mrs. Latham, Barbara Stanton; Trina, Mrs. Margolin, Judy Clegg; Pat, Robert Dannenberg.

A Comedy in 2 acts. The action takes place at the present time in the apartment and Office of Ann Stanley in NYC, after a prologue somewhere in the Greek islands.

Company Manager: Robert Hulter
Press: Harvey B. Sabinson, Lee Solters, Bernard Simon
Stage Managers: Heinz Hohenwald, Phil Laurenson

For original NY production, see THEATRE WORLD, Vol. 25.

Bert Andrews Photos

156 Robert Darnell, Barbara Britton Above: Ed Fuller, Minette Hirsch, Robert Dannenberg, Barbara Britton

Nancy Cushman, Tracy Brooks Swope Top Left: Hugh Reilly, Barbara Britton, Robert Dannenberg, Tracy Brooks Swope, Nancy Cushman

Tony Tanner, Gloria LeRoy

GEORGE M!

Book, Michael Stewart, John and Fran Pascal; Music and Lyrics, George M. Cohan; Lyric and Musical Revisions, Mary Cohan; Director, Billy Matthews; Designed by Leo B. Meyer; Lighting, Ralph Alswang; Musical Direction, Milton Setzer; Costumes, Sanjora; Associate Producer, Jane Friedlander; Musical Supervision and Additional Orchestrations, Julian Stein; Dances and Musical Numbers Staged by Robert Pagent; Presented by Tom Mallow; Tour Management, American Theatre Productions; Assistant Conductor, Robert Billig; Opened KRNT Theatre, Des Moines, Iowa, Sept. 25, 1970, and closed Apr. 10, 1971 in Civic Opera House, Chicago.

CAST

Jerry Cohan	Ray D'Amore
Nellie Cohan	Gloria LeRoy
George M. Cohan	Tony Tanner
Josie Cohan	Maureen Maloney
Archie	Doug Newton
E. F. Albee	B. J. Harrod
Madame Grimaldi	Harriet Leider
Mrs. Laughing Water	Rita Abrams
Ethel Levey	Sally Soldo
Mr. Behman	Henry Victor
Agnes Nolan	Andrea Duda
Louie	Bob La Croix
Freddie	Arthur Whitfield
Sam Harris	Ken Starrett
Faye Templeton	Donna Sanders
Actor on strike	Joe La Vigna
Walt	Richard Northcutt

SINGERS AND DANCERS: Rita Abrams, Betty Chambers, Charon Lee Cohen, Robbee Fian, Ellen Greene, B. J. Harrod, Lois Hathaway, Denise Hefner, Elizabeth Hines, Art Hutchinson, Bob La Croix, Harriet Leider, Sandy Levitt, Pamela McLernon, Doug Newton, Richard Northcutt, Henry Victor, Joe LaVigna, James E. Rogers, Arthur Whitfield

UNDERSTUDIES: George M., James E. Rogers; Jerry, B. J. Harrod; Nellie, Betty Chambers; Josie, Lois Hathaway; Ethel, Denise Hefner; Agnes, Elizabeth Hines, Faye, Ellen Greene; Grimaldi, Betty Chambers

MUSICAL NUMBERS: "Always Leave Them Laughing," "The Two of Us," "The Four of Us," "Musical Moon," "Oh, You Wonderful Boy," "Musical Comedy Man" "All Aboard Broadway," "Virginia," "Twentieth Century Love," "My Home Town," "Billie," "Push Me along in My Pushcart," "Ring to the Name of Rosie," "Popularity," "Give My Regards to Broadway," "45 Minutes from Broadway," "Down by the Erie," "Mary's a Grand Old Name," "So Long, Mary," "Yankee Doodle Dandy," "Nellie Kelly," "Harrigan," "Johnny Get Your Gun," "Over There," "Grand Ol' Flag," "Musical Time Change," "I'd Rather Be Right," Finale.

A Musical in 2 acts. The action takes place between 1878 and 1937.

Company Manager: James Preston
Press: F. B. Kelley, Bernard Simon
Stage Managers: Rodger Franklin, Robert Bruce Holley, Richard Northcutt

For original NY production, see THEATRE WORLD, Vol. 24.

Bert Andrews Photos

Donna Sanders
Above: Sally Soldo Top: Tony Tanner, Maureen Maloney, Ray D'Amore, Gloria LeRoy

HADRIAN VII

By Peter Luke; Based on the works of Fr. Rolfe (Baron Corvo); Director, Henry T. Weinstein; Scenery and Lighting, John Pitts; Costumes, Brooks-Van Horne; Assistants to the Producers, Janice Stanton, Judy McAllister; Tour Management, American Theatre Productions; Promotion Manager, Bernard Simon; Presented by Theo Barnes; Opened Thursday, Jan. 14, 1971 in Page Auditorium, Durham, N.C., closed Mar. 28 1971 in Powers Auditorium, Youngstown, O.

CAST

Father William Rolfe ....Theo Barnes
Mrs. Crowe ....Parker McCormick
Bailiffs ....Joseph Maher, Guy Spaull†1
Jeremiah Sant ....John Leighton
Cardinal-Archdeacon................................J. Frank Lucas†2
Dr. Talacryn, Bishop of Caerleon..............Joseph Maher
Dr. Courtleigh, Cardinal Archbishop of Pimlico ....Guy Spaull + 1
Father St. Albans ....Robert Cessna
Cardinal Ragna ....Stephen Pearlman
Cardianl Berstein ....Dennis Helfend
Rector St. Andrew's College...........................Guy Arbury
George Arthur Rose ....Phillip Schopper

CARDINALS, GUARDS, ACOLYTES: John Bentley, Hubert Bland, Jerry Hopkins, Dennis Kennedy, Donald Keyes, Barry Molitch, David Rosenbaum, Ira Rubin.

UNDERSTUDIES: Rolfe, Berstein, Dennis Kennedy; Mrs Growe, Helen Verlenden Alexander; Talacryn, Ira Rubin; Courtleigh, J. Frank Lucas; Sant, John Bentley; St. Alabans, Dennis Helfend; Ragna, David Rosenbaum; Rector, Donald Keyes; Rose, Barry Molitch

A Play presented in two acts.

Company Manager: Johanna Pool
Press: Lee Solters, Harvey B. Sabinson,
Ralph Roseman
Stage Managers: Larry Pool, Hubert Bland,
Barry Molitch

† Succeeded by: 1. J. Frank Lucas, 2. Guy Spaull

For original NY production, see THEATRE WORLD, Vol. 25

Bert Andrews Photos

John Leighton, Theo Barnes

Theo Barnes, Joseph Maher, Guy Spaull

HELLO, DOLLY!

Book, Michael Stewart; Based on play "The Matchmaker" by Thornton Wilder; Music and Lyrics, Jerry Herman; Originally Directed and Choreographed by Gower Champion; Re-Staged by Lucia Victor; Settings, Oliver Smith; Costumes, Freddy Wittop; Lighting, Jean Rosenthal; Dance and Incidental Music Arrangements, Peter Howard; Musical Direction, Alfonso Cavaliere; Orchestrations, Philip J. Lang; Original Cast Album by RCA Victor; A David Merrick and Champion-Five Production; Presented by David Merrick; Opened in O'Keefe Auditorium, Toronto, Can., Tuesday, May 25, 1971, closed July 24, 1971 at San Diego Community Center

CAST

Mrs. Dolly Levi	Pearl Bailey
Ernestina	Lil Greenwood
Ambrose Kemper	Howard Porter
Horse	Celestine Winters, Fran Loeb
Horace Vandergelder	Cab Calloway
Ermengarde	Tina Andrews
Cornelius Hackl	Nat Gales
Barnaby Tucker	Damon Evans
Irene Molloy	Ernestine Jackson
Minnie Fay	Marki Bey
Mrs. Rose	Marie Bryant
Rudolph	Jim Watkins
Judge	Rudy Challenger
Court Clerk	James Kennon-Wilson

TOWNSPEOPLE: Lana Caradimas, Trudi Green, Verlynne Hutson, Nancy Keller, Irma Kingsley, Jane Lambert, LaVerne Ligon, Fran Loeb, Janice Painchaud, Jacqueline Payne, Zelda Pulliam, Renee Robin, Celestine Winters, Darcel Wynne, Guy Allen, Toney Brealond, Tedd Carrere, Chuck Cissel, Don Coleman, Richard Dodd, Ray Gilbert, Jim Hovis, James Kennon-Wilson, Alton Lathrop, Richard Maxon, Charles Neal, Richard Schneider, E. B. Smith, Kenny Steed, Luke Stover, Richard Wlaker, Edmond Wesley, Jonathan Wynne, Jerome Young

UNDERSTUDIES: Vandergelder, Jim Watkins; Irene, Rene Robin; Cornelius, Luke Stover; Barnaby, Chuck Cissel; Minnie Fay, Zelda Pulliam; Ermengarde, Verlynne Hutson; Ambrose, Don Coleman; Rudolph, Guy Allen; Judge, E. B. Smith; Ernestine, Laverne Ligon

MUSICAL NUMBERS: "I Put My Hand In" "It Takes a Woman," "Put on Your Sunday Clothes," "Ribbons Down My Back," "Motherhood," "Dancing," "Before the Parade Passes By," "Elegance," "The Waiters' Gallop," "Hello, Dolly!," "It Only Takes a Moment," "So Long Dearie," Finale

A Musical in 2 acts and 15 scenes. The action takes place in the past in Yonkers and New York City.

General Manager: Jack Schlissel
Company Manager: Harold O. Kusell
Press: Harvey B. Sabinson, Lee Solters, Maurice Turet
Stage Managers: Pat Tolson, Bob Vandergriff, Peter B. Mumford

Friedman-Abeles Photos

For original NY production see THEATRE WORLD, Vol. 20

Top Right: Pearl Bailey, and Below with chorus in title number

Cab Calloway, Pearl Bailey

HAIR

Book and Lyrics, Gerome Ragni, James Rado; Music, Galt MacDermot; Director, Tom O'Horgan; Musical Director, Steve Gillette; Executive Producer, Bertrand Castelli; Dances Re-Staged by Jerry Combs; Costumes, Nancy Potts; Scenery, Robin Wagner; Lighting, Jules Fisher; Sound, Abe Jacob; Presented by Michael Butler in association with Marshall Naify; Opened Friday, Aug. 29, 1969, at the Geary in San Francisco, and still playing May 31, 1971.

CAST

Claude	Eron Tabor
Berger	Bruce Hyde†1
Woof	Karl Richey†2
Hud	Philip M. Thomas†3
Sheila	Lydia Phillips†4
Jeanie	Marsha Faye
Crissy	Jolie Kanat†5
Mother	Marsha Faye, Reggie Mack, James Wigfall†6
Father	Michael B. Brown†7, Star Donaldson†8, Soni Moreno
Principal	Gayle Hayden, Arsenio S. Avizado†9, James Wigfall†10
Tourist Couple	Tom Bullock, Robert Marcum†11
Supremes	Paulette Ellen Jones, Merria A. Ross, Jeannie Wood
Young Recruit	Michael B. Brown†12
Maria	Maria-Elene Cordero
Nancy	Nancy Blossom
Roger	Roger Kent Cruz
General Grant	James Wigfall†6
Abraham Lincoln	Annie Sampson
Booth	Susan Madley†13
Coolidge	Elizabeth Caveness†14
Gable	Paulette Ellen Jones
Scarlet	Gayle Hayden
Butterfly McQueen	Toad Attell
Custer	Marsha Faye
Sergeant	Charles Weldon†15

and Shezwae Powell, Johnnie Keyes, Jennifer Lee, Candi, Thatcher Baker, Debi Dye, Greta Stewart, Roscoe Blount, Ken Ortega, Michael Owen, Winston Tong

UNDERSTUDIES: Berger, Roger Kent Cruz; Claude, Bill Windsor; Woof, Reggie Mack; Hud, Johnnie Keyes; Jeanie, Toad Attell; Sheila, Nancy Blossom; Crissy, Jennifer Lee

MUSICAL NUMBERS: "Aquarius," "My Donna," "Hashish," "Sodomy," "Colored Spade," "Manchester," "Ain't Got No," "Dead End," "Air," "Initials," "I Got Life," "Going Down," "Hair," "My Conviction," "Easy to Be Hard," "Don't Put It Down," "Frank Mills," "Hare Krishna," "Where Do I Go?" "Electric Blues," "Black Boys," "White Boys," "Walking in Space," "Abie Baby," "3-5-0-0," "What a Piece of Work Is Man," "Good Morning Starshine," "The Bed," "Flesh Failures," "Let the Sunshine In."

The American Tribal Love-Rock Musical in two acts.

Press: Claire Harrison Reed, Nan Hohenstein
Stage Managers: Neil Phillips, Fred Kopp, Larry Spiegel

† Succeeded by: 1. Philip Thomas, 2. Arsenio Avizado, 3. Roscoe Blount, 4. Maria-Elena Cordero, 5. Soni Moreno, 6. Joey Richards, 7. Light Brown, 8. Tom Bullick, 9. Reggie Mack, 10. Jennifer Lee, 11. Michael Owen, 12. Light Brown, 13. Candi, 14. Jennifer Lee, 15. Roscoe Blount

For original NY production, see THEATRE WORLD. Vol. 24.

Freda Walker, Bruce Govan, Harry Perry, David Lasley, Sundiata Mausi

Detroit "Hair" company

HAIR

Re-Staged by Armand Coullet; Dances Re-Staged by
Rhonda Oglesby, after Julie Arenal; Musical Director,
Dennis Smith; Regional Director, Jonathan Banks;
Presented by Michael Butler; Opened at Vest Pocket
Theatre, Detroit, June, 1970, and still playing May 31,
1971.

CAST

Claude	David Patrick Kelly
Berger	Michael Campbell
Woof	Danny Miller
Hud	Stanley Ramsey
Sheila	Stoney
Jeanie	Linda Deater
Crissy	Debbie Andrews
Mother	Stanley Ramsey, Linda Deater, Meat Loaf
Father	Audrey Mitchell, Jody Pearlman, Bruce Govan
Principal	Signa Joy, Denny Fairchild, Corky
James Brown	Dwight Hankins
Tourist Lady	David Lasley
Hubert	David Stidwill
Supremes	Betty Lloyd, Audrey Mitchell, Sheilla Royster
Booth	Michael Brown
Ulysses S. Grant	Meat Loaf
Abraham Lincoln	Audrey Mitchell
Coolidge	Gloria Goldman
Gable	Sheilla Royster
Scarlett	Suzi Stern
Custer	Linda Deater
Teddy Roosevelt	Freda Walker
Sergeant	Stanley Ramsey
Indians	Signa Joy, Stanley Ramsey, Corky, Debbie Andrews

and Gayle Riffle, Deborah Hampton, Dwight Hankins,
Gloria Goldman, Harry Perry, Alfie Hughes, Farmer
Al, Edward, Sundiata Mausi, Suzi Stern

UNDERSTUDIES: Claude, Bruce Govan; Berger, Harry
Perry; Woof, Denny Fairchild; Hud, Dwight Hankins;
Sheila, Linda Deater; Crissy, Suzi Stern; Jeanie, Jody
Pearlman

Company Manager: John Corkill
Press: Fred Weterick, John Bagdasarian
Stage Managers: Ed Fisher, Henderson Davis, Jr.

For original NY production, see THEATRE WORLD,
Vol. 24.

HAIR

Book and Lyrics, Gerome Ragni, James Rado; Music,
Galt MacDermott; Director, Tom O'Horgan; Executive
Producer, Bertrand Castelli; Musical Direction, Fred
Waring, Jr.; Dance Director, Julie Arenal; Sound, Abe
Jacob; Costumes, Nancy Potts; Scenery, Robin Wagner;
Lighting, Jules Fisher, Presented by Michael Butler;
Opened Hanna Theatre, Cleveland, Ohio, Mar. 9, 1971,
and still playing May 31, 1971.

CAST

Claude	Del Cunningham, John Jerzog
Berger	Richard Almack, Doug Rowell
Woof	Jonathon Johnson
Hud	Johnnie Keyes
Sheila	Debbie Dye, Marsha Faye
Jeannie	Marsha Faye, Debbie Dye
Crissy	Jo Ann Harris
Mother	Jeanie, Reggie Mack, David Molina
Father	John Dickson, Betty Lloyd, Richard Almack
Principal	John Dickson, John David Yarbrough, Rose Marie Barbee
Tourist Couple	Danny Kantner, John David Yarbrough
Supremes	Betty Lloyd, Linda Gaines, Rose Marie Barbee
Abraham Lincoln	Linda Gaines
Sergeant	Arthur Dillingham
Recruit Parents	Susan Gaynes, John Dickson

and Leo Elmore, Ursula Szlagowski, Cecelia Eaves,
Zora Rasmussen, Ben Lautman, Doug Rowell, Miss
Alaina Reed

Company Manager: Jerry Arrow
Press: Michael Gifford, Horace Geeley NcNab
Stage Managers: Russell Carlson, Barry Kearsley,
Jim Emanuel

For original NY production, see THEATRE WORLD,
Vol. 24.

Patty Kean

KNICKERBOCKER HOLIDAY

Words, Maxwell Anderson; Music, Kurt Weill; Director, Albert Marre; Choreography, Donald Saddler; Settings and Lighting, Howard Bay; Costumes, Freddy Wittop; Musical Arrangements, Harper MacKay; Musical Direction, Jack Lee; Dance Arrangements, Richard DeBenedictis; Production Coordinator; Herbert K. Adams; Technical Director, Warren Merkle; Stage Managers: Bill Holland, Larry Dean, Tom Gleason; Producer, Glenn Jordan; Opened Tuesday, May 11, 1971 in Curran Theatre, San Francisco and still playing May 31, 1971.

CAST

Washington Irving	David Holliday
Corlear	John Ferrante
Mynheer Tienhoven	Jack Collins
Roosevelt	Gino Conforti
Van Rensselaer	John Wheeler
Vanderbilt	Jerry Mann
Van Cortlandt	Eric Brotherson
DePeyster	Robert Miller Driscoll
Marshal Schermerhorn	Dale Malone
Brom Broeck	David Holliday
Mistress Schermerhorn	Ruth Kobart
Tina Tienhoven	Anita Gillette
Governor Pieter Stuyvesant	Burt Lancaster
Surrogates	Lonnie Chase, John Frayer, Mark Hudson, Roger Wade
Sailors	Michael Shanahan, Sam Weber
Guards	Gene Brundage, Kirk Norman
Builders of Nieuw Amsterdam	Bjarne Buchtrup, Richard Grimm, Ted Sprague, Steve Ward
Gentlemen of Nieuw Amsterdam, Tom Jepperson, Tom McKinney, Carl Lindstrom	

MAIDENS OF NIEUW AMSTERDAM: Miriam Boyer, Sharon Daniels, Kelley Gazze, Margit Haut, Kathleen Knight, Roberta Silbert, Barbara Ludwig, Trish Mahoney, Pamela Sousa, Sandra Voris, Polly Wood

ADVERSARIES: Bjarne Buchtrup, Lonnie Chase, John Frayer, Richard Grimm, Mark Hudson, Michael Shanahan, Ted Sprague, Roger Wade, Steve Ward, Sam Weber

MUSICAL NUMBERS: "Washington Irving Song," "Hush-Hush," "It Never Was You," "Will You Remember Me?," "One Touch of Alchemy," "The One Indispensable Man," "Young People Think About Love," "September Song," "How Can You Tell an American?," "All Hail the Political Honeymoon." "There's Nowhere to Go but Up," "Sitting in Jail," "We Are Cut in Twain," "To War!," "Our Ancient Liberties," "Pavane," "The Scars," "The Attack," "Dirge for a Soldier," "No, Ve Vouldn't Gonto Do It," Finale

A Musical in 2 acts and 20 scenes.

Top Left: David Holliday, Burt Lancaster

David Holliday

Marge Redmond, Jack Weston

LAST OF THE RED HOT LOVERS

By Neil Simon; Director, Robert Moore; Scenery, Oliver Smith; Costumes, Donald Brooks; Lighting, Peggy Clark; Presented by Saint-Subber; Opened Monday, Sept. 28, 1970 at National Theatre, Washington, D. C., and still playing May 31, 1971.

CAST

Barney Cashman ....Jack Weston
Elaine Navazio...Rosemary Prinz†
Bobbi Michele...Ginger Flick
Jeanette Fisher..Marge Redmond

STANDBYS: Barney, Kenneth McMillan; Elaine, Jeanette, Holly Harris; Bobbi, Susan Lee-Wallack

A Comedy in three acts. The action takes place at the present time in NYC apartment in the East Thirties.

General Manager: C. Edwin Knill
Company Manager: Morry Efron
Press: Harvey B. Sabinson, Lee Solters, Robert Reud
Stage Managers: Charles Durand, Ted Sheraton

† Succeeded by Elaine Hyman.

For original NY production, see THEATRE WORLD, Vol. 26.

Zodiac Photos

Jack Weston, Ginger Flick
Above: Rosemary Prinz, Jack Weston

163

NATIONAL SHAKESPEARE COMPANY

Artistic Director, Philip Meister; Managing Director, Elaine Sulka; General Manager, Albert Schoemann; Tour Director, Vincent Wagner; Business Manager, Lloyd Kay; Program Director, Maurice Edwards; Production Coordinator, Judy Schoen; Technical Director, William Lambert; Stage Manager, Richard Beebe; Opened Oct. 5, 1970 and closed May 7, 1971.

HAMLET

(Director, Philip Meister; Set, William Pitkin; Costumes, Clyde Wachsberger; Lighting, William Lambert)

CAST

Claudius	Stephen Klein
Hamlet	Rod Loomis
Polonius	James Bailey
Horatio	Ollie Nash
Laertes	Christopher Root
Rosencrantz	Harlan Schneider
Guildenstern	Douglas Cheek
Osric	Harlan Schneider
Marcellus	Wes Finlay
Players	Judith Hink, Wes Finlay, Christopher Root
Norwegian Captain	Wes Finlay
Sailor	Wes Finlay
Gertrude	Saax Bradbury
Ophelia	Eren Ozker

MUCH ADO ABOUT NOTHING

(Director, Mario Siletti; Costumes and Scenery, Clyde Wachsberger; Lighting, William Lambert)

CAST

Leonato	James Bailey
Borachio	Ollie Nash
Hero	Eren Ozker
Beatrice	Judith Hink
Margaret	Saax Bradbury
Don Pedro	Stephen Klein
Claudio	Douglas Cheek
Benedick	Wes Finlay
Don John	Harlan Schneider
Dogberry	Richard Beebe
Verges	Christopher Root
Friar Francis	Rod Loomis

OEDIPUS REX

(By Sophocles; Director, Malcolm Black; Set, Clyde Wachsberger; Costumes, Judith Haugan; Lighting, William Lambert; Music, Arnold Black)

CAST

Oedipus	Rod Loomis
Jocasta	Judith Hink
Antigone	Eren Ozker
Ismene	Saax Bradbury
Creon	Richard Beebe
Tiresias	Ollie Nash
Priest	Wes Finlay
Messenger	James Bailey
Herdsman	Harlan Schneider
Chorus Leader	Stephen Klein
Servant	Douglas Cheek
Boy	Christopher Root

Top Right: Rod Loomis, Eren Ozker, Saax Bradbury, Stephen Klein in "Hamlet" Below: Wes Finlay, Saax Bradbury, Douglas Cheek, Eren Ozker, Judith Hink, Ollie Nash in "Much Ado About Nothing"

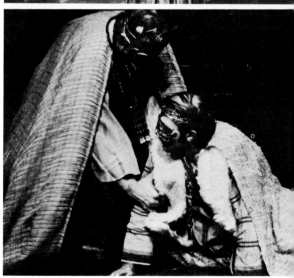

Rod Loomis, Harlan Schneider in "Oedipus Rex"

NO PLACE TO BE SOMEBODY

By Charles Gordone; Director, Mr. Gordone; Set, John Retsek; Lighting, Conrad Penrod; Associate Producer, Albie Baker; Production Associate, Linda J. Friedman; Presented by Ashton Springer, Jeanne Warner; Opened Monday. Sept. 14, 1970 and still playing May 31, 1971.

CAST

Gabe Gabriel	Christopher Williams
Shanty Mulligan	John Tracy
Johnny Williams	Ben Vereen
Dee Jacobson	Carole Thompson
Evie Ames	Carolyn Blakey
Cora Beasely	Ebony Wright
Melvin Smeltz	John Moore
Mary Lou Bolton	Andrea Schmid
Sweets Crane	Melvin Stewart
Mike Maffucci	Len Pera
Louie	Richard Burgess
Judge Bolton	Michael Donn
Sgt. Cappaletti	Richard Curtis
Harry	Jerry Gardner

A Drame in 3 acts. The action takes place 15 years ago in Johnny's Bar in West Greenwich Village, NYC.

Company Manager: Stan Hilton
Press: Claire Harrison Reed, Nan Hohenstein
National Press Representative: Robert Ganshaw
Stage Managers: G. Tito Shaw, Jerry Gardner

Gabe Gabriel	Nick Smith
Shanty Mulligan	Ronnie Thompson
Johnny Williams	William Jay
Dee Jacobson	Susan G. Pearson
Evie Ames	Sylvia Soares
Cora Beasley	Marge Eliot
Melvin Smeltz	Henry Baker
Mary Lou Bolton	Susan Willerman
Sweets Crane	Julius W. Harris
Mike Maffucci	Nick Lewis
Louie	Jim Jacobs
Judge Bolton	Ed Van Nuys
Sgt. Cappaletti	Peter Savage
Harry	Malcolm Hurd

Company Manager: Douglas Helgeson
National Press: Robert Ganshaw
Press: Guy Livingston
Stage Managers: Garland Lee Thompson,
Malcolm Hurd

Gabe Gabriel	Philip M. Thomas
Shanty Mulligan	Ian Sander
Johnny Williams	Terry Alexander
Dee Jacobson	Robin Lane
Evie Ames	Paulette Jones
Cora Beasley	Mary Alice
Melvin Smeltz	Richard Lawson
Mary Lou Bolton	Susan Sparling
Sweets Crane	W. Benson Terry
Mike Maffucci	Larry Gorodkin
Louie	Rik Lawrence
Judge Bolton	Philip Hanson
Sgt. Cappaletti	Richard Finkelstein
Harry	Winston Young

Company Manager: Jack Reed
National Press Representative: Robert Ganshaw
Stage Manager: Clyde Houston, Richard Finkelstein

For original NY production, see THEATRE WORLD, Vol. 25.

Rik Lawrence Photos

Top Right: Marge Eliot, Ronnie Thompson
Below: Philip Thomas, W. Benson Terry, Terry
Alexander

Robin Lane, Terry Alexander, Paulette Jones

PLAY IT AGAIN, SAM

By Woody Allen; Director, Ben Gerard; Settings, William Ritman; Lighting, Martin Aronstein; Costumes, Ann Roth; Associate Producer, Samuel Liff; Presented by David Merrick in association' with Jack Rollins and Charles Joffre; Opened Tuesday, Sept. 15, 1970 at Blackstone Theatre, Chicago, and closed Feb. 27, 1971 at the Huntington Hartford in Los Angeles.

CAST

Allan Felix	Red Buttons
Nancy Felix	Connie Day
Bogey	Peter DeMaio
Dick Christie	William Bogert
Linda Christie	Deborah Deeble
Dream Sharon	Glory McRae
Sharon Lake	Rebecca Shaw
Gina	Kathie Savage†1
Vanessa	Sarah Chattin†2
Go-Go Girl	Marika Choma
Museum Girl	Patricia Earnest†3
Barbara Tyler	Glory McRae

STANDBYS AND UNDERSTUDIES: Allan, Frank Giordano; Nancy, Rebecca Shaw; Linda, Julie Prince; Sharon, Barbara, Jan Cobler; Sharon, Vanessa, Tanya Duncan

A Comedy in 3 acts and 3 scenes. The action takes place at the present time in the apartment of Allan Felix on West 10th Street in NYC.

General Manager: Jack Schlissel
Company Manager: Boris Bernardi
Press: Harvey B, Sabinson, Lee Solters, Willard Keefe
Stage Manager: Patrick Tolson

† Succeeded by: 1. Tanya Duncan, 2. Jan Cobler, 3. Julie Prince For original NY production see THEATRE WORLD, Vol 25.

**Deborah Deeble, Red Buttons, Marika Choma,
William Bogert**

**Peter DeMaio, Red Buttons
Top Left: Kathie Savage, Red Buttons**

PLAZA SUITE

By Neil Simon; Director, Stanley Prager; Scenery, Oliver Smith; Lighting, Jean Rosenthal; Costumes, Patricia Zipprodt; Production Assistant, Donal Rothey; Presented by Saint-Subber; A Nancy Enterprises Production; Tour Direction, National Performing Arts Inc.; NY Promotion Manager, Bernard Simon; Opened Friday, Oct. 16, 1970 in Academy of Music, Northampton, Mass., and closed Apr. 25, 1971 in Vestal, NY Community Center.

CAST

"Visitor from Mamaroneck"
Bellhop...Ronn Cummins
Karen Nash..Betty Garrett
Sam Nash..Larry Parks
Waiter..Burton Ovington
Jean McCormack................................Valerie Von Volz
"Visitor from Hoolywood":
Waiter..Burton Ovington
Jesse Kiplinger ...".................................Larry Parks
Muriel Tate..Betty Garrett
"Visitor from Forest Hills"
Norma Hubley.....................................Betty Garrett
Roy Hubley...Larry Parks
Borden Eisler....................................Ronn Cummins
Mimsi Hubley....................................Valerie Von Volz

STANDBYS: Mr. Parks, Alan North; Miss Garrett, June Miller; Miss Von Volz, Lynn Martin; Mr. Cummins, Garrett C. Parks.

Three one-act comedies with the action taking place in a suite in the Plaza Hotel in NYC at the present time

General Manager: C. Edwin Knill
Company Manager: L. Liberatore
Press: Harvey B. Sabinson. Lee Solters, Paul G. Anglim
Stage Managers: Wally Peterson, Garrett C. Parks

For original NY production, see THEATRE WORLD, Vol. 24.

Zodiac Photos

Larry Parks, Valerie von Volz, Betty Garrett
Above: Ronn Cummins, Betty Garrett, Larry Parks

Betty Garrett, Larry Parks

PROMISES, PROMISES

Book, Neil Simon; Based on screenplay "The Apartment" by Billy Wilder, I. A. L. Diamond; Music, Burt Bacharach; Lyrics, Hal David; Director, Robert Moore; Musical Numbers Staged by Michael Bennett; Settings, Robin Wagner; Costumes, Donald Brooks; Lighting, Martin Aronstein; Dance Arrangements, Harold Wheeler; Orchestrations, Jonathan Tunick; Musical Direction, Don Jennings; Associate Producer, Samuel Liff; Hairstylist, Joe Tubens; Presented by David Merrick; Opened Monday, May 11, 1970 in Civic Auditorium, San Diego, and still touring May 31, 1971.

CAST

Chuck Baxter	Anthony Roberts†
J. D. Sheldrake	Bob Holiday
Fran Kubelik	Melissa Hart
Bartender Eddie	James Celmayster
Mr. Dobitch	David Sabin
Sylvia Gilhooley	Susan Luckey
Mr. Kirkeby	Larry Douglas
Mr. Eichelberger	Thomas Batten
Vivien Della Hoya	Joyce Driscoll
Dr. Dreyfuss	Jack Krushchen
Jesse Vanderhof	Barney Martin
Dentist's Nurse	Eva Sue Newcomer
Company Nurse	Nancy Pivarunas
Company Doctor	Gerry O'Hara
Peggy Olson	Diane Findlay
Lum Ding Hostess	Zuzane Knych
Waiter	Paul–Patrick Benjamin
Madison Square Garden Attendant	Paul Kastl
Dining Room Hostess	Eva Sue Newcomer
Miss Polansky	Eva Sue Newcomer
Miss Blackwell	Maureen Cavanaugh
Bartender Eugene	Edward Pfeiffer
Marge MacDougall	Kelly Britt
Helen Sheldrake	Susanne Carroll
Karl Kubelik	James Celmayster
New Young Executive	Joe Yanello
Orchestra Voices	Linda McClure, Sharon Navratil, Marcia Gallis
Interns and Dates	Mark Goldman, Paul-Patrick Benjamin, Ginger Brown, Eva Sue Newcomer
Clancy's Employees	Nancy Pivarunas, Paul Kastl, Eva Sue Newcomer

CLANCY'S PATRONS: Ginger Brown, Maureen Cavanaugh, Danny Ramey, Paul-Patrick Benjamin, Joe Yanello, Mark Goldman, Camille Roncek, Susanne Carroll

UNDERSTUDIES: Chuck, Tom Foral; Fran, Marcia Callis; Dreyfuss, Barney Martin; Dobitch, Kirkeby, Eichelberger, Vanderhof, Tom Boyd; Sheldrake, Gerry O'Hara; Peggy, Susan Luckey; Marge, Diane Findlay; Karl, Paul Kastl; Vivien, Maureen Cavanaugh, Swing Dancers, Zuzane Knych, Gerry O'Hara

A Musical in 2 acts and 14 scenes. The action takes place at the present time in NYC.

General Manager: Jack Schlissel
Company Manager: Al Rosen
Press: Harvey B. Sabinson, Lee Solters, Gertrude Bromberg
Stage Managers Bill O'Brien, William Letters, Tom Boyd

† Succeeded by Anthony Teague

For original NY production, see THEATRE WORLD, Vol. 25.

**Top Left: Kelly Britt, Anthony Teague
Below: Bob Holliday, Melissa Hart**

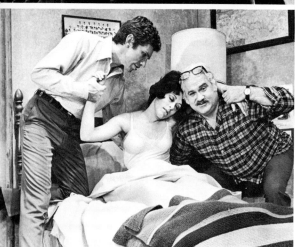

Anthony Teague, Melissa Hart, Jack Kruschen

WILL ROGERS' U. S. A.

Adapted and Directed by Paul Shyre; Designed by Eldon Elder; Associate Producer, Bryan Sterling; Presented by George Spota and Marc Merson; Opened Wednesday, Sept. 16, 1970 in Ford's Theatre, Washington, D. C., and closed Jan. 2, 1971 in Los Angeles Music Center.

CAST

JAMES WHITMORE

A One-man show presented in two acts.

General Manager: Seth Schapiro
NY Promotion Manager: Bernard Simon
Stage Manager: James Whitmore III

James Whitmore

YOUR OWN THING

Book, Donald Driver; Suggested by Shakespeare's "Twelfth Night'; Music and Lyrics, Hal Hester, Danny Apolinar; Director, Richard Nagel; Choreography, George Bunt; Settings, Robert Guerra; Technical Director, Richard Taylor; Presented by Empire Theatrical Corp; Opened Oct. 3, 1970 at University of Pittsburgh, and closed Apr. 28, 1971 at Wake Forest University, Winston-Salem, N.C.

CAST

Danny	Marc Allen III[1]
John	Kris Johnson
Michael	Ronnie Hall
Orson	Will Jacobs[2]
Olivia	June Compton
Viola	Elaine Petricoff[3]
Sebastian	Jon Stevens
Purser	Jerry Lee
Nurse	Linda Maasser[4]
Stage Manager	Jerry Lee

MUSICAL NUMBERS: "No One's Perfect," "The Flowers," "I'm Me," "Baby! Baby!," "Come Away, Death," "I'm on the Way to the Top," "Let It Be," "She Never Told Her Love," "Be Gentle," "What Do I Know," "The Now Generation," "The Middle Years," "When You're Young and in Love," "Hunca Munca," "Don't Leave Me," "Do Your Own Thing," "Flowers."

A Musical presented without intermission.

NY Promotion Manager: Bernard Simon
Stage Managers: Jack Rimp, Richard Taylor

† Succeeded by: 1. Randy Herron, 2. Gary McKim, 3. Vicki Nunis, 4. Patti Littlefield

For original NY production, see THEATRE WORLD, Vol. 24

Bert Andrews Photos

Jon Stevens, Ronnie Hall, Will Jacobs, Marc Allen III, Elaine Petricoff, Kris Johnson, June Compton

1776

Book, Peter Stone; Based on conception by Sherman Edwards; Music and Lyrics, Sherman Edwards; Scenery and Lighting, Jo Mielziner; Costumes, Patricia Zipprodt; Musical Direction, Jonathan Anderson; Orchestrations, Eddie Sauter; Director, Peter Hunt; Musical Numbers Staged by Onna White; Presented by Stuart Ostrow; Opened Thursday, Apr. 23, 1970 at the Curran in San Francisco, and still touring May 31, 1971.

CAST

John Hancock	David Ford†1
Dr. Josian Bartlet	Lee Winston
John Adams	Patrick Bedford
Stepehn Hopkins	Truman Gaige
Roger Sherman	Stanley Simmonds
Lewis Morris	Ray Lonergan
Robert Livingstone	Larry Devon
Rev. John Witherspoon	Robert Goss
Benjamins Franklin	Rex Everhart
John Dickinson	George Hearn
James Wilson	Ed Preble
Caesar Rodney	William Boesen†2
Col. Thomas McKean	Gordon Dilworth
George Read	Michael Shaw
Samuel Chase	Leon Spelman
Richard Henry Lee	Gary Oakes
Thoas Jefferson	Jon Cypher†3
Joseph Hewes	Walter Charles
Edward Rutledge	Jack Blackton
Dr. Lyman Hall	Richard Mathews
Charles Thomson	Louis Beachner†4
Andrew McNair	Stuart Germain
A Leather Apron	Michael Makman†5
Courier	Ty McConnell†6
Abigail Adams	Barbara Lang
Martha Jefferson	Pamela Hall†7

UNDERSTUDIES: Adams, Richard Mathews; Franklin, Dickinson, Gordon Dilworth; Rutledge, Lee Winston; McKean, Hancock, Walter Charles; Jefferson, Hopkins, Thomson, Hall, Lee, Robert Goss; Abigail, Martha, Victoria Hall; Rodney, Stanley Simmonds; Bartlettt, Larry Devon; McNair, Michael Shaw; Courier, James Ferrier; Wilson, Ray Lonergan; Hewes, Livingstone, Witherspoon, Read, Sherman, Chase, Morris, John Dorrin

A Musical Play in 2 acts and 7 scenes. The action takes place for two months before and up to July 4, 1776.

General Managers: Joseph Harris, Ira Bernstein
Company Manager: Milton M. Pollack
Press: Lee Solters, Harvey B. Sabinson, Harry Davies
Stage Managers: Ben D. Kranz, Patricia Drylie, John Dorrin

† Succeeded by: 1. Jack Murdock, s. Douglas Gordon, 3. Robert Elston, 4. John Eames, 5, James Ferrier, 6. Michael Glenn–Smith, 7. Kristen Banfield

For original NY production, see THEATRE WORLD, Vol. 25.

Top Left: Jack Murdock, George Backman, Patrick Bedford

Kristen Banfield, Rex Everhart, Patrick Bedford

Reid Shelton, Paul Tripp, John Adams Right: Jerry Lanning Below: Don Perkins, Paul Tripp, Pat Gorman

1776

Director, Gordon Hunt; Musical Direction, Glene Clugston; Presented by Stuart Ostrow in association with Theater Now, Inc.; Opened Sept. 18, 1970 in Masonic Auditorium, Scranton, Pa., and closed May 14, 1971 at Palace Theatre, Albany, N.Y.

CAST

John Hancock	William Kiehl
Dr. Josiah Bartlett	Gary Beach†1
John Adams	Don Perkins
Stephen Hopkins	Tom Gorman
Roger Sherman	Dan Entriken
Lewis Morris	Reg Perry
Robert Livington	James Todkill
Rev. John Witherspoon	Joneal Joplin
Benjamin Franklin	Paul Tripp†2
John Dickinson	Patrick Hines
James Wilson	W. P. Dremak
Caesar Rodney	Roland Ireland
Col. Thomas McKean	James F. Cade
George Read	Kevin O'Leary
Samuel Chase	Tom Sinclair
Richard Henry Lee	Reid Shelton
Thomas Jefferson	William Jennings
Joseph Hewes	Dan Merriman
Edward Rutledge	Jerry Lanning†3
Dr. Lyman Hall	K. C. Wilson
Secretary Charles Thomson	William Major
Custodian Andrew McNair	Skedge Miller
Leather Apron	Bryan Young
Courier	Larry Small
Abigail Adams	Ann Clements†4
Martha Jefferson	Pat Gorman

Company Manager: Oscar Berlin
Press: Harvey B. Sabinson, Lee Solters,
Robert W. Jennings
NY Promotion Manager: Bernard Simon
Stage Managers: Paul Waigner, Jane Squire,
Bryan Young, Joneal Joplin

† Succeeded by: 1. John Almberg, 2. Sam Kressen, 3. Gary Beach, 4. Mara Worth

Martha Swope Photos

James Todkill, Kevin O'Leary, W. P. Dremak, William Kiehl, Reg Perry, Patrick Hines, Dan Merriman, Jerry Lanning, K. C. Wilson

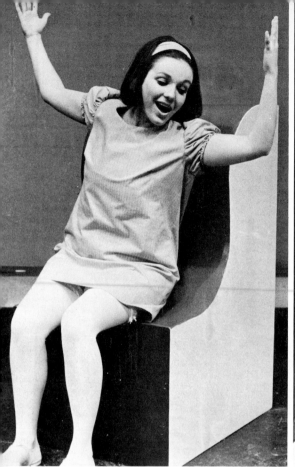

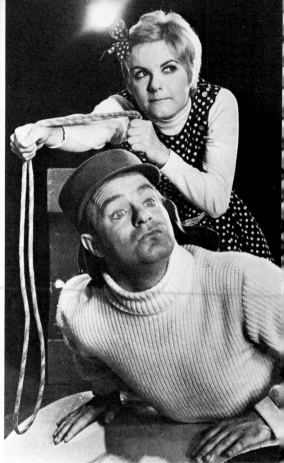

YOU'RE A GOOD MAN, CHARLIE BROWN

Book, John Gordon; Based on comic strip "Peanuts" by Charles M. Schulz; Music and Lyrics, Clark Gesner; Sets and Costumes, Alan Kimmerl; Lighting, Jules Fisher; Director, Joseph Hardy; Musical Staging, Patricia Birch; Musical Coordinator, Edmund Assaly; Musical Supervision, Arrangements, Additional Material, Joseph Raposo; Press, Max Eisem; Original Cast Album on MGM Records; Presented by Arthur Whitelaw, Gene Persson; Opened Wednesday, Sept. 17, 1970 and closed at the Mendelssohn Auditoriu, Ann Arbor, Mich., on Dec. 13, 1970.

CAST

Linus	Derek McGrath
Charlie Brown	Richard Whelan
Patty	Marylu Moyer
Schroeder	Dennis Phillips
Snoopy	Grant Cowan
Lucy	Cathy Wallace

MUSICAL NUMBERS: "You're a Good Man, Charlie Brown," "Schroeder," "Snoopy," "My Blanket and Me," "Kite," "Dr. Lucy," "Book Report," "The Red Baron," "T.E.A.M.," "Glee Club Rehearsal," "Little Known Facts," "Suppertime," "Happiness"

A Musical in two acts. The action takes place at the present time and is an average day in the life of Charlie Brown.

**Richard Whelan Top: (L) Cathy Wallace, (R)
Grant Cowan, Marylu Moyer**

ZORBA

Book, Joseph Stein; Music, John Kander; Lyrics, Fred Ebb; Adapted from "Zorba the Greek" by Nikos Kazantzakis; Director, Ruth Mitchell; Choreographer, Ron Field; Dances and Musical Numbers Re-Staged by George Martin; Scenic Design, Boris Aronson; Production Adaption, Leo B. Meyer; Costumes, Patricia Zipprodt; Lighting, Ralph Alswang; Musical Direction, Harold Hastings; Musical Director, Albert L. Fiorillo; Orchestrations, Don Walker; Dance Music Arranged by Dorothea Freitag; Associate Producer, Jane Friedlander; Presented by Tom Mallow; Tour Management, American Theatre Production; Opened Sept. 11, 1970 in Bushnell Auditorium, Hartford, Conn. and closed May 18, 1971 in Memorial Auditorium, Worcester, Mass.

CAST

Constable	John A. Duval
Nikos	Thom Koutsoukos
Hortense	Vivian Blaine
Manolako	Abraham Cohen†1
Panayotis	Jeff Phillips
Irini	Deborah St. Darr
Mimiko	Vaughn Martinez
Kostandi	Joe Vaccarella
Widow	Vilma Vaccaro
Drummer	Ali Hafid
Leader	Margalit Ankory
Loukas	Frank Torren
Fivos	Tony Falcone
Sofia	Jouce Tomanec
Zorba	Michael Kermoyan
Antonias	Harriett Conrad
Aliki	Susan Currier
Grigoris	Robert Land†2
Pavli	Joseph Neal
Thanos	John Terranova
Despo	Beverly Hand
Mavrodani	John F. Roberson†3
Vasilis	Donald Mark
Katapolis	Patrick McCann
Marina	Judith Ann Davies
Father Zacharia	Christopher Cable
Meropi	Wendy Kamron†4
Anagnosti	Richard Folmer

MUSICAL NUMBERS: "Life Is," "The First Time," "The Top of the Hill," "No Boom, Boom," "Vive La Difference," "The Butterfly," "Goodbye Canavarro," "Belly Dance," "Grandpapa," "Only Love," "The End in the Road," "Bouboulina," "Why Can't I Speak?," "Mine Celebration," "The Crow," "Happy Birthday," "I Am Free."

A Musical in two acts.

Company Manager: Jerry Livengood
Press: John L. Toohey
NY Promotion Manager: Bernard Simon
Stage Managers: Jack Rimp, Richard Taylor
Christopher Cable

† Succeeded by: 1. Robert Land, 2. Fabian Stuart, 3. Richard Folmer, 4. Gloria Franco
For original NY production, see THEATRE WORLD, Vol. 25.

Bert Andrews Photos

Deborah St. Darr, Margalit Ankory, Jeff Phillips
Top Right: Deborah St. Darr, Michael Kermoyan
(R)

Vivian Blaine, Michael Kermoyan, also above
with Thom Koutsoukos

173

PRETTYBELLE

Book and Lyrics, Bob Merrill; Based on novel of same name by Jean Arnold; Music, Jule Styne; Staged by Gower Champion; Designed by Oliver Smith; Costumes, Ann Roth; Lighting, Nananne Porcher; Musical Direction and Incidental Music Arranged by Peter Howard; Orchestrations, Elliot Lawrence, Jack Cortner; Production Supervisor, Jerry Adler; Associate Producer, Hildy Parks; A Gower Champion Production; Presented by Alexander H. Cohen; Opened Monday, February 1, 1971 at the Shubert, Boston, and closed there Mar. 6, 1971.

CAST

Henry Baines	William Larsen
Sybil Mae Asch	Barbara Ann Walters
Prettybelle Sweet	Angela Lansbury
Nurses	Susan Plantt, Linda Lubera
Dr. Dimmer	Richard Kuss
Mayor	Chad Block
Mother Sweet	Charlotte Rae
Lovey Sweet	Renee Lippin
John Sweet	Dean Crane, Jr.
Ray Schaeffer	Jon Cypher
Willy Thomas	Joe Morton
Cully Hart	Igors Gavon
Huey Lipscombe	Robert Karl
Bubba Rawlings	Jan Leighton
Boy Scout	Brian Hall
Folksinger	Michael Jason
Leroy Sweet	Mark Dawson
GoGo Girls	Susan Plantt, Linda Lubera, Chris Cooper
Bouncer	Joe Milan
Pool Hall Mexican	Chad Block
Mason	Peter Lombard
Marie	Chris Cooper
Jesus	Bert Michaels
Motel Clerk	George Blackwell
Bellhop	Bobby Lee
Motel Doorman	Howard Porter
Deputies	Chad Block, Robert Karl, Joe Milan
Magistrate	Richard Kuss
Bud Michaels	Sean Walsh

STANDBYS AND UNDERSTUDIES: Prettybelle, Marijane Maricle; Ray, Mason, Sean Walsh; Mother, Sybil Mae; Maggie Task; Lovey, Mimi Wallace; Jesus, Bobby Lee

MUSICAL NUMBERS: "Manic Depressives," "Policeman's Hymn," "Prettybelle," "To a Small Degree," "You Ain't Hurtin' Your Ole Lady None," "How Could I Know What Was Goin' On?," "I Never Did Imagine," "In the Japanese Gardens," "An Individual Thing," "I Met a Man," "The No-Tell Motel," "I'm in a Tree," "When I'm Drunk," Finale.

A Musical in 2 acts and 17 scenes.

General Manager: Roy A. Somlyo
Company Manager: Seymour Herscher
Press: James D. Proctor, Bob Ullman, Richard Hummler
Stage Managers: Marnel Summer, Edward Julien, David Gold

Zodiac Photos

Top Right: Mark Dawson, Igors Gavon, Jan Leighton, Bob Karl, Jon Cypher Below: Renee Lippin, Angela Lansbury, Charlotte Rae

George Blackwell, Angela Lansbury, Howard Porter

LOLITA, MY LOVE

Book and Lyrics, Alan Jay Lerner; Based on Vladimir Nabokov novel "Lolita"; Music, John Barry; Staged by Tony Capobianco; Choreography, Danny Daniels; Musical Direction, Herbert Grossman; Orchestrations, Eddie Sauter; Settings; Ming Cho Lee; Costumes, Jose Varona; Lighting, Jules Fisher; Dance Arrangements, John Morris; Audio Design, Jack Shearing; Associate Producer, Stone Widney; Production Associate, Larry Coleman; Presented by Norman Twain; Opened Feb. 16, 1971 at the Shubert in Philadelphia, and closed there Feb. 27, 1971 for revisions; Re-opened at the Shubert in Boston, Mar. 23, 1971 and closed there Mar. 27, 1971.

CAST

Humbert Humbert	John Neville
Mona Dahl	Kendall March[†1]
Quincey	Dan Siretta
Nelson Quimby	Irwin Pearl
Claire Quilty	Leonard Frey
Vivian Darkbloom	Velerie Camille
Charlotte Haze	Dorothy Loudon
Lolita	Annette Ferra[†2]
Rev. Dr. Neiling	Josh Wheeler
Young Man	Lance Westergard
Neighbor	David Thomas
Mrs. Thornbush	Fran Stevens
Camp Counsellors	Jacqueline Johnson, Jacqueline Britt
Mr. Bliss	Neil McNelis[†3]
Bellboys	John Mineo, Irwin Pearl
Amy Pratt	Gretel Cummings
Dick Schiller	John Withman
Bill Crest	Daniel Walsh
Policemen	Adam Petroski, Frank Bouley

SINGERS: Frank Bouley, Jacqueline Britt, Walter P.Brown, Rhoda Butler, Jacque Dean, Lynn East, Linda Ellis, Robert Hultman, Jacqueline Johnson, Neil McNelis, Irwin Pearl, Adam Petroski, Meg Scanlon, Fran Stevens, David Thomas, Trudy Wallace, Daniel Walsh, Josh Wheeler, John Witham

DANCERS: Velerie Camille, Carol Conte, Larry Grenier, Mickey Gunnerson, Carolin Kirsch, John Mineo, Jo Anne Ogawa, Pamela Peadon, Don Percassi, Rosalin Ricci, Dan Siretta, Patrick Spohn, Jill Streisant, Lance Westergard, Lee Wilson

MUSICAL NUMBERS: "Lolita," "Going Going Gone," "In the Broken Promise Land of Fifteen," "The Same Old Song," "Mother Needs a Boyfriend," "Dante, Petrarch and Poe," "Sur Les Quais," "Charlotte's Letter," "Farewell, Little Dream," "Have You Got What You Came With?," "At the Bed-D-By Motel," "Tell Me Tell Me," "Buckin' for Beardsley," "Beardsley School for Girls," "It's a Bad, Bad World," "How Far Is It to the Next Town?"

A Musical in 2 acts and 15 scenes.

† For the Boston opening, succeeded by: 1. Jill Streisant, 2. Denise Nickerson, 3. John Witham. Director, Noel Willman; Choreographer, Dan Siretta

Denise Nickerson

John Neville, Annette Ferra (also above)

AMERICAN SHAKESPEARE FESTIVAL
Stratford, Connecticut
Joseph Verner Reed, Executive Producer
Michael Kahn, Artistic Director
June 16 through Sept. 6, 1970

Managing Producer, Berenice Weiler; Production Manager, Lo Hardin; Production Assistants, Bill Capobianco, Barry Schear; Press, Reginald Denenholz, Ellen Levene; Music Director and Conductor, Conrad Susa; Stage Managers, Nikos Kafkalis, Walter W. Meyer; Costumes, Jane Greenwood; Lighting, John Gleason; Choreography, William Burdick.

COMPANY

Charles Berendt, J. Kenneth Campbell, Paul Corum, Jill Clayburgh, James Cromwell, Danny Davis, Bernard Frawley, Moses Gunn, Margaret Hamilton, Eva LeGallienne, Joseph Maher, Roberta Maxwell, Jan Miner, Ken Parker, Wyman Pendleton, Mary Ellen Ray, Lee Richardson, David Selby, Josef Sommer, Tom Tarpey, Amy Taubin, Peter Thompson, John Tillinger, John Ventantonio, Josef Warik.

Maureen Anderman, Ron Lohse, Gary Poe, Tim Riley, Garland Wright, Mary Wright, Robert Blumenfield, Eugene Brezany, Patricia Callahan, Jack Heifner, Edwin McDonough, Lizabeth Mackay, William Merritt, Jonathan Morgan, Mark Niedzolkowski, John Ogden, Ralph Redpath, Paul Shutt.

PRODUCTIONS

"All's Well that End Well" (Director, Michael Kahn; Scenery, Marshal L. Eck), "Othello" (Director, Michael Kahn; Scenery, Karl Eigsti), "The Devil's Disciple" (Director, Cyril Ritchard; Scenery, William Ritman).

Martha Swope Photos

Top Right: Eva LeGallienne, Roberta Maxwell, Peter Thompson, Josef Sommer in "All's Well that Ends Well" Below: Cyril Ritchard, Lee Richardson, Jill Clayburgh, David Selby in "The Devil's Disciple"

Cyril Ritchard, Margaret Hamilton
in "The Devil's Disciple"

Roberta Maxwell, Moses Gunn in
"Othello"

DELACORTE THEATER

Opened Tuesday, June 23, 1970.
The New York Shakespeare Festival in cooperation with the City of New York presents:

HENRY VI, PART I

By William Shakespeare; Director, Stuart Vaughan; Setting, Ming Cho Lee; Lighting, Martin Aronstein; Costumes, Theoni V. Aldredge; Music, John C. Rigliano; Fights, James Sloyan; Technical Coordinator, Michael Hopper; Assistant Director, Amy Saltz.

CAST

Duke of Bedford	David Byrd
Humphrey, Duke of Gloucester	Robert Gerringer
Duke of Exeter	John Carpenter
Cardinal Beaufort	Patrick Hines
Sir William Lucy	David Snell
Duke of Buckingham	Howard Green
Young John Talbot	Leon Russom
Prince Charles of France	Don Perkins
Duke of Alencon	Drew Snyder
Reignier, Duky of Anjou	Alexander Panas
Bastard of Orleans	Tom Sawyer
Joan La Pucelle	Gretchen Corbett
First Warder	Rocky Anderson
Gloucester's First Man	James DeMarse
Second Warder	Stuart Pankin
Woodville	Frank Borgman
Mayor of London	Charles Durning
Master Gunner of Orleans	Jeff Peters
His Son	David Aaron
Lord Salisbury	John LaGioia
Lord Talbot	Robert Burr
Messenger to Talbot	Brian Calloway
French Sergeant	John W. Davis
French Sentinel	Christopher Leahy
English Soldier	James Keach
Countess' Messenger	Peter Reznikoff
Talbot's Captain	Albert Hall
Countess of Auvergne	Sasha Von Scherler
Countess' Porter	Jeff Peters
Richard Plantagenet	Paul Sparer
William De La Pole	Jack Ryland
Duke of Somerset	Gregory Abels
Earl of Warwick	David Hooks
Vernon	Ronny Cox
A Lawyer	Mervyn Haines, Jr.

Henry VI	Nicholas Kepros
Bishop's Servingman	Albert Quinton
Gloucester's Second Man	Fred Morsell
Basset	Mike Moran
Governor of Paris	George Spelvin
Messenger to Richard	John Allee
Joan's Friends	Christopher Burgess, Sarah Jane Eigerman, Sally Westerman
Margaret	Barbara Caruso
Joan's Father	Albert Quinton
Papal Legate	Fred Morsell
Earl of Salisbury	William Myers
Eleanor, Duchess of Gloucester	Patricia Falkenhain
John Hume	Dan Durning
First Petitioner	Albert Quinton
Second Petitioner	Mike Moran
Peter	Christopher Leahy
Thomas Horner	Mervyn Haines, Jr.
Bolingbroke	David Snell
Margaret Jourdain	Bette Henritze
John Southwell	Stuart Pankin
Townsman	John Allee
Saunder Simpcox	John W. Davis
Wife to Simpcox	Anne Thompson
Mayor of St. Albans	Jeff Peters
Beadle	James Keach
Neighbors	Ronny Cox, John LaGioia, Mike Moran
First Petitioner	David Aaron
Second Petitioner	George Spelvin
Sheriff	Frank Borgman
Sir John Stanley	Albert Hall
Post	Fred Morsell

ENSEMBLE: David Aaron, John Allee, Rocky Anderson, JoAnne Astrow, Christopher Burgess, Brian Calloway, John W. Davis, James DeMarse, Sarah Jane Eigerman, Rennie Elmar, John Ferraro, David Guzman, Albert Hall, Michael Hayes, James Keach, Kevin Kline, Christopher Leahy, Fred Morsell, Stuart Pankin, Jeff Peters, Peter Reznikoff, Mark Robinson, Mark Russel, Kathy Sillaway, Stephen Snow, Rafael Triana, Sally Westerman, Erik White.

Presented in two parts. The action takes place in Fifteenth Century France and England.

General Manager: David Black
Press: Merle Debuskey, Faith Geer
Stage Manager: R. Derek Swire, Dean Compton, Judy Rasmuson

Zodiac Photos

David Hooks, Gretchen Corbett   **Nicholas Kepros**

in "Henry VI"

DELACORTE THEATER

Opened Wednesday, June 24, 1970.
The New York Shakespeare Festival in
cooperation with the City of New York presents:

HENRY VI, PART II

By William Shakespeare; Director, Stuart Vaughan;
Setting, Ming Cho Lee; Lighting, Martin Aronstein;
Costumes, Theoni V. Aldredge; Music, John Corigliano;
Fights, James Sloyan; Choreography, Diane Adler;
Technical Coordinator, Michael Hopper; Assistant Director, Amy Saltz.

CAST

First Murderer	George Spelvin
Second Murderer	Alexander Panas
William De La Pole	Jack Ryland
King Henry VI	Nicholas Kepros
Queen Margaret	Barbara Caruso
Cardinal Beaufort	Patrick Hines
Duke of Somerset	Gregory Abels
Duke of Buckingham	Howard Green
Earl of Warwick	David Hooks
Earl of Salisbury	William Myers
Duke of Gloucester	Robert Gerringer
Duke of Exeter	John Carpenter
Sea Captain	John LaGioia
First Gentleman	John Allee
Second Gentleman	Brian Calloway
Master	Albert Hall
Mate	Albert Quinton
Walter Whitmore	John W. Davis
George Bevis	Ronny Cox
John Holland	Mike Moran
Jack Cade	Charles Durning
Dick the Butcher	Mervyn Haines, Jr.
Smith the Weaver	Don Perkins
Clerk of Chatham	Dan Durning
Michael	James Keach
Sir Humphrey Stafford	Jeff Peters
William Stafford	Stuart Pankin
Lord Say	David Byrd
Messenger to King Henry	John Allee
Another Messenger	Brian Calloway
Cade Rebel	Rocky Anderson
First Rebel	James DeMarse
Second Rebel	Peter Reznikoff
Lord Clifford	Frank Borgman
Messenger	Fred Morsell

Alexander Iden	David Snell
Ricahrd Plantagenet, Duke of York	Paul Sparer
Edward, Earl of March	Tom Sawyer
George, Duke of Clarence	Drew Snyder
Richard, Duke of Gloucester	Donald Madden
Young Clifford	John LaGioia
Duke of Norfolk	John W. Davis
Earl of Westmoreland	Jeff Peters
Earl of Northumberland	Alexander Panas
Edward, Prince of Wales	Leon Russom
Edmund, Earl of Rutland	David Aaron
Duchess of York	Bette Henritze
Messenger to York	Albert Hall
Sir John Mortimer	Stuart Pankin
Sir Hugh Mortimer	Rocky Anderson
Tutor	James DeMarse
Son who killed his father	Christopher Leahy
Father who killed his son	Albert Quinton
Humphrey	Mike Moran
Sinkloe	Ronny Cox
Lady Grey	Jeanne Hepple
A Nobleman	John Allee
Lewis XI, King of France	Dan Durning
Bona	Anne Thompson
Messenger to France	James De Marse
Earl of Oxford	Gregory Abels
Governor of Paris	George Spelvin
Lord Hastings	David Byrd
First Watchman	James Keach
Second Watchman	James DeMarse
Young Duke of Somerset	Don Perkins
Lord Rivers	Frank Borgman
Sir Thomas Stanley	Rocky Anderson
A Huntsman	Kevin Kline
Sir Robert Brackenbury	Howard Green
Henry, Earl of Richmond	John Allee
Messenger to Warwick	Fred Morsell
Mayor of York	Dan Durning
Sir John Montgomery	Robert Gerringer
Soldier	Kevin Kline
First Messenger to Warwick	Rocky Anderson
Second Messenger to Warwick	Christopher Leahy
Marquess of Montague	Ronny Cox

Presented in two parts. The action takes place in
Fifteenth Century England.

General Manager: David Black
Press: Merle Debuskey, Faith Geer
Stage Manager: R. Derek Swire, Dean Compton,
Judy Rasmuson

Zodiac Photos

Barbara Caruso, Nicholas Kepros

Donald Madden, David Snell

in "Henry VI"

DELACORTE THEATER

Opened Thursday, June 25, 1970.*
The New York Shakespeare Festival in cooperation with the City of New York presents:

RICHARD III

By William Shakespeare; Director, Stuart Vaughan; Setting, Ming Cho Lee; Lighting, Martin Aronstein; Costumes, Theoni V. Aldredge; Music, John Carigliano; Fights, James Sloyan.

CAST

Duke of Gloucester, afterward Richard III	Donald Madden
George, Duke of Clarence	Drew Snyder
Sir Robert Brakenbury	Howard Green
Lord Hastings	David Byrd
Lady Anne	Susan McArthur
Berkley	James Keach
Tressel	Kevin Kline
Lord Rivers	Frank Borgman
Lord Grey	Ronny Cox
Queen Elizabeth	Jeanne Hepple
Marquis of Dorset	Peter Reznikoff
Duke of Buckingham	Robert Gerringer
Sir William Stanley	John Carpenter
Queen Margaret	Barbara Caruso
Catesby	Jack Ryland
First Murderer	Leon Russom
Second Murderer	George Spelvin
King Edward IV	Tom Sawyer
Sir Richard Ratcliff	Mervyn Haines, Jr.
Mayor of London	Albert Quinton
First Citizen	Jeff Peters
Scrivener	Mike Moran
Bishop of Ely	Dan Durning
Richard, Duke of York	Robert Benson Ross Burr
Duchess of York	Bette Henritze
Messenger to Bishop	James DeMarse
Edward, Prince of Wales	David Aaron
Messenger to Hastings	Stuart Pankin
Mistress Shore	Sally Westerman
Sir Thomas Vaughan	John W. Davis
Lord Lovel	Don Perkins
Page	Christopher Leahy
Sir James Tyrell	Alexander Panas
Messengers to Richard III	John Allee, Brian Calloway, Albert Hall
Earl of Richmond, later Henry VII	David Snell
Earl of Oxford	Gregory Abels
Sir Walter Herbert	Stuart Pankin
Sir James Blunt	Rocky Anderson
Earl of Surrey	John LaGioia
Duke of Norfolk	John W. Davis
Ghost of Henry VI	Nicholas Kepros
Ghost of Prince Edward	Leon Russom

Presented in two parts. The action takes place in England during the late 15th Century.

General Manager: David Black
Press: Merle Debuskey, Faith Geer
Stage Managers: R. Derek Swire, Dean Compton, Judy Rasmuson

Zodiac Photos

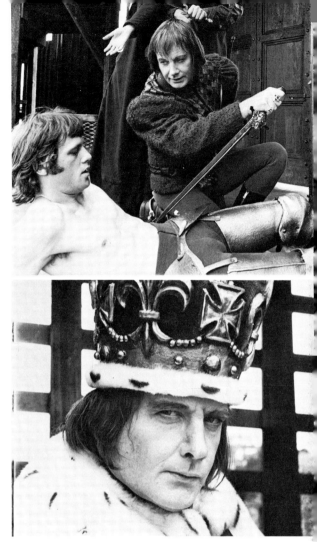

Donald Madden, and above with Leon Russom in "Richard III"

MOBILE THEATER

Opened Tuesday, July 14, 1970.*
The New York Shakespeare Festival (Joseph Papp, Producer) presents:

SAMBO

Music, Ron Steward, Neal Tate; Lyrics, Ron Steward; Director, Michael Schultz; Choreography, Tommy Jonsen; Setting, Ming Cho Lee; Costumes, Milo Morrow; Lighting, Lawrence Metzler; Musical Director, Margaret Harris; Associate Producer, Bernard Gersten.

CAST

Sambo	Ron Steward
Bo Peep	Veronica Redd
Jack Horney	George Turner
Untogether Cinderella	Judy White
Miss Sally Muffat	Jane Stuart
Tiger Lady	Sandi Morris
Tiger Man	Joe Darby
Musicians	Margaret Harris, Fred Waits, Ted Dunbar, Reggie Johnson, Hal Vick, Wood Shaw

Press: Merle Debuskey, Faith Geer
Stage Manager: Ken Glickfeld

* Closed Aug. 8, 1970 after playing parks and playgrounds of the five boroughs.

Sandi Morris, Joe Darby, Judy White, Ron Steward, Jane Stuart

Zodiac Photo

NORTH SHORE SHAKESPEARE FESTIVAL
Beverly, Massachusetts
Stephen Slane, Managing Director
April 26 through May 29, 1971
Ninth Season

Presented by The North Shore Community Arts Foundation; Director, Philip Lawrence; Sets, Eve Lyon; Costumes, Jay Liebman; Lighting, Theda Taylor; Press, Eva T. Slane; Stage Manager, Robert Bruyr

COMPANY

Leta Bonynge, Amanda Bruce, Dixie Carter, David Chaney, Gene Galusha, Diane Gardner, Russell Gold, Ken Kliban, John P. LaGioia, Dennis Lipscomb, Douglas Marland, John Mintun, Seymour Penzner, Stuart Craig Wood

PRODUCTIONS

"Romeo and Juliet," "Twelfth Night"

Ulrike Welsch Photos

Right: Russell Gold in "Twelfth Night"

Douglas Marland, Seymour Penzner (top), Dennis Lipscomb, Diane Gardner, John Mintun, Russell Gold (Friar)

Top: David Hutchison, Stuart Craig Wood, Amanda Bru Center: Dixie Carter, Russell Gold, Gene Galusha, Joh Mintun, Seymour Penzner, Front: Diane Gardner, Dennis Lipscomb in "Twelfth Night"

180

OREGON SHAKESPEARE FESTIVAL
Ashland, Oregon

Angus L. Bowmer, Producing Director
May 22 through Sept. 13, 1970
Thirtieth Season

Managing Director, William W. Patton; Directors, Angus L. Bowmer, Nagle Jackson, Larry Oliver, Raye Birk, Peter Nyberg; Costume Designer, Jean Schultz Davidson; Stage Designers, Clayton L. Karkosh, Richard L. Hay; Technical Director, Larry Davidson; Lighting Designer, Steven A. Maze; Musical Arranger, Composer, Director, W. Bernard Windt; Choreographer, Jo Bailey Guthrie; Press, Robert F. Knoll, Anne Batzer.

COMPANY

Joe Abramczyk, Robert B. Alto, John Arnone, Diana Bellamy, Candace Birk, Raye Birke, Mark Blankfield, Ron Boussom, Jerry Brown, Larry Carpenter, Kit Carson, Clinton Cochran, John R. Darrah, Philip Davidson, Tom Donaldson, Dorothy French, Craig Gardner, Gregory Grove, Ric Hamilton, Bradley High, Andy Kallok, Frank Kelly, Vivian Sally Kemp, Katherine King, Roger Kozol, Christopher Leggette, Catherine Lincoln, Richard Lincoln, Julian Lopez-Morillas, James McLure, William Molloy, Mark D. Murphey, Rick Newman, Fredi Olster, Michael O'Sullivan, Shirley Patton, Kenneth Perez, Corey Phelps, Jolene Phelps, Julie Rogers, William Rohrig, Schuyler M. Roll, Elaine Sawyer, Gregory Ward Schroeder, John Sheehan, J. W. Swearingen, Greg Temple, J. Steven White, Loyd Williamson, Michael Winters, Richard Yarnell, Pamela R. Carson

PRODUCTIONS

"The Merchant of Venice," "The Comedy of Errors," "Julius Caesar," "Richard II," "Rosencrantz and Guildenstern Are Dead," "The Imaginary Invalid"

Carolyn Mason Jones Photos

**Philip Davidson, Ric Hamilon
in "Julius Caesar"**

**Fredi Olster, Richard Lincoln
in "Merchant of Venice"**

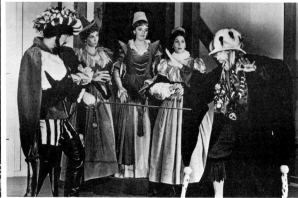

**Gregory Ward Schroeder, Michael O'Sullivan in
"Richard II"**

**Mark D. Murphy, Shirley Patton, Candace Birk,
Catherine Lincoln, Michael O'Sullivan
in "Comedy of Errors"**

181

SAN DIEGO NATIONAL SHAKESPEARE FESTIVAL
San Diego, Calif. Craig Noel, Producing Director
June through Sept. 1970
Twenty-first Season

Directors, Craig Noel, Louis Criss, Pirie MacDonald, Stephen Porter; Settings and Costumes, Peggy Kellner, John Conklin, Douglas Russell; Lighting, Bruce Kelley; Music Composed by Ken Benshoof; Choreographer, Jillana; Stage Managers, Robert Stevenson, Michael Vine, Tom Corcoran, Robert Bonaventura, John David Peters; Assistant to Producing Director, Michael Phillips; Technical Director, Gene Reilly; Sound Technician, Ross Houtz.

COMPANY

Stephen C. Bradbury, Pat Brown, Paul Baccus, Michael Biers, Leon Charles, C. Wayland Capwell, Richard Council, Eugene Carroll, James Degan, Donna Couchman, David Dukes, Marley Days, Alan Fudge, Ellen Geer, Larry Golden, Martin Gerrish, Yvonne Gregerson, Dale Helward, Stephen Hawxhurst, Charles F. Hutchins, Thomas Kopache, Richard Kneeland, Michael Keenan, William Lehrke, Charlie Moll, Tom McCorry, John McMurtry, James McHugh, Ian Manos, Elizabeth Myers, Stephen D. Newman, Michael Phillips, Philip Shofner, Charles Shockley, Don Sparks, Christopher Shelton, Theodore Sorel, David Stutz, Joyce Schumaker, Tom Toner, Susan Tanner, Susan Taylor, Randy Wagner, Moira Wylie

PRODUCTIONS

"Cymbeline," "Much Ado about Nothing," "King Richard II," "Charley's Aunt"

Right: Richard Kneeland, Stephen D. Newman in "Richard II"

Ellen Geer, Theodore Sorel in "Cymbeline"

John McMurtry, Tom Toner in "Much Ado about Nothing"

STRATFORD FESTIVAL OF CANADA
Jean Gascon, Artistic Director
June 8 through Oct. 10, 1970
Eighteenth Season

General Manager, William Wylie; Administrative Director, Victor Polley; Production Director, John Hayes; Press, Mary Webb; Anne Selby; Administrator, Andree Gingras; Production Manager, Jack Hutt; Company Managers, Cedric Fresco, Max Helpmann; Stage Managers, Thomas Hooker, Ross Hill, Patrick McEntee, Christopher Root, Nora Polley, Ann Skinner; Technical Director, Robert M. Hall.

COMPANY

Malcolm Armstrong, Bernard Behrens, Christine Bennett, Colin Bernhardt, Mervyn Blake, Roger Blay, Pamela Brook, Blair Brown, Douglas Campbell, Joyce Campion, Helen Carey, Jane Casson, Leo Ciceri, Stanley Coles, Patrick Crean, Richard Curnock, Donald Davis, Zulema Dene, Eric Donkin, Ronald East, James Edmond, Bernard Engel, Donald Ewer, Alfred Gallagher, Pat Galloway, Robin Gammell, John Gardiner, Roland Hewgill, Mary Hitch, Dominic Hogan, Eric House, James Hurdle, Anne Ives, Gordon Jackson, Joel Kenyon, Salem Ludwig, Barry MacGregor, Stephen Markle, Robin Marshall, Gillian Martell, Elizabeth Milne, Melanie Morse, Stephen Murray, William Needles, Maureen O'Brien, Bette Oliver, Leon Pownall, Kate Reid, Joseph Rutten, Arnold Soboloff, Don Sutherland, Dolores Sutton, Powys Thomas, Joseph Totaro, Kenneth Welsh, Irene Worth, Carolyn Younger

PRODUCTIONS

"The Merchant of Venice," "The School for Scandal," "Hedda Gabler," "Vatzlav," "The Architect and The Emperor of Assyria," "The Friends," "Cymbeline"

Robert C. Ragsdale, Douglas Spillane Photos

**Right: Leo Ciceri, Maureen O'Brien
in "Cymbeline"**

**Leo Ciceri, Irene Worth, Gillian Martell
in "Hedda Gabler"**

**Roger Blay, Arnold Soboloff in "The Architect
and the Emperor of Assyria"**

**Bernerd Engel, Leo Ciceri, Donald Davis
in "Merchant of Venice"**

ACTORS THEATRE OF LOUISVILLE
Louisville, Kentucky
Jon Jory, Producing Director
Sept. 24, 1970 through May 9, 1971

General Manager, Alexander Speer; Press, Trish Pugh; Administrative Director, Vaughn McBride; Sets, John Jensen, James Edmund Brady, Grady Larkins, Hal Tine; Costumes, Will Walker, John Jensen, James Edmund Brady; Lighting and Technical Director, Johnny Walker; Assistant, Geoffrey T. Cunningham; Stage Managers, David Semonin, Charles Traeger; Properties, Debbie Shoss; Costume Assistants, Jania Szatanski, Judy Babnick, Jean Bross; Technical Assistant, Mark Luking, Gary Fox; Directors, Jon Jory, Dennis Rosa, Sue Lawless, Ken Jenkins, Christopher Murney

COMPANY

Hugh Alexander, Stanley Anderson, Armand Assante, Jusef Bulos, David C. Burrow, Dale Carter Cooper, Al Corbin, Peggy Cowles, George Ede, Lee Anne Fahey, Sam Freed, Joe Hindy, Katharine Houghton, Jean Inness, Ken Jenkins, Victor Jory, Ken Kliban, Judith Long, Patricia McAneny, Vaughn McBride, Sandy McCallum, Roger Miller, Christopher Murney, Adale O'Brien, Gretchen Oehler, Michael Parish, Benjamin H. Slack, William Swetland, Charles Traeger, Paul Villani, Eleanor Wilson, Nan Withers, Max Wright

PRODUCTIONS

"The Taming of the Shrew," "Charley's Aunt," "Our Town," "The Lion in Winter," "Thurber Carnival," "Tenth Man," "Feiffer's People," "Joe Egg," "Major Barbara," "Dracula'

Gavin C. Whitsett Photos

Right: Sandy McCallum, Ken Jenkins, George Ede, Stanley Anderson in "The Tenth Man"
Above: Lee Anne Fahey, George Ede in "Dracula"

Victor Jory
in "Our Town"

Ken Jenkins, Katharine Houghton
in "Taming of the Shrew"

ALLEY THEATRE
Houston, Texas
Nina Vance, Producing Director
Oct. 22, 1970 through June 20, 1971

Managing Director, Iris Siff; Business Manager, Bill Pogue; Press, Bob Feingold, Claudia Autrey; Merry-Go-Round Directors, Bettye Gardner, Ellenore Flynn; Producing Associate, H. Wilkenfeld; Production Manager, Bettye Fitzpatrick; Company Manager, Bob Leonard; Stage Managers, John Hagan, Henry Westin; Lighting, Richard D. Cortright, John Hagan, Jonathan Duff; Designers, Jerry Williams, Richard H. Graham, Jr.; Technical Directors, John Hagan, Paul Prentiss; Directors, Nina Vance, Beth Sanford, William Hardy, R. Edward Leonard, Burry Fredrik

COMPANY

Linda Brumfield, Rutherford Cravens, George Ebeling, Lillian Evans, Bettye Fitzpatrick, Robyn Goodman, William Hardy, I. M. Hobson, Nancy Evans Leonard, James Richard Morgan, Fred Morrow, Donna O'Connor, Woody Skaggs, Joel Stedman, Ray Stricklyn, William Trotman, James Broderick, Jeannette Clift, Karen Filer, Joe Finkelstein, Gertrude Flynn, Mary K. Isaacs, R. Edward Leonard, Beth Sanford, Melissa Weaver, Grace Chapman, Kendall Clark, Joe Isaacs, Michael Moriarty, Charles Robinson, Allen Amason, Clint Anderson, John Goldsmith, Malcolm McGee, Ann Minor, Fred Morrow, Joel Ontiberoz, Michel Rutrough, Bob Larkin, John Milford, Patricia Pearcy, Nancy Spivay, Jack Bell, Jonathan Farwell, Garry Phillips

PRODUCTIONS

"Mourning Becomes Electra," World Premiere of "Ring Round the Bathtub" by Jane Trahey(Dec. 3, 1970), "The Night Thoreau Spent in Jail," "Our Town," "The Prime of Miss Jean Brodie," "Tango," "Dial 'M' for Murder"

Right: Michael Moriarty, George Ebeling in "The Night Thoreau Spent in Jail" Above: Donna O'Connor, I. M. Hobson, Bettye Fitzpatrick, Rutherford Cravens in "Tango"

Ray Stricklyn, Lillian Evans in "Mourning Becomes Electra"

Jeannette Clift, Mary K. Isaacs, James Broderick, Gertrude Flynn in "Ring Round the Bathtub"

185

AMERICAN CONSERVATORY THEATRE
San Francisco, California
William Ball, General Director
Nov. 14, 1970 through May 8, 1971
Fifth Bay Area Season

Executive Producer, James B. McKenzie; Executive Director, Edward Hastings; Conservatory Director, Allen Fletcher; General Manager, Charles Dillingham; Production Director, Benjamin Moore; Press, Cheryle Elliott; Writer, Dennis Powers; Designers, Robert Darling, Robert Fletcher, Ann Roth, James Tilton, Walter Watson; Lighting, Ward Russell, Jackson DeGovia; Sound, Charles Richmond; Stage Managers, Eugene Barcone, Dorothy Fowler, Helaine Head; Directors, William Ball, Allen Fletcher, Edward Hastings, Ellis Rabb

COMPANY

Jim Baker, Martin Berman, Joseph Bird, Carolyn Blakey, Nancy Blossom, Mark Bramhall, Light Brown, Joy Carlin, Michael Cavenaugh, Jeff Chandler, Suzanne Collins, Peter Donat, Jay Doyle, Robert Fletcher, David Gilliam, Jerry Glover, Patrick Gorman, John Hancock, Kathleen Harper, Dudley Knight, Anne Lawder, Michael Learned, Fanny Lubritsky, Winifred Mann, Lee McCain, Frank Ottiwell, William Paterson, Ken Ruta, Josef Sommer, Deborah Sussel, Scott Thomas, Ann Weldon, Mark Wheeler, G. Wood

PRODUCTIONS

In rotating repertory: "The Merchant of Venice," "Hadrian VII," "The Relapse," "The Tempest," "The Latent Homosexual," "The Time of Your Life," "An Enemy of the People," World Premiere of "The Selling of the President" by Stuart Hample; Suggested by Joe McGinniss' book; Music and Lyrics, Bob James, Jack O'Brien.

Hank Kranzler Photos

Left: William Paterson, Ken Ruta in 'Time of Your Life' Top: Peter Donat (C), Ken Ruta (R) in 'Merchant of Venice'

Jay Doyle in 'The Relapse'

Martin Berman, William Paterson in 'The Selling of the President'

ARENA STAGE
Washington, D. C.
Zelda Fichandler, Producing Director
Oct. 23, 1970 through July 18, 1971

Directors, Gene Frankel, Norman Gevanthor, Gene Lesser, Gilbert Moses, Mel Shapiro, David William; Sets, Bennet Averyt, David R. Ballou, John Conklin, Leo Kerz, Eugene Lee, Franne Newman, Ming Cho Lee; Costumes, Marjorie Slaiman, Gwynne Clark, Theoni V. Aldredge, Linda Fisher; Lights, Vance Sorrells, Martin Aronstein, Henry R. Gorfein, Hugh Lester, Lee Watson; Production Manager, Hugh Lester; Stage Managers, Elizabeth Darr, Florine Pulley, Simon Siegl; Technical Director, Henry R. Gorfein; Executive Director, Thomas C. Fichandler; Press, Alton Miller

COMPANY

Dan Ahearn, Richard Bauer, Ned Beatty, Leslie Cass, Jill Eikenberry, Morris Engle, Michael Fairman, Grayce Grant, Michael Lewis, Robert Prosky, Richard Sanders, Donegan Smith, Michael Tucker, Howard Witt
GUEST ARTISTS: Jane Alexander, Viveca Lindfors, Douglas Rain, Shepperd Strudwick, Jack MacGowran

PRODUCTIONS

Professional World Premiere of "The Night Thoreau Spent in Jail," World Premiere of new adaptation of "Mother Courage," American Premiere of "The Ruling Class," World Premiere of "Pueblo," "Jack MacGowran in the Works of Beckett," American Premiere of "Wipe-Out Games," "Awake and Sing," "What the Butler Saw," "The Sign in Sidney Brustein's Window"

Fletcher Drake Photos

Left: 'The Night Thoreau Spent in Jail' Top: World Premiere of 'Pueblo'

Jane Alexander, Richard Bauer, Viveca Lindfors, Frank Adu, Michael Tucker, Lee Clark in 'Mother Courage'

Zina Jasper, Michael Fairman in 'The Sign in Sidney Brustein's Window'

ASOLO, THE STATE THEATER COMPANY
Sarasota, Florida
Richard G. Fallon, Executive Director
June 1, 1970 through Sept. 5, 1971

Managing Director, Howard J. Millman; Artistic Directors, Robert Strane, Eberle Thomas; Director Children's Theatre, Moses Goldberg; Designers, Holmes Easley, Catherine King; Business Manager, R. B. Mussar; Press, Edith N. Anson; Technical Directors, Victor Meyrich, Steve Hogan; Lighting, John D. Gowans, James Meade; Sound, Peter J. Morere; Properties, Bob Naismith; Stage Managers, Marian Wallace, Sethia Hardesty; Directors, Richard G. Fallon, Richard D. Meyer, Moses Goldberg, Peter Frisch, Bradford Wallace, Robert Lanchester, Howard J. Millman, Eberle Thomas, Robert Strane, Jon Spelman, Holmes Easley.

COMPANY

Robert Britton, Stuart Culpepper, Patrick Egan, David Mallon, Macon McCalman, William Pitts, Barbara Redmon, Sharon Spelman, Henry Strozier, Isa Thomas, Bradford Wallace, Carol Williard, Robert Strane, Eberle Thomas, Joyce Millman, Polly Holliday, Walter Rhodes, William Leach, Robert Lanchester, James L. Sutorius, Kathleen O'Meare Noone, Bill E. Noone, Richard Hopkins, Susan Sandler, Devora Millman

PRODUCTIONS

"Blithe Spirit," "Glass Menagerie," "Misalliance," "The Physicists," "Oh, Dad, Poor Dad...," "Dr. Faustus," "A Flea in Her Ear," "Life with Father," "All's Well that Ends Well," "The Price," "The Tortoise and The Hare," "Born Yesterday," "Candida," "Joe Egg," "Comedy of Errors," "Love for Love," "The Subject Was Roses," "Charley's Aunt," "Our Town," "Indians," "Puppet Prince," "Snow Queen'

Wayne Manley, Henry Waitt Photos

Right: Isa Thomas, Stuart Culpepper, Bradford Wallace in "All's Well That Ends Well" Above: Robert Stane, Bill E. Noone, Barbara Redmond, Sharon Spelman, Robert Lanchester, James L. Sutorius, Kathleen O'Meara Noone in "Comedy of Errors"

188

Patrick Egan, Eberle Thomas in "Dr. Faustus"

Devora Millman, Patrick Egan, Robert Lanchester, Polly Holliday in "Joe Egg"

BARTER THEATER
Abingdon, Virginia
Robert Porterfield, Founder-Director
April through October 1970
38th Season

Managing Director, Robert Porterfield; Business Manager, Pearl P. Hayter; Press, Owen Phillips; Sets, Bennett Averyt, Frank Moss; Costumes, Lynn Sams; Lighting, Robert Marshall, Jr.; Stage Managers, Bruce Blakemore, Thomas D. Moore III; Directors, Robert Porterfield, Owen Phillips

COMPANY

Antonie Becker, Roger Brown, Dale Carter Cooper, Jane Cronin, Jeff Dalton, James W. Gillespie, Ronald Hale, James Kleeman, Michael Rives, William Schilling, Gene Richard Snow, Anna Stuart, Milton Tarver, Walter Williamson, Paul Woodville, Nell Virginia Bowen, Marlene Caryl, Roy Clary, Robert J. Foley, Liz Ingleson, John H. Milligan, Michael Norell, Jerry Oddo, James Anthony Smith

PRODUCTIONS

"Much Ado about Nothing," "Arsenic and Old Lace," "Plaza Suite," World Premiere of "A Stand in the Mountains" by Peter Taylor, "Lion in Winter," "Petrified Forest," "World of Carl Sandburg," "The Stolen Prince," "Rumpestiltskin," World Premiere of "Rat Race" by Paul Dellinger, "Star Spangled Girl," "Peter of the Round Table'

Larry D. Webster Photos

Right: "The Petrified Forest" Above: Jane Cronin, William Schilling, Roger Brown in "Plaza Suite"

"The Lion in Winter"

"Rat Race"

BUCKS COUNTY PLAYHOUSE
New Hope, Pa.
Lee R. Yopp, Producer-Director
June 1, 1970 through May 31, 1971
Thirty-second Season

Associate Producer, Albert G. Effrat; Press, Carol J. Gilbert, Victoria Grove Shuman; Directors Theatre in Education, Marsha Frazier, Nancy W. Bousum; Designer-Technical Director, Jack Wikoff; Lighting, Don Yopp; Sound, Robert Saviers; Costumes, Shan Willson; Properties, Sharon Ryterband; Stage Managers, Don Yopp, George Dannenberg

COMPANY

Robert Councill, Minerva Davenport, Louis John Deszeran, Edward Earle, Dennis M. Fitzpatrick, Joe Flynn, Michelle Gianinni, Philip Kellman, Marcia Mahon, Frederic Major, William Parent, William Simington, Gloria Willis

GUEST ARTISTS: Donald Moffatt, Chester Morris, Imogene Coca, Manu Tupou, Gloria DeHaven

PRODUCTIONS

"The Roar of the Greasepaint...," "Stop the World...," "Hadrian VII," "The Magistrate," "Odd Couple," "Barefoot in the Park," "Come Blow Your Horn," "Star Spangled Girl," "Caine Mutiny Court Martial," "Never Too Late," "Prime of Miss Jean Brodie," "Hamlet," "Boys in the Band," "I Do! I Do!," "Oedipus Rex," "Ridiculous Young Ladies," "Christmas Carol," "Adaptation/Next," World Premiere of "When Do the Words Come True?," "Our Town," "Zoo Story/American Dream," "Luv," "Indians," "Billy Budd.'

Left: Bill Gerber, Gloria DeHaven, Paul Keith in "When Do the Words Come True?" Above: Norman Kelley, Edward Earle, Sharon Ryterband in "Man of LaMancha"

Gloria Willis, Louis Criscuolo in "Next"

Donald Moffatt as Hadrian VII

CENTER STAGE
Baltimore, Maryland
Peter W. Culman, Producing Director
Oct. 23, 1970 through Apr. 25, 1971

Artistic Director, John Stix; General Manager, David Frank; Directors, Peter W. Culman, Robert Lewis, Sheldon Patinkin, John Stix, Richard Ward; Designers, Eldon Elder, Leo Kerz, Thom Lafferty, Whitney J. LeBlanc; David Mitchell, Joan Olsson, Jay Scott, Preston Sisk, Charles Vanderpool; Musical Director, William Bland; Technical Director, Dennis Shenk; Stage Managers, Andrew Friedlander, Cindy Kite, Shana Sullivan; Press, Flo Harbold; Workshop Director, Vivienne Shub

COMPANY

Mathew Anden, Peter Bailey Britton, Sally Cotton, Carolan Daniels, Barbara Frank, Steven Gilborn, Bert Houle, Douglas Jones, Wil Love, John Newton, Robert R. Reilly, Jonathan Slade, Betsy Stoll, Henry Strozier, Shana Sullivan, Dan Tyra, Sophie Wibaux GUEST ARTISTS: Lee Allen, Rae Allen, Nell Carter, Frederick Coffin, Darryl Croxton, Bob Delegall, Valerie French, Ken Gilman, Robert Guillaume, Hurd Hatfield, Bette Howard, Eric Kilpatrick, Margaret Phillips, Carol Fox Prescott, Dan Priest, Peter Strauss, John Tillinger, Irv Turner, Richard Ward

PRODUCTIONS

"A Cry of Players," "Marat/deSade," "Twelfth Night," "The Collection/The Lover," "Ceremonies in Dark Old Men," World Premiere of "Fire in the Mindhouse" with Lyrics by Arnold Borget and Music by Lance Mulcahy, "Mimes and Pantomimes," "The Private Ear,' "Children's Story   Theatre"

C. B. Nieberding Photos

Left: Margaret Phillips, Wil Love in "The Collection" Above: Nell Carter, Lee Allen, Robert Guillaume, Carol Fox in "Fire in the Mindhouse"

Peter Strauss, Rae Allen, Sharon Kovens
in "A Cry of Players"

Hurd Hatfield, Carolan Daniels, Peter Bailey
Britton in "Marat/deSade"

CENTER THEATRE GROUP
Ahmanson Theatre
Music Center of Los angeles
Elliott Martin, Director
Oct. 13, 1970 through May 1, 1971
Fourth Season

Manager, Charles Mooney; Assistant Manager, Barbara Stocks; Press, Rogers, Cowan & Brenner, Dale Olson, Peter Frisch; Technical Supervisor, H. R. Poindexter; Administrative Assistant, Brenda Ferencz; Sound, Jack Mitnick; Stage Managers, Lo Hardin, Walter W. Meyer, Robert Linden, Alan Hall.

PRODUCTIONS AND CASTS

"ABELARD AND HELOISE" (See Broadway Calendar)

"FORTY CARATS" (see National Touring Companies)

World Premiere of "REMOTE ASYLUM" by Mart Crowley; Director, Edward Parone; Setting, Ming Cho Lee; Costumes, Donald Brooks; Lighting, Thomas Skelton. CAST: Anne Francis (Diana), William Shatner (Tom), Ralph Williams (Michael), Nancy Kelly (Irene), Arthur O'Connell (Ray), Carlos Rivas (Carlos), Joaquin Vallarte (Jose), Roberto Roberi (Juan), Anette Cardona (Peasant) A Play in 3 acts.

"Abelard and Heloise" (See Broadway Calendar)

"DESIGN FOR LIVING" by Noel Coward; Director, Peter Wood; Sets and Costumes, Mago; Lighting, Thomas Skelton CAST: Maggie Smith (Gilda), Robert Stephens (Otto), Denholm Elliott (Leo), Roderick Cook (Ernest), Liza Cole (Miss Hodge), Peter Church (Birbeck) Jess Nichols (Photographer), Kevin Tighe (Henry), Doria Cook (Helen), Nan Martin (Grace), Jess Nichols (Delivery Man), Gene Simms (Matthew)

"COMPANY" (see National Touring Companies)

**Right: Maggie Smith, Robert Stephens
Above: Denholm Elliott, Maggie Smith
in "Design for Living"**

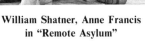
**William Shatner, Anne Francis
in "Remote Asylum"**

**Arthur O'Connell, Ralph Williams
in "Remote Asylum"**

192

CENTER THEATRE GROUP
Mark Taper Forum
Gordon Davidson, Artistic Director
June 1, 1970 through May 31, 1971

General Manager, Francis von Zerneck, David Lunney; Press, Richard Kitzrow, Brooke Karzen, Susan Cobb, Farrar Cobb; Design Consultant, Peter Wexler; Lighting, Tharon Musser; Technical Supervisor, H. R. Poindexter; Production Manager, John DeSantis; Stage Managers, David Barger, Tom A. Larson, Don Winton, Madeline Puzo, Dom Salinaro; Assistant Directors, Wallace Chappell, Alfred Rossi

PRODUCTIONS AND CASTS

"PAUL SILL'S STORY THEATRE" (See Broadway Calendar)

World Premiere of "THE DREAM ON MONKEY MOUNTAIN" by Derek Walcott; Director, Michael A. Schultz; Designers, Edward Burbridge, Lewis Brown, Tharon Musser; Choreography, Mary Barnett;

CAST: Afolabi Ajayi, Andrew Beddeay, Roscoe Lee Browne, K. Lawrence Dunham, Antonio Fargas, Santiago A. Gonzales III, Herbert Jefferson, Jr., Ron O'Neal, Esther Rolle, Charles Turner, James A. Watson, Jr., Anne Worthington, Cinque Attucks, Deborah Brooks, Charlette Cooke, Fred Grey, Ed Mock, Philomena Nowlin, Freda Vanterpool

World Premiere of "ROSENBLOOM" by Harvey Perr; Director, Gordon Davidson; Designers, Michael Devine, Peter Wexler, Tharon Musser; Songs, Randy Newman. CAST: Sheree North, Nehemiah Persoff, Ron Rifkin, Carrie Snodgress

"METAMORPHOSES" (See Broadway Calendar)

"OTHELLO" by William Shakespeare; Director, John Berry; Designers, Peter Larkin, Dorothy Jeakins, Martin Aronstein. CAST: Penelope Allen, Phillip Clark, Jill Clayburgh, Carolan Daniels, Edgar Daniels, Michael Graves, James Earl Jones, Konrad Matthaei, Alan Oppenheimer, Joseph Ruskin, Anthony Zerbe, Al Alu, Timothy Burns, Lee Corrigan, Joseph Culliton, Lou fant, Peter Jacob, Adair Jameson, Flora Plumb, Jack Swanson, Sam Vlahos, Craig Bovia, David Clegg, Michael Landrum, James McHugh, Gerald P. Quinn, Danny Romero, Anthony Rutledge, Harv Selsby

Top Left: George Morgan, Lesley Warren, Avery Schreiber, John Rubinstein, George Gaynes, Paula Kelly, Bill Callaway, Judi West, Bernie Casey, Michael Greene in "Metamorphoses" Below: Carrie Snodgress, Sheree North, Nehemiah Persoff, Ron Rifkin in "Rosebloom"

James Earl Jones, Jill Clayburgh
in "Othello"

Antonio Fargas, Roscoe Lee Browne
in "Dream on Monkey Mountain"

CENTER THEATRE GROUP
New Theatre for Now
Edward Parone, Director
June 1, 1970 through May 31, 1971

"L. A. UNDER SIEGE" by Mayo Simon; Director, Edward Parone; Designers, Michael Devine, Tharon Musser, Pete Menefee, Don Morand, Tom A. Larson; Manager, Ellen Tarlow. CAST: Frank Aletter, Helen Page Camp, Naomi Hirshhorn, Allyn Ann McLerie, Fredricka Myers, David Sachs, Brian Taggert, Malachi Throne, Douglass Watson

World Premiere of "THE TRIAL OF THE CATONSVILLE 9" by Daniel Berrigan; Director, Gordon Davidson; Designers, Michael Davien, Tharon Musser; Music, Joseph Byrd; Film Sequences, Sterling Johnson, Patrick Crawford, Group One Productions. CAST: Gwen Arner, Beau Bridges, Paul Carr, Matt Clark, Mariclare Costello, James Daly, Mary Jackson, John Lasell, Davis Roberts, William Schallert, Peter Strauss, Tom Troupe, Anthony Zerbe

World Premiere of "FATHER'S DAY" by Oliver Hailey; Director, Michael Montel; Designers, Robert Moore, Michael Garrett, Jeffrey Jones. CAST: Barbara Colby, Ellen Geer, Donald Moffat, Lawrence Pressman, John Saxon, Diana Webster

"CAFETERIA STYLE LUNCH" by David Trainer, "MOMSIE AND THE MIDNIGHT BRIDE" by Alan Ormsby; Directed by Wallace Chappell; "BLACK JUDAS" by Robert Valine; Director, Alfred Rossi; Designers, Robert Moore, Michael Garrett, Jeffrey Jones; Music, Santiago A. Gonzales III; Choreography, Maryellen Clemons. CAST: Helen Page Camp, Steve Franken, Santiago A. Gonzales III, Ben Hammer, Kelly Jean Peters, Barbara Press, John Ritter, Paul Winfield

"WHO WANTS TO BE THE LONE RANGER" by Lee Kalcheim; Director, Edward Parone; Designers, Donald Harris, Tharon Musser, William Barbe. CAST: Bob Balaban, Bill Callaway, Helen Page Camp, Dana Elcar, Dana Ewing, Pippa Scott, Joyce Van Patton, Judi West

Tom Troupe, Anthony Zerbe, Gwen Arner, Paul Carr, Matt Clark, Beau Bridges, Peter Strauss, Mariclare Costello, James Daly in "Trial of the Catonsville 9"

Tom Troupe, James Daly in "Trial of the Catonsville 9"

Allyn Ann McLerie, Frank Aletter in "Under Siege"

CHARLES PLAYHOUSE
Boston, Massachusetts
Frank Sugrue, Producing Director
Apr. 7, 1970 through June 27, 1971

Executive Director, William Floyd; General Manager, Peter Henderson; Press, Leslie Gifford, Mary Jane Cotton, Elise Chedekel, David Wynne; Administrative Assistant, Hilary Fradis; Stage Managers, John Dobbins, Patricia Moeser, Leon Leake, Steve McCorkle; Artistic Adviser, Louis Criss; Sets and Lighting, David Shaver, John Jacobsen; Costumes, Peter Wingate; Directors, Moni Yakim, Peter Wingate

PRODUCTIONS AND CASTS

"JACQUES BREL IS ALIVE AND WELL AND LIVING IN PARIS" with Goerge Ball, Denise LeBrun, Bob Jeffrey, Sally Cooke, Shawn Elliott, Annette Pirrone

World Premiere of "IN 3 ZONES" by Wilford Leach; Director, Louis Criss; Music, John Herbert McDowell; Film Sequences, Brian Kaufman. CAST: Alice Drummond, David Dukes, Clarence Felder, Alan Fudge, June Gable, Nicholas Kepros, Joan Tolentino, Alaina Warren

William L. Smith Photos

Right: Shawn Elliott, Annette Pirrone, Denise LeBrun, J. T. Cromwell Above: Bob Jeffrey, Denise LeBrun, Annette Pirrone, George Ball in "Jacques Brel is Alive and Well and Living in Paris"

Alice Drummond
in "In 3 Zones"

David Dukes, June Gable, Nicholas Kepros
in "In 3 Zones"

CIRCLE IN THE SQUARE AT FORD'S THEATRE
Washington, D. C.
Theodore Mann, Artistic Director
Sept. 15 through May 31, 1971

Managing Director, Paul Libin; Settings and Costumes, Marsha L. Eck; Lighting, David F. Segal; Music and Musical Direction, John Duffy; Movement, Peter Maloney; Director, Theodore Mann; Press, Judy Clericuzio, Jan DuPlain.

PRODUCTIONS AND CASTS

"WILL ROGERS' U.S.A." with James Whitmore (see National Touring Companies)

"ARSENIC AND OLD LACE" with Pamela Simpson, Jack Fletcher, Paul Haney, Walter Flanagan, Jerrold Ziman, Cynthia Latham, Stockard Channing, Edward Herrmann, Alexander Reed, Stefan Gierasch, Peter Bosche, Marlow Ferguson, Hansford Rowe

"FESTIVAL AT FORD'S" with Andy Williams, James Stewart, Pearl Bailey, Tennessee Ernie Ford, Bobbie Gentry, Henry Mancini, The Supremes, Dionne Warwicke

"JOHN AND ABIGAIL" with Michael Higgins, Salome Jens, Daniel Cohen, Julia Fremon, Baxter Harris, Jayne Haynes, Keren Liswood, Michael Pendrey, Ellen Schindler, Roger Sewall, Sylvia Soares

"MAX MORATH AT THE TURN OF THE CENTURY" with Max Morath

"YOU'RE A GOOD MAN, CHARLIE BROWN" with Nancy Fox, Douglas Houston, Barnaby Millard, Trip Plymale, Chip Zien, Carol Ziske

Tom Barnett Photos

Left: Chip Zien in "You're a Good Man, Charlie Brown" Above: Cynthia Latham, Pamela Simpson in "Arsenic and Old Lace"

James Whitmore in "Will Rogers' U.S.A."

Max Morath

CLEVELAND PLAYHOUSE
Cleveland, Ohio
Richard Oberlin, Managing Director
Sept. 11, 1970 through May 23, 1971
55th Season

Business Manager, James Sweeney; Company Manager, Nelson Isekeit; Press, Kathleen Kennedy, Bonnie Jacobs; Production Coordinator, Larry Tarrant; Consultant, Rex Partington; Directors, Jonathan Bolt, John Going, Richard Oberlin, Robert Snook, Larry Tarrant; Designers, Eugene Hare, Joe Dale Lunday, Marla Nedelman; Costumes, Joe Dale Lunday, Harriet Cone; Technical Directors, John Flynn, Ben Letter; Lighting, Jeffrey Dallas; Properties, Leslie Leonelli; Stage Managers, Jonathan Bolt, Allen Leatherman, Ben Letter, Evie McElroy, Bjorn Pernvik, Larry Tarrant

COMPANY

Robert Allman, Jean Barrett, Nolan D. Bell, David Berman, Jonathan Bolt, John Buck, Jr., Susan Burkhalter, Margaret Christopher, David Frazier, Mary Gallagher, June Gibbons, Jana Gibson, John Going, Richard Halverson, Charlotte Hare, Myrna Kaye, Allen Leatherman, Evie McElroy, Vincent Michaels, Bob Moak, Richard Oberlin, Edith Owen, Dorothy Paxton, Mary Shelley, Robert Snook, Vivienne Stotter, Larry Tarrant, Robert Thorson

GUEST ARTISTS: Leif Ancker, Roy Clary, Ted Hallaman, Tom Keena, Shela Russell, Tom Carson

PRODUCTIONS

"The Huff and the Puff" and "Whatever Happened to Hugging and Kissing?," "Don Juan in Hell," "Threepenny Opera," "Fallen Angels," "Gallows Humor," "Endgame," "Lysistrata," "Except for Susie Finkel," "You Know I Can't Hear You when the Water's Running," "Spoon River Anthology," "Summer and Smoke," "White House Murder Case," "Beyond the Fringe," "Devil's Disciple," "The Promise," "Plaza Suite"

Guest Performance of "Songs from Milkwood" and "Woyzeck" by the National Theatre of the Deaf

David M. Novak Photos

Top Left: "Threepenny Opera" Below: Robert Thorson, John Buck, Jr., Myriam Lipari in "The Promise"

Ronald Greene, Robert Thorson in "White House Murder Case"

Susan Burkhalter, Tom Keena, Mary Shelley in "Except for Susie Finkel"

COMPANY THEATRE
Los Angeles California
June 1, 1970 through May 31, 1971

Artistic Directors, Stephen Bellon, William Hunt, Steven Kent; Administrative Director, Barry Opper; Lance Larsen; Directors, Stephen Bellon, Steven Kent, Jack Rowe; Designers, Donald Harris, Russell Pyle; Costumes, Boyd Clopton,Steven Kent; Lighting, Donald Harris; Musical Arrangements, Stephen Bellon, Lance Larsen, Jack Rowe, Bob Walter, Steven Kent, Sam Eisenstein, George Herbert, William Hunt, Roxanne Pyle, Daniel Sonneborn

COMPANY

Arthur Allen, Roger Barnes,Stephen Bellon, Suzanne Benoit, Gar Campbell, Nina Carozza, Toby Coleman, Bill Dannevik, Barbara Grover, Donald Harris, Nancy Hickey, Larry Hoffman, William Hunt, Steven Kent, Lori Landrin, Lance Larsen, Candace Laughlin, Polita Marks, Sandra Morgan, Marcina Motter, Barry Opper, Don Opper, Michael Carlin Pierce, Roxanne Pyle, Russell Pyle, Dennis Redfield, Wiley Rinaldi, Jack Rowe, Richard Serpe, Trish Soodik, Michael Stefani, Bob Walter

PRODUCTIONS

"Narrow Road to the Deep North" by Edward Bond, "James Joyce Memorial Liquid Theatre Volume II," "Children of the Kingdom" by Don Keith Opper, "The Plague" by Sam Eisenstein,"The Emergence" by Amagiesta Fleming,

Right: Lance Larsen, Gar Campbell, Jack Rowe in "Narrow Road to the Deep North" Above: Dennis Redfield (L) in "The Emergence"

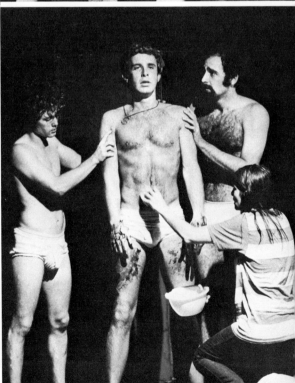

Sandra Morgan, Gar Campbell in "Children of the Kingdom" Above: Gar Campbell, Lance Larsen in "The Plague"

"The James Joyce Memorial Liquid Theatre"

DALLAS THEATER CENTER
Dallas, Texas
Paul Baker, Managing Director
Sept. 15, 1970 through Aug. 14, 1971

Assistant Director, Mary Sue Jones; Directors, Paul Baker, Ken Latimer, Ryland Merkey, Sally Netzel, Campbell Thomas; Designers, Mary Sue Jones, John Henson, Johanna Stalker, A. J. Rogers, Kathleen Latimer; Costumes, Mary Sue Jones, John Henson, Michael Wray, Lynn Lester, Kathleen Latimer; Lighting, Randy Moore, Robyn Baker Flatt, Sally Netzel

COMPANY

Judith Davis, Michael Dendy, Kaki Dowling, John Figlmiller, Robyn Baker Flatt, Mary Sue Jones, Preston Jones, Kathleen Latimer, Ken Latimer, Gene Leggett, John Logan, Ryland Merkey, Randy Moore, Louise Mosley, Sally Netzel, Synthia Rogers, Frank Schaefer, Randolph Tallman, Campbell Thomas, Jacque Thomas, Lynn Trammell, Ronald Wilcox, David Pursley, Mona Pursley

GUEST ARTISTS: Theodore Mann, Stratis Karras

PRODUCTIONS

"Little Murders," "Boys from Syracuse," "Farce 'n' Flick and Fantoccini," "Hamlet ESP," "Peter Pan," "The Seagull," "Harvey," "The Night Thoreau Spent in Jail," "The Night Watchman," "Joe Egg," "The Late Christopher Bean," "Waiting for Godot," "Anna Christie," "Dear Liar," "The Attendant"

Andy Hanson Photos

Right: Randy Moore, Steven Mackenroth in "Waiting for Godot" Above: Ella-Mae Brainard, Margaret Yount, Ryland Merkey in "Harvey"

Mary Sue Jones, Christopher Hendrie in "The Sea Gull"

Gene Leggett, Reginald Montgomery, Randolph Tallman, Jim Progar in "Hamlet"

DETROIT REPERTORY THEATRE
Detroit, Michigan
Bruce E. Millan, Artistic Director
Oct. 1, 1970 through May 29, 1971

Director, Bruce Millan; Scenery, John Knox, Bruce Millan, David Stoller; Lighting, Dick Smith

COMPANY

W. Paul Unger, Council Cargle, Barbara Busby, Colleen Cain, Denise Delaney, Harrison Avery, Dee Andrus, Don Annis, Jesse Newton, William Boswell, Robert Williams, Charles Roseborough, John D. Carter, Jr., Gregory Edward Gray, Margo Coley, Cliff Roquemore, Barbara Jacobs

PRODUCTIONS

"Slow Dance on the Killing Ground," "No Flowers in Cement," "Ceremonies in Dark Old Men"

Left: W. Paul Unger, Robert Williams in "No Flowers in Cement"

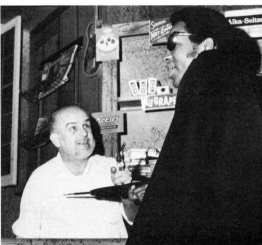

Cliff Roquemore, John D. Carter, Jr. in "Ceremonies in Dark Old Men"

Barbara Busby, Council Cargle Above: W. Paul Unger, Council Cargle in "Slow Dance on the Killing Ground"

GOODMAN THEATRE
Chicago, Illinois
John Reich, Producing Director
Oct. 12, 1970 through June 27, 1971

Associate Producing Director, Douglas Seale; Managing Director, Sheldon Kleinman; Press, Mel Kopp, Rhona Berkowitz; Directors, Douglas Campbell, Patrick Henry, Douglas Seale; Sets, Marc Cohen, Alicia Finkel, Sandro LaFerla, James Maronek; Costumes, Alicia Finkel, Virgil Johnson, Daniel Pugh; Lighting, Jerrold Gorrell, G. E. Naselius, Bengt Nygren, Wayne Tignor; Stage Managers, Patricia Christian, George Boyd, Lois Nygren

COMPANY

Loyse Anderson, Susan Batson, Dale Benson, Eric Berry, Douglas Campbell, Ann Casson, Leonardo Cimino, Maurice Copeland, Richard Curnock, Donna Curtis, David Dwight, June Gable, Jack Godby, Jo Henderson, Max Howard, Ronald Jones, Art Mellor, Gerald Alan Miller, Russell Nype, Vincent Park, Nick Polus, LuAnn Post, John Reymont, Ira Rogers, Kathleen Rostrom, Carol Ruth, Suzi Schelly, Joseph Shaw, Veronica Skowronski, Rebecca Taylor, Robert Theis, Jerry Tulles, Christopher Walken, Laneri Walker, David Whitaker, Donald Woods

PRODUCTIONS

"The Threepenny Opera," "Twelfth Night," "The Night Thoreau Spent in Jail," "Marching Song," "Poor Bitos," "Lady Audley's Secret'

David H. Fishman Photos

Top Left: Douglas Campbell, Leonardo Cimino in "Marching Song" Below: Eric Berry, Richard Curnock, Jo Henderson, Dale Benson in "Twelfth Night"

Terry Lomax, Donna Curtis, Russell Nype, June Gable in "Lady Audley's Secret'

Lu Anne Post, Christopher Walken in "The Night Thoreau Spent in Jail"

GUTHRIE THEATER COMPANY
(formerly Minnesota Theatre Company)
Minneapolis, Minnesota
Donald Schoenbaum, Managing Director
June 18, 1970 through Dec. 12, 1970

Production Manager, Gordon Smith; Press, Thomas Gifford, Charlotte Solomon; Technical Director, Robert Scales; Directors, Robert David Macdonald, Israel Hicks, Philip Minor, John Hirsch, Michael Langham; Sets and Costumes, Gordon Micunis, John Jensen, Geraldine Cain, Eoin Sprott; Lighting, Robert Scales; Stage Managers, Ron Bruncati, Milton Commons, Jon Cranney, Marc Rush, Patrick Stansfield, Gordon Smith

COMPANY

Paul Ballantyne, Emery Battis, Fran Bennett, Robert Benson, Ed Bernard, Ross Bickell, Gerry Black, Barbara Bryne, Timothy Casey, Jon Cranney, Joseph Culliton, Lance Davis, Allan Estes, David Feldshuh, Katherine Ferrand, Warren Frost, Allison Giglio, Maxwell Glanville, Ron Glass, Peter Michael Goetz, Ellin Gorky, Allen Hamilton, Eric House, Bette Howard, Charles Keating, Stephen Keep, Linda Kelsey, James J. Lawless, William Levis, Noel McCoy, Leroy McDonald, Biff McGuire, Michael Parish, Robert Pastene, Briain Petchey, Ken Pogue, Marc Rush, Michele Shay, Fern Sloan, Sander Szabo, Arnold Wilkerson

PRODUCTIONS

"The Venetian Twins," "Ceremonies in Dark Old Men," "The Tempest," "A Man's a Man," "A Play"

Right: Arnold Wilkerson, Maxwell Glanville, Bette Howard in "Ceremonies in Dark Old Men" Above: Timothy Casey, Leroy McDonald, Allan Estes, Ross Bickell, Peter Michael Goetz, Charles Keating in "A Man's a Man"

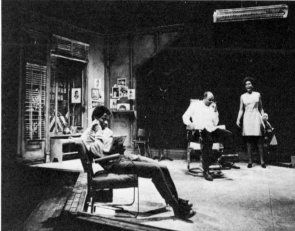

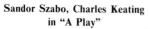

Sandor Szabo, Charles Keating in "A Play"

Britain Petchey, Emery Battis in "The Venetian Twins"

202

HARTFORD STAGE COMPANY
Hartford, Connecticut
Paul Weidner, Producing Director
Oct. 15, 1970 through June 20, 1971
Eighth Season

Managing Director, William Stewart; Press, Ann Vermel, Ellen Jones; Production Manager, Harold Courchene; Settings and Costumes, Santo Loquasto, Linda Fisher, Colleen Callahan, Lawrence King; Lighting, Joe Pacitti, Larry Crimmins, John Wright Stevens, Peter Hunt; Directors, Paul Weidner, Philip Minor, Jacques Cartier, Nagle Jackson; Stage Managers, Fred Hoskins, Nancy Dobak, Marc Rush, Gary Lamagna; Technical Director, Peter Wrenn-Meleck, Craig Watson.

COMPANY

Jeremiah Sullivan, John Colenback, Henry Thomas, Christopher Andrews, John Dignan, Michael Dryansky, Richmond Hoxie, Larry Pertilla, Herve Villechaize, Tana Hicken, John MacAllan, Richard Jamieson, Vivian Reis, David O.Petersen, Donald Bell, Mary Dawn Ames, Robin Murphy, Stephen Nasuta, Kermit Brown, Charlotte Moore, Darthy Blair, Jill Tanner, James Carruthers, Katharine Houghton, Edith Gresham, Ted Graeber, Robert Moberly, James Valentine, Ron Frazier, Michael Esterson, Robert Pastene, Teresa Wright, Tom Atkins, John Glover, Lois de Banzie, Peter Duncan, Josephine Nichols, Anthony Heald, Mark Dempsey, Paul Rudd, Lisle Wilson, Jr., Michael Nouri

PRODUCTIONS

"Rosencrantz and Guildenstern are Dead," "Ring 'Round the Moon," World Premiere of "A Gun Play" by Yale M. Udoff, "Long Day's Journey into Night, "Blithe Spirit," "The Boys in the Band'

David Robbins Photos

Right: Tom Atkins, John Glover, Teresa Wright, Robert Pastene in "Long Day's Journey into Night" Above: Ron Frazier, Tana Hicken, Charlotte Moore, Darthy Blair in "A Gun Play"

Katharine Houghton, Jeremiah Sullivan in "Ring Round the Moon"

David O. Petersen, Ron Frazier, Henry Thomas in "Boys in the Band"

203

INNER CITY REPERTORY THEATER
Los Angeles, Calif.
C. Bernard Jackson, Executive Director
Fourth Season

General Manager, Josie Dotson; Producing Director, Jay Stephens; Press, Bruce Feldman, Clifford Choice; Musical Director, Margaret Bonds; Technical Director, Lupre Autajay; Sets, Lorentz Gonzalez; Lighting, Rae Creevey; Costumes, Betye Saar; Stage Manager, Jeanne Joe, Annette Ensley

COMPANY

Ronald Allen, Sheila Antoine, Chris Calloway, Mel Carter, Clifford Choice, Jack Crowder, Dalyce Curry, Tony de Costa, Sumi Haru, Robert Ito, Edith Hernandez, Waltye Johnson, Muriel Landers, Esther Martinez, Wardell Howard, Olga James, Ruby Millsap, Delilah Moseley, Conrad Parham, Dennis Parnell, Michael Richards, Natividad Vacio, Clarence Whitmore, Danny Williams, Adolph Caeser, Isabel Sanford, Ruth Warshawsky

PRODUCTIONS

"Street Scene," "The Alligators Are Coming," Premiere of "One Is A Crowd" by Beah Richards, "The Madman and the Nun," "Gallows Humor"

Lyn Smith Photos

Left: Olga James, Robert Ito Below: Esther Martinez, Natividad Vacio, Mel Carter, Sheila Antoine in "Street Scene"

Ruth Warshawsky, Isabel Sanford, Adolph Caeser in "The Alligators Are Coming"

Jack Crowder, Beah Richards in "One is a Crowd"

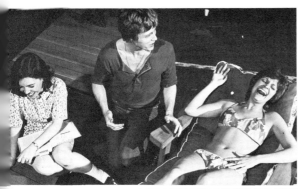

Harriet Hall, Nancy Coleman, Larry Gates, Mark Lamos,
John Saxon in "Another Part of the Forest"

IVANHOE THEATRE
Chicago, Illinois
George Keathley, Producer
June 23, 1970 through May 31, 1971

President, Richard D. Jansen; Associate Producer, Aaron Gold; Press, Gold/Wilson; Technical Director, Ivan Carlson; Stage Managers, Thomas M. Guerra, Charles F. Christensen; Sets, Wrick Paul; Costumes, Georgiana Jordan; Directors, George Keathley, Warren Enters.

PRODUCTIONS AND CASTS

"A SHOT IN THE DARK" with Tom Bosley, Anne Rogers, Werner Klemperer, Lake Bobbitt, George Womack, Jacquebeth Benton, Helen Meier, Georgiana Jordon

"LEMON SKY" with Christopher Walken, James Broderick, Patricia Peardon, Lee McCain, Kathryn Baumann, Michael Lang, Gleen Carl Russell

"BUS STOP" with Sandy Dennis, Ben Piazza, Mary Michaels, Marrian Walters, Doug Alleman, Bob Thompson, Don Marston, George Womack

"WHO'S AFRAID OF VIRGINIA WOOLF?" with Eileen Herlie, James Broderick, Ben Piazza, Rebecca Taylor

"THE INNOCENTS" with Piper Laurie, Geraldine Kay, Bambi Holzer, Craig Taylor, Linda Willner, David Whitaker

"THE BIGGEST THIEF IN TOWN" with John McGiver, Bob Thompson, Shelley Long, Robert Urich, Edgar Meyer, Marji Bank, Doug Alleman, George Womack, Dick Stadelmann, Jack Reidy

"THE EFFECT OF GAMMA RAYS ON MAN-IN-THE—MOON MARIGOLDS" with Irene Dailey, Marla Friedman, Adrienne Kent, Beatrice Fredman

"ANOTHER PART OF THE FOREST" with John Saxon, Larry Gates, Nancy Coleman, Harriet Hall, Judd Reilly, Louise Jenkins, Bob Curry, Bob Thompson, Mark Lamos, Dennis Kennedy, Karin Woodward

Dick Klein Photos

Top Left: Doug Alleman, Mary Michaels, Bob Thompson, George Womack, Marrian Walters, Sandy Dennis, Ben Piazza in "Bus Stop"

Ben Piazza, Eileen Herlie, James Broderick in "Who's Afraid of Virginia Woolf?" Above: Kathryn Baumann, Christopher Walken, Lee McCain in "Lemon Sky"

Beatrice Fredman, Irene Dailey in "The Effect of Gamma Rays on Man-in-the-moon Marigolds"

LONG WHARF THEATRE
New Haven, Connecticut
Arvin Brown, Artistic Director
Oct. 23, 1970 through May 28, 1971

Executive Director, M. Edgar Rosenblum; Artistic Directors of Children's Theatre, Isaac Schambelan, Peter J. Hajduk; Directors, Jeff Bleckner, Gilbert Cates, Ted Cornell, Eddy Gilbert, Brian Murray; Sets, John Conklin, Virginia Dancy, Kert Lundell, Hal Tine, Elmon Webb, Peter Wingate; Costumes, Whitney Blausen, Santo Loquasto, Lewis Rampino, Peter Wingate; Lighting, Ronald Wallace, Judy Rasmuson; Stage Managers, William Garry, Jean Weigel; Press, Margery A. Colloff; Administrative Assistant, Susan Tabler

COMPANY

Madeleine de Jean Adams, Tom Atkins, Emery Battis, Ronald Bishop, Peter Brouwer, Shirley Bryan, John Cazale, Olivia Cole, Tom Crawley, William Cwikowski, Joyce Ebert, Marjorie Lynne Feiner, Will Fenno, Elizabeth Foster, John Glover, Christopher Hastings, Frank Hooper, Paul Henry Itkin, Laurie Kennedy, Heidi Mefford, Carol Morell, Jeffrey Nelson, Patricia Pearcy, Michael Procaccino, Judith Resnick, Grant Roll, Martha Schlamme, Terrence Sherman, William Swetland, Carol Teitel, Henry Thomas, Richard Venture, Edward Zang, Cindy Veazey

GUEST ARTISTS: Morris Carnovsky, Charles Cioffi, David Clennon, John Cromwell, Mildred Dunnock, Richard Dysart, Alvin Epstein, Zakes Mokae, Ruth Nelson, Will Lee

PRODUCTIONS

"The Skin of Our Teeth," "Yegor Bulichov" (U. S. Premiere), "A Place without Doors" (U.S. Premiere), "She Stoops to Conquer," "The Blood Knot," World Premiere of "Solitaire/Double Solitaire," "Heartbreak House," "The Price," "Winnie the Pooh," "Wind in the Willows," "Thirteen Clocks," "Go Jump in the Lake," "Hansel and Gretel"

William L. Smith Photos

Right: Richard Venture, Martha Schlamme in "Heartbreak House" Above: Alvin Epstein, Mildred Dunnock in "A Place without Doors"

Joyce Ebert, Tom Atkins in "She Stoops to Conquer"

Richard Venture in "Solitaire/Double Solitaire"

McCARTER THEATER
Princeton, N. J
Arthur Lithgow, Executive Director
Oct. 16, 1970 through Apr. 24, 1971

Business Manager, Nancy Shannon; Press, Selika C. Conover; Production Director, John C. Schenck III; Technical Director, Timothy O'Brien; Sets and Costumes, James Edmund Brady, Grady Larkins, Mil Mikulewicz, Douglas Cooper, Susan Shaughnessy; Lighting, F. Mitchell Dana, Garry Holfeltz, Stage Managers, Nina Seely, Anne Keefe; Production Assistant, Margery Burt; Directors, Arthur Lithgow, Eric Krebs, Robert Blackburn, Russell L. Treyz, Louis Criss

COMPANY

Robert Blackburn, Scotty Bloch, Tom Brennan, Brendan Burke, Leila Cannon, Beth Dixon, Alice Elliott, Donald Gantry, Richard Jamieson, W. G. McMillan, Tennyson Moore, Fred Morsell, Seymour Penzner, Richard Pilcher, Bob Schmidbauer, Tazewell Thompson, Joan Weisberg

PRODUCTIONS

"All My Sons," "A Raisin in the Sun," "The Show-off," "Little Murders," "The Importance of Being Earnest," "The Homecoming," "Macbeth," and World Premiere of "Caesar at the Rubicon" by Theodore H. White

Jim McDonald Photos

Left: Tom Brennan, Richard Pilcher, Robert Blackburn in "Caesar at the Rubicon" Above: Seymour Penzner, Madge Grant, Dorothy Chace, Robert Blackburn in "All My Sons"

Fred Morsell, Sam Stokes, Sylvia Soares
in "A Raisin in the Sun"

Joan Weisberg, Richard Jamieson
in "The Homecoming"

MEADOW BROOK THEATRE
Rochester, Michigan
Terrance Kilburn, Artistic Director
Nov. 5, 1970 through June 20, 1971

Managing Director, Frank F. Bollinger; Business Manager, Alfred J. Mercieca; Press, Robert J. Kraus; Costumes, Veronica Gustaff; Scenery and Lighting, Richard Davis; Technical Director, Lyalls Phillips; Stage Managers, Ralph H. Valatka, Jr., Donna M. Ryan, John B. O'Reilly, Jr.; Directors, John Ulmer, Joseph Shaw

COMPANY

Elisabeth Orion, Diane Bugas, Glynis Bell, Elizabeth Oustinoff, Susan Thorne, Andrea Stonorov, Toby Tompkins, Robert Englund, Richmond F. Johnson, Philip Mallet, Michael Tolaydo, David Himes

GUEST ARTISTS: Peter Brandon, Priscilla Morrill, Harry Ellerbe, Barbara Quinn, William LeMassena, Joseph Shaw

PRODUCTIONS

"The Skin of Our Teeth," "Life with Father," "The Crucible," "Tartuffe," "The Rainmaker," "Who's Afraid of Virginia Woolf?," "A Thousand Clowns, " "The Fantasticks"

Left: William LeMassena, Diane Bugas in "The Rainmaker" Below: (L) Glynis Bell, Michael Tolaydo, Defoy Glenn, John B. O'Reilly, Jr., Richmond F. Johnson, Harry Ellerbe, Elisabeth Orion in "The Skin of Our Teeth" (R) Diane Bugas, Elisabeth Orion, Toby Tompkins, Glynis Bell, Susan Thorne, Michael Tolaydo in "Tartuffe"

Glynis Bell, Donna M. Ryan, Angel Menzie, Richmond F. Johnson, Robert Englund in "The Crucible"

Michael Tolaydo, Robert Englund, Andrea Stonorov, Diane Bugas in "Life with Father"

MILWAUKEE REPERTORY THEATER COMPANY
Milwaukee, Wisconsin
Tunc Yalman, Artistic Director
Sept. 25, 1970 through May 30, 1971

Managing Director, Charles Ray McCallum; Press, Donald Donne; Directors, Ronald L. Hufham, Timothy S. Mayer, John Pasquin, Paul Weidner, Tunc Yalman; Designer, William James Wall; Lighting, William Mintzer; Stage Managers, Merry Tigar, Margie Perkins; Assistant Set Designer, Christopher M. Idoine; Associate Costume Designer, Janet C. Warren

COMPANY

Gary Bayer, Dale J. Bellaire, Linda Carlson, Sirin Devrim, Elizabeth Franz, Joan Graves, Rob Harland, Sindy Hawke, Jim Jansen, Gertrude Jeannette, Stuart Kendall, Charles Kimbrough, Mary Jane Kimbrough, Stephanie Lewis, Judith Light, Philip MacKenzie, Arthur McFarland, William McKereghan, Mark Metcalf, Kevin O'Connor, Maggie Olesen, Penelope Reed, Anne Shropshire, Charles E. Siegel, Kerry Welch, Alan Zampese

PRODUCTIONS

"Medea," "You Can't Take It with You," "As You Like It," "Spoon River Anthology," "The Liar," "A Doll's House," "Interview," "The Zoo Story," "Winging It'

Jack Hamilton Photos

Left: Penelope Reed, William McKereghan in "Spoon River Anthology" Below: "The Liar"

"Medea"

Charles and Mary Jane Kimbrough in "A Doll's House"

MUMMERS THEATRE
Oklahoma City, Okla.
Mack Scism, Producer-Director
Dec. 4, 1970 through May 2, 1971

Associate Artistic Director, John Wylie; Director, Saylor Creswell; Costumes, William Schroder; Sets, Robert Steinberg; Press, Midge Richards, Pat Shoemaker; Stage Manager, Robert J. Fahey.

COMPANY

Anne Ault, Charles Berendt, Saylor Creswell, Robert Machray, Mary Michaels, Christopher Shelton, Benjamin Slack, Louise Speed, Angela Wood, Claude Woolman, John Wylie, Jon Bergman, Jo Leffingwell, Mary Ed Porter, Scott Porter, Dana Roberts, Nick Roberts, Susan Tanner, Scott Wagner.

GUEST ARTIST: Edward Mulhare

PRODUCTIONS

"A Man for All Seasons," "Dear Liar," "The Rivalry," "The World of Carl Sandburg," "The Misanthrope," "A Phoenix Too Frequent," "Bedtime Story," "Arsenic and Old Lace," "Star Spangled Girl," "See How They Run"

Left: Edward Mulhare in "A Man for All Seasons" Below: Nick Roberts, Charles Berendt, Anne Ault in "World of Carl Sandburg" Right: Clarence Felder, Earl Hindman in "The Rivalry"

Rudolph Willrich, Angela Wood in "A Phoenix Too Frequent"

Jo Leffingwell, Christopher Shelton in "The Misanthrope"

PAF PLAYHOUSE
Huntington Station, N.Y.
Clint Marantz, Executive-Artistic Director
June 1, 1970 through May 31, 1971

Directors, William Pardue, Clint Marantz, Clement Fowler; Sets, Lighting and Technical Direction, John W. Shane

COMPANY

Clement Fowler, Sean Griffin, Lauren Levian, Roger Middleton, William Pardue, Kelly Patton, Mary Lou Schertz, Dawn Horwitz

GUEST ARTISTS: Marian McPartland, Tony Montanaro, Martin Josman, Thomas James, Edith Macy, Eric Nebbia, Nicholas Zaninovic

PRODUCTIONS

"Spoon River Anthology," "Summertree," "Aria da Capo," "The Adam and Eve Diary"

Joan Ames Photos

Right: Sean Griffin, Mary Lou Schertz, Lauren Levian, Roger Middleton, Kelly Patton, William Pardue, Clement Fowler in "Spoon River Anthology" Below Left: Clement Fowler, Thomas James in "Summertree"

CLEMENT FOWLER

PAF's Adaptation

Spoon River Anthology

Sean Griffin, Lauren Levian
in "Aria da Capo"

Mary Lou Schertz, Roger Middleton
in "The Adam and Eve Diary"

211

PITTSBURGH PLAYHOUSE
Pittsburgh, Pa.
S. Joseph Nassif, Executive Producer
37th Season

Associate Producer, Ken Costigan; Assistant to Producer, Dianne Wrocklage; Business Manager, Richard Davis; Press, Will Disney; Production Manager, W. Valentine Mayer; Directors, Ken Costigan, S. Joseph Nassif, Tom Thomas, W. Valentine Mayer, Will Disney, Joseph Talarowski, William Glennon; Musical Director, James Reed Lawlor; Designers, Mary Ellen Kennedy, Leonard Feldman; Technical Director, Bob Kuiper; Costumes, Frank Childs; Sound, Jeff Weissert; Stage Managers, Sue Carroll, Rodney J. Loucks, William C. Thobaben

COMPANY

Nan Mason, Paul Greeno, George McGuire, Shirley Haviland, Wayne Darby Cook, Daniel Madia, Rich Cleary, Joy Ann Allen, Ted Kubiak, Leland Starnes, Mary Eythe Glick, Alan Clary, Helen V. Carson, David Novich, Marcia Collins, Harry McVeety, Peggy Gordon, Anthony Powell, David Tompkins, Robin Richards, Ken Costigan, Val Mayer, William Becze, Eddie Steinfeld, John Dorish, Joe Schad, Colette di Giosio, Susan Silversmith, Jonathan Margret, Vic Mangan, Herman Sadwick, George Lester, John-Lindsay McCormick, Jim Marcus, Helen Wayne Rauh, Lenora Nemetz, George Maguire, Jerry Morris, Robert Watts, Beth Austin, Enrico Bello, Wayne Claeren, Will Disney, Soralie Levin, Nina Kay Menning, William C. Thobaben, Ann Muffly, Lincoln Maazel, Lenora Nemetz, Barbara Ellenberger, Lee Ann Moffett, Coco Holette, Barney McKenna, Scott Davis, Dan Madia, Ed West, George Di Cenzo, Lynn George, Hal Robinson, John Remme, Betty Aberlin, Jim Horne.

PRODUCTIONS

"Your Own Thing," "Everthing in the Garden," "Room Service," "No Strings," "Catch Me if You Can," "The Hostage," "Luv," "Guys and Dolls."

Guild Photos

Right: Geoff Garland, Ann Muffly in 'The Hostage' Top: George DiCenzo, Ken Costigan in 'Luv'

Nan Mason, Paul Greeno in 'Your Own Thing'

Eddie Steinfeld, Jimmy Marcus, Ken Costigan in 'Room Service'

PLAYHOUSE IN THE PARK
Cincinnati, Ohio
Word Baker, Director
April 9, 1970 through May 31, 1971

Company Manager, Dan Early; Press, Patricia Gerhardt, Ike Feather, M. J. Boyer; General Manager, William Craver; Stage Manager, Sherman F. Warner; Directors, Word Baker, Jeff Blechner, Dan Early, Michael Flanagan, Brooks Jones, Eugene Lesser, Brian Murray, Anthony Perkins, Marc Primus, Moni Yakim; Sets, Jay Depenbrock, Holly Haas Donaldson, Tom Oldendick, Robert V. Taylor, Ed Wittstein, Stuart Wurtzel; Costumes, Patrizia von Bradenstein, Galey Summers, Annie Warner; Lighting, Leo Bonamy, Jay Depenbrock, Phillip Price, Owen Ryan; Props, Tom Oldendick; Casting, Michael Flanagan

COMPANY

George Addis, Afolabi Ajayi, David Ault, George Ball, Donna Barry, Tom Belleville, Paul Benedict, Tom Berns, Ronald Bishop, Roscoe Lee Browne, Amanda Bruce, Cecil Cabot, Madelyn Cain, Carolyn Coates, Helmar Cooper, Bill Copeland, J. T. Cromwell, Leora Dana, Anita Dangler, Diane Danzi, Roger DeKoven, Roni Dengel, Martin DiMartino, Alma Durand, Laura Esterman, Patricia Feldman, Jack Fletcher, Don Gantry, Candide Lee Gauger, Garry George, John Glover, Karen Grassle, Jack Gwillim, William Hansen, Susan Harting, Little Joe Heideman, Lon Heineman, Leonard Hicks, Denny Horton, David Huffman, Ken Jenkins, Daniel Landis, Jim Leahly, Gilbert Lewis, David Little, Sun Luck, Leopoldo Mandeville, Kevin Mathews, Bill McClaren, Barney McFadden, DeAnn Mears, Eda Reiss Merin, Mary Lynn Metton, Paul Milikin, Harold Miller, Barbara Montgomery, Bill Moor, Per Neuman, Tom Neuman, Leonard Norris, Gary O'Dell, Don Oliver, Richard Ooms, Bernie Passeltiner, Lisa Petlett, Roddy Quinn, Charlotte Rae, Frank Raiter, Lester Rawlins, Betty Rhodes, Gil Rogers, Ed Rombola, Beth Rosenberg, Gastone Rossilh, Sarallen, Pamela Simpson, Betty Sinclair, Steve Skiles, Jeff van Sluys, Tonia Smith, Howard L. Sponseller, Jr., Robert Stocking, Michael Stoddard, James Lee Strong, Patrick Tovatt, John Towey, Barbette Tweed, Cicely Tyson, Fran Uditsky, James Valentine, Jewel Walker, Anitra Walsh, Cecilia Ward, Marlene Warfield, Walt Weidenbacker, Harry Weingartner, Grenna Whitaker, Larry White, James Wigfall, Ian Wilder, David Wiles, Stan Wilson, Beatrice Winde, Bernard Wurger

PRODUCTIONS

"Pygmalion," "Off-Off-Broadway Season," "Ardele," "Many Happy Returns, A Review of Revues," "Come Back, Little Sheba," "He Who Gets Slapped," "Tobacco Road," "The Blacks," "As You Like It," "Jacques Brel Is Alive and Well...," "Angel Street," "Slow Dance on the Killing Ground'

Walt Burton Photos

Top Right: Roni Dengel, Bill Moor in 'Angel Street' Below: 'Many Happy Returns--A Review of Revues'

Gastone Rosselli, Gary George, George Addis, Richard Ooms in 'As You Like It'

Leora Dana in 'Tobacco Road'

REPERTORY THEATRE NEW ORLEANS
New Orleans, La.
June Havoc, Artistic Director
Nov. 19, 1970 through Apr. 25, 1971

General Manager, James Bernard; Sets, Ashton Smith; Costumes, Frank Bennett; Technical Director, Tom Saunders; Stage Managers, William Dolive, Mitchell Edmonds, Ray Atherton, Gerald McRaney; Directors, June Havoc, Wendell Phillips, Maurice Kowaleski

COMPANY

June Havoc, Michael Ebert, Sandra Seacat, Elaine Kerr, Gerald McRaney, Jan Buttram, Patsi Bertucci, Frank Bennett, Blair Ziegler, George Taylor, Wendell K. Phillips, Fred Chappell, Sylvia Kuumba Williams, Marya Marlowe, Linda Cook, Christian Grant, Timothy Meyers, Paul Bernard, Rodney Robinson, Harold Marchand, The Pineapple Kids, Leif Anderson, Joan McCrae, Mary Sauves, Teresa Kelly, Gerald Wilson, James Mapes

PRODUCTIONS

"The Skin of Our Teeth," "Angel Street," "The Elinor Glyn Liquid Memorial Love Regatta," "The Burd," "As You Like It," "Androcles and the Lion," "The Stolen Prince," "Pinocchio"

Left: June Havoc in "The Skin of Our Teeth"

"Love Regatta" company: front: Ann Buckholtz, Mel Marvin, June Havoc, Tom Buckholtz, Ashton Smith second row: Timothy Meyers, Leif Anderson, Jan Buttram back row: Frank Bennett, Marcus Baynes, Bill McCarthy, Bayne Keenan, Tommy Woodin

SEATTLE REPERTORY THEATRE
Seattle, Washington
W. Duncan Ross, Artistic Director
Oct. 21, 1970 through Apr. 18, 1971

Producing Director, Peter Donnelly; Guest Directors, Arne Zaslove, Nagle Jackson, Robert Loper, Israel Hicks; Sets, Jason Phillips; Costumes, Ritchie M. Spencer, James Crider; Lighting, Mark S. Krause, William Mintzer, Steven A. Maze; Technical Director, Floyd Hart; Stage Manager, John Page Blakemore; Press, Shirley Dennis

COMPANY

Sian Barbara Allen, John Aylward, Hopeton Bonar, Clayton Corzatte, Ted D'Arms, Margaret Hilton, John Kauffman, Robert Loper, Anne Murray, Gary Reineke, Randall Rickman, Marc Singer, Jeffrey Tambor, Christopher Bailey, Robert Cornthwaite, T. J. Escott, Allan Hunt, Garrett Myles, John Oldham, Stephen Parr, Tom Toner

GUEST ARTISTS: Richard Chamberlain, Douglass Watson, Manu Tupou, Geraldine Court, Michael O'Sullivan, Joan White, Maureen O'Sullivan, Albert Ottenheimer, Eve Roberts

PRODUCTIONS

"Richard II," "Indians," "A Flea in Her Ear," "The Miser," "Hay Fever," "The Price," "Happy Ending"

"Day of Absence" with Gerry Black, Joe Fields, Gus Fleming, Ron Glass, Hilda Haynes, Glenn Johnson, Hazel Medina, Joseph Mydell, Beatrice Winde

CameraCraft Photos

Top left: (C) Gerald Henry, Douglass Watson in "Indians" Below: Ted D'Arms, Clayton Corzatte, Jeffrey Tambor, Richard Chamberlain in "Richard II"

Randall Rickman, Anne Murray, Robert Loper, Clayton Corzatte in "A Flea in Her Ear"

Joan White, Michael O'Sullivan in "The Miser" Above: Hilda Haynes, Ron Glass, Joe Fields, Beatrice Winde in "Happy Ending"

STAGE/WEST
West Springfield, Mass.
Stephen E. Hays, Producing Director
Nov. 14, 1970 through Apr. 4, 1971

Artistic Director, John Ulmer; Sets, Robert Federico, Richard Blair, William Hatch; Stage Manager, William Guild; Sales Promotion, Wilma Barrows

COMPANY

Armande Assante, Carole Couche, Peter Blaxill, Hannah Brandon, Max Gulack, Jerry Hardin, Dianne Hill, Leon Stevens, Eric Taveres, Vinnie Holman

PRODUCTIONS

"Hamlet," "Lovers," "Light Up the Sky," "Tartuffe," "The Price," "A Thousand Clowns"

Pecum Photos

Right: Leon B. Stevens, Jerry Hardin in "The Price"

Max Gulack, Dianne Hill, Hannah Brandon, Armand Assante, Vinnie Holman, Jerry Hardin, Eric Tavaris (front) in "Tartuffe"

STUDIO ARENA THEATRE
Buffalo, N.Y.
Neal Du Brock, Executive Producer
Sept. 29, 1970 through May 30, 1971

General Manager, Robert Tolan; Assistant Director, Kathryn Kingdon; Press, Blossom Cohan; William E. Lurie, Business Manager; Administrative Assistant, James Payne; Associate Director, Warren Enters; Director Emeritus, Jane Keeler; School Director, Norman Sandler; Stage Managers, Ingrid von Wellesheim Cantarella, Richard Mueller; Technical Directors, Harold Head, Peter Politanoff; Settings and Costumes, John Wright Stevens, Stephen J. Hendrickson, Peter Harvey, Larry Aumen, Duane Andersen, Douglas Higgins, Carrie F. Robbins, Les Lawrence, Timothy Miller, Douglas Lebrecht; Lighting, David Zierk; Directors, Neal Du-Brock, Clarke Gordon, Moni Yakim, Warren Enters, Louis Criss, Chuck Gnys, Don Price.

PRODUCTIONS AND CASTS

"DAMES AT SEA" with Brenda Broome, Richard Balin, Tommy Breslin, Jerry Grant, Corinne Kason, Page Miller

World Premiere of "SCENES FROM AMERICAN LIFE" by A. R. Gurney, Jr. with Bill Abrams, Terry Burns, Nancy Donohue, Robert Einenkel, Jane Hallaren, Roy London, Caroline McWilliams, Steve Nelson, Patricia O'Connell

World Premiere of "THE SURVIVAL OF ST. JOAN" (Book and Lyrics, James Lineberger; Music, Hand and Gary Ruffin) with F. Murray Abraham, Bill Braden, Mary Carter, Tom Carter, John A. Coe, Gretchen Corbett, Patrick Ford, Judith Granite, Peter Lazer, Dennis Lipscomb, Mack McMack, George Pentecost, Janet Sarno, Julia Willis

"THE PRICE" with Jack Gilford, Shepperd Strudwick, Richard McKenzie, Eve Collyer

"L.A. UNDER SIEGE" with Cathryn Damon, Bill Moor, Janet Dowd, Michael (M.P.) Murphy, Trinity Thompson, Tom Rosqui, Christine Joyce, Peter Gorwin

"JACQUES BREL IS ALIVE AND WELL AND LIVING PARIS" with Stan Porter, Henrietta Valor, George Lee Andrews, Fran Uditsky

"OTHELLO" with Clebert Ford, Nicholas Kepros, Erika A. Slezak, Bryan Hull, Carol Mayo Jenkins, Stephen Keep, John McMurtry, Robert Patterson, Tom V. V. Tammi, Frederic Warriner, Nancy Zala, David Zirlin

"THE EFFECT OF GAMMA RAYS ON MAN-In-THE-MOON MARIGOLDS" with Jo Van Fleet, Kathryn Baumann, Pamela Kingsley, Elizabeth Sanders, Ethel Woodruff

World Premiere of "THE NEPHEW" by James Purdy with James Patterson, Wallace Rooney, Margaret Brewster, Margaret Hamilton, Mary Bell, Laurinda Barrett, Barbara Sharpe, Spencer Davis, Page Johnson, Roger DeKoven, Sally Rubin

"SCUBA DUBA" with F. Murray Abraham, Peter DeMaio, Clarke Gordon, Paul Knowles, Eve McVeagh, Tom Mafdirosian, John Newton, Elizabeth Perry, Kelly Swartz, K. C. Townsend, James Wigfall

"INDIANS" with Stan Porter, Alan Mixon, Robert Darnell, Leslie Woolf, Muni Seroff, Jack Axelrod, Mel Haynes, Peter H. Clune, Alex Czernikow, Larry Manning, Roger Miller, Mike Nelson, J. R. Marks, Kelly Karson, K. Lype O'Dell, Betty Lutes, Justine Surbone, Raphael Triana, Robert Shea, John Cassese, Barry Douglas, Peter Gatto, Ric Cane

"The Doctor in spite of Himself," "Aladdin," "The Pied Piper of Hamlin"

Greenberg-May Photos

Top Right: Jo Van Fleet in "The Effect of Gamma Rays on Man-in-the-moon Marigolds"
Below: Shepperd Strudwick, Jack Gilford, Richard McKenzie in "The Price"

Paul Knowles, James Wigfall, F. Murray Abraham in "Scuba Duba"

SYRACUSE REPERTORY THEATRE
Syracuse, N. Y.
Rex Henriot, Managing Director
March 5 through May 9, 1971

Artistic Director, G. F. Reidenbaugh; Acting Artistic Director, Leonard Dryansky; Business Manager, Walter Innes; Press, Kittie Sine; Sets, Leonard Dryansky, Robert Lewis Smith; Lighting Robert Alexander; Costumes, Richard Hieronymus; Technical Director, Robert Lewis Smith; Stage Manager, Diann Fay; Properties, Elizabeth Foster; Directors, Rex Henriot, Gary Gage

COMPANY

Samuel As-Said, Joe Bellomo, Clayton Corbin, Jack Collard, James Callahan, David Deardorff, Patrick Desmond, Richard Fancy, Gary Gage, Zoaunne LeRoy Henriot, Joyce Krempel, Valerie Lee, Sandy McCallum, Roger Miller, David Moody, Ron Prather, Gerald Richards, Victor Raider-Wexler, James Wilcher, John Thomas Waite

PRODUCTIONS

"The Fantasticks," "The Indians," "The Time of Your Life," "The Tavern," "Room Service'

Rick Graves Photos

Left: Gerald Richards in "Indians"

**Ron Prather
in "The Fantasticks"**

**Sandy McCallum, James Callahan,
Jack Collard in "Room Service"**

THEATRE COMPANY OF BOSTON
Boston, Mass.
David Wheeler, Artistic Director
Feb. 10 through Apr. 4, 1971

Producer, Sara O'Connor, Production Manager, Helaine Witkind; Press, Bonnie Jacob; Directors, Paul Benedict, David Wheeler, Designers, Roy Cato, Sr., John Thornton; Costumes, Lewis D. Rampino; Lighting, John R. Fishback; Stage Manager, Helaine Witkind; Technical Directors, Gary Casarella, Gary W. Miller

COMPANY

Richard Allert, Terence Blackburn, Larry Bryggman, Robert Collinge, Jan Egleson, Stefan Fischer, Marc Frasier, Lee Goncharoff, Max Gulack, Lance Hendriksen, Leslie Hurley, Paul Henry Itkin, Brent Jennings, Allan Johnson, Gustave Johnson, Andreas Katsulas, Lee Kissman, David Kneuss, Josephine Lane, Forrest Logan, Sumner McClain, Carolyn Pickman, Catherine Sella, James Spruill, William Young, James R. Zepp, Mindy Zepp

PRODUCTIONS

"Landscape," "Silence," "La Turista," "Saved," "The Burghers of Calais'

William L. Smith Photos

Right: Brent Jennings, Leslie Hurley, James Spruill, Forrest Logan in "The Burghers of Calais" Below Left: Roberta Collinge, Lee Kissman, William Young, Lee Goncharoff in "La Turista"

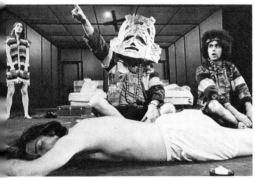

James Spruill, Catherine Sella, Roberta Collinge in "The Burghers of Calais"

Roberta Collinge, Lance Henriksen in "Saved"

THEATRE OF THE LIVING ARTS
Philadelphia, Pa.
Samuel Rulon, Manager
March 19 through May 31, 1971

General Manager, Marvin Krauss; Company Manager, Joe Turowsky; Press, Stan Hurwitz, Max Eisen; Sets and Costumes, Alan Kimmel; Stage Manager, Suzanne Egan

PRODUCTION AND CAST

"YOU'RE A GOOD MAN, CHARLIE BROWN" with Ann Hodapp, Janice Lorri, Peter Platten, Don Potter, Jim Ricketts, George Ryland

Right: Janice Lorri, Don Potter in "You're a Good Man, Charlie Brown"

Jim Ricketts, Don Porter, Janice Lorri, George Ryland, Ann Hodapp, Peter Platten in "You're a Good Man, Charlie Brown"

TRINITY SQUARE REPERTORY COMPANY
Providence, R. I.
Adrian Hall, Artistic Director
Oct. 14, 1970 through May 8, 1971

Administrative Director, Marion Simon; General Manager, Lamont E. Smith; Press, David Wynne; Musical Director, Richard Cumming; Sets, Eugene Lee, Robert D. Soule; Lighting, Roger Morgan; Costumes, John Lehmeyer, Franne Newman; Stage Managers; Franklin Keyser, Robert Applegarth, William Radka, Bree Cavazos; Directors, Adrian Hall, Philip Minor, Wayne Carson, William Cain

COMPANY

Leta Anderson, Beatrice Ballance, Ruth Benson, Robert Black, William Cain, Michael Champagne, Robert J. Colonna, Timothy Crowe, William Damkoehler, David Davies, Dortha Duckworth, James Eichelberger, James Gallery, Ed Hall, Richard Jenkins, David C. Jones, Richard Kavanaugh, David Kennett, Jon Kimball, Richard Kneeland, Marguerite Lenert, Howard London, Mina Manente, George Martin, Thomas Mason, Barbara Meek, Marian Mercer, Martin Molson, Elizabeth Moore, Barbara Orson, Edie Pool, Donald Somers, Jill Tanner, Cynthia Wells, Joanna Williams

PRODUCTIONS

"You Can't Take It with You," "Son of Man and the Family" (Premiere), "Little Murders," "The Taming of the Shrew," "Adaptation/Next," "Love for Love," "The Good and Bad Times of Cady Francis McCullum and Friends" (Premiere), "Threepenny Opera," "Harvey"

* Still playing May 31, 1971.

† Succeeded by: 1. Michael Price, 2. J. M. Jonas

William L. Smith Photos

Top Right: (C) Ed Hall, Marian Mercer, Richard Kneeland in "The Good and Bad Times of Cady Francis McCullum and Friends" Below: "Son of Man and the Family"

Cynthia Wells, George Martin
in "Love for Love"

Robert J. Colonna, Barbara Orson in "You Can't Take It With You" Above: William Cain, Marian Mercer in "Taming of the Shrew"

WASHINGTON THEATER CLUB
Washington, D. C.
Hazel H. Wentworth, Executive Director
June 3, 1970 through May 30, 1971
Tenth Season

Artistic Director, Davey Marlin-Jones; Managing Director, Bill Walton; Press, Leo Sullivan, Lillian Miller; Manager, Bryan E. Clark; Designer, James Parker; Technical Director, Steve Ayers; Stage Manager, Robert H. Leonard; Costumes, Joyce Wilsie; Sound, F. Kieran Killiam

PRODUCTIONS AND CASTS

"EXIT THE KING" with Ned Beatty, Anne Chodoff, Howard Jerome, Bob Spencer, Trinity Thompson, Marcia Wood

"BEFORE YOU GO" with Ralph Strait and Marcia Wood

"THE BLACK EXPERIENCE COMPANY": Damon W. Brazwell, Hattie Winston, Dave Connel, J. Herbert Herr, Buddy Butler

"THE EFFECT OF GAMMA RAYS ON MAN-IN-THE-MOON MARIGOLDS" with Helena Carroll, Fran Brill, Marie Carroll, Francesca James, Patricia Pearcy

"THE LAST SWEET DAYS OF ISAAC" with Christian Grey, Carole Prandis, Michael Forella, Delores St. Amand, Jamil Zakkai

"A FIFTH OF SPREAD EAGLE" with Michael Forella, Brendan Hanlon, Mickey Hartnett, Delores St. Amand, Laura Waterbury, Jamil Zakkai

"LITTLE BOXES" with Ronald Dawson, Pat Gebhard, Dorothea Hammond, Brendan Hanlon, J. S. Johnson, Ruth Maynard, Margaret Winn, Jamil Zakkai, Suzanne Zenor

"THE WEB AND THE ROCK" with Delores Sutton, Stephen McHattie, Michael Forella, Jamil Zakkai, Margaret Winn, Ruth Maynard, J. S. Johnson, Suzanne Zenor

"THE CHINESE" AND "DR. FISH" with Marie Carroll, Michael Forella, Sally-Jane Heit, J. S. Johnson, Suzanne Zenor

"FATHER'S DAY"

Left: J. S. Johnson, Marie Carroll, Michael Forella, Sally-Jane Heit in 'Dr. Fish' Top: Michael Forella, Mickey Hartnett in 'A Fifth of Spread Eagle'

Ruth Maynard, Brendan Hanlon in 'Coffee Lace'

Helena Carroll, Fran Brill in 'The Effect of Gamma Rays on Man-in-the-Moon Marigolds'

YALE REPERTORY THEATRE
New Haven, Connecticut
Robert Brustein, Artistic Director
Oct. 8, 1970 through June 5, 1971

Managing Director, Thomas B. Burrows, Jr.; Press, Howard Rogut; Directors, Larry Arrick, Robert Brustein, Alvin Epstein, Tom Haas, Michael Posnick; Designers, Santo Loquasto, Edgar Swift, Ariel Ballif, William B. Warfel, Steven Rubin, Dennis G. Daluiso, Leo Yoshimura, Michael Yeargan, Kenneth Thompson, Paul Butler, Robert W. Scheeler; Stage Managers, Frank S. Torok, Carol M. Waaser

COMPANY

David Ackroyd, Peter Covette, Barbara Damashek, Carmen DeLavallade, Robert Drivas, Alvin Epstein, Jeremy Geidt, Kenneth Haigh, James Naughton, Elizabeth Parrish, Louis Plante, Lee Richardson, Charles Turner, Stephen Van Benschoten, Henry Winkler, James Brick, Lisa Carling, Lydia Fisher, Maxine Lieberman

PRODUCTIONS

"The Revenger's Tragedy," "Macbeth," "Woyzeck," "Play," "The Seven Deadly Sins" Premieres of "Gimpel the Fool" by Isaac Bashevis Singer, adapted by Larry Arrick; "Saint Julian the Hospitaler" by Gustave Flaubert, adapted by Kenneth Cavander; "Olympian Games" written and composed by Kenneth Cavander and Barbara Damashek, based on Ovid's "Metamorphoses"; "Where Has Tommy Flowers Gone?" by Terrence McNally; "The Little Mahagonny" by Bertolt Brecht and Kurt Weill

Michael Shane Photos

Left: Louis Plante, Carmen DeLavallade, Jeremy Geidt, Henry Winkler, David Ackroyd, Elizabeth Parris in 'Olympian Games' Top: Stephen Van Benschoten, Robert Drivas in 'Where Has Tommy Flowers Gone?'

Theodore Ravinett, Maxine Lieberman, William Duvall, Stephanie Cotsirilos in 'The Little Mahagonny'

Alvin Epstein in 'Gimpel the Fool'

PULITZER PRIZE PLAYS

1918-Why Marry?, 1919-No award, 1920-Beyond the Horizon, 1921-Miss Lulu Bett, 1922-Anna Christie
1923-Icebound, 1924-Hell-Bent Fer Heaven, 1925-They Knew What They Wanted, 1926-Craig's Wife, 1927-In Abraham's Bosom, 1928-Strange Interlude, 1929-Street Scene, 1930-The Green Pastures, 1931-Alison's House, 1932-Of Thee I Sing, 1933-Both Your Houses, 1934-Men in White, 1935-The Old Maid, 1936-Idiot's Delight, 1937-You Can't Take It With You, 1938-Our Town, 1939-Abe Lincoln in Illinois, 1940-The Time of Your Life, 1941-There Shall Be No Night, 1942-No award, 1943-The Skin of Our Teeth, 1944-No award, 1945-Harvey, 1946-State of the Union, 1947-No award, 1948-A Streetcar Named Desire, 1949-Death of a Salesman, 1950-South Pacific, 1951-No award, 1952-The Shrike, 1953-Picnic, 1954-The Teahouse of the August Moon, 1955-Cat on a Hot Tin Roof, 1956-The Diary of Anne Frank, 1957-Long Day's Journey into Night, 1958-Look Homeward, Angel, 1959-J. B., 1960-Fiorello!, 1961-All the Way Home, 1962-How to Succeed in Business without Really Trying, 1963-No award, 1964-No award, 1965-The Subject Was Roses, 1966-No award, 1967-A Delicate Balance, 1968-No award, 1969-The Great White Hope, 1970-No Place to Be Somebody, 1971-The Effect of Gamma Rays on Man-in-the-Moon Marigolds

NEW YORK DRAMA CRITICS CIRCLE AWARD PLAYS

1936-Winterset, 1937-High Tor, 1938-Of Mice and Men, Shadow and Substance, 1939-The White Steed, 1940-The Time of Your Life, 1941-Watch on the Rhine, The Corn is Green, 1942-Blithe Spirit, 1943-The Patriots, 1944-Jacobowsky and the Colonel, 1945-The Glass Menagerie, 1946-Carousel, 1947-All My Sons, No Exit, Brigadoon, 1948-A Streetcar Named Desire, The Winslow Boy, 1949-Death of a Salesman, The Madwoman of Chaillot, South Pacific, 1950-The Member of the Wedding, The Cocktail Party, The Consul, 1951-Darkness at Noon, The Lady's Not for Burning, Guys and Dolls, 1952-I Am a Camera, Venus Observed, Pal Joey, 1953-Picnic, The Love of Four Colonels, Wonderful Town, 1954-Teahouse of the August Moon, Ondine, The Golden Apple, 1955-Cat on a Hot Tin Roof, Witness for the Prosecution, The Saint of Bleecker Street, 1956-The Diary of Anne Frank, Tiger at the Gates, My Fair Lady, 1957-Long Day's Journey into Night, The Waltz of the Toreadors, The Most Happy Fella, 1958-Look Homeward Angel, Look Back in Anger, The Music Man, 1959-A Raisin in the Sun, The Visit, La Plume de Ma Tante, 1960-Toys in the Attic, Five Finger Exercise, Fiorello!, 1961-All the Way Home, A Taste of Honey, Carnival, 1962-Night of the Iguana, A Man for All Seasons, How to Succeed in Business without Really Trying, 1963-Who's Afraid of Virginia Woolf?, 1964-Luther, Hello, Dolly!, 1956-The Subject Was Roses, Fiddler on the Roof, 1966-The Persecution and Assassination of Marat as Performed by the Inmates of the Asylum of Charenton under the Direction of the Marquis de Sade, Man of La Mancha, 1967-The Homecoming, Cabaret, 1968-Rosencrantz and Guildenstern Are Dead, Your Own Thing, 1969-The Great White Hope, 1776, 1970-The Effect of Gamma Rays on Man-in-the-Moon Marigolds, Borstal Boy, Company, 1971-Home, Follies, The House of Blue Leaves

AMERICAN THEATRE WING
ANTOINETTE PERRY (TONY) AWARD PLAYS

1948-Mister Roberts, 1949-Death of a Salesman, Kiss Me, Kate, 1950-The Cocktail Party, South Pacific, 1951-The Rose Tattoo, Guys and Dolls, 1952-The Fourposter, The King and I, 1953-The Crucible, Wonderful Town, 1954-The Teahouse of the August Moon, Kismet, 1955-The Desperate Hours, The Pajama Game, 1956-The Diary of Anne Frank, Damn Yankees, 1957-Long Day's Journey into Night, My Fair Lady, 1958-Sunrise at Campobello, The Music Man, 1959-J. B., Redhead, 1960-The Miracle Worker, Fiorello tied with Sound of Music, 1961-Becket, Bye Bye Birdie, 1962-A Man for All Seasons, How to Succeed in Business without Really Trying, 1963-Who's Afraid of Virginia Woolf?, A Funny Thing Happened on the Way to the Forum, 1964-Luther, Hello, Dolly!, 1965-The Subject Was Roses, Fiddler on the Roof, 1966-The Persecution and Assassination of Marat as Performed by the Inmates of the Asylum of Charenton under the Direction of the Marquis de Sade, Man of La Mancha, 1967-The Homecoming, Cabaret, 1968-Rosencrantz and Guildenstern Are Dead, Hallelujah, Baby!, 1969- The Great White Hope, 1776, 1970-Child's Play, Applause, 1971-Sleuth, Company

PAUL ZINDEL
author of "The Effect of Gamma Rays on Man-in-the-moon Marigolds"
1971 Pulitzer Prize play

Anne Bancroft

Robert Goulet

Sandy Duncan

Charlton Heston

Rosemary Harri

PREVIOUS THEATRE WORLD AWARD WINNERS

1944-45: Betty Comden, Richard Davis, Richard Hart, Judy Holliday, Charles Lang, Bambi Linn, John Lund, Donald Murphy, Nancy Noland, Margaret Phillips, John Raitt

1945-46: Barbara Bel Geddes, Marlon Brando, Bill Callahan, Wendell Corey, Paul Douglas, Mary James, Burt Lancaster, Patricia Marshall, Beatrice Pearson

1946-47: Keith Andes, Marion Bell, Peter Cookson, Ann Crowley, Ellan Henley, John Jordan, George Keane, Dorothea MacFarland, James Mitchell, Patricia Neal, David Wayne

1947-48: Valerie Bettis, Edward Bryce, Whitfield Connor, Mark Dawson, June Lockhart, Estelle Loring, Peggy Maley, Ralph Meeker, Meg Mundy, Douglas Watson, James Whitmore, Patrice Wymore

1948-49: Tod Andrews, Doe Avedon, Jean Carson, Carol Channing, Richard Derr, Julie Harris, Mary McCarty, Allyn Ann McLerie, Cameron Mitchell, Gene Nelson, Byron Palmer, Bob Scheerer

1949-50: Nancy Andrews, Phil Arthur, Barbara Brady, Lydia Clarke, Priscilla Gillette, Don Hanmer, Marcia Henderson, Charlton Heston, Rick Jason, Grace Kelly, Charles Nolte, Roger Price

1950-51: Barbara Ashley, Isabel Bigley, Martin Brooks, Richard Burton, James Daly, Cloris Leachman, Russell Nype, Jack Palance, William Smithers, Maureen Stapleton, Marcia Van Dyke, Eli Wallach

1951-52: Tony Bavaar, Patricia Benoit, Peter Conlow, Virginia de Luce, Ronny Graham, Audrey Hepburn, Diana Herbert, Conrad Janis, Dick Kallman, Charles Proctor, Eric Sinclair, Kim Stanley, Marian Winters, Helen Wood

1952-53: Edie Adams, Rosemary Harris, Eileen Heckart, Peter Kelley, John Kerr, Richard Kiley, Gloria Marlowe, Penelope Munday, Paul Newman, Sheree North, Geraldine Page, John Stewart, Ray Stricklyn, Gwen Verdon

1953-54: Orson Bean, Harry Belafonte, James Dean, Joan Diener, Ben Gazzara, Carol Haney, Jonathan Lucas, Kay Medford, Scott Merrill, Elizabeth Montgomery, Leo Penn, Eva Marie Saint

1954-55: Julie Andrews, Jacqueline Brookes, Shirl Conway, Barbara Cook, David Daniels, Mary Fickett, Page Johnson, Loretta Leversee, Jack Lord, Dennis Patrick, Anthony Perkins, Christopher Plummer

1955-56: Diane Cilento, Dick Davalos, Anthony Franciosa, Andy Griffith, Laurence Harvey, David Hedison, Earle Hyman, Susan Johnson, John Michael King, Jayne Mansfield, Sarah Marshall, Gaby Rodgers, Susan Strasberg, Fritz Weaver

1956-57: Peggy Cass, Sydney Chaplin, Sylvia Daneel, Bradford Dillman, Peter Donat, George Grizzard, Carol Lynley, Peter Palmer, Jason Robards, Cliff Robertson, Pippa Scott, Inga Swenson

1957-58: Anne Bancroft, Warren Berlinger, Colleen Dewhurst, Richard Easton, Timmy Everett, Eddie Hodges, Joan Hovis, Carol Lawrence, Jacqueline McKeever, Wynne Miller, Robert Morse, George C. Scott

1958-59: Lou Antonio, Ina Balin, Richard Cross, Tammy Grimes, Larry Hagman, Dolores Hart, Roger Mollien, France Nuyen, Susan Oliver, Ben Piazza, Paul Roebling, William Shatner, Pat Suzuki, Rip Torn

1959-60: Warren Beatty, Eileen Brennan, Carol Burnett, Patty Duke, Jane Fonda, Anita Gillette, Elisa Loti, Donald Madden, George Maharis, John McMartin, Lauri Peters, Dick Van Dyke

1960-61: Joyce Bulifant, Dennis Cooney, Nancy Dussault, Robert Goulet, Joan Hackett, June Harding, Ron Husmann, James MacArthur, Bruce Yarnell

1961-62: Elizabeth Ashley, Keith Baxter, Peter Fonda, Don Galloway, Sean Garrison, Barbara Harris, James Earl Jones Janet Margolin, Karen Morrow, Robert Redford, John Stride, Brenda Vaccaro

1962-63: Alan Arkin, Stuart Damon, Melinda Dillon, Robert Drivas, Bob Gentry, Dorothy Loudon, Brandon Maggart, Julienne Marie, Liza Minnelli, Estelle Parsons, Diana Sands, Swen Swenson

1963-64: Alan Alda, Gloria Bleezarde, Imelda De Martin, Claude Giraud, Ketty Lester, Barbara Loden, Lawrence Pressman, Gilbert Price, Philip Proctor, John Tracy, Jennifer West

1964-65: Carolyn Coates, Joyce Jillson, Linda Lavin, Luba Lisa, Michael O'Sullivan, Joanna Pettet, Beah Richards, Jaime Sanchez, Victor Spinetti, Nicholas Surovy, Robert Walker, Clarence Williams III

1965-66: Zoe Caldwell, David Carradine, John Cullum, John Davidson, Faye Dunaway, Gloria Foster, Robert Hooks, Jerry Lanning, Richard Mulligan, April Shawhan, Sandra Smith, Lesley Ann Warren

1966-67: Bonnie Bedelia, Richard Benjamin, Dustin Hoffman, Terry Kiser, Reva Rose, Robert Salvio, Sheila Smith, Connie Stevens, Pamela Tiffin, Leslie Uggams, Jon Voight, Christopher Walken

1967-68: Pamela Burrell, Sandy Duncan, Julie Gregg, Bernadette Peters, Alice Playten, Brenda Smiley, David Birney, Jordan Christopher, Jack Crowder, Stephen Joyce, Mike Rupert, Rusty Thacker

1968-69: Jane Alexander, David Cryer, Ed Evanko, Blythe Danner, Ken Howard, Lauren Jones, Ron Leibman, Marian Mercer, Jill O'Hara, Ron O'Neal, Al Pacino, Marlene Warfield

1969-70: Susan Browning, Donny Burks, Catherine Burns, Len Cariou, Bonnie Franklin, David Holliday, Katharine Houghton, Melba Moore, David Rounds, Lewis J. Stadlen, Kristoffer Tabori, Fredricka Weber

Paul Newman

Audrey Hepburn

Eli Wallach

Carol Lawrence

Fritz Weaver

1971 THEATRE WORLD AWARD WINNERS

CLIFTON DAVIS
of "Do It Again"

JULIE GARFIELD
of "Uncle Vanya"

MARTHA HENRY
of Lincoln Center Repertory Company

MICHAEL DOUGLAS
of "Pinkville"

227

JAMES NAUGHTON
of "Long Day's Journey into Night"

TRICIA O'NEIL
of "Two by Two"

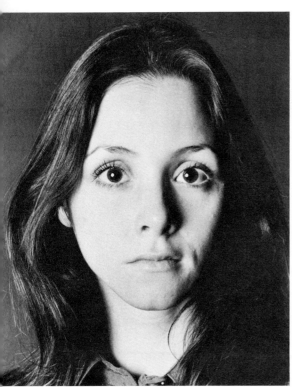

AYN RUYMEN
of "The Gingerbread Lady"

KIPP OSBORNE
of "Butterflies Are Free'

ROGER RATHBURN
of "No, No, Nanette"

Zodiac Photo

JENNIFER SALT
of "Father's Day"

JOAN VAN ARK
of "School for Wives"

WALTER WILLISON
of "Two by Two"

1971 THEATRE WORLD AWARD PARTY

Van Williams Photos

Roger Rathburn, Carol Channing,
and below with Tricia O'Neil

Julie Garfield, Carol Channing,
below: Martha Henry, David Birney

Kipp Osborne, Carol Channing,
and below with Ayn Ruymen

Boni Enten, Kristoffer Tabori,
Carol Channing, Alice Playten

Brenda Vaccaro, Maureen Stapleton,
James Coco

Michael Douglas, Carol Channing Below: Susan
Browning, Walter Willison, Victor Spinetti

James Naughton, Carol Channing Below: James
Coco, David Cryer, James Naughton, Bill Barnes

Sheila Smith, Walter Willison,
Ed Evanko

Igors Gavon, Frances Keys, Jacques
Crampon, Mary Ann Niles

•Bill Abrams   Maureen Anderman   Jere Admire   Nancy Andrews   Robert Anthony

BIOGRAPHIES

OF THIS SEASON'S CAST

AARON, JACK. Born May 1, 1933 in NYC. Attended Hunter Col., Actors Workshop. Off-Bdwy in "Swim Low Little Goldfish," "Journey of the Fifth Horse," "The Nest," "One Flew Over the Cuckoo's Nest."

ABRAHAM, F. MURRAY. Born Oct. 24, 1939 in Pittsburgh. Attended U. Tex. Off-Bdwy bow 1967 in "The Fantasticks," followed by "An Opening in the Trees," "The Fourteenth Dictator," "Young Abe Lincoln," "Tonight in Living Color," "Adaptation," "Survival of St. Joan." Bdwy debut in "The Man In The Glass Booth" (1968).

ABRAMS, BILL. Born Aug. 25, 1943 in Boone, NC. Graduate St. Andrews, Yale. NY debut Off-Bdwy in "Of Thee I Sing," followed by "This Is the Rill Speaking," "Now Is the Time for All Good Men."

ACKERMAN, LONI ZOE. Born Apr. 10, 1949 in NYC. Attended New School. Bdwy debut 1968 in "George M!", followed by "Dames at Sea" (OB), "No, No, Nanette."

ADAMS, MASON. Born Feb. 26, 1919 in NYC. Graduate U. Wisc. Neighborhood Playhouse. Has appeared in "Get Away, Old Man," "Public Relations," "Career Angel," "Violet," "A Shadow of My Enemy," "Tall Story," "Inquest," "Trial of Catonsville 9" (OB).

ADMIRE, JERE. Born Apr. 29 in Ft. Worth, Tex. Graduate TCU. Bdwy bow 1959 in "Greenwillow," followed by "Tenderloin," "Sail Away," "No Strings," "Here's Love," "Do I Hear A Waltz?," "Royal Hunt of the Sun," "Cabaret," OB in "On the Town," "Boys in the Band," "Steambath."

ALBRECHT, JOHANNA. Born July 30, 1940 in Mass. Graduate Smith Col. NY debut Off-Bdwy 1971 in "Six."

ALDREDGE, TOM. Born Feb. 28, 1928 in Dayton, O. Attended Dayton U., Goodman Theatre. Bdwy bow 1959 in "The Nervous Set," followed by "UTBU," "Slapstick Tragedy," "Everything In The Garden," "Indians," "Engagement Baby," "How the Other Half Loves," Off-Bdwy in "The Tempest," "Between Two Thieves," "Henry V," "The Premise," "Love's Labour's Lost," "Troilus and Cressida," "Butter and Egg Man," "Ergo," "Boys In The Band," "Twelfth Night," "Colette."

ALEXANDER, C. K. Born May 4, 1920 in Cairo, Egypt. Graduate American U. Bdwy debut 1946 in "Hidden Horizon," followed by "The Happy Time," "Flight into Egypt," "Mr. Pickwick," "Can Can," "Fanny," "The Matchmaker," "La Plume de Ma Tante," "Rhinoceros," "Carnival," "Tovarich," "The Dragon," "Corruption in the Palace of Justice" (OB), "Poor Bitos," "Ari."

ALLEN, MARC III. Born Mar. 3, 1943 in Los Angeles. Attended Mt. San Antonio Col. NY bow Off-Bdwy 1969 in "Your Own Thing," followed by "Promenade," "Journey of Snow White," Bdwy debut in "Look to the Lilies."

ALLEN, RAE. Born July 3, 1926 in Brooklyn. Attended Hunter College, AADA. Credits: "Where's Charley?," "Alive and Kicking," "Call Me Madam," "Pajama Game," "Damn Yankees," "Pictures In The Hallway" and "I Knock At the Door" (OB), "Oliver!," "Traveller Without Luggage," "On A Clear Day You Can See Forever," APA, "Henry IV" (CP) "Fiddler On The Roof," "And Miss Reardon Drinks A Little."

ALLINSON, MICHAEL. Born in London; attended Lausanne U, RADA. Bdwy bow 1960 in "My Fair Lady," followed by "Importance of Being Earnest" (OB), "Hostile Witness," "Come Live with Me," "Coco."

ALLSBROOK, BILL. Born May 21, 1945 in Roanoke Rapids, NC. Graduate Temple U. Bdwy bow 1968 in "Cabaret," followed by "Applause."

AMIC-ANGELO, ANDREW. Born Feb. 27, 1943 in Boston. Attended Leland Powers School. Appeared in "A View from the Bridge" (OB), Bdwy debut in "The Unknown Soldier and His Wife" (1967), "Skye" (OB).

ANANIA, JOHN. Born July 12, 1923 in Sicily. Attended HB Studio. Bdwy bow 1947 in "Sweethearts," followed by "Christine," "What A Killing" (OB), "Little Me," "Fly Blackbird" (OB), "Cafe Crown," "Skyscraper," "Breakfast at Tiffany's," "Golden Rainbow," "The Penny Wars," "Applause."

ANDERMAN, MAUREEN. Born Oct. 26, 1946 in Detroit. Graduate U Mich. Bdwy debut 1970 in Am. Shakespeare Festival's "Othello."

ANDERSON, JUDITH. Born in Adelaide, Aust., Feb. 10, 1898. NY debut 1923 in "Peter Weston," followed by "Cobra," "The Dove," "Strange Interlude," "As You Desire Me," "Firebird," "The Mask and the Face," "Come of Age," "The Old Maid," "Family Portrait," "Hamlet," "Macbeth," "The Three Sisters," "Medea," "Tower Beyond Tragedy," "John Brown's Body," "In the Summer House," "Chalk Garden," "Comes A Day," "Elizabeth the Queen" (CC'66), as Hamlet (1971).

ANDERSON, THOMAS. Born in Pasadena, Cal. Bdwy debut 1934 in "4 Saints in 3 Acts," followed by "Roll Sweet Chariot," "Cabin In The Sky," "Native Son," "Set My People Free," "How Long Till Summer," "A Hole In The Head," "The Great White Hope," "70, Girls, 70," Off-Bdwy: "Conquering Thursday," "The Peddler" and "The Dodo Bird."

ANDREWS, MARIE. Born in NYC. Graduate Queens Col., U Wisc. Debut Off-Bdwy 1954 in "The Way of the World," followed by "Thieves Carnival," "World of Sholom Aleichem," "Electra," "Agamemnon," "An Evening of Katherine Mansfield," Bdwy debut 1970 in "Les Blancs."

ANDREWS, NANCY. Born Dec. 16, 1924 in Minneapolis. Attended Pasadena Playhouse. Bdwy debut in "Hilarities," followed by "Touch and Go" for which she received a THEATRE WORLD Award, "Gentlemen Prefer Blondes," "Hazel Flagg," "Plain and Fancy," "Pipe Dream," "Juno," "Christine," "Flower Drum Song," "Little Me," "70 Girls 70," Off-Bdwy in "Threepenny Opera," "Tiger Rag," "Madame Aphrodite," "Say Nothing," "How Much, How Much?"

ANGELA, JUNE. Born Aug. 18, 1959 in NYC. Bdwy debut 1970 in "Lovely Ladies, Kind Gentlemen."

ANTHONY, ROBERT. Born May 10, 1941 in Newark, N.J. Attended Boston U, AADA. Off-Bdwy in "Jerico-Jim Crow," "Bugs and Veronica," "Dirty Old Man," "Hamlet" and "Othello" (CP), "Scuba Duba," Bdwy bow in "The Man in the Glass Booth" ('68), "Butterflies Are Free."

| Paulette Attie | Johnny Armen | Adrienne Barbeau | Luis Avalos | Yolande Bavan |

APLON, BORIS. Born July 14 in Chicago. Attended U. Chicago, Goodman Theatre. Off-Bdwy in "Makrapoulos Secret," "King of the Whole Damn World," at CC in "Carousel" and "Show Boat," on Bdwy in "Candide," "Anya," "Fiddler on the Roof."

ARLISS, DIMITRA. Born in Lorain, O. Attended Goodman Theatre. NY debut Off-Bdwy 1964 in "Trojan Women," followed by Bdwy bow in "Indians," "Antigone" (LC).

ARMEN, JOHNNY. Born Jan. 4, 1938 in NYC. Graduate Fordham U. Bdwy debut 1971 in "Lenny."

ARNOLD, JEANNE. Born July 30 in Berkeley, Calif. Graduate U. Cal. NY debut off Bdwy 1955 in "Threepenny Opera," followed by "Take Five," "Demi-Dozen," "Medium Rare," "Put It In Writing," on Bdwy in "The Happy Time," "Coco."

ARNOLD, MADISON. Born Feb. 7, 1935 in Allentown, Pa. Attended Columbia, U Vienna, U Berlin. Bdwy bow 1968 in "Man in the Glass Booth," OB in "Lower Depths," "Much Ado about Nothing," "The Gamblers," "The Marriage," "Macbeth" (CP), "Ride a Black Horse."

ASHER, JANE. Born Apr. 5, 1946 in London. Began career at 5. NY debut with Bristol Old Vic in "Romeo and Juliet" and "Measure for Measure" (CC'67), followed by "The Philanthropist."

ASTREDO, HUMBERT ALLEN. Born in San Francisco. Attended SFU. NY debut in "Arms and the Man" (OB'67), followed by "Fragments," Bway bow in "Les Blancs" ('70).

ATKINSON, DAVID. Born in Montreal, Oct. 20, 1921. Attended McGill U., Pasadena Playhouse. Credits: "Inside U.S.A.," "Girl In Pink Tights," "The Vamp," CC revivals of "Carousel," "Kiss Me, Kate," "Brigadoon," and "Annie Get Your Gun," "Man of LaMancha."

ATKINSON, MATTHEW. Born July 23, 1963 in NYC. Debut Off-Bdwy 1970 in "Rag Doll," followed by "Greenwillow" (ELT).

ATTIE, PAULETTE. Born Brooklyn, July 25, 1936. Graduate UCLA. NY debut OB 1964 in "La Vie Parisienne," followed by "The Bald Soprano," "The Old Maid and the Thief," "Diary of Adam and Eve," "Sensations."

ATTLE, JOHN C. Born in Tacoma, Wash. Graduate U. Wash. Bdwy bow 1964 in "Fiddler On The Roof," followed by "Jacques Brel Is Alive and Well and Living In Paris" (OB).

AUBERJONOIS, RENE. Born June 1, 1940 in NYC. Graduate Carnegie Inst. With LCRep in "A Cry of Players" and "King Lear," on Bdwy in "Fire," "Coco."

AVALOS, LUIS. Born Sept. 2, 1946 in Havana. Graduate NYU. Debut at CC in "Never Jam Today," followed by "Rules for the Running of Trains" (OB), and LC's "Camino Real," "Beggar on Horseback," "Good Woman of Setzuan."

AXELROD, JACK. Born Jan. 25, 1930 in Los Angeles. Graduate U Calif. Debut Off-Bdwy 1969 in "Macbeth," followed by "Gandhi."

BACALL, LAUREN. Born Sept 16, 1924 in NYC. Attended AADA. Bdwy debut 1942 in "Johnny 2 x 4," followed by "Goodbye Charlie," "Cactus Flower," "Applause."

BACKUS, RICHARD. Born Mar. 28, 1945 in Goffstown, NH. Harvard graduate. Bdwy debut 1971 in "Butterflies Are Free."

BAIN, CONRAD. Born Feb. 4, 1923 in Lethbridge, Can. Attended AADA. Credits: "Sixth Finger In A Five Finger Glove," "Candide," "Hot Spot," "Advise and Consent," "The Cuban Thing." Off-Bdwy: "The Makropoulous Secret," "The Queen and The Rebels," "Hogan's Goat," "The Kitchen," "Scuba Duba," "Nobody Hears A Broken Drum," "Steambath," "Play Strindberg" (LC).

BAKER, LENNY. Born Jan. 17, 1945 in Boston. Graduate Boston U. Bow Off-Bdwy 1969 in "Frank Gagliano's City Scene," followed by "The Year Boston Won The Pennant" (LC); "The Time of Your Life" (LC), "Summertree," "Early Morning," "Survival of St. Joan."

BALLANTYNE, PAUL. Born July 8, 1909 in Boorhead, Iowa. Among his many credits are "The Strong Are Lonely," "Brown Danube," "St. Joan," "Richard III," "The Enchanted" (OB), "Mary Stuart," "Elizabeth the Queen," "House of Atreus," "Arturo Ui," "School for Wives."

BARBEAU, ADRIENNE. Born June 11, 1945 in Sacramento, Cal. Attended Foothill Col. Bdwy debut 1968 in "Fiddler on the Roof," followed by "Stag Movie" (OB).

BARBOUR, THOMAS. Born July 25, 1921 in NYC. Graduate Princeton and Harvard. Credits: Off-Bdwy "Twelfth Night," "Merchant of Venice," "The Admirable Bashville," "River Line," "The Lady's Not For Burning," "The Enchanted," "Antony and Cleopatra," "The Saintliness of Margery Kemp," "Dr. Willy Nilly," "Under The Sycamore Tree," "Epitaph For George Dillon," "Thracian Horse," "Old Glory," "Sjt. Musgrave's Dance." Bdwy: "Portrait of A Queen," "The Great White Hope," "Scratch."

BARRETT, RAINA. Born Jan. 5, 1941 in Detroit. Graduate Ithaca Col. Debut 1968 Off-Bdwy in "Recess," followed by "Oh! Calcutta!"

BARRIE, BARBARA. Born May 23, 1931 in Chicago. Graduate U. Tex. Bdwy debut 1955 in "The Wooden Dish," followed by "Happily Never After," "Company." Off-Bdwy in "The Crucible," "The Beaux Stratagem," "Taming of The Shrew" and "All's Well That Ends Well" (CP), "Horseman, Pass by," "Twelfth Night" (CP).

BARRS, NORMAN. Born Nov. 6, 1917 in London. NY debut 1948 with Dublin Gate Co. in "The Old Lady Says No!" and "Where Stars Walk," followed by "Now I Lay Me Down To Sleep," "The Little Glass Clock," "The Apple Cart," "The Little Moon of Alban," "Kwamina," "Poor Bitos," "The Zulu and the Zayda," "Hostile Witness," "Loot," OB in "Little Boxes," "Saved," "Homecoming."

BARTENIEFF, GEORGE. Born Jan. 24, 1933 in Berlin. Bdwy bow 1947 in "The Whole World Over," followed by "Venus Is," "All's Well That Ends Well," "Walking To Waldheim" (OB), "Memorandum" (OB), "Quotations From Chairman Mao Tse-Tung," "Death of Bessie Smith," "Cop-Out," "The Increased Difficulty of Concentration" (LC), "Room Service," "Trelawny of The Wells" (OB).

BARTLETT, MICHAEL. Born Aug. 23, 1901 in North Oxford, Mass. Attended Princeton. Bdwy debut 1930 in "Through the Years," followed by "Three Waltzes," "Cat and the Fiddle," "School for Husbands," "Follies."

BARTOW, ARTHUR. Born June 15, 1935 in Cushing, Okla. Graduate U Okla. Bdwy debut 1964 in "Ben Franklin in Paris," followed OB by "Sensations," "Look Where I'm At".

BASSIE, JOAN. Born July 22, 1939 in Chicago. Attended RADA. NY debut 1964 in "Arms and the Man"(OB), followed by Bdwy bow 1967 in "The Imaginary Invalid" and "Tonight at 8:30," "Not Now, Darling."

BAVAN, YOLANDE. Born June 1, 1942 in Ceylon. Attended U. Colombo. NY debut 1964 in "A Midsummer Night's Dream" (CP), followed by Off-Bdwy's "Jonah," "House of Flowers," "Salvation," "Tarot," "Back Bog Beast Bait."

BAXTER, KEITH. Born Apr. 29, 1935 in Newport, Wales. Graduate RADA. Bdwy debut 1961 in "A Man for All Seasons" for which he received a THEATRE WORLD Award, followed by "The Affair," "Avanti," "Sleuth."

| Reathel Bean | Shirl Bernheim | Sidney Ben-Zali | Donna Olivia Black | Jay Bonnell |

BEAL, JOHN. Born Aug. 13, 1909 in Joplin, Mo. Graduate U. Pa. Many credits include "Wild Waves," "Another Language," "She Loves Me Not," "Russet Mantle," "Soliloquy," "Miss Swan Expects," "Liberty Jones," "Voice of The Turtle," "Lend An Ear," "Teahouse of The August Moon," "Calculated Risk," "Billy," "Our Town" (1970). Off-Bdwy in "Our Town," "Wilder's Triple Bill," "To Be Young, Gifted and Black," "Candyapple," "Long Day's Journey into Night."

BEAN, REATHAL. Born Aug. 24, 1942 in Mo. Graduate Duke U. Appeared (OB) in "America Hurrah," "San Francisco's Burning," "The Love Cure," "Henry IV" (CP), "In Circles," "Peace," "Journey of Snow White."

BEARD, JAMES. Born Feb. 27 in NYC. Off-Bdwy in "The Scarecrow," "Henry V" (CP), "Him." "Smiling The Boy Fell Dead," "Taming of The Shrew" (CP), "My Fair Lady" (CC'68), on Bdwy in "The Egg," "Don't Drink The Water," "Hello, Dolly!"

BECKER, EDWARD. Born in Astoria, N.Y. Attended Am. Theatre Wing. Bdwy bow 1951 in "Paint Your Wagon," followed by "Silk Stockings," "Happy Hunting," "Body Beautiful," "Whoop-Up," "Bye Bye Birdie," "Family Affair," "Camelot," "Here's Love," "Illya Darling," "Brigadoon" (CC '67), "Mame," "Jimmy," "Ari."

BECKER, RAY. Born May 18, 1934 in NYC. Attended HB Studio. Bdwy bow in "How To Succeed . . . ," followed by "Curley McDimple" (OB), "George M!," "Applause."

BEDFORD, BRIAN. Born Feb. 16, 1935 in Morley, Eng. Attended RADA. NY bow 1960 in "Five Finger Exercise," followed by "Lord Pengo," "The Private Ear," "The Knack" (OB). "The Astrakhan Coat," "The Unknown Soldier and His Wife," "Seven Descents of Myrtle," with APA in "Misanthrope," "Cocktail Party," and "Hamlet," "Private Lives," "School for Wives."

BENJAMIN, FRED. Born Sept. 8, 1944 in Boston. Has appeared in "We're Civilized" (OB), "Hello, Dolly!," "Promises, Promises."

BENSON, ROBBY. Born Jan. 21, 1956 in Dallas, Tex. Attended AADA. Bdwy bow 1969 in "Zelda," followed by "The Rothschilds."

BEN-ZALI, SIDNEY. Born Dec. 20, 1945 in Rio de Janeiro. NY debut Off-Bdwy 1965 in "Lorenzaccio," Bdwy bow 1971 in "The Rothschilds."

BERDEEN, ROBERT. Born Aug. 6 in Arlington, Va. Attended Neighborhood Playhouse. Credits: "A Dream of Swallows" (OB), "The Passion of Josef D," "Fiddler on the Roof," "Royal Hunt of the Sun," "Billy," "Me and Juliet" (ELT), "Ballad of Johnny Pot" (OB).

BERNHEIM, SHIRL. Born Sept. 21, 1921 in NYC. Studied with Ouspenskaya. Debut Off-Bdwy 1967 in "A Different World," followed by "Stag Movie."

BERRY, ERIC. Born Jan. 9, 1913 in London. Graduate RADA. NY debut 1954 in "The Boy Friend," followed by "Family Reunion," "The Power and the Glory," "Beaux Stratagem," "Broken Jug," "Pictures in the Hallway," "Peer Gynt," "Great God Brown," "Henry IV," "The White House," "White Devil," "Charley's Aunt," "The Homecoming" (OB).

BIRNEY, DAVID. Born Apr. 23, 1939 in Washington, D.C. Graduate Dartmouth, UCLA. Off-Bdwy with NYSF in "Comedy of Errors," "Titus Andronicus," and "King John" and in "Mac-Bird," "Ceremony of Innocence," "Summertree" for which he received a THEATRE WORLD Award, "The Miser" (LC), "Crimes of Passion" (OB), "Playboy of The Western World," "Good Woman of Setzuan," "An Enemy of The People," and "Antigone" (LC).

BISHOP, RONALD. Born Mar. 28, 1923 in New Haven, Conn. Graduate Ithaca Col. Bdwy bow 1943 in "Othello," followed by "Julius Caesar," "The Visit," "Galileo" (LC), "St. Joan" (LC), "Survival of St. Joan" (OB).

BLACK, DONNA OLIVIA. Born Dec. 28, 1948 in NYC. Attended NYU. Debut Off-Bdwy 1971 in "In New England Winter."

BLACKTON, JACK. Born Mar. 16, 1938 in Colorado Springs. Graduate U. Colo. Off-Bdwy in "Put It In Writing," "Jacques Brel Is Alive . . . " Bdwy bow 1966 in "Mame."

BLOCK, CHAD. Born May 1, 1938 in Twin Falls, Ida. Bdwy bow 1954 in "The Vamp," followed by "Li'l Abner," "Destry Rides Again," "Take Me Along," "Do Re Mi," "Come On Strong," "Hello, Dolly!," "Walking Happy," "Hallelujah, Baby!," "Coco."

BLOOM, CLAIRE. Born Feb. 15, 1931 in London. Bdwy debut 1956 with Old Vic in "Romeo and Juliet" and "Richard II," followed by "Rashomon," OB in "A Doll's House," "Hedda Gabler."

BLUMENFELD, ROBERT. (formerly Robert Fields) Born Feb. 26, 1943 in NYC. Graduate Rutgers, Columbia. Debut Off-Bdwy 1965 with American Savoyards, Bdwy bow 1970 in "Othello" (ASF).

BOLSTER, STEPHEN. Born Apr. 7, 1933 in Cambridge, Mass. Attended Harvard. Has appeared in "Enemy of the People" ('58 OB), "Big Fish, Little Fish," "Education of Hyman Kaplan," "Lovely Ladies, Kind Gentlemen."

BOND, SUDIE. Born July 13, 1928 in Louisville, Ky. Attended Rollins Col. Off-Bdwy: "Summer and Smoke," "Tovarich," "American Dream," "Sandbox," "Endgame," "Theatre of The Absurd," "Home Movies," "Softly and Consider The Nearness," "The Memorandum," "The Local Stigmatic," On Bdwy in "Waltz of The Toreadors," "Auntie Mame," "The Egg," "Harold," "My Mother, My Father and Me," "The Impossible Years," "Keep It In the Family," "Quotations From Chrmn. Mao Tse-Tung," "American Dream," "Forty Carats," "Hay Fever."

BONERZ, PETER. Born Aug. 6, 1938 in Portsmouth, NH. Graduate Marquette U. NY bow Off-Bdwy 1961 in "The Premise," followed by "The White House Murder Case," Bdwy debut 1970 in "Story Theatre."

BONNELL, JAY. Born Apr. 12, 1932 in Passaic, NJ. Graduate Seton Hall U. Debut Off-Bdwy 1958 in "Member of the Wedding," followed by "Escape Me Never," "Look After Lulu," "Fire Brand," "Shoestring Revue," "Meeow!"

BOOTH, SHIRLEY. Born Aug. 30, 1907 in NYC. Bdwy debut 1925 in "Hell's Bells," followed by "Bye Bye Baby," "Laff That Off," "War Song," "Too Many Heroes," "Three Men on a Horse," "Excursion," "Philadelphia Story," "My Sister Eileen," "Tomorrow the World," "Hollywood Pinafore," "Land's End," "Goodbye, My Fancy," "Love Me Long," "Come Back, Little Sheba," "A Tree Grows in Brooklyn," "Time of the Cuckoo," "By the Beautiful Sea," "Miss Isobel," "Juno," "Second String," "Look to the Lilies," "Hay Fever."

BORRELLI, JIM. Born Apr. 10, 1948 in Lawrence, Mass. Graduate Boston Col. NY debut Off-Bdwy 1971 in "Subject to Fits."

BOSCO, PHILIP. Born Sept 26, 1930 in Jersey City, NJ. Graduate Catholic U. Credits: "Auntie Mame," "Rape of The Belt," "Ticket of Leave Man" (OB), "Donnybrook," "Man For All Seasons," with LCRep in "The Alchemist," "East Wind," "Galileo," "St. Joan," "Tiger At The Gates," "Cyrano," "King Lear," "A Great Career," "In The Matter of J. Robert Oppenheimer," "The Miser," "The Time of Your Life," "Camino Real," "Operation Sidewinder," "Amphitryon," "An Enemy of the People," "Playboy of the Western World," "Good Woman of Setzuan," "Antigone."

Margaret Braidwood   Barry Bostwick   Dell Brownlee   Norman Bush   Rosalind Breslow

BOSTWICK, BARRY. Born Feb. 24, 1945 in San Mateo, Cal. Graduate Cal-Western, NYU. Bdwy debut with APA in "War and Peace," "Pantagleize," "Misanthrope." "Cock-A-Doodle Dandy," "Hamlet," OB in "Salvation," "Colette," "Soon."

BOZYK, ROSE. Born in Poland May 13, 1914. Star of many Yiddish productions before 1966 Bdwy debut in "Let's Sing Yiddish," followed by "Sing, Israel, Sing," "Mirele Efros" (OB), "Light, Lively and Yiddish."

BRAIDWOOD, MARGARET. Born Sept. 30, 1924 in Liverpool, Eng. Credits: "Tamburlaine the Great," "A Loss of Roses," "Duel of Angels," "Passage to India," "Dylan," "Traveller Without Luggage," "How's the World Treating You?," "The Astrakhan Coat," "Rosencrantz and Guildenstern Are Dead," Off-Bdwy in "Red Peppers," "Saved," "AC/DC."

BRASWELL, CHARLES. Born Sept. 7 in McKinney, Tex. Attended Arlington State Col. Bdwy bow 1960 in "A Thurber Carnival," followed by "Wildcat," "Sail Away," "Hot Spot," "Here's Love," "I Had A Ball," "Me and Thee," "Mame," "Company."

BRAUNSTEIN, ALAN. Born Apr. 30, 1947 in Bklyn. Debut Off-Bdwy 1962 in "Daddy Come Home," followed by Bdwy bow 1970 in "Hair."

BREMERS, BEVERLY ANN. Born Mar. 10, 1950 in Chicago. Attended HB Studio. NY debut 1969 in "Hair," followed by "The Me Nobody Knows".

BREMSETH, LLOYD. Born July 27, 1948 in Minneapolis. Attended U Minn. Debut Off-Bdwy 1968 in "Kiss Rock," followed by "Klara," "Sweet Shoppe Myriam," "Kiss Now."

BRESLIN, TOMMY. Born Mar. 24, 1946 in Norwich, Conn. Attended Iona Col. Off-Bdwy in "For Love or Money," "Freedom Is A Two-Edged Sword," "Who's Who, Baby?" "Beggar on Horseback" (LC), "Moon Walk," Bdwy bow 1971 in "70 Girls 70."

BRESLOW, ROSALIND. Born in N.J. Attended Oberlin, AADA. NY debut Off-Bdwy 1970 in "Heloise."

BRIGHT, RICHARD. Born June 28, 1937 in Bklyn. Off-Bdwy in "The Balcony," "Does A Tiger Wear a Necktie?," "The Beard," "Survival of St. Joan."

BRINK, ROBERT. Born Nov. 9, 1944 in Milwaukee, Wisc. Yale graduate. Off-Bdwy in "Awakening of Spring," "Shout from the Rooftops," with American Savoyards, "The Nuns."

BROCHU, JAMES. Born Aug. 16, 1946 in NYC. Graduate St. Francis Col. Attended AADA. Debut Off-Bdwy 1968 in "Endecott and The Red Cross," followed by "Taming of the Shrew," "Unfair to Goliath," "Skye," "To Be or Not To Be," "Greenwillow."

BRODERICK, JAMES. Born Mar. 7, 1928 in Charlestown, NH. Attended UNH, Neighborhood Playhouse. Bdwy bow 1953 in "Maggie," followed by "Johnny No Trump," off-Bdwy in "A Touch of the Poet," "Two by Saroyan," "The Firebugs," "Rooms," "The Time of Your Life" (LC), "Scenes from American Life" (LC).

BROOKES, JACQUELINE. Born July 24, 1930 in Montclair, NJ. Graduate U. Iowa, RADA. Bdwy debut 1955 in "Tiger at the Gates," followed by "Watercolor," "Abelard and Heloise," Off-Bdwy in "The Cretan Woman" for which she received a THEATRE WORLD Award, "The Clandestine Marriage," "Measure for Measure," "Duchess of Malfi," "Ivanov," "Six Characters in Search of an Author," "An Evening's Frost," "Come Slowly, Eden," "The Increased Difficulty of Concentration" (LC), "The Persians," "Sunday Dinner."

BROWN, GRAHAM. Born Oct. 24, 1924 in NYC. Graduate Howard U. Off-Bdwy: "Widower's Houses," "The Emperor's Clothes," "Time of Storm," "Major Barbara," "A Land Beyond The River," "The Blacks," "The Firebugs," "God Is A (Guess What?)," "An Evening of One Acts," "Man Better Man," "Behold! Cometh the Vanderkellans," "Ride a Blackhorse," Bdwy in "Weekend," "The Man In The Glass Booth."

BROWN, R. G. Born April 24, 1933, in Flint, Mich. Attended LACC, U. Mich. Bdwy bow in "New Faces of 1962," followed by "A Great Career" (LC), OB in "Spiro Who?," "Whispers on the Wind."

BROWNING, SUSAN. Born Feb. 25, 1941 in Baldwin, NY. Graduate Penn. State. Bdwy bow 1963 in "Love and Kisses," followed by "Company" for which she received a THEATRE WORLD Award, Off-Bdwy roles in "Jo," "Dime A Dozen," "Seventeen," "Boys from Syracuse," "Collision Course."

BROWNLEE, DELL. Born in Paris. Attended Marymount, Neighborhood Playhouse. Bdwy debut 1961 in "The Unsinkable Molly Brown," followed by "Carnival," "Here's Love," "Fade Out, Fade In," "Man of La Mancha."

BRUNO, JEAN. Born Dec. 7, 1926 in Bklyn. Attended Hofstra Col., Feagin School. Bdwy debut 1960 in "Beg, Borrow or Steal," followed by "Midgie Purvis," "Music Man," "Family Affair," "Minnie's Boys," OB in "All That Fall," "Hector," "Hotel Paradiso," "Pidgeons in the Park," "Ergo," "Trelawny of the Wells."

BRUNS, PHILIP. Born May 2, 1931 in Pipestone, Minn. Graduate Augustana College, and Yale. Bdwy bow 1964 in "The Deputy," Off-Bdwy in "Mr. Simian," "The Cradle Will Rock," "He Who Gets Slapped," "Dr. Willy Nilly," "Come Play With Me," "Listen To The Mocking Bird," "The Bald Soprano," "Jack Or The Submission," "Endgame," "Servant of Two Masters," "Pantomania," "Square In The Eye," "The Butter and Egg Man," "Spitting Image," "Henry V," "A Dream Out of Time."

BRYGGMAN, LARRY. Born Dec. 21, 1938 in Concord, Cal. Attended CCSF, Am. Theatre Wing. NY bow 1962 Off-Bdwy in "A Pair of Pairs," followed by "Live Like Pigs," "Stop, You're Killing Me!" "Mod Donna," "Waiting for Godot."

BUCKLEY, BETTY. Born July 3, 1947 in Big Spring, Tex. Graduate TCU. Bdwy debut 1969 in "1776," followed by "Ballad of Johnny Pot" (OB).

BUKA, DONALD. Born in Cleveland, O. Attended Carnegie Tech. Has appeared in "Twelfth Night," "The Corn Is Green," "Bright Boy," "Helen Goes to Troy," "Sophie," "Live Life Again," "Those That Play the Clowns," "Heritage" (OB).

BURR, ROBERT. Born in Jersey City, NJ. Attended Colgate U. Has appeared in "Cradle Will Rock," "Mister Roberts," "Romeo and Juliet," "Picnic," "The Lovers," "Anniversary Waltz," "Top Man," "Remains to Be Seen," "The Wall," "Andersonville Trial," "A Shot in the Dark," "A Man for All Seasons," "Luther," "Hamlet," "Bajour," "White Devil," "Royal Hunt of the Sun," "Dinner at 8," "King John" (CP), "Henry VI" (CP).

BUSH, NORMAN. Born Apr. 11, 1933 in Louisville, Ky. Attended AADA. NY bow Off-Bdwy 1960 in "The Goose," followed by "The Connection," "Funny House of a Negro," "The Toilet," and NEC's "Daddy Goodness," "Kongi's Harvest," "Summer of the 17th Doll," "Song of the Lusitanian Bogey," "God Is A(Guess What?)," "Malcochon," "Man Better Man," "Day of Absence," "Brotherhood," "Akokawe," "In New England Winter"

BYRD, CARL. Born Aug. 10, 1935 in Jackson, Miss. Attended Roosevelt U. Debut Off-Bdwy in "The Blacks" (1961), followed by "A Good Place to Raise a Boy," "Behold! Cometh the Vanderkellans."

| Gaylea Byrne | Carl Byrd | Maureen Byrnes | John Call | Helena Carroll |

BYRNE, GAYLEA. Born in Baltimore, Md. Graduate Peabody Conservatory. NY debut Off-Bdwy 1961 in "All In Love," followed by "Music Man" (CC), "Man of LaMancha."

BYRNES, MAUREEN. Born May 14, 1944 in Chicago. Bdwy debut 1965 in "La Grosse Valise," followed by "Oh, Calcutta!"

CABLE, CHRISTOPHER. Born Mar. 18, 1930 in Alameda, Cal. Graduate U Cal. NY debut Off-Bdwy 1965 in "Garden of Heavenly Faucets," followed by "The Drunkard."

CAESAR, SID. Born Sept. 8, 1922 in Yonkers, NY. Bdwy debut 1944 in "Tars and Spars," followed by "Make Mine Manhattan," "Little Me," "Four on a Garden."

CAINE, RICHARD. Born Oct. 25, 1940 in Rochester, NY. Graduate Northwestern U. NY debut Off-Bdwy 1966 with American Savoyards, followed by "Shoestring Revue" (ELT).

CAIRNS, ANGUS. Born Mar. 29, 1910 in Fitchburg, Mass. NY debut 1941 in "Othello" (CC), followed by ART's "Henry VIII," "What Every Woman Knows," "Androcles and the Lion," "Yellow Jack," "Alice in Wonderland," and "Mock Turtle," "Brigadoon," "Kiss Me, Kate," "Paint Your Wagon," "Threepenny Opera" (OB), The Engagement Baby," "Soon" (OB).

CALBES, ELEANOR. Born Feb. 20, 1940 in Aparri, PI. Graduate U Phil., Royal Conservatory of Toronto. Appeared in CC revivals of "South Pacific," "The King and I," and Bdwy debut 1970 in "Lovely Ladies, Kind Gentlemen."

CALL, JOHN. Born Nov. 3, 1915 in Philadelphia. Attended U Pa. Appeared in "Father Malachy's Miracle," "Merchant of Yonkers," "As You Like It," "Be So Kindly," "But for the Grace of God," "Flying Gerardos," "So Proudly We Hail," "Bet Your Life," "Bloomer Girl," "Pipe Dream," "A Touch of the Poet," "Oliver," "Pickwick," "Time for Singing," NYSF's "Comedy of Errors" and "Hamlet," "Any Resemblance to Persons Living or Dead" (OB).

CALVERT, HENRY. Born Jan. 8, 1920 in Chicago. Attended Dramatic Workshop, Theatre Wing. Off-Bdwy in "The Prodigal," "Hamlet," "Miss Julia," "The Country Girl," "There Is No End," "America Hurrah," "Spiro Who?" "And Whose Little Boy are You?"

CARA, IRENE. Born Mar. 18, 1959 in NYC. Bdwy debut 1968 in "Maggie Flynn," followed by "The Me Nobody Knows."

CAREW, PETER. Born Nov. 8, 1922 in Old Forge, Pa. Graduate NYU. NY bow 1948 in "The Coffee House" (OB), followed by "Street Scene," "Ah, Wilderness," "Antigone," "Waiting for Lefty," "12 Angry Men," "Falling from Hell," "Go Show Me a Dragon," "A Stage Affair," "King of the Whole Damn World," "Purple Canary," "Kiss Mama," "A View from the Bridge," "He Who Gets Slapped," "Istanboul," Bdwy debut 1969 in "Great White Hope."

CAREY, DAVID. Born Nov. 16, 1945 in Brookline, Mass. Graduate Boston U., Ohio U. Debut 1969 Off-Bdwy in "Oh,

What a Wedding," followed by "Let's Sing Yiddish," "Dad, Get Married," "Light, Lively and Yiddish."

CARIOU, LEONARD. Born Sept. 30, 1939 in Winnipeg, Can. Bdwy debut 1968 with Minn. Theatre Co. in "House of Atreus," followed by "Henry V.," "Applause" for which he received a THEATRE WORLD Award.

CARRADINE, DAVID. Born Dec. 8, 1940 in Hollywood, Cal. Attended San Francisco State Col. Bdwy bow 1964 in "The Deputy," followed by "The Royal Hunt of the Sun" for which he received a THEATRE WORLD Award, Off-Bdwy in "The Transgressor Rides Again," "Ballad of Johnny Pot."

CARROLL. HELLENA. Born in Glasgow, Scot. Attended Weber-Douglas School of Drama, London. Came to US with Dublin Players. Founded, directed, acted with Irish Players Off-Bdwy. Bdwy debut 1956 in "Separate Tables," followed by "Happy as Larry," "A Touch of the Poet," "Little Moon of Alban," "The Hostage," "Oliver!," "Pickwick," "Three Hand Reel" (OB), "Something Different," "Georgy," "Borstal Boy," "Pictures in the Hallway" (LC).

CASH, ROSALIND. Born Dec. 31, 1938 in Atlantic City, NJ. Attended CCNY. Bdwy debut 1966 in "The Wayward Stork," followed by Off-Bdwy in "Junebug Graduates Tonight," "Fiorello" (CC), "To Bury A Cousin," with NEC in "Song of The Lusitanian Bogey," "Kongi's Harvest," "Ceremonies In Dark Old Men," "An Evening of One Acts," "Man Better Man," "The Harangues," "Day of Absence," "Brotherhood."

CASON, BARBARA. Born Nov. 15, 1933 in Memphis, Tenn. Graduate Iowa U. Bdwy debut 1967 in "Marat/Sade," followed by "Jimmy Shine," OB in "Firebugs," "Spitting Image," "Enemy of the People" (LC).

CASS, PEGGY. Born May 21, 1926 in Boston. Attended Wyndham. Appeared in "Touch and Go," "Live Wire," "Bernardine," "Phoenix '55" (OB), "Othello," "Henry V." "Auntie Mame" for which she received a THEATRE WORLD Award, "A Thurber Carnival," "Children From Their Games," "Don't Drink The Water," "The Front Page" ('69), "Plaza Suite".

CATLETT, MARY JO. Born Sept. 2, 1938 in Denver, Colo. Graduate Loretto Hts. Col. Has appeared in "Along Came A Spider" (OB), "New Girl In Town," "Fiorello," "Pajama Game," "Hello, Dolly!" "Canterbury Tales," "Promenade" (OB), "Greenwillow" (ELT).

CAVANAUGH, MICHAEL. Born in NYC. Attended San Francisco State Col. NY bow 1969 in "Oh! Calcutta!"

CHANG, TISA. Born Apr. 5 in Chungking, China. Attended CCNY. Bdwy debut 1970 in "Lovely Ladies, Kind Gentlemen."

CHANNING, CAROL. Born Jan. 31, 1921 in Seattle, Wash. Graduate Bennington Col. Bdwy debut 1941 in "No for an Answer," followed by "Let's Face It," "Proof Through the Night," "Lend an Ear" for which she received a THEATRE WORLD Award, "Gentlemen Prefer Blondes," "Wonderful Town," "The Vamp," "Show Girl," "Hello Dolly!," "Four on a Garden."

CHARNEY, JORDAN. Born in NYC. Graduate Bklyn Col. Off-Bdwy in "Harry, Noon and Night," "A Place for Chance," "Hang Down Your Head and Die," "The Pinter Plays," "Telemachus Clay," "Zoo Story," "Viet Rock," "MacBird," "Red Cross," "The Glorious Ruler," "Waiting for Godot," "Slow Memories." Bdwy in "Slapstick Tragedy," "The Birthday Party."

CHILD, MARILYN. Born in Santa Monica, Cal. Graduate U Cal. Bdwy debut 1960 in "Do Re Mi," followed by "Hot Spot," "The Mad Show" (OB), "New Faces of 1968," "Nevertheless, They Laugh" (OB).

CHRIS, MARILYN. Born May 19, 1939 in NYC. Attended CCNY. Has appeared in "The Office," "Birthday Party," "7 Descents of Myrtle," OB in "Nobody Hears a Broken Drum," "Fame," "Judas Applause," "Junebug Graduates Tonight," "Man Is Man," "In the Jungle of Cities," "Good Soldier Schweik," "The Tempest," "Ride a Black Horse."

CHRISMAN, CAROLYN. Born in NYC. Appeared Off-Bdwy in "Games," "Fantastic Gardens," "Home Again," "Something for Kitty Genovese," "Greenwillow." "

Grant Code	Tisa Chang	Alex Colon	Margery Cohen	C. David Colson

CHRISTIAN, ROBERT. Born Dec. 27, 1939 in Los Angeles. Attended UCLA. Off-Bdwy in "The Happening," "Hornblend," "Fortune and Men's Eyes," "Boys in The Band," "Behold! Cometh The Vanderkellans." Bdwy in "We Bombed In New Haven," "Does A Tiger Wear A Necktie?"

CIOFFI, CHARLES. Born Oct. 31, 1935 in NYC. Graduate of U. Minn. With LCRep in "A Cry of Players," "King Lear," "In The Matter of J. Robert Oppenheimer," "Antigone," and OB in "Whistle in the Dark."

CLAIRE, LUDI. Born Apr. 15 in Ind. Attended Ecole Internationale, Geneva. Appeared in "The Small Hours," "Gramercy Ghost," "Tower Beyond Tragedy," "Venus Observed," "Someone Waiting," "Legend of Lovers," "Silk Stockings," "First Gentleman," "Country Wife," "Duel of Angels," "Hamlet."

CLARK, OLIVER. Born Jan. 4, 1939 in Buffalo, NY. Graduate Buffalo U. Bdwy bow 1963 in "Arturo Ui," followed by "Ben Franklin In Paris," "Caucasian Chalk Circle" (LCRep), "Don't Drink The Water," Off-Bdwy in "Spiro Who?," "Two Times One," "Passing Through from Exotic Places," "Next."

CLARKE, RICHARD. Born Jan. 31, 1933 in Eng. Graduate UReading. With LCRep in "St. Joan," "Tiger at the Gates," and "Cyrano de Bergerac," on Bdwy 1970 in "Conduct Unbecoming."

CLAYBURGH, JILL. Born Apr. 30, 1944 in NYC. Graduate Sarah Lawrence. Bdwy debut 1968 in "The Sudden and Accidental Re-Education of Horse Johnson," "The Rothschilds." Off-Bdwy in "It's Called the Sugar Plum," "Calling in Crazy" and "The Nest."

CLYDE, JEREMY. Born Mar. 22, 1941 in Dorney, Eng. Attended Grenoble U. Bdwy debut 1970 in "Conduct Unbecoming."

COATES, CAROLYN. Born Apr. 29, 1930 in Oklahoma City. Attended UCLA. Off-Bdwy in "The Innocents," "The Balcony," "Electra," "The Trojan Women" for which she received a THEATRE WORLD Award, "A Whitman Portrait," "Party On Greenwich Avenue," "The Club Bedroom," "A Scent of Flowers," "The Effect of Gamma Rays on Man-in-the-Moon Marigolds," with LCRep in "The Country Wife," "Condemned of Altona," "The Caucasian Chalk Circle," and "The Disintegration of James Cherry," on Bdwy in "Death of Bessie Smith," "American Dream," "Fire!," "All Over."

COCO, JAMES. Born Mar. 21, 1930 in NYC. On Bdwy in "Hotel Paradiso," "Everybody Loves Opal." "A Passage To India," "Arturo Ui" "The Devils," "The Astrakhan Coat," "Here's Where I Belong," "The Last of the Red Hot Lovers," Off-Bdwy in "Moon In The Yellow River," "That 5 A.M. Jazz," "Lovey," "Squat Betty and The Sponge Room," "Salome," "Fragments," "Witness," and "Next."

CODE, GRANT. Born Mar. 2, 1896 in LaCrosse, Wis. Harvard graduate. Appeared in "Too Late the Phalarope," "The Hostage," "Galileo," "Dylan," "Legend of Lizzie," "Lost in the Stars," "Summer and Smoke" (ELT), OB in "In the Jungle of Cities" "Trelawny of the Wells."

COFFIELD, PETER. Born July 17, 1945 in Evanston, Ill. Graduate of Northwestern and UMich. NY debut with APA in "The Misanthrope," "Cock-A-Doodle Dandy" and "Hamlet," followed by "Abelard and Heloise."

COFFIN, FREDERICK. Born Jan. 16, 1943 in Detroit. Graduate U Mich. Debut 1971 Off-Bdwy in "Basic Training of Pavlo Hummel."

COHEN, MARGERY. Born June 24, 1947 in Chicago. Attended U. Wisc., U. Chicago, HB Studio. Bdwy debut 1968 in "Fiddler on the Roof," followed by "Jacques Brel Is Alive and Well . . . " (OB).

COLES, ZAIDA. Born Sept. 10, 1933 in Lynchburg, Va. Off-Bdwy in "The Father," "Pins and Needles," "The Life and Times of J. Walter Smintheus," on Bdwy in "Weekend," "Zelda."

COLEY, THOMAS. Born July 29, 1918 in Bethayres, Pa. Attended Washington and Lee U. Bdwy debut 1935 in "Taming of the Shrew," followed by "Swingin' the Dream," "Return Engagement," "Cue for Passion," "My Fair Ladies," "Mr. Peebles and Mr. Hooker," "Portrait in Black," "Harvey," "I Never Sang for My Father," "Our Town" ('69), "A Passage to E. M. Forster" (OB).

COLON, ALEX. Born Jan. 26, 1941 in Patillas, PR. Attended Hunter Col. Off-Bway in "Macbeth," "Winterset," "Crossroads," "Golden Streets," "Hatful of Rain," Bdwy debut 1970 in "The Gingerbread Lady."

COLTON, CHEVI. Born in NYC. Attended Hunter Col. Off-Bdwy in "Time of Storm," "Insect Comedy" (CC). "The Adding Machine," "O Marry Me," "Penny Change," "The Mad Show," "Jacques Brel Is Alive . . . ," on Bdwy in "Cabaret."

COLSON, C. DAVID. Born Dec. 23, 1941 in Detroit. Graduate U. Mich. NY bow 1970 in "The Last Sweet Days of Isaac" (OB), Bdwy debut 1970 in "Purlie."

CONDOS, DIMO. Born Feb. 29, 1932 in NYC. Off-Bdwy in "The Celebration," "O'Flaherty," "The Cannibals," "Moths," "Pinkville."

CONNELL, JANE. Born Oct. 27, 1925 in Berkeley, Cal. Attended UCal. Off-Bway in "Shoestring Revue," "Threepenny Opera," "Pieces of Eight," "Demi-Dozen," "She Stoops to Conquer," on Bdwy in "New Faces of 1956," "Drat! The Cat!," "Mame," "Dear World."

CONNOLLY, THOMAS. Born in NYC; attended NYU. Debut OB in "The Moon in Yellow River," followed by "The Miracle Worker," "Riot Act," "Never Too Late," "Philadelphia, Here I Come," "What the Butler Saw" (OB).

CONWAY, KEVIN BRYAN. Born May 29, 1942 in NYC. Debut 1968 off-Bdwy in "Muzeeka," on Bdwy 1969 in "Indians," followed by "Saved" (OB).

COOK, JAMES. Born Mar. 7, 1937 in NYC. Attended AADA. Off-Bdwy in "The Fantasticks," "Goa," with LCRep in "Cyrano," "A Cry of Players," "King Lear," "The Miser," "Playboy of the Western World," "Good Woman of Setzuan," "Enemy of the People," and "In the Matter of J. Robt. Oppenheimer," on Bdwy in "The Great White Hope," "The Wrong Way Light Bulb."

COONAN, SHEILA. Born June 28, 1922 in Montreal, Can. Attended McGill U. Has appeared in "Red Roses For Me," "A Taste of Honey," "The Hostage," "Hogan's Goat" (OB), "The Great White Hope," "Macbeth" (OB).

COOPER, MARILYN. Born Dec. 14, 1936 in NYC. Attended NYU. Appeared in "Mr. Wonderful," "West Side Story," "Brigadoon" (CC), "Gypsy," "I Can Get It For You Wholesale," "The Mad Show" (OB), "Hallelujah, Baby!," "Golden Rainbow," "Mame," "A Teaspoon Every 4 Hours," "Two by Two."

COOPER, MELVILLE. Born Oct. 15, 1896 in Birmingham, Eng. Bdwy bow 1935 in "Laburnum Grove," followed by "Jubilee," "The Merry Widow," "While the Sun Shines," "Firebrand of Florence," "Pygmalion," "Gypsy Lady," "The Haven," "An Inspector Calls," "The Liar," "Day after Tomorrow," "Make a Wish," "Much Ado about Nothing," "Escapade," "My Fair Lady," "Hostile Witness," "Charley's Aunt."

COOPER, PEGGY. Born Mar. 31, 1931 in Huntington, W Va. Graduate Baldwin-Wallace Conserv. Bdwy debut 1968 in "Zorba," followed by "La Strada," "The Rothschilds."

Nora Coppola **Sam Coppola** **Paddy Croft** **Paul Corum** **Diane Cypkin**

COPELAND, JOAN. Born June 1, 1922 in NYC. Attended Bklyn Col., AADA. Appeared in "How I Wonder," "Sundown Beach," "Detective Story," "Handful of Fire," "Tovarich," "Something More," "The Price," "Two by Two."

COPPOLA, NORA. Born in Van Nuys, Cal. Attended San Fernando State Col. Bdwy debut 1971 in "Abelard and Heloise."

COPPOLA, SAM J. Born July 31, 1935 in NJ. Attended Actors Studio. NY bow 1968 Off-Bdwy in "A Present from Your Old Man," followed by "Things That Almost Happen."

CORBETT, GRETCHEN. Born Aug. 13, 1947 in Portland, Ore. Attended Carnegie Tech. Off-Bdwy in "Arms and The Man," "The Bench," "Iphigenia In Aulis," "Survival of St. Joan," on Bdwy in "After The Rain," "Forty Carats."

CORDNER, BLAINE. Born Aug. 21, 1901 in Jacksonville, Fla. Appeared in "We, the People," "Bridal Quilt," "Blow, Ye Winds," "The World Waits," "First Flight," "A New Life," "Arsenic and Old Lace," "Bloomer Girl," "Set My People Free," "An Enemy of the People" (LC).

CORUM, PAUL. Born Aug. 8, 1943 in Los Angeles. Yale graduate. Bdwy debut 1970 with ASF "Othello," followed by "The Philanthropist."

COSTER, NICOLAS. Born Dec. 3, 1934 in London. Attended Neighborhood Playhouse. Bdwy bow 1960 in "Becket," followed by "90 Day Mistress," "But Seriously," Off-Bway in "Epitaph for George Dillon," "Shadow and Substance," "Thracian Horses," "O, Say Can You See," "Happy Birthday, Wanda June."

COVER, FRANKLIN. Born Nov. 20, 1928 in Cleveland, O. Graduate of Denison, Western Reserve U. Off-Bdwy in "Julius Caesar," "Henry IV," "She Stoops To Conquer," "The Plough and The Stars," "The Octoroon," "Hamlet," and "Macbeth," Bdwy bow 1962 in "Giants, Sons of Giants," followed by "Calculated Risk," "Abraham Cochrane," "Any Wednesday," "The Investigation," "Forty Carats,"

COWAN, GRANT. Born Aug. 20, 1935 in Winnipeg, Can. Attended U. Manitoba, Bristol Old Vic. Bdwy bow 1971 in "You're a Good Man, Charlie Brown."

CRAIG, NOEL. Born Jan. 4 in St. Louis, Mo. Attended Northwestern, Goodman Theatre, Guildhall School London. Bdwy debut 1967 in "Rosencrantz and Guildenstern Are Dead," followed by "A Patriot for Me," "Conduct Unbecoming."

CRANE, DEAN.. Born Jan. 5, 1932 in Denver, Colo. Made Bdwy debut 1953 in "John Murray Anderson's Almanac," followed by "Fanny," "Lute Song" (CC'59), "Carnival" (1968 CC), "Nevertheless, They Laugh" (OB).

CROFT, PADDY. Born in Worthing, Eng. Attended Avondale Col. Off-Bdwy 1961 "The Hostage," followed by "Billy Liar," "Live Like Pigs," "Hogan's Goat," "Long Day's Journey into Night," with APA, on Bdwy in "The Killing of Sister George," "The Prime of Miss Jean Brodie."

CROMWELL, J. T.. Born Mar. 4, 1935 in Ann Arbor, Mich. Graduate U Cinn. Bdwy bow 1965 in "Half A Sixpence," followed by "Jacques Brel Is Alive . . . " (OB).

CRONYN, TANDY. Born Nov. 26, 1945 in Los Angeles Attended Central School of Speech and Drama in London. Bdwy debut 1969 in "Cabaret," followed by LCRep productions of "Playboy of the Western World," "Good Woman of Setzuan," "An Enemy of the People," and "Antigone."

CRYER, DAVID. Born Mar. 8, 1936 in Evanston, Ill. Attended DePauw U. Off-Bdwy in "The Fantasticks," "Streets of New York," "Now Is The Time For All Good Men" and "Whispers on The Wind," on Bdwy in "110 In The Shade," "Come Summer," for which he received a THEATRE WORLD Award, "1776," "Ari."

CULLUM, JOHN. Born Mar. 2, 1930 in Knoxville, Tenn. Graduate U. Tenn. Bdwy bow 1960 in "Camelot," followed by "Infidel Caesar," "The Rehearsal," Burton's "Hamlet," "On A Clear Day You Can See Forever," for which he received a THEATRE WORLD Award, "Three Hand Reel" (OB), "Man of LaMancha," "1776 . . "

CUNNINGHAM, JOHN. Born June 22, 1932 in Auburn, NY. Graduate of Dartmouth and Yale. Off-Bdwy in "Love Me Little," "Pimpernel," "The Fantasticks," "Love and Let Love," on Bdwy in "Hot Spot," "Zorba," "Company," "1776."

CURTIS, KEENE. Born Feb. 15, 1925 in Salt Lake City. Graduate U. Utah. Bdwy bow 1949 in "Shop At Sly Corner," joined APA 1960 and appeared in "School For Scandal," "The Tavern," "Anatole," "Scapin," "Right You Are," "The Importance of Being Earnest," "Twelfth Night," "King Lear," "The Seagull," "Lower Depths," "Man and Superman," "Judith," "War and Peace," "You Can't Take It With You," "Pantagleize," "The Cherry Orchard," "The Misanthrope," "The Cocktail Party," "Cock-A-Doodle Dandy," and "Hamlet," followed by "A Patriot for Me," "Colette" (OB), "The Rothschilds."

CYPHER, JON. Born Jan. 13, 1932 in Brooklyn. Graduate U. Vt. Bdwy bow 1958 in "The Disenchanted," followed by "The Wives" (OB), "The Great Western Union" (OB), "Jennie," "Night of The Iguana," "Man of LaMancha," "Sherry!," "The Great White Hope," "1776," "Coco."

CYPKIN, DIANE. Born Sept. 10, 1948 in Munich, Ger. Attended Bklyn Col. Bdwy debut 1966 in "Let's Sing Yiddish," followed by "Papa Get Married," "Light, Lively and Yiddish."

CZAKO, GLENN R.. Born May 26, 1949 in NYC. Graduate CCNY. Debut OB 1962 in "Miracle of Christmas," followed by "Happy Ending," "Day of Absence," "Uncle Vanya."

DABDOUB, JACK. Born Feb. 5 in New Orleans. Graduate Tulane U. Off-Bdwy in "What's Up," "Time For The Gentle People," "The Peddler" and "The Dodo Bird," on Bdwy in "Paint Your Wagon," "My Darlin' Aida," "Happy Hunting," "Hot Spot," "Camelot," "Baker Street," "Anya," "Annie Get Your Gun" (LC), "Her First Roman" "Man of LaMancha," "Coco."

DAMON, CATHRYN. Born Sept. 11 in Seattle, Wash. Bdwy debut 1954 in "By The Beautiful Sea," followed by "The Vamp," "Shinbone Alley," "A Family Affair," "Foxy," "Flora, The Red Menace," "UTBU," "Come Summer," "Criss-Crossing," "A Place for Polly," "Last of the Red Hot Lovers," Off-Bdwy in "Boys from Syracuse," "Secret Life of Walter Mitty," "Show Me Where The Good Times Are," "Effect of Gamma Rays on Man-in-the-Moon Marigolds".

DANIELE, GRACIELA. Born Dec. 8, 1939 in Buenos Aires. Bdwy debut 1964 in "What Makes Sammy Run?" followed by "Here's Where I Belong," "Promises, Promises," "Follies."

DANIELS, WILLIAM.. Born Mar. 31, 1927 in Brooklyn. Graduated Northwestern U. Bdwy bow 1943 in "Life With Father," followed by "Richard II," "Seagulls Over Sorrento," "Legend of Lizzie," "Cat On A Hot Tin Roof," "A Thousand Clowns," "The Zoo Story" (OB), "The Iceman Cometh" (OB), "Look Back In Anger" (OB), "Dear Me, The Sky Is Falling," "One Flew Over The Cuckoo's Nest," "On A Clear Day You Can See Forever," "Daphne In Cottage D," "1776."

DANNER, BLYTHE. Born in Philadelphia. Graduate of Bard Col. Debut Off-Bdwy 1966 in "The Infantry," followed by "Collision Course," "Summertree," "Up Eden," "Someone's Comin' Hungry," with LC Rep in "Cyrano," and "The Miser" for which she received a THEATRE WORLD Award, Bdwy debut 1969 in "Butterflies Are Free."

DARDEN, NORMA. Born Nov. 4 in Newark, NJ. Sarah Lawrence graduate. Bdwy debut 1968 in "Weekend," Off-Bdwy in "Underground."

| Bob Delegall | Norma Darden | Mark Dempsey | Cherry Davis | Robert DeNiro |

DARVAS, LILI. Born Apr. 10, 1906 in Budapest. Bdwy debut 1944 in "Soldier's Wife," followed by "Hamlet," "Bravo," "Cry of the Peacock," "Horses in Midstream," "Hidden River," "Waltz of the Toreadors," "Cheri," "Far Country," "First Love," "My Mother, My Father, and Me," "Happiness" (OB), "The Miser" (LC), "Les Blancs."

DA SILVA, HOWARD. Born May 4, 1909 in Cleveland, O. Attended Carnegie Tech. Debut with Civic Rep Co., followed by "Ten Million Ghosts," "Golden Boy," "The Cradle Will Rock," "Casey Jones," "Abe Lincoln In Illinois," "Summer Night," "Two On An Island," "Oklahoma!," "Shootin' Star," "Burning Bright," "The Unknown Soldier and His Wife," "Compulsion," "Fiorello," "Romulus," "In The Counting House," "Dear Me, The Sky Is Falling," "Hamlet" (CP), "1776." Off-Bdwy in "World of Sholom Aleichem," "The Adding Machine," "Diary of A Scoundrel," and "Volpone,"

DAVID, CLIFFORD. Born June 30, 1932 in Toledo, O. Attended Toledo U., Actors Studio. Bdwy bow 1960 in "Caligula," followed by "Wildcat," "The Aspern Papers," "Boys From Syracuse" (OB), "On A Clear Day You Can See Forever," "A Joyful Noise," "1776," "Camino Real" (LC).

DAVID, JEAN. Born May 4, 1931 in Denver, Colo. Graduate of Columbia. Debut 1963 Off-Bdwy in "Six Characters in Search of an Author," followed by "Miss Julie," "Hobbies," "Jack," "Oedipus," "Epitaph for George Dillon," "Now You See It," "Moondreamers," "Istanboul," "Triple Image," "Beelch," "Finnegan's Wake," "Dark of the Moon," "Subject to Fits."

DAVID, JEFF. Born Sept. 16, 1940 in Philadelphia. Graduate Carnegie Tech. Off-Bdwy in "Arms and the Man," "Phaedra," "Country Wife," "Caucasian Chalk Circle," "The Butter and Egg Man," "Francesca de Remini," "Hamlet," "Pequod," "Memory Bank," "Perry's Mission."

DAVID, THAYER. Born Mar. 4, 1927 in Medford, Mass. Harvard graduate. Appeared in "The Relapse," "King Lear," "Mr. Johnson," "Protective Custody," "A Man for All Seasons," "Andorra," "The Seagull," "The Crucible," "Royal Hunt of the Sun," "Those That Play the Clowns," OB in " "Carefree Tree," "White Devil," "Oscar Wilde," "The Bench," "Uncle Vanya."

DAVIS, CHERRY. Born in Independence, Mo. Attended RADA. OB in "Young Abe Lincoln," "Threepenny Opera," "Corner of the Morning," "As You Like It," "Your Own Thing," on Bdwy in "Gypsy," "Oliver," "George M!"

DAVILA, DIANA. Born Nov. 5, 1947 in NYC. Bdwy debut 1967 in "Song of The Grasshopper," followed by "The Prime of Miss Jean Brodie," OB in "What the Butler Saw," "The Refrigerators".

DAVIS, CLIFTON. Born Oct. 4 in Chicago. Attended Oakwood Col. NY debut Off-Bdwy 1968 in "How to Steal an Election," followed by "Horseman, Pass By," "To Be Young, Gifted and Black," "No Place to Be Somebody," "Do It Again!" for which he received a THEATRE WORLD Award. on Bdwy in "Hello, Dolly!" "Jimmy Shine," "Look to the Lilies," "The Engagement Baby."

DAWSON, CURT.. Born Dec. 5, 1941 in Kansas, Graduate RADA. NY bow 1968 Off-Bdwy in "Futz," followed by "Boys in the Band," "Not Now, Darling,"

DeCARLO, YVONNE. Born Sept. 1, 1924 in Vancouver, BC. Attended Vancouver School of Drama. Bdwy debut 1971 in "Follies."

DEE, RUBY.. Born Oct. 27 in Cleveland, O. Graduate Hunter Col. Bdwy debut 1946 in "Jeb," followed by "Anna Lucasta," "The Smile of the World," "A Long Way Home," "The World of Sholom Aleichem" (OB), "A Raisin in the Sun," "Purlie Victorious," "Boesman and Lena" (OB).

DeKOVEN, ROGER. Born Oct. 22, 1907 in Chicago, Attended U. Chicago, Northwestern, Columbia. Bdwy bow 1926 in "Juarez and Maximilian," followed by "Mystery Man," "Once in a Lifetime," "Counsellor-at-Law," "Murder in the Cathedral," "Eternal Road," "Brooklyn, USA," "The Assassins," "Joan of Lorraine," "Abie's Irish Rose," "The Lark," "Hidden River," "Compulsion," "Miracle Worker," "Fighting Cock," "Tovarich," "Arturo Ui," "Funny Girl," Off-Bdwy in "Deadly Game," "Steal the Old Man's Bundle," with LCRep in "St. Joan," "Tiger at the Gates," "Walking to Waldheim," "Cyrano, and "An Enemy of The People."

DELEGALL, BOB. Born July 24, 1945 in Philadelphia. Debut Off-Bdwy 1971 in "The Basic Training of Pavlo Hummel."

DELLA SORTE, JOSEPH. Born May 5, 1940 in Yonkers, NY. Graduate Boston U., Neighborhood Playhouse. Bdwy bow 1961 in "Ross," followed by "Taming of the Shrew" (CP), "South Pacific" (LC), "Billy," "The Man with the Flower in His Mouth" (OB), "Ari."

DEL MEDICO, MICHAEL. Born Oct. 3, 1933 in Chicago. Attended DePaul U, American Theatre Wing. Bdwy bow 1956 in "Inherit the Wind," followed by "The Disenchanted," Off-Bdwy in "Cicero," "Rise, Marlowe," "Go Show Me A Dragon," "Witches' Sabbath," "Burn Me to Ashes," "Line," "I Dreamt I Dwelt in Bloomingdale's," "Line."

DEMPSEY, MARK. Born Jan. 29, 1936 in Hollywood, Calif. Graduate U. Wash. NY debut 1969 Off-Bdwy in "Oh! Calcutta!"

DENGEL, JAKE. Born June 19, 1933 in Oshkosh, Wis. Graduate Northwestern U. NY bow OB in "The Fantasticks," followed by "Red Eye of Love," "Fortuna," "Abe Lincoln in Illinois," "Dr. Faustus," "An Evening with Garcia Lorca," "The Shrinking Bride," Bdwy in "Royal Hunt of the Sun," with APA in "Cock-a-doodle Dandy" and "Hamlet."

DENGEL, RONI. Born Nov. 16, 1942 in Hartsdale, NY. Attended Columbia, Royal Ballet School. Bdwy debut 1953 in "Mrs. McThing," followed by "Remarkable Mr. Pennypacker," "Sunrise at Campobello," "Not Now, Darling."

DeNIRO, ROBERT. Born Aug. 17, 1943 in NYC. Studied with Stella Adler. Debut Off-Bdwy 1970 in "One Night Stands of a Noisy Passenger."

DENNIS, RONALD. Born Oct. 2, 1944 in Dayton, O. Has appeared in "Show Boat" (LC'66), OB in "Of Thee I Sing," "Moon Walk."

DENNIS, SANDY. Born Apr. 27, 1937 in Hastings, Neb. Has appeared in "Dark at the Top of the Stairs," "Burning Bright" (OB), "Face of a Hero," "Complaisant Lover," "A Thousand Clowns" for which she received a THEATRE WORLD Award, "Any Wednesday," "Daphne in Cottage D," "How the Other Half Loves."

DESPO. Born July 13, 1922 in Piraeus, Greece. Appeared in films and with Greek Ntl. Theatre before Bdwy bow in 1967 in "Illya, Darling," followed by "Istanboul" (OB).

DEWHURST, COLLEEN. Born in Montreal, Can. Attended Downer Col., AADA. Bdwy debut 1952 in "Desire under the Elms," followed by "Tamburlaine the Great," "Country Wife," "Caligula," "All the Way Home," "Great Day in the Morning," "Ballad of the Sad Cafe," "More Stately Mansions," "All Over," Off-Bdwy in "Taming of the Shrew," "The Eagle Has Two Heads," "Camille," "Macbeth," "Children of Darkness" for which she received a THEATRE WORLD Award, "Antony and Cleopatra" (CP), "Hello and Goodbye," "Good Woman of Setzuan" (LC).

DIAMOND, MICHAEL. Born July 18, 1945 in Bklyn. Attended UNH. NY bow 1969 Off-Bdwy in "King Lear," followed by "Henry V," "Heloise" (ELT).

Samantha Doane

Charles Durning

Katharine Dunfee

Ray Edelstein

Ronnie Claire Edwar

DIETZ, EILEEN. Born in NYC; attended Neighborhood Playhouse, AADA. Appeared OB in "Come Back, Little Sheba," "Steambath."

DILLON, MELINDA. Born Oct. 13, 1939 in Hope, Ark. Attended Goodman Theatre School. Bdwy debut 1962 in "Who's Afraid of Virginia Woolf?" for which she received a THEATRE WORLD Award, followed by "You know I Can't Hear You When The Water's Running" "A Way of Life," "A Round with Ring" (OB), "Paul Sills' Story Theatre," "Metamorphoses."

DIXON, MacINTYRE. Born Dec. 22, 1931 in Everett, Mass. Graduate Emerson Col. Off-Bdwy in "Quare Fellow," "Plays for Bleecker St.," "Stewed Prunes," "Cat's Pajamas," "Three Sisters," "3 X 3," "Second City," "Mad Show," "Meeow!," on Bdwy in "Xmas in Las Vegas, " "Cop-Out," "Story Theatre," "Metamorphoses."

DOANE, SAMANTHA. Born Nov. 29, 1946 in Harlan, Ky. Graduate U. Ky., Neighborhood Playhouse. Bdwy debut 1971 in "Abelard and Heloise."

DONHOWE, GWYDA. Born Oct. 20, 1933 in Oak Park, Ill. Attended Drake U. Goodman Theatre, Bdwy debut 1957 in "Separate Tables," followed by "Half a Sixpence," "The Flip Side," "Paris Is Out," "Applause," with APA in "The Showoff," "War and Peace," "Right You Are...," "You Can't Take It with You," Off-Bdwy in "Philosophy in the Boudoir," "Rondelay."

D'ORSAY, FIFI. Born Apr. 16, 1904 in Montreal, Can. After long and successful career in films, made Bdwy debut 1971 in "Follies."

DOUGLAS, MICHAEL. Born Sept. 25, 1944 in New Brunswick, NJ. Graduate U Cal. NY debut 1969 Off-Bdwy in "City Scene," followed by "Pinkville" for which he received a THEATRE WORLD Award.

DOVA, NINA. Born Jan. 15, 1926 in London. Attended Neighborhood Playhouse. Debut Off Bdwy in "I Feel Wonderful," followed by Bdwy in "Zorba," "The Rothschilds."

DOW, R. A. Born Aug. 30, 1941 in Cambridge, Mass. Graduate U Pa. NY bow Off-Bdwy 1970 in "The Dirtiest Show in Town."

DOWD, MEL. Born Feb. 2 in Chicago. Attended Goodman Theatre. Off-Bdwy in "Macbeth," "A Midsummer Night's Dream," "Romeo Juliet," "Julius Caesar," "Royal Gambit," "The Emperor," "Invitation To A Beheading," "Mercy Street," Bdwy debut 1958 in "Methuselah," followed by "A Case of Libel," "Sweet Bird of Youth," "Camelot," "The Right Honourable Gentleman," "The Sound of Music" (CC), with LCRep in "The Unknown Soldier and His Wife," and "Tiger At The Gates," "Everything In The Garden," "Dear World," "Not Now, Darling."

DOWNING, DAVID. Born July 21, 1943 in NYC. Off-Bdwy: with NEC in "DAY of Absence," "Happy Ending," "Song of The Lusitanian Bogey," and "Ceremonies in Dark Old Men," "Man Better Man," "The Harangues," "Brotherhood," "Perry's Mission," "Rosalee Pritchett," "Dream on Monkey Mt.," "Ride a Black Horse."

DRISCHELL, RALPH. Born Nov. 26, 1927 in Baldwin, NY. Attended Carnegie Tech. Off-Bdwy in "Playboy of The Western World," "The Crucible," "The Balcony," "Time of Vengeance," "Barroom Monks," "Portrait of The Artist As A Young Man," "Abe Lincoln In Illinois," "The Caretaker," "A Slight Ache," "The Room," on Bdwy in "Rhinoceros," "All In Good Time," "Rosencrantz and Guildenstern Are Dead," with LCRep in "The Year Boston Won the Pennant," "The Time of Your Life," "Camino Real, "Operation Sidewinder," "Beggar on Horseback."

DRUMMOND, ALICE. Born May 21, 1929 in Pawtucket R.I. Attended Pembroke Col. Off-Bdwy with Phoenix Co., and in "Royal Gambit," "Go Show Me A Dragon," "Sweet of You to Say So," "Gallows Humor," "American Dream," "Giants' Dance," "The Carpenters," "Charles Abbott & Son," Bdwy debut 1963 in "Ballad of the Sad Cafe," followed by "Malcolm," "The Chinese."

DUEL, WILLIAM. Born Aug. 30, 1923 in Corinth, NY. Attended Ill. Wesleyan, Yale. Off-Bdwy in: "Three-penny Opera," "Portrait Of The Artist As A Young Man," "Barroom Monks." "A Midsummer Night's Dream," "Henry IV," "Taming of The Shrew," "The Memorandum," on Bdwy in "A Cook For Mr. General," "Ballad of The Sad Cafe," "Ilya Darling," "1776."

DUNCAN, SANDY. Born Feb 20, 1946 in Henderson, Tex. Attended Len Morris Col. NY debut in "The Music Man" (CC'65), followed by its revivals of "Carousel," "Finian's Rainbow," "Sound of Music,' "Wonderful Town," and "Life With Father," Off-Bdwy in "Ceremony of Innocence" for which she received a THEATRE WORLD Award, "Your Own Thing," Bdwy debut 1969 in "Canterbury Tales," followed by "Love is A Time of Day," "The Boy Friend."

DUNFEE, KATHARINE. Born Aug. 26, 1948 in Santa Monica, Cal. Attended NYU. Bdwy debut 1957 in "Under Milk Wood," followed by "The Visit" (CC), OB in "Mod Donna," "Subject to Fits."

DUNNOCK, MILDRED. Born Jan. 25 in Baltimore, Md. Graduate Goucher Col., Columbia. Bdwy debut 1932 in "Life Begins," followed by "The Corn is Green," "Richard III," "Only the Heart," "Foolish Notion," "Lute Song," "Another Part of the Forest," "The Hallams," "Death of a Salesman," "Pride's Crossing," "The Wild Duck," "In the Summer House," "Cat on a Hot Tin Roof," "Child of Fortune," "The Milk Train Doesn't Stop Here Anymore," "Traveller without Luggage," Off-Bdwy in "The Trojan Women," "Phedre," "Willie Doesn't Live Here Anymore," " Colette," "A Place Without Doors."

DURNING, CHARLES. Born Feb. 28, 1933 in Highland Falls, NY. Attended Columbia. NYU, Bdwy credits: "Poor Bitos," "Drat! The Cat!," "Pousse Cafe," "The Happy Time," "Indians," Off-Bdwy in NYSF productions, "Two By Saroyan," "The Child Buyer," "An Album of Gunther Grass," "Huui, Huui," "An Invitation To A Beheading," "Lemon Sky," "Henri VI," "Happiness Cage."

DUSSAULT, NANCY. , Born June 30, in Pensacola, Fla. Graduate Northwestern. NY debut 1958 (OB) in "Diversions," followed by "Street Scene"(CC), "Dr. Willy Nilly, "The Cradle Will Rock," "No For an Answer," "Whispers on the Wind," "Trelawny of the Wells," on Bdwy in "Do Re Mi" for which she received a THEATRE WORLD Award, "Sound of Music, " "Bajour," CC revivals of "Carousel," "Finian's Rainbow."

DUSSEAU, JOANNE. Born Mar. 15, 1942 in Houston, Tex. Graduate U Colo. Debut 1971 Off-Bdwy in "Any Resemblance to Persons Living or Dead."

EATON, SALLY. Born Apr. 6, 1947 in Warren, Pa. NY debut Off-Bdwy 1967 in "Hair."

EDELSTEIN, RAY. Born Sept. 6, 1937 in Roanoke,Va. NY debut 1970 in "Candyapple" (OB), followed by "Oh! Calcutta!"

EDWARDS, RONNIE CLAIRE. Born Feb. 9, 1933 in Oklahoma City. Graduate U Okla. Debut 1963 in "Paint Your Wagon," followed by "Trial of the Catonsville 9."

ELDRIDGE, ELAINE. Born in Glendale, NY. Attended Hunter Col. Bdwy debut 1935 in "Dance of Death," followed by "Traveller without Luggage," OB in "Clerambard," "Juno and the Paycock," "Red Roses for Me," "Johnny Summitt," "Every Other Evil," "Triple Play," "Caucasian Chalk Circle," "Country Wife" "Trelawny of the Wells."

Josip Elic   Laura Esterman   Albert Fann   Pauline Flanagan   Richard Fasciano

ELIC, JOSIP. Born Mar. 10, 1921 in Butte, Mont. Attended Wisc U., Faigan School. NY bow (OB) in "Threepenny Opera," followed by "Don Juan in Hell," "Leave It to Jane," "Comic Strip," "Coriolanus," "Too Much Johnson," "Stag Movie," Bdwy in "Hamlet," "Baptiste," "West Side Story," "Sign in Sidney Brustein's Window," "Kelly."

ELIZONDO, HECTOR. Born Dec. 22, 1936 in NYC. Attended CCNY. Off-Bdwy in "Drums In The Night," "Steambath," on Bdwy in "The Great White Hope."

ELLIN, DAVID. Born Jan. 10, 1925 in Montreal, Can. Attended AADA. Appeared in "Swan Song," "West Side Story," "The Education of Hyman Kaplan," "Light, Lively and Yiddish," Off-Bdwy in "The Trees Die Standing," "Mirele Efros," and "The End of All Things Natural."

ELLIOTT, BOB. Born Mar. 26, 1923, in Boston. Attended Feagan School. On radio from 1942. Bdwy debut 1970 in "Bob and Ray--The Two and Only."

ELLIOTT, PATRICIA. Born July 21, 1942 in Gunnison, Colo. Graduate U. Colo., London Academy. NY debut with LCRep 1968 in "King Lear," and "A Cry of Players," followed by OB in "Henry V," "The Persians," "A Doll's House," "Hedda Gabler."

ENGEL, ROBERT. Born Oct. 7, 1948 in Chicago. Attended UWisc. Debut Off-Bdwy 1971 in "Candide."

EPSTEIN, ALVIN. Born May 14, 1925 in NYC. Attended Queens Col., Decroux School of Mime, Habimah Theatre. Appeared with Marcel Marceau, and in "King Lear," "Waiting for Godot," "From A to Z," "No Strings," "The Passion of Josef D.," "Postmark Zero," Off-Bdwy in "Purple Dust," "Pictures in a Hallway," "Clerambard," "Endgame," "Whores, Wares and Tin Pan Alley," "A Place Without Doors."

ESTERMAN, LAURA. Born Apr. 12, 1945 in NYC. Attended Radcliffe, London AMDA. NY debut 1969 with LCRep in "The Time of Your Life," followed OB by "The Pig Pen", "The Carpenters."

EVANS, DICKIE. Born Nov. 24, 1950 in Baltimore, Md. Attended Boston Conserv. Debut 1971 Off-Bdwy in "A Day in the Life of Just about Everyone."

EVANS, HARVEY. Born Jan. 7, 1941 in Cincinnati, O. Bdwy debut 1957 in "New Girl in Town," Followed by "West Side Story," "Redhead," "Gypsy," "Anyone Can Whistle," "Hello Dolly!," "George M!," "Our Town," "The Boy Friend," "Follies,"

EVERHART, REX. Born June 13, 1920 in Watseka, Ill. Graduate U. Mo., NYU. Bdwy bow 1955 in "No Time For Sergeants," followed by "Tall Story," "Moonbirds," "Tenderloin," "A Matter of Position," "Rainy Day In Newark," "Skyscraper," "How Now, Dow Jones?," "1776."

EWER, DONALD. Born Sept. 10, 1923 in London. Attended RADA. Bdwy debut 1957 in "Under Milk Wood," followed by "Alfie," "Billy Liar" (OB), "Saved" (OB).

FANN, ALBERT. Born Feb. 21, 1933 in Cleveland, O. Attended Cleveland Inst. of Music. Debut Off-Bdwy 1970 in "King Heroin."

FASCIANO, RICHARD. Born Mar. 18, 1943 in Ansonia, Conn. Graduate U Conn. Bdwy debut 1970 in "Butterflies Are Free."

FAYE, JOEY. Born July 12, 1910 in NYC. Bdwy bow 1938 in "Sing Out The News," followed by "Room Service," "Meet The People," "The Man Who Came To Dinner," "The Milky Way," "Boy Meets Girl," "Streets of Paris," "Allah Be Praised," "The Duchess Misbehaves," "Tidbits of 1948," "High Button Shoes," "Top Banana," "Tender Trap," "Man of LaMancha," "Lyle" (OB), "70, Girls, 70."

FEINER, MARJORIE LYNNE. Born June 26, 1948 in Bklyn. Attended Buffalo U. Debut Off-Bdwy 1971 in "False Confessions."

FELLOWS, DON. Born Dec. 2, 1922 in Salt Lake City. Attended U Wisc. Appeared in "Mister Roberts," "South Pacific," "Only in America," "Marathon '33," "Friday Night" (OB). "Generation," "My House Is Your House" (OB).

FENNESSY, JOHN. Born Aug. 5, 1946 in Bklyn. Attended NYU, AADA. Debut 1970 Off-Bdwy in "Greenwillow."

FERNANDEZ, JOSE. Born Aug. 19, 1948 in Havana, Cuba. Attended HB Studio. Appeared Off-Bdwy in "Dark of the Moon," "The Me Nobody Knows."

FIELD, BETTY. Born Feb. 8, 1918 in Boston. Attended AADA. Bdwy debut 1934 in "Page Miss Glory," followed by "3 Men on a Horse," "Room Service," "What a Life," "Primrose Path," "2 on an Island," "Flight to the West," "A New Life," "Voice of the Turtle," "Dream Girl," "Rat Race," "Not for Children," "Fourposter," "Ladies of the Corridor," "Festival," "Waltz of the Toreadors," "A Touch of the Poet," "A Loss of Roses," "Strange Interlude," ('63), "Where's Daddy?" "Birthday Party" (LC), "Landscape" (LC)," "All Over."

FIORE, FRANK. Born Nov. 15, 1953 in Kew Gardens, NY. Attended Drama Workshop, Juilliard. Bdwy debut 1970 in "Child's Play."

FISHER, DOUGLAS. Born July 9, 1934 in Bklyn. Attended St. John's U., AADA. Debut (OB) 1963 in "Best Foot Forward," followed by "Frere Jacques," "Devils' Disciple," "Accent on Youth," "Lost in the Stars," "Say, Darling," "Shoestring Revue."

FITZGERALD, GERALDINE. Born Nov. 24, 1914 in Dublin, Ire. Bdwy debut 1938 in "Heartbreak House," followed by "Sons and Soldiers," "Doctor's Dilemma," "King Lear," "Hide and Seek," Off-Bdwy in "The Cave Dwellers," "Pigeons," "Long Day's Journey into Night,"

FITZGERALD, NEIL. Born Jan. 15, 1898 in Tipperary, Ire. Attended Trinity Col. Appeared in "Leave Her To Heaven," "The Wookey," "Without Love," "Ten Little Indians," "Plan M," "You Touched Me," "The Play's The Thing," "Design For A Stained Glass Window," "The High Ground," "To Dorothy, A Son," "Mr. Pickwick," "Witness For The Prosecution," "Little Moon of Alban," "Hadrian VII," "The Mundy Scheme," "All Over," Off-Bdwy in "Portrait Of The Artist As A Young Man," "Three Hand Reel," "Carricknabauna."

FITZPATRICK, KELLY. Born Dec. 31, 1937 in Mt. Kisco, NY. Graduate Hobart Col., Dublin Workshop. Bdwy debut 1971 in "Abelard and Heloise."

FLANAGAN, PAULINE. Born June 29, 1925 in Sligo, Ire. Debut Off-Bdwy 1958 in "Ulysses in Nighttown," followed by "Pictures in the Hallway," "Antigone" (LC), on Bdwy in "God and Kate Murphy," "The Living Room."

FLIPPIN, LUCY LEE. Born July 23, 1943 in Philadelphia. Graduate Northwestern U. Debut Off-Bdwy 1970 in "The Playground," followed by "Shoestring Revue."

FLYNN, THOMAS F. Born Dec. 16, 1946 in Albany, NY. Graduate Union Col., Neighborhood Playhouse Debut 1970 Off-Bdwy in "House of Blue Leaves."

FORD, DAVID. Born Oct. 30, 1929 in LaJolla, Calif. Attended Ariz. State, U S. Dak. NY bow Off-Bdwy in "Billy Budd," followed by "Tea Party," on Bdwy in "The Physicists," "1776."

FORD, SYDNEY. Born Feb. 28, 1938 in London. NY debut Off-Bdwy 1953 in "Private Secretary," followed by "The Bells," "Silver Nails," "Trilby," "Heloise."

FORLOW, TED. Born Apr. 29, 1931 in Independence, Mo. Attended Baker U. Bdwy debut 1957 in "New Girl In Town," followed by "Juno," "Destry Rides Again," "Subways Are For Sleeping," "Can-Can," "Wonderful Town" (CC), "A Funny Thing Happened On The Way To The Forum," "Milk And Honey," "Carnival" (CC'68), "Man of La Mancha."

Ed Forman   **Charlotte Frazier**   **Ronald Frazier**   **Beulah Garrick**   **John Gallagher**

FORMAN, ARTHUR EDMUND. Born Aug. 9, 1918 in Scranton, Pa. Attended U Minn., Neighborhood Playhouse. Debut 1969 Off-Bdwy in "Tango," followed by "Scuba Duba," "Uncle Vanya."

FORREST, MILTON EARL. Born Apr. 21, 1946 in NYC. Attended CUNY. Debut off-Bdwy 1968 in "The David Show," followed by "The Way It Is," "The Pen," "As You Like It," "Pinkville."

FORSYTHE, HENDERSON. Born Sept. 11, 1917 in Macon, Mo. Attended U. Iowa. Off-Bdwy in "The Iceman Cometh," "The Collection," "The Room," "A Slight Ache," "Happiness Cage", "Waiting for Godot", on Bdwy in "The Cellar and the Well," "Miss Lonelyhearts," "Who's Afraid of Virginia Woolf?," "Malcolm," "Right Honourable Gentleman," "Delicate Balance," "Birthday Party," "Harvey," "Engagement Baby."

FOSTER, FRANCES. Born June 11 in Y.onkers, NY Bdwy debut 1955 in "The Wisteria Trees," followed by "Nobody Loves An Albatross," "Raisin In The Sun," Off-Bdwy in "Take a Giant Step," "Edge of the City," "Tammy and The Doctor," "The Crucible," NEC's "Happy Ending," "Day of Absence," "An Evening of One Acts," "Man Better Man," "Brotherhood," "Akokawe," and "Rosalee Pritchett," "Good Woman of Setzuan" (LC), "Behold! Cometh the Vanderkellans" (OB).

FOSTER, HERBERT. Born May 14, 1936 in Winnipeg, Can. With Natl. Rep. Theatre 1967 in "The Imaginary Invalid," "A Touch of The Poet," and "Tonight At 8:30," followed by "Papers" (OB) "Henry V." LC's "Playboy of the Western World," "Good Woman of Setzuan," and "Scenes from American Life."

FOWKES, CONARD. Born Jan. 4, 1933 In Washington, D.C. Yale Graduate. Bdwy bow 1958 in "Howie," followed by "The Wall," "Minor Miracle," Off-Bdwy in "Look Back in Anger," "That Thing at the Cherry Lane," "America Hurrah," "The Reckoning," "Istanboul."

FRANKLIN, BONNIE. Born Jan. 6, 1944 in Santa Monica, Cal. Attended Smith Col. UCLA. Debut Off-Bdwy 1968 in "Your Own Thing," followed by "Dames at Sea," Bdwy bow 1970 in "Applause" for which she received a THEATRE WORLD Award.

FRANKLIN, NANCY. Born in NYC. On Bdwy in "Happily Never After," "The White House," "Never Live Over A Pretzel Factory," Off-Bdwy in "Buffalo Skinner," "Power of Darkness," "Oh Dad, Poor Dad---," "Theatre of Peretz," "Seven Days of Mourning," "Here Be Dragons."

FRAZIER, CHARLOTTE. Born Aug. 13, 1939 in Philadelphia. Graduate Lebanon Valley Col. Bdwy debut in "Bye Bye Birdie," followed by "How to Succeed in Business . . . ," "Company."

FRAZIER, RONALD CORDELL. Born Feb. 18, 1942. Graduate Carnegie Tech. Bdwy debut 1970 in "Wilson in the Promise Land," followed by "Enemy of the People" (LC).

FREEMAN ANN. Born in Portsmouth, Eng. NY debut 1967 in revival of "Life with Father" (CC), followed by "Present Laughter" (OB).

FRENCH, ARTHUR. Born in NYC. Attended Bklyn Col. Off-Bdwy in "Raisin' Hell In the Sun," "Ballad of Bimshire," "Day of Absence," "Happy Ending," "Jonah." with NEC in "Ceremonies In Dark Old Men," "An Evening of One Acts," "Man Better Man," "Brotherhood," "Perry's Mission," "Rosalee Pritchett."

FRENCH, VALERIE. Born in London. Bdwy debut 1965 in "Inadmissible Evidence," followed by "Help Stamp Out Marriage," OB in "Tea Party," "Mother Lover," "Trelawny of the Wells,"

FRY, RAY. Born Feb. 22, 1923 in Hebron, Ind. Graduate SF State Col.,Northwestern. Bdwy bow 1944 in "Hickory Stick," followed by "Cyrano," "The Cradle Will Rock," with LCRep in "Danton's Death," "The Country Wife," "Caucasian Chalk Circle," "The Alchemist," "Galileo," "St. Joan," "Tiger At The Gates," "Cyrano," "A Cry of Players," "Bananas," "The Miser," "Operation Sidewinder," "Beggar on Horseback," "Playboy of the Western World," "Good Woman of Setzuan," "Birthday Party," "Antigone."

FULLER, PENNY. Born 1940, in Durham, NC. Attended Northwestern. Appeared in "Barefoot in the Park," "Cabaret," NYSF's "Richard III," "As You Like It," and "Henry IV," "Applause."

GABLE, JUNE. Born June 5, 1945 in NY. Graduate Carnegie Tech. Appeared Off-Bdwy in "MacBird," "Jacques Brel Is Alive and Well and Living In Paris."

GABOR, ZSA ZSA. Born Feb. 6, 1923 in Budapest, Hungary. Bdwy debut 1970 in "40 Carats."

GALLAGHER, HELEN. Born in Brooklyn, 1926. Bdwy debut 1947 in "Seven Lively Arts," followed by "Mr. Strauss Goes To Boston," "Billion Dollar Baby," "Brigadoon," "High Button Shoes." "Touch and Go," "Make A Wish," "Pal Joey," "Hazel Flagg," CC revivals of "Guys and Dolls," "Finian's Rainbow," and "Oklahoma," "Pajama Game," "Bus Stop," "Portofino," "Sweet Charity," "Mame," "Cry For Us All," " No, No, Nanette."

GALLAGHER, JOHN. Born Mar. 27, 1947 in Trenton, NY. Attended HB Studio. Debut Off-Bdwy 1971 in "Underground."

GARDENIA, VINCENT. Born Jan. 7 in Italy. NY bow Off-Bdwy 1956 in "Man With The Golden Arm," followed by "Brothers Karamazov," "Power of Darkness," "Machinal," "Gallows Humor," "Endgame," "Little Murders," "Passing Through from Exotic Places," "Carpenters," on Bdwy in "The Visit" (1957), "The Cold Wind and The Warm," "Rashomon," "Only In America," "The Wall," "Daughters of Silence," "Seidman and Son," "Dr.Fish."

GARFIELD, DAVID. Born Feb. 6, 1941 in Brooklyn. Graduate Columbia, Cornell. Off-Bdwy in "Hang Down Your Head and Die," Bdwy bow l967 in "Fiddler on the Roof," followed by "The Rothschilds."

GARFIELD, JULIE. Born Jan. 10, 1946 in Los Angeles. Attended U Wisc., Neighborhood Playhouse. NY debut 1969 in "Honest-to-God Schnozzola," followed by "Uncle Vanya" for which she received a THEATRE WORLD Award.

GARLAND, GEOFF. Born June 10, 1932 Warrington, Eng. NY bow Off-Bdwy 1961 in "The Hostage," on Bdwy in "Hamlet," NRT's "The Imaginary Invalid," "A Touch of The Poet," and "Tonight At 8:30," "The Front Page" ('69), "Trelawny of the Wells" (OB).

GARRETT, JOY. Born Mar. 2, 1945 in Ft. Worth, Tex. Graduate Tex. Wesleyan, AADA. NY bow Off-Bdwy 1969 in "Gertrude Stein's First Reader," followed by "The Drunkard," "Candyapple."

GARRICK BEULAH. Born June 12, 1921 in Nottingham, Eng. NY debut 1959 in "Shadow and Substance," followed by "Auntie Mame," "Juno," "Little Moon of Alban," "High Spirits," "The Hostage," "Funny Girl," "Lovers," "Abelard and Heloise."

GASSELL, SYLVIA. Born July 1, 1923 in NYC. Attended Hunter, New School. Bdwy debut 1952 in "The Time of The Cuckoo," followed by "Sunday Breakfast," "Fair Game For Lovers," "Inquest," Off-Bdwy in "U.S.A.," "Romeo and Juliet," "Electra," "A Darker Flower," "Fragments," "Goa," "God Bless You, Harold Fineberg," "Philosophy In The Boudoir," "Stag Movie."

Judy Gibson	**Edmund Gaynes**	**Ruth Gillette**	**Gene GeBauer**	**Bette Glenn**

GAVON, IGORS. Born Nov. 14, 1937 in Latvia. Bdwy bow 1961 in "Carnival," followed by "Hello, Dolly!" "Marat/DeSade," "Billy," Off-Bdwy in "Your Own Thing," "Promenade," "Exchange," "Nevertheless, They Laugh."

GAYNES, EDMUND. Born May 14, 1947 in Brooklyn. Graduate CCNY. Bdwy bow 1958 in "Body Beautiful," followed by "Greenwillow," "The Fig Leaves Are Falling," Off Bdwy in Bartleby," "Best Foot Forward," "Promenade," "Now Is the Time"

GeBAUER, GENE. Born June 28, 1934 in Ord, Neb. NY bow 1960 in "Machinal" (OB), followed by "Once Upon a Mattress," "Stag Movie," on Bdwy in "Camelot," "No Strings," "Hello, Dolly!" "Oh! Calcutta!"

GEER, WILL. Born Mar. 9, 1902 in Frankfort, Ind. Attended U Chicago, Columbia, Oxford. Bdwy bow 1924 in "Uncle Tom's Cabin," followed by "Merry Wives of Windsor," "Let Freedom Ring," "Bury the Dead," "200 Were Chosen," "A House in the Country," "Of Mice and Men," "Steel," "Freedom of the Press," "The Cradle Will Rock," "Sing Out the News," "Tobacco Road," "The More the Merrier," "Moon Vine," "Sophie," "Flamingo Road," "On Whitman Avenue," "Hope Is the Thing . . . ," APA productions, "The Vamp," "Ponder Heart," "No Time for Sergeants," "110 in the Shade," "An Evening's Frost" (OB), "Horseman,Pass by" (OB), "Scratch."

GELFAND, CAROL. Born Aug. 16, 1937 in Chicago. Attended U. Ill., Columbia. Debut off-Bdwy 1961 in "The Cage," Bdwy bow 1970 in "Company."

GENTLES, AVRIL. Born Apr. 2, 1929 in Upper Montclair, NJ. Graduate U NC. Bdwy debut 1955 in "The Great Sebastians," followed by "Nude With Violin," "Present Laughter," "Dinny and The Witches" (OB), "My Mother, My Father and Me," "The Wives" (OB), "Jimmy Shine," "Grin and Bare It," "Now Is the Time" (OB).

GERSTAD, JOHN. Born Sept. 3, 1925 in Boston. Attended Harvard. Bdwy bow 1943 in "Othello," followed by "Dark of The Moon," "Joy To The World," "Not For Children," "The Male Animal" (CC'52), "Golden Fleecing," "Trial of Lee Harvey Oswald," "Come Summer," "Penny Wars," "Oklahoma!" (LC), "All Over."

GIBBS, ANN. Born Sept. 26 in Oklahoma City. Attended U. Okla. Debut off-Bdwy 1969 in "You're a Good Man, Charlie Brown."

GIBSON, JUDY. Born Sept. 11, 1947 in Trenton, NJ. Graduate Rider Col. Bdwy debut 1970 in "Purlie," followed OB by "Sensations," and "Manhattan Arrangement."

GIELGUD, JOHN. Born Apr. 14, 1904 in London. Attended RADA. NY debut 1928 in "The Patriot," followed by "Hamlet," "Importance of Being Earnest," "Love for Love," "Crime and Punishment," "The Lady's Not for Burning," "Medea" "Ages of Man," "School for Scandal," "Homage to Shakespeare," "Tiny Alice," "Ivanov," "Home."

GIERASCH, STEFAN. Born Feb. 5, 1926 in NYC. Appeared in "Kiss and Tell," "Snafu," "Billion Dollar Baby," "Montserrat," "Night Music," "Hatful of Rain," "Compulsion," "Shadow of a Gunman," "War and Peace" (APA), "7 Days of Mourning" (OB), "AC/DC" (OB).

GILBERT, LOU. Born Aug. 1, 1909 in Sycamore, Ill. Appeared in "Common Ground," "Beggars Are Coming To Town," "Truckline Cafe," "The Whole World Over," "Volpone," "Hope's The Thing With Feathers," "Detective Story," "His and Hers," "The Great White Hope," Off-Bdwy in "A Month In The Country," "Big Man," "Dynamite Tonight," "Good Woman of Setzuan" (CC).

GILFORD, JACK. Born July 25 in NYC. Bdwy bow 1940 in "Meet the People," followed by "They Should Have Stood in Bed," "Count Me In," "The Live Wire," "Alive and Kicking," "Once Over Lightly," "Diary of Anne Frank," "Romanoff and Juliet," "The Tenth Man," "A Funny Thing Happened . . . ," "Cabaret," "3 Men on a Horse," "No, No, Nanette."

GILLETTE, ANITA. Born Aug. 16, 1938 in Baltimore. Debut Off-Bdwy 1960 in "Russell Patterson's Sketchbook" for which she received a THEATRE WORLD Award. followed by "Carnival," "All American," "Mr. President," "Guys and Dolls" (CC'55), "Don't Drink The Water," "Cabaret," "Jimmy."

GILLETTE, RUTH. Born Aug. 16 1906 in Chicago. Attended Northwestern. Bdwy debut in "Passing Show of 1924," followed by "Gay Paree," "Passions of 1926," "Carousel," "My Maryland," "Pajama Game," "Gazebo," "Mame," "70, Girls, 70."

GLENN, BETTE. Born Dec. 13, 1946 in Atlantic City, NJ. Graduate Montpelier Col. Debut Off-Bdwy 1971 in "Ruddigore" (ELT.)

GLOVER, JOHN. Born Aug. 7, 1944 in Kingston, NY. Attended Towson State Col. Debut Off-Bdwy 1969 in "A Scent of Flowers," followed by "Subject to Fits" "House of Blue Leaves."

GORDON, PEGGY. Born Dec. 26, 1949 in NYC. Attended Carnegie Tech. Debut Off-Bdwy 1971 in "Godspell."

GORMAN, CLIFF. Born Oct. 13, 1936 in NYC. Attended UCLA. Off-Bdwy in "Hogan's Goat," "Boys in the Band," "Ergo," Bdwy bow 1971 in "Lenny."

GOULD, GORDON. Born May 4, 1930 in Chicago. Yale graduate. From 1963 with APA in "Man and Superman," "War and Peace," "Judith," "Lower Depths," "Right You Are," "Scapin," "Impromptu at Versailes," "You Can't Take It with You," "The Hostage," "The Tavern," "Midsummer Night's Dream," "Merchant of Venice," "Richard II," "Much Ado about Nothing," "Wild Duck," "The Show-Off" and "Pantagleize," followed by "School for Wives."

GOULD, HAROLD. Born Dec. 10, 1923 in Schenectady, N.Y. Graduate SUNY, Cornell. NY bow 1969 at Lincoln Center in "The Increased Difficulty of Concentration," and "Amphitryon," followed by "House of Blue Leaves" (OB).

GOZ, HARRY G. Born June 23, 1932 in St. Louis. Attended St. Louis Inst. of Music. NY bow 1957 in "Utopia Limited," followed by "Bajour," "Fiddler on the Roof," "Two by Two."

GRAHAM, JUNE. Born in St. Louis. Attended U Wash., U Iowa. Debut 1967 Off-Bdwy in "When Did You Last See My Mother?." followed by "War Games," "My House Is Your House."

GRANT,MICKI. Born June 30 in Chicago. Attended U. Ill., Geller School. Bdwy debut 1963 in "Tambourines to Glory," Off-Bdwy in "Fly Blackbird," "The Blacks," "Brecht on Brecht," "Jerico-Jim Crow," "The Cradle Will Rock," "Leonard Bernstein's Theatre Songs," "To Be Young, Gifted and Black," "Don't Bother Me."

GREEN, HOWARD. Born Mar. 9, 1936 in Detroit. Graduate U Mich, Off-Bdwy in "Darkness at Noon," "Cyrano" (LC), "Ceremony of Innocence," "Henry VI" (CP), "Richard III" (CP)

GREEN, MARTYN. Born Apr. 22, 1899 in London. Attended Royal Col. Appeared with D'Oyly Carte (1934-51), Chartok's Gilbert & Sullivan Co., "Misalliance," "Shangri-La," "Child of Fortune," "A Visit to a Small Planet," "Black Comedy," "Canterbury Tales," "Charley's Aunt," Off-Bdwy in "Drums under the Windows," "Red Roses for Me," "Carricknabauna."

Reuben Greene   **Pamela Hall**   **John Grigas**   **Jill Harmon**   **Jack Harrold**

GREENE, JAMES. Born Dec. 1, 1926 in Lawrence, Mass. Graduate Emerson Col. Off-Bdwy in "The Iceman Cometh," "American Gothic," "The King and the Duke," "The Hostage," "Plays for Bleecker St.," "Moon in the Yellow River," "Misalliance," with LCRep 2 years, with APA in "You Can't Take It with You," "School for Scandal," "Wild Duck," "Right You Are," "The Show-Off" "and "Pantagleize." on Bdwy in "Romeo and Juliet," "Girl on Via Flaminia," "Compulsion," "Inherit the Wind," "Shadow of a Gunman," "Andersonville Trial," "Night Life," "School for Wives."

GREENE, MARTY. Born June 19, 1909 in Bklyn. Bdwy debut 1940 in "Summer Night," followed by "Night Music," "Golden Boy," "Enter Laughing," "Threepenny Opera" (OB), "Out West of Eighth," "God Bless You, Harold Fineberg" and "Whose Little Boy Are You? (OB).

GREENE, REUBEN. Born Nov. 24, 1938 in Philadelphia. With APA in "War and Peace," "You Can't Take It With You," and "Pantagleize," Off-Bdwy in "Jericho-Jim Crow," "Happy Ending," "The Boys In The Band."

GREENHOUSE, MARTHA. Born June 14 in Omaha, Neb. Attended Hunter Col., Am. Th. Wing. Appeared in "Sons and Solders," "Clerambard" (OB), "Our Town" (OB), "Dear Me, the Sky Is Falling," "Family Way," "Woman Is My Idea," "3 by Ferlinghetti" (OB).

GRIGAS, JOHN. Born Feb. 16, 1930 in Shenandoah, Pa. Bdwy debut 1956 in "Plain and Fancy," followed by "My Fair Lady," "Milk and Honey," "Baker Street," "It's Superman," "Man of LaMancha," "Dear World," "Follies."

GRIMALDI, DENNIS. Born Sept. 30, 1947 in Oak Park, Ill. Graduate Goodman School. Debut 1970 Off-Bdwy in "Me and Juliet" (ELT).

GRODIN, CHARLES. Born Apr. 21, 1935 in Pittsburgh. Attended U Miami, Pittsburgh Playhouse. Bdwy debut 1962 in "Tchin-Tchin," followed by "Absence of a Cello," Off-Bdwy in "Hooray! It's a Glorious Day," "Steambath."

GROVER, STANLEY. Born Mar. 28, 1926 in Woodstock, Ill. Attended U Mo. Appeared in "Seventeen," "Wish You Were Here," "Time Remember'd," "Candide," "13 Daughters," "Mr. President," CC revivals of "South Pacific," "Finian's Rainbow," and "King and I," "Lyle" (OB), "Company."

GRUET, ALLAN. Born Mar. 22, 1945 in Paterson, NJ. Graduate Boston U. Bdwy debut 1968 in "Fiddler on the Roof," followed by "The Rothschilds."

GUNN, MOSES. Born Oct. 2, 1929 in St. Louis. Graduate Tenn. AIU, U. Kan. Off-Bdwy in "Measure For Measure," "Bohikee Creek," "Day of Absence," "Happy Ending," "Baal," "Hard Travelin'," "Lonesome Train," "In White America," "The Blacks," "Titus Andronicus" (CP), Bdwy debut 1966 in "A Hand Is On the Gate," with NEC in "Song of The Lusitanian Bogey," "Summer of 17th Doll," "Kongi's Harvest," and "Daddy Goodness," OB in "Cities In Bezique," "Perfect Party," "To Be Young, Gifted and Black," ASF's "Othello" on Bdwy.

GUERRERO, DANNY. Born Oct. 14, 1945 in Tucson, Ariz. Attended UCLA, Pasadena Playhouse. Off-Bdwy in "Hello, Tourista," "Two Gentlemen of Verona," "Devil's Disciple," "Who's Who, Baby," "Manhattan Arrangement."

GUSS, LOUIS. Born Jan. 4 in NYC. Credits: "Girl on the Via Flaminia," "Handful of Fire," "One More River," "Once There Was a Russian," "Night of the Iguana," "Odd Couple," "Flora the Red Menace," "But Seriously," "Gandhi" (OB).

HAILEY, MARIAN. Born Feb. 1, 1941 in Portland, Ore. U. Wash graduate. Bdwy debut 1965 in "Mating Dance," followed by "Any Wednesday," "Best Laid Plans," "Keep It In The Family," "Harvey," "Company," Off-Bdwy in "Under the Yum Yum Tree," "Thornton Wilder's Triple Bill," "Castro Complex."

HAINES, A. LARRY. Born Aug. 3, 1917 in Mt. Vernon, NY. Attended CCNY. Bdwy bow 1962 in "A Thousand Clowns," followed by "Generation," "Promises, Promises," "Last of the Red Hot Lovers."

HAINES, MERVYN, JR. Born Aug. 20 1933 in Newark, NJ. Attended AADA. With NYSF in "All's Well That Ends Well," "Measure For Measure," "Richard III," "Henry VI," with LCRep in "King Lear," "A Cry of Players," "Henry V."

HALL, ALBERT. Born Nov. 10, 1937 in Boothton, Ala. Columbia graduate. Debut 1971 Off-Bdwy in "Basic Training of Pavlo Hummel."

HALL, MARK. Born June 10, 1955 in Boston, Mass. Debut Off-Bdwy 1968 in "As You Like It," Bdwy bow 1970 in "Child's Play."

HALL, PAMELA. Born Oct. 16, 1947 in Champaign, Ill. Attended U Ill. Off-Bdwy in "Harold Arlen Songbook," "Frere Jacques," "A Month of Sundays," on Bdwy in "Dear World," "1776."

HAMILL, MARY. Born Dec. 29, 1943 in Flushing, NY. Graduate U Dallas. Debut Off-Bdwy in "Spiro Who?" followed by "What the Butler Saw," and Bdwy bow 1971 in "4 on a Garden."

HAMILTON, JOHN. Born Dec. 11, 1940 in Lowell, Mass. Attended U Hartford. NY bow 1971 in "Now Is the Time for All Good Men" (OB).

HAMILTON, ROGER. Born in San Diego, Cal., May 2, 1928. Attended San Diego Col., RADA. Off-Bdwy in "Merchant of Venice," "Hamlet," "Live Like Pigs," "Hotel Passionato," "Sjt. Musgrove's Dance," on Bdwy in "Someone Waiting," "Separate Tables," "Little Moon of Alban," "Luther," "The Deputy," "Rosencrantz and Guildenstern Are Dead," "The Rothschilds."

HANLEY, ELLEN. Born May 15, 1926 in Lorain, O. Attended Juilliard. Bdwy debut 1946 in "Annie Get Your Gun," followed by "Barefoot Boy with Cheek" for which she received a THEATRE WORLD Award, "High Button Shoes," "Two's Company," "First Impressions," "Fiorello!", "The Boys from Syracuse" (OB), "1776."

HANSON, PHILIP. Born Oct. 11, 1924 in Everett, Wash. Graduate U Ill. Debut Off-Bdwy 1961 in "Moby Dick," followed by "A Christmas Carol," "Seven Pillars of Wisdom," "Heloise" (ELT).

HARMON, JILL. Born in NYC, Apr. 25, 1949. Attended Northwestern. Debut 1962 Off-Bdwy in "Black Monday," followed by "Rate of Exchange," Bdwy debut in "Fiddler on the Roof."

HARRIS, JULIE. Born Dec. 2, 1925 in Grosse Point, Mich. Attended Yale. Bdwy debut 1945 in "It's A Gift," followed by "Henry V," "Oedipus," "The Playboy of The Western World," "Alice In Wonderland," "Macbeth," "Sundown Beach" for which she received a THEATRE WORLD Award. "The Young and The Fair," "Magnolia Alley," "Montserrat," "The Member of The Wedding," "I Am A Camera," "Mlle. Colombe," "The Lark," "The Country Wife," "The Warm Peninsula," "Little Moon of Alban," "A Shot In The Dark," "Marathon '33," "Ready When You Are, C.B.," "Hamlet" (CP), "Skyscraper," "40 Carats," "And Miss Reardon Drinks A Little."

HARROLD, JACK. Born June 10, 1920 in Atlantic City, NJ. Bdwy debut 1943 in "The Merry Widow," followed by "Carousel," "Mr. Strauss Goes to Boston," "The Chocolate Soldier," "Lady from Paris," "The Vamp," "Unsinkable Molly Brown," "Rugantino," "The Cradle Will Rock," NYC Opera, "Good Woman of Setzuan" (LC).

HAYLE, DOUGLAS. Born Jan. 11, 1942 in Trenton, NJ. AADA graduate. With NYSF in "Henry IV," "Romeo and Juliet," LCRep. in "King Lear," "A Cry of Players," "In the Matter of J. Robert Oppenheimer," and "The Miser," "Trelawny of the Wells" (OB).

Eileen Heckart   Edward Herrmann   Katherine Helmond   Bolen High   Jeanne Hepple

HECHT, PAUL. Born Aug. 16, 1941 in London. Attended McGill U. With NYSF, Off-Bdwy in "Sjt. Musgrave's Dance" and "MacBird." On Bdwy in "Rosencrantz and Guildenstern Are Dead," "1776," "The Rothschilds."

HECKART, EILEEN. Born Mar. 29, 1919 in Columbus, O. Graduate Ohio State. Debut Off-Bdwy in "Tinker's Dam," followed by "Our Town" (CC), "They Knew What They Wanted," "The Traitor," "Hilda Crane," "In Any Language," "Picnic" for which she received at THEATRE WORLD Award, "The Bad Seed," "A View From The Bridge," "The Dark At The Top of The Stairs," "Invitation To A March," "Pal Joey" (CC), "Everybody Loves Opal," "A Family Affair," "Too True To Be Good," "And Things That Go Bump In The Night," "Barefoot In The Park," "You Know I Can't Hear You When The Water's Running," "The Mother Lover," "Butterflies Are Free."

HEFFERNAN, JOHN,. Born May 30, 1934 in NYC. Attended CCNY, Columbia, Boston U. Off-Bdwy in "The Judge," "Julius Caesar," "Great God Brown," "Lysistrata," "Peer Gynt," "Henry IV," "Taming of The Shrew," "She Stoops To Conquer," "The Plough and The Stars," "The Octoroon," "Hamlet," "Androcles and the Lion," "A Man's A Man," "Winter's Tale," "Arms and The Man," "St. Joan" (LCRep), "Peer Gynt" (CP), "The Memorandum," "Invitation To A Beheading," on Bdwy in "Luther," "Tiny Alice," "Postmark Zero," "Woman Is My Idea," "Morning, Noon and Night," "Purlie,"

HEFLIN, MARTA. Born Mar. 29, 1945 in Washington, DC. Attended Northwestern, Carnegie Tech. NY debut 1967 in "Life With Father" (CC), followed by Salvation" (OB), "Soon" (OB).

HELMERS, JUNE. Born Oct. 21, 1941 in Middletown, O. Attended Carnegie Tech. Bdwy debut 1967 in "Hello Dolly!" followed by "Oklahoma!" (LC), "Johnny Johnson" (OB).

HELMOND, KATHERINE. Born in Galveston, Tex. Off-Bdwy in "Orpheus Descending," "Trip to Bountiful" "The Time of Your Life," "Another Part of the Forest," "Mousetrap," "House of Blue Leaves."

HEMSLEY, SHERMAN. Born Feb. 1, 1938 in Philadelphia. Attended Phila. Academy of Dramatic Arts. NY bow 1968 Off-Bdwy in "The People vs. Ranchman," Bdwy 1970 in "Purlie."

HENDERSON, MELANIE. Born Sept. 20, 1957 in NYC. Debut 1970 in "The Me Nobody Knows."

HENGST, MARILYN. Born Feb. 22, 1946 in West Frankfort, Ill. Graduate SIU. Bdwy debut 1970 in "Not Now, Darling."

HENRITZE, BETTE. Born May 3 in Betsy Layne, Ky. Graduate U. Tenn. Off-Bdwy: "Lion In Love," "Abe Lincoln In Illinois," "Othello," "Baal," "Long Christmas Dinner," "Queens of France," "Rimers of Eldritch," "The Displaced Person," "The Acquisition," "Crime of Passion," "Happiness Cage," NYSF in "Henry VI," "Richard III," on Bdwy in "Jenny Kissed Me," "Pictures In The Hallway," "Giants, Sons of Giants," "Ballad of a Sad Cafe," "The White House," "Dr. Cook's Garden," "Here's Where I Belong."

HENRY, MARTHA. Born Feb. 17, 1938 in Detroit, Mich. Graduate Carnegie Tech. NY debut 1971 with LCRep in "Playboy of the Western World," "Scenes from American Life," and "Antigone" for which she received a THEATRE WORLD Award.

HEPBURN, KATHARINE. Born Nov. 9, 1909 in Hartford, Conn. Attended Bryn Mawr. Bdwy debut 1928 in "Night Hostess," followed by "A Month in the Country," "Art and Mrs. Bottle," "The Warrior's Husband," "The Lake" "Philadelphia Story," "Without Love," "As You Like It," "The Millionairess," "Coco."

HEPPLE, JEANNE. Born in London and attended its Univ. Bdwy debut 1965 in "Inadmissable Evidence," followed by "Sjt. Musgrave's Dance" (OB), "A Touch of the Poet," "Tonight at 8:30," "Imaginary Invalid," NYSF's "Henry VI," and "Richard III," "Early Morning" (OB), "How the Other Half Loves."

HERMAN, MAXINE. Born Aug. 17, 1948 in NYC. Attended NYU. Debut Off-Bdwy 1970 in "The Nuns," followed by "Tarot."

HERRMANN, EDWARD. Born July 21, 1943 in Washington, DC. Graduate Bucknell U., London AMDA. Debut 1970 Off-Bdwy in "Basic Training of Pavlo Hummel"

HEWITT, ROBERT. Born Aug. 12, 1922 in Sydney, Aust. Member of Old Vic, London. Bdwy bow 1963 in "Chips With Everything," followed by "The Zulu and The Zayda," "Hadrian VII," "Conduct Unbecoming."

HEYMAN, BARTON. Born Jan. 24, 1937 in Washington, DC. Attended UCLA. Off-Bdwy 1967 in "A Midsummer Night's Dream," Bdwy debut 1969 in "Indians," followed by "Trial of Catonsville 9." (OB)

HICKEY, WILLIAM. Born in Bklyn. Studied at HB Studio. Bdwy bow 1951 in "St. Joan," followed by "Tovarich," "Miss Lonelyhearts," "Body Beautiful," "Make a Million," "Not Enough Rope," "Moonbirds," "Step on a Crack," OB in "On the Town," "Next," "Happy Birthday, Wanda June."

HIGGINS, DENNIS. Born Aug. 25, 1942 in Washington, DC. Attended G Wash U.,AADA. Debut 1969 Off-Bdwy in "Tom Jones," followed by "Greenwillow" (ELT).

HIGH, BOLEN. Born Nov. 27, 1945 in Houston, Tex. Graduate U Denver, Goodman Theatre. Bdwy debut 1969 in "Henry V," followed by "Meeow!" (OB).

HILL, RALSTON. Born Apr. 24, 1927 in Cleveland, O. Graduate Oberlin Col. Off-Bdwy in "The Changeling," "Streets of New York," "Valmouth," "Carousel," (LC'65), on Bdwy in "1776."

HINCKLEY, ALFRED. Born Sept. 22, 1920, in Kalamazoo, Mich. Graduate NYU. Bdwy bow 1959 in "Legend of Lizzie," followed by "Subways Are for Sleeping," "Man for All Seasons," OB in "A Clearing in the Woods," "Long Voyage Home," "Cockeyed Kite," "Come Share My House," "Night of the Dunce," "Rimers of Eldritch," "People vs. Ranchman," "Steambath."

HINGLE, PAT. Born July 19, 1923 in Denver. Graduate Tex. U. Made Bdwy bow 1953 in "End As A Man," followed by "Festival," "Cat On A Hot Tin Roof," "Girls of Summer," "The Dark At The Top of The Stairs," "J.B.," "Deadly Game," "Strange Interlude" ('63), "Blues For Mr. Charlie," "A Girl Could Get Lucky," "The Glass Menagerie" ('65), "Johnny No Trump," "The Price," "Child's Play."

HINKLEY DEL. Born July 24, 1930 in Indianapolis. Attended Butler and Ind U. Bdwy bow 1967 in "Sherry!," followed by "How to Steal an Election," and "Soon" Off-Bdwy.

HINNANT, BILL. Born Aug. 28, 1935 on Chincoteague Island, Va. Yale graduate. Appeared in "No Time for Sergeants," followed by "Here's Love," "Frank Merriwell," Off-Bdwy in "All Kinds of Giants," "Put It in Writing," "You're A Good Man, Charlie Brown," "American Hamburger League."

HINSON, BONNIE. Born Oct. 11, 1946 in Charlotte, NC. Graduate U Cin. NY debut 1970 in "Me and Juliet" (ELT), followed by "Now Is the Time for All Good Men" (OB).

HO, WAI CHING. Born Nov. 16, 1943 in Hong Kong. Graduate UHK, AADA. Debut Off-Bdwy 1968 in "People vs. Ranchman," followed by "Moon on a Rainbow Shawl."

HOBSON, JAMES. Born Nov. 28, 1938 in Hamilton, Ont. Studied at HB Studio. Debut in "Most Happy Fella" (CC'66), followed by "Mahagonny" (OB), Bdwy bow in "Lovely Ladies, Kind Gentlemen" (1970).

HODAPP, ANN. Born May 6, 1946 in Louisville, Ky. Attended Hunter, NYU. Debut Off-Bdwy 1968 in "You're A Good Man, Charlie Brown," followed by "A Round with Ring," "House of Leather," "Shoestring Revue" (ELT).

245

Laurie Hutchinson   John Cecil Holm   Anne Ives   Carl Hunt   Mary Jackson

HOFFMAN, JANE. Born July 24 in Seattle, Wash. Attended U. Cal. Bdwy debut 1940 in "Tis of Thee," followed by "Crazy With The Heat," "Something For The Boys," "One Touch of Venus," "Calico Wedding," "Mermaids Singing," "A Temporary Island," "Story For Strangers," "Two Blind Mice," "The Rose Tattoo," "The Crucible," "Witness For the Prosecution," "Third Best Sport," "Rhinoceros," "Mother Courage and Her Children," "Fair Game For Lovers," "A Murderer Among Us," Off-Bdwy in "The American Dream," "The Sandbox," "Picnic on the Battle-field," "Theatre of The Absurd," "The Child Buyer," "A Corner of The Bed," "Someone's Comin' Hungry," "The Increased Difficulty of Concentration" (LC), "American Hamburger League," "Slow Memories."

HOLGATE, RONALD. Born May 26, 1937 in Aberdeen, S.D. Attended Northwestern U., New Eng. Cons. Debut 1961 Off-Bdwy in "Hobo," followed by "A Funny Thing Happened On The Way To The Forum." "Milk and Honey," "Hooray, It's A Glorious Day" (OB), "1776."

HOLLAND, ANTHONY. Born Oct. 17, 1933 in Brooklyn. Graduate U Chicago. Off-Bdwy: "Venice Preserved," "Second City," "Victim of Duty," "The New Tenant," "Dynamite Tonight," "The Quare Fellow," "White House Murder Case," "Waiting For Godot," on Bdwy in "My Mother, My Father and Me," "We Bombed in New Haven."

HOLLIDAY, DAVID. Born Aug. 4, 1937 in Illinois. Attended Carthage Col. After appearing in London, made Bdwy bow 1968 in "Man of La Mancha," followed by "Coco" for which he received a THEATRE WORLD Award, "Nevertheless, They Laugh" (OB).

HOLM, JOHN CECIL. Born Nov. 4, 1904 in Philadelphia. Attended U Pa. Bdwy bow 1929 in "The Front Page," followed by "Whirlpool," "Penal Law 2010," "The Up and Up," "Wonder Boy," "Bloodstream," "Dangerous Corner," "Mary of Scotland," "Midgie Purvis," "Gramercy Ghost," "Mr. President," "The Advocate," "A Mighty Man Is He." "Philadelphia, Here I Come!," "Forty Carats."

HORTON, RUSSELL. Born Nov. 11, 1941 in Los Angeles. UCLA graduate. NY bow 1966 in "Displaced Person" (OB), followed by "How's the World Treating You?," "Galileo" (LC), "What Did We Do Wrong?"," "Antigone" (LC).

HOWARD, KEN. Born Mar. 28, 1944 in El Centro, Calif. Graduate Amherst and Yale. Bdwy debut 1968 in "Promises, Promises," followed by "1776" for which he received a THEA-TRE WORLD Award, "Child's Play,"

HOWLAND, BETH. Born May 28, 1941 in Boston. Debut Off-Bdwy 1960 in "Once Upon A Mattress," followed by Bdwy in "Bye, Bye, Birdie," "High Spirits," "Drat! The Cat!," "Darling of the Day," "Company."

HUDDLE, ELIZABETH. Born Jan. 20, 1940 in Redding, Cal. Attended U Pacific. With LCRep in "Danton's Death," "Country Wife," "Condemned of Altona," "Caucasian Chalk Circle," "Alchemist," "Yerma," "Good Woman of Setzuan," "Playboy of the Western World," "Scenes from American Life," on Bdwy in "Little Murders."

HUDSON, CHARLES. Born Mar. 29, 1931 in Thorpsprings, Tex. Attended AADA, Am. Th.Wing. Bdwy bow 1951 in "Billy Budd," followed by OB in "The Streets of New York," "Summer of Daisy Miller," "Great Scot!," "Any Resemblance to Persons Living or Dead."

HUGHES, BARNARD. Born July 16, 1915 in Bedford Hills, N.Y. Attended Manhattan Col. Off-Bdwy credits: "Rosmersholm," "A Doll's House," "Hogan's Goat," "Line," on Bdwy in "The Ivy Green," "Dinosaur Wharf," "Teahouse of The August Moon" (CC'56), "A Majority of One," "Advise and Consent," "The Advocate," "Hamlet" ('64), "I Was Dancing," "Generation," "How Now, Dow Jones?," "Wrong Way Light Bulb," "Sheep On The Runway," "Abelard and Heloise."

HUGHES, TRESA. Born Sept. 17, 1929 in Washington, DC. Attended Wayne U. Off-Bdwy in "Electra," "The Crucible," "Hogan's Goat," "Party On Greenwich Avenue," "Fragments," "Passing Through from Exotic Places," "Beggar On Horseback" (LC), "Early Morning," On Bdwy in "The Miracle Worker," "The Devil's Advocate," "Dear Me, The Sky Is Falling," "The Last Analysis," "Spofford," "The Man In The Glass Booth."

HUGO, LAURENCE. Born Dec. 22, 1917 in Berkeley, Cal. Attended U Cal, Neighborhood Playhouse. Bdwy bow 1941 in "The Distant City," Followed by "Skin of Our Teeth," "I'll Take the High Road," "Decision," "Born Yesterday," "Stalag 17," "Double in Hearts," "U.S.A." (OB), "There's a Girl in My Soup," "Hamlet" with Judith Anderson.

HUNT, CARL. Born June 21, 1941 in Boston. Graduate U Minn., Temple U. Debut Off-Bdwy 1971 in "The House of Blue Leaves."

HUSMANN, RON. Born June 30, 1937 in Rockford, Ill. Attended Northwestern. In "Fiorello!," "Greenwillow," "Tenderloin" for which he received a THEATRE WORLD Award, "All Ameri-can," "Lovely Ladies, Kind Gentlemen," "Look Where I'm At" (OB).

HUSTON, PHILIP. Born Mar. 14, 1910 in Goshen, Va. Bdwy debut 1934 in "Strange Orchestra," followed by "Macbeth," "Twelfth Night," "Othello," "Catherine Was Great," "The Tempest," "Winter's Tale," "The Father," "With a Silk Thread," "Tower Beyond Tragedy," "The Shrike," CC's "Cyrano" and "Richard III," "And Whose Little Boy Are You?" (OB).

HUTCHINSON, LAURIE. Born Jan. 4, 1945 in Cleveland, O. Graduate Stephens Col. Debut 1967 Off-Bdwy in "Under Gas-light," followed by "Up Eden," "Les Jardins Publique," "Green-willow" (ELT).

HYMAN, EARLE. Born Oct. 11, 1926 in Rocky Mt., NC. Attended New School, Am. Th. Wing. Bdwy bow 1943 in "Run, Little Chillun," followed by "Anna Lucasta," "Climate of Eden," "Merchant of Venice," "Othello," "Julius Caesar," "The Tem-pest," "No Time for Sergeants," "Mr. Johnson" for which he received a THEATRE WORLD Award, "St. Joan," "Hamlet," "Waiting for Godot," "Duchess of Malfi," "Les Blancs," OB in "The White Rose and the Red," "The Worlds of Shakespeare," "Jonah," "The Life and Times of J. Walter Smintheus."

HYMAN, ELAINE. Born in Detroit. Columbia Graduate. Bdwy debut 1962 in "General Seeger," followed by "Say Darling," Off-Bdwy in "Javelin," "Night of the Dunce," "What the Butler Saw."

ING, ALVIN. Born May 26, 1938 in Honolulu. Columbia Gradu-ate. Bdwy debut 1959 in "World of Suzie Wong," Off-Bdwy in "Tenth of an Inch," "Cranes and Peonies," "Coffins for Butter-flies," "Six."

IRVING, GEORGE S. Born Nov. 1, 1922 in Springfield, Mass. Attended Leland Powers Sch. Bdwy bow 1943 in "Oklahoma!," followed by "Call Me Mister," "Along Fifth Avenue," "Two's Company," "Me and Juliet," "Can-Can," "Shinbone Alley," "Bells Are Ringing," "The Good Soup," "Tovarich," "A Murderer Among Us," "Alfie," "Anya," "Galileo" (LC), "The Happy Time," "Up Eden" (OB), "Promenade" (OB), "4 on a Garden."

IVES, ANNE. Born in Providence, RI. Attended Sargent's School, Am. Th. Wing. Bdwy debut 1906 in "The Chorus Lady," after many years in London and regional theatre, in 1952 returned to Bdwy in "Point of No Return," followed by "Masquerade," "The Crucible" (OB), "The Effect of Gamma Rays on Man-in-the-Moon Marigolds," (OB), "Good Woman of Setzuan" (LC).

JACKSON, MARY. Born Nov. 22, 1915 in Milford, Mich. Graduate Western Col. Bdwy debut 1944 in "Kiss and Tell," followed by "Eastward in Eden," "Flowering Cherry," "Trial of the Catonsville 9" (OB).

Page Johnson   Justine Johnston   Tom Lee Jones   Janet Kapral   Michael Karm

JARRETT, JERRY. Born Sept. 9, 1918 in Brooklyn. Attended New Theatre School. Off-Bdwy in "Waiting For Lefty," "Nat Turner," "Me Candido," "That 5 A.M. Jazz." Bdwy bow 1948 in "At War With the Army," followed by "Gentlemen Prefer Blondes," "Stalag 17," "Fiorello," "Fiddler On The Roof."

JASPER, ZINA. Born Jan. 29, 1939 in the Bronx. Attended CCNY. Bdwy debut 1967 in "Something Different," followed by "Paris Is Out," OB in "Saturday's Children," "Moondreamers," "A Dream Out of Time."

JAY, WILLIAM. Born May 15, 1935 in Baxter Springs, Kan. Attended Off-Bdwy 1963 in "Utopia," followed by "The Blacks," "Loop The Loop," "Happy Ending," "Day of Absence," "Hamlet" (CP), "Othello" (CP), NEC's "Song of The Lusitanian Bogey", "Ceremonies In Dark Old Men," "Man Better Man," "The Harangues," "Brotherhood," "Perry's Mission," and "Rosalee Pritchett."

JAYE, L. ERROL. Born Feb. 7, 1928 in Jacksonville, Fla. Graduate Fisk U., AMDA. Debut 1966 Off-Bdwy in "Happy Ending" and "Day of "Absence," followed by NYSF's "Troilus and Cressida" and "Henry V," "Who's Got His Own," "The Electronic Nigger and Others," "A Black Quartet," "5 on the Blackhand Side," "Moon on a Rainbow Shawl," Bdwy debut 1968 in "The Great White Hope."

JENSEN, STERLING. Born Mar. 15, 1925 in San Diego, Cal. Bdwy debut 1955 in "Desk Set," followed by OB in "Mime Theatre," "The Father," "The Miser," "Peleas and Melisande," "The Bond," "King Lear," "Journey's End," "Dance of Death," "Trumpets and Drums," "Macbeth," "Oedipus," "Lady from Maxim's," "Hamlet," "Uncle Vanya."

JOHNS, CLAY. Born June 6, 1934 in Lima, O. Off Bdwy in "Tiger at the Gates," "The Disenchanted," "Under the Gaslight," "The Queen and the Rebels," "The Drunkard," "Johnny Johnson,"

JOHNSON, KAREN. Born July 18, 1939 in Kane, Pa. Graduate Holyoke Col. Debut 1965 Off-Bdwy in "The 4th Pig," followed by "Plain and Fancy" (ELT), "You're a Good Man, Charlie Brown."

JOHNSON, PAGE. Born Aug. 25 1930 in Welch, W.Va. Graduate Ithaca Col. Bdwy bow 1951 in DeHavilland's "Romeo and Juliet," followed by "Electra," "Oedipus," "Camino Real," "In April Once" for which he received a THEATRE WORLD Award, "Red Roses For Me," "The Lovers," Off-Bdwy in "Military Taps," "The Enchanted," "Guitar," "4 In 1," "Journey of The Fifth Horse," "Yucca Trail," and "Ruby's Revenge," with APA in "School For Scandal," "The Tavern" and "The Seagull," "The Odd Couple," "The Boys In The Band."

JOHNSTON, JUSTINE. Born June 13 in Evanston, Ill. Off-Bdwy in "Little Mary Sunshine," "The Time of Your Life" (LC), on Bdwy in "Pajama Game," "Milk and Honey," "Follies."

JONES, CHARLOTTE. Born Jan. 1 in Chicago. Attended Loyola, DePaul U. Off-Bdwy in "False Confessions," "Sign of Jonah," "Girl on the Via Flaminia," "Red Roses for Me," "Night Is Black Bottles," "Camino Real," "Plays for Bleecker St.," "Pigeons," "Great Scot!," "Sjt. Musgrave's Dance," "Papers," "Johnny Johnson," on Bdwy in "Camino Real," "Buttrio Square," "Mame," "How Now Dow Jones."

JONES, JAMES EARL. Born Jan. 17, 1931 in Arkabutla, Miss. Graduate Mich U. Off-Bdwy credits: "The Pretender," "The Blacks" "Clandestine On The Morning Line," "The Apple," "A Midsummer Night's Dream," "Moon On A Rainbow Shawl" for which he received a THEATRE WORLD Award. "PS 193," "The Last Minstrel," "The Love Nest," "Bloodknot," "Othello," "Baal," "Danton's Death" (LCRep), "Boesman and Lena," on Bdwy in "The Egghead," "Sunrise At Campobello," "The Cool World," "A Hand Is On The Gate," "The Great White Hope," "Les Blancs."

JONES, PAUL. Born Feb. 24, 1942 in Portsmouth, Eng. Attended Jesus Col. Bdwy debut 1970 in "Conduct Unbecoming."

JONES, TOM LEE. Born Sept. 15, 1946 in San Saba, Tex. Harvard graduate. Bdwy debut 1969 in "A Patriot for Me," followed by "4 on a Garden."

JONES, NEIL. Born May 6, 1942 in Boston. Attended Boston Cons. Appeared in "The Music Man," "Hello, Dolly!," "Promises, Promises."

JORDAN, RICHARD. Born July 19, 1938 in NYC. Attended Harvard. Bdwy bow 1961 in "Take Her, She's Mine," followed by "Bicycle Ride to Nevada," APA's "War and Peace" and "Judith," "Generation," "All's Well That Ends Well" (NYSF), "A Patriot for Me," "Trial of Catonsville 9" (OB).

JOYCE, STEPHEN. Born Mar. 7, 1933 in NYC. Attended Fordham. Bdwy bow 1966 in "Those That Play the Clowns," followed by "The Exercise," Off-Bdwy in "Three Hand Reel," LCRep's "Galileo" and "St. Joan," "Stephen D" for which he received a THEATRE WORLD Award, "Fireworks," "School for Wives."

JULIA, RAUL. Born Mar. 9, 1940 in San Juan, PR. Graduate UPR. Off-Bdwy in "Macbeth" "Titus Andronicus" (CP), "Theatre In The Streets," "Life Is A Dream" "Blood Wedding," "The Ox Cart," "No Exit," "The Memorandum," "Frank Gagliano's City Scene," "Your Own Thing," "The Persians," "Castro Complex," "Pinkville," Bdwy bow 1968 in "The Cuban Thing," followed by "Indians."

KAHL, HOWARD,. Born Sept 17, 1930 in New Albany, Ind. Graduate Ind. U. Bdwy debut 1962 in "Camelot," followed by "Hot Spot," "Fade Out-Fade In," "Pleasures and Palaces," "Anya," "On A Clear Day You Can See Forever," "Cabaret," "Applause."

KAHN, MADELINE. Born Sept. 29, 1942 in Boston. Graduate Hofstra U. Bdwy debut in "New Faces of 1968," followed by "Promenade" (OB), "2 by 2."

KAISER, ARDYTH. Born in Evansville, Ind. Graduate Northwestern. Debut Off-Bdwy 1965 in "The Parasite," followed by Bdwy 1970 in "Not Now Darling."

KAPRAL, JANET. Born in Brno, Czech. Graduate Marquette U. Debut Off-Bdwy 1970 in "Trelawny of the Wells."

KARIN, RITA. Born Oct. 24, 1919 in Warsaw, Poland. Bdwy debut 1960 in "The Wall," followed by "A Call On Kuprin," "The Penny Wars," Off-Bdwy in "The Pocket Watch," "Scuba Duba," "House of Blue Leaves."

KARM, MICHAEL. Born Oct. 24, 1941 in Chicago. Attended U Ill. NY bow 1963 Off-Bdwy in "Best Foot Forward," "followed by "South Pacific" (CC), "How to Succeed . . ." (CC), "South Pacific" (LC), "Mad Show" (OB), "Salvation" (OB), Bdwy debut 1970 in "Two by Two."

KASON, CORINNE. Born Mar. 10 in San Francisco. Attended San Jose State Col. Debut 1968 OB in "Futz" followed by "By Jupiter," "Unfair to Goliath," Bdwy bow 1969 in "Fiddler on the Roof."

KAVANAUGH, DORRIE. Born July 12, Attended Tulane U. Graduate Neighborhood Playhouse. Bdwy debut 1969 in "Fire," followed by "Saved" (OB).

KAYE, DANNY. Born Jan. 18, 1913 in Bklyn. Appeared in vaudeville before 1939 Bdwy debut in "Left of Broadway," followed by "Straw Hat Revue," "Lady in the Dark," "Let's Face It," "Two by Two."

KEACH, STACY. Born June 2, 1941 in Savannah, Ga. Graduate U. Cal. Yale, London Acad. Off-Bdwy in "MacBird," "The Niggerlovers," "Henry IV" (CP), with LCRep in "The Country Wife," "King Lear," "Peer Gynt" (CP), "Long Day's Journey into Night," Bdwy debut in "Indians" (1969).

| Gene Kelton | Gail Kellstrom | Edward Kovens | Christal Kim | John LaGioia |

KEELER, RUBY. Born Aug. 25, 1910 in Halifax, N.S., Can. Bdwy debut 1923 in "The Rise of Rosie O'Reilly," followed by "Show Girl," "Bye Bye, Bonnie," "Lucky," "Sidewalks of New York" "Hold on to Your Hats," a career in films, retirement, and "No, No, Nanette" in 1970.

KELLSTROM, GAIL. Born June 24, 1944 in Newark, NJ. Graduate Rutgers, Penn State. Debut Off-Bdwy 1970 in "Second Cummings," followed by "Yerma."

KELLY, PATSY. Born Jan. 12, 1910 in Bklyn. Appeared in vaudeville before 1928 Bdwy debut in "Three Cheers," followed by "Earl Carroll's Sketch Book," "Vanities," "Wonder Bar," "Flying Colors," a long career in films, "Dear Charles," "No, No, Nanette."

KELTON, GENE. Born Oct. 21, 1938 in Flag Staff, Ariz. Appeared in "Once Upon a Mattress," "Destry Rides Again," "Subways Are for Sleeping," "Here's Love," "Fade Out-Fade In," "Skyscraper," "Mame," "Dear World," "Applause."

KERCHEVAL, KEN. Born July 15, 1935 in Indiana. Attended Pacific U., Neighborhood Playhouse. Off-Bdwy credits: "Dead End," "Young Abe Lincoln," "Black Monday," "A Man's A Man," "23 Pat O'Brien Movies," "Father Uxbridge Wants to Marry," "Horseman, Pass By," "Who's Happy Now?," on Bdwy in "Something About A Soldier," "Fiddler On The Roof," "Happily Never After," "The Apple Tree," "Cabaret," "Father's Day."

KERR, PHILIP. Born Apr. 9, 1940 in NYC. Attended Harvard, London AMDA. Bdwy bow 1969 with ACT in "Tiny Alice," "A Flea in Her Ear," "The Three Sisters," followed by "Hamlet" (OB).

KERT, LARRY. Born Dec. 5, 1934 in Los Angeles. Attended LACC. Bdwy bow 1953 in "John Murray Anderson's Almanac," followed by "Ziegfeld Follies," "Mr. Wonderful," "Walk Tall," "Look Ma, I'm Dancin'," "Tickets, Please," "West Side Story," "A Family Affair," "Breakfast at Tiffany's," "Cabaret," "La Strada," "Company."

KESTELMAN, SARA. Born May 12, 1944 in London. Attended Central School of Speech. Bdwy debut 1971 in RSC's "A Midsummer Night's Dream."

KEYES, DANIEL. Born Mar. 6, 1914 in Concord, Mass. Attended Harvard. Bdwy bow 1954 in "The Remarkable Mr. Pennypacker," followed by "Bus Stop," "Only In America," "Christine," "First Love," "Take Her, She's Mine," "Baker Street," "Dinner At 8," "I Never Sang For My Father," "Wrong Way Light Bulb," "A Place For Polly," "Scratch," Off-Bdwy in "Our Town," "Epitaph For George Dillon," "Plays For Bleecker St.," "Hooray, It's A Glorious Day!," "Six Characters In Search of An Author," "Sjt. Musgrave's Dance," "Arms and The Man."

KIDWELL, GENE. Born Oct. 14, 1946 in Lafayette, Ind. Attended Ind. U. Debut 1968 in "You're A Good Man, Charlie Brown." (OB)

KIM, CHRISTAL. Born Sept. 25, 1916 in Kalamazoo, Mich. Attended Professional Children's School, NYC. Bdwy debut 1953 in "Teahouse of the August Moon," followed by "Basic Training of Pavlo Hummel" (OB).

KIMBROUGH, CHARLES. Born May 23, 1936 in St. Paul, Minn. Graduate Ind. U., Yale. Off-Bdwy in "All In Love," "Struts and Frets," Bdwy bow 1969 in "Cop-Out," followed by "Company."

KIMMINS, GRACE. Born July 2, 1942 in Philadelphia, Pa. Graduate Catholic U. NY debut 1969 in "Impressions on Love" (LC), followed by "Adaptation" (OB).

KIRKLAND, SALLY. Born Oct. 31, 1944 in NYC. Member Actors Studio. Bdwy debut 1961 in "Step on a Crack," followed by "Bicycle Ride to Nevada," "Marathon '33," "Off-Bdwy in "Midsummer Night's Dream," "Fitz," "Bitch of Waverly Place," "Tom Paine," "Futz," "Sweet Eros," "Witness," "One Night Stands of a Noisy Passenger."

KIRSCH, CAROLYN. Born May 24, 1942 in Shreveport, La. Attended Ballet Russe School. Bdwy debut 1963 in "How to Succeed . . . ," followed by "Folies Bergere," "La Grosse Valise," "Skyscraper," "Breakfast at Tiffany's," "Sweet Charity," "Hallelujah, Baby!," "Dear World," "Promises, Promises," "Coco."

KISER, TERRY. Born Aug. 1, 1939 in Omaha, Neb. Graduate U. Kan. NY bow 1966 Off-Bdwy in "Night of The Dunce," followed by "Fortune and Men's Eyes" for which he received a THEATRE WORLD Award, "Horseman, Pass By," "Frank Gagliano's City Scene," "The Ofay Watcher," "Castro Complex," Bdwy debut 1970 in "Paris Is Out."

KNIGHT, WILLIAM. Born Dec. 6, 1934 in Los Angeles. Graduate LACC. NY debut 1970 in "Oh! Calcutta!"

KOVENS, EDWARD. Born June 26, 1934 in NYC. Attended NYS Inst. of Arts. On Bdwy in "Three Sisters," Off-Bdwy in "Modern Statuary," "Never Ending Rain," "Waiting for Godot," "Dirty Hands," "Country Girl" (CC), "Deer Park," "Fortune and Men's Eyes."

KRAMER, LLOYD. Born Nov. 25, 1947 in Lynn, Mass. Graduate Trinity Col. Bdwy debut 1970 in "Child's Play."

KRAWFORD, GARY. Born Mar. 23, 1941 in Kitchener, Can. Debut Off-Bdwy 1968 in "The Fantasticks," followed by "Manhattan Arrangement," on Bdwy in "Pousse Cafe," "The Education of Hyman Kaplan."

KROSS, RONALD. Born Feb. 24, 1936 in Nanticoke, Pa. Graduate Wilkes Col., Penn. State. Bdwy debut 1969 in "1776."

KUHNER, JOHN. Born Dec. 27, 1942 in Cleveland, O. Graduate Denison U. Debut 1968 Off-Bdwy in "Your Own Thing," followed by "House of Leather," "Tarot."

KUPPERMAN, ALVIN. Born Oct. 14, 1945 in Brooklyn. Graduate Emerson Col. Off-Bdwy in "If We Grow Up," Bdwy debut 1970 in "Minnie's Boys," "A Dream Out of Time" (OB).

KURTZ, SWOOSIE. Born Sept. 6, 1944 in Omaha, Nebr. Attended U SCal. London Academy. Debut Off-Bdwy 1968 in "The Firebugs," followed by "The Effect of Gamma Rays on Man-in-the-Moon Marigolds."

KUSSACK, ELAINE. Born Dec. 30 in Brooklyn. Graduate Hunter Col., Columbia. Bdwy debut 1969 in "Fiddler on the Roof."

LAGERFELT, CAROLYN. Born Sept. 23, in Paris. Graduate AADA. Bdwy debut 1971 in "The Philanthropist," followed by "4 on a Garden."

LaGIOIA, JOHN P.. Born Nov. 24, 1937 in Philadelphia. Graduate Temple U. Off-Bdwy in "Keyhole," "Lovers in the Metro," "The Cherry Orchard," "Titus Andronicus," "Henry VI," "Richard III." (NYSF), Bdwy bow 1969 in "Henry V."

LAMONT, ROBIN. Born June 2, 1950 in Boston, Attended Carnegie-Mellon U. Debut Off-Bdwy 1971 in "Godspell."

LANCASTER, LUCIE. Born Oct. 15, 1907 in Chicago. Bdwy debut 1947 in "Heads or Tails," followed by "Mr. Pickwick," "Girl Who Came to Supper," "Bajour," "How Now, Dow Jones," "Little Boxes" (OB), "70, Girls, 70."

Susan Lehman

Bill LaVallee

Gloria LeRoy

Robert Legionaire

Abby Lewis

LANCHESTER, ROBERT. Born Aug. 2, 1941 in Boston. Graduate MIT, UC Berkeley. Bdwy debut 1969 with ACT in "A Flea in Her Ear" and "Three Sisters," followed by "Greenwillow" (ELT).

LANE, GENETTE. Born Oct. 13, 1940 in Bklyn, Md. Attended Peabody Conserv., Am. Th. Wing. Off-Bdwy in "Peter Rabbit," "The Adventures of High Jump," "The Drunkard," "Ruddigore" (ELT).

LAUGHLIN, SHARON. Graduate U. Wash. Bdwy debut 1964 in "One by One," Off-Bdwy in "Henry IV" (NYSF), "Huui, Huui," "Mod Donna," "Subject to Fits".

LaVALLEE, BILL. Born June 13, 1943 in Baton Rouge, La. Attended LSU. Debut Off-Bdwy 1968 in "Redhead," followed by "God Bless You, Harold Fineberg," "Shoestring Revue" (ELT).

LAVIN, LINDA. Born Oct. 15, 1939 in Portland, Me. Graduate William & Mary Col. Bdwy bow 1962 in "A Family Affair," followed by "The Riot Act," "Wet Paint" (OB) for which she received a THEATRE WORLD Award, "The Game Is Up," "Hotel Passionato," "The Mad Show" (OB), "It's Superman!," "On A Clear Day You Can See Forever," "Something Different," "Little Murders" (OB), "Cop-Out," "Last of the Red Hot Lovers," "Story Theatre."

LAVREN, CHRISTINE. Born Sept. 7, 1944 in Victoria, Tex. Studied with Allan Miller. Bdwy debut 1971 in "4 on a Garden."

LAWSON, LEE. Born Oct. 14, 1941 in NYC. Attended Bost U. Columbia. Off-Bdwy in "Firebugs," "The Knack," "Birthday Party" (LC), "Scenes from American Life" (LC), Bdwy bow 1966 in "Agatha Sue, I Love You," followed by "Cactus Flower," "My Daughter, Your Son."

LAZER, PETER. Born Apr. 12, 1946 in NYC. Attended NYU. Bdwy debut 1957 in "Hide and Seek," followed by "Miss Isobel," "Watercolor," "Criss-Crossing," "Survival of St. Joan."

LEACH, MARJORIE. Born Dec. 15, 1902 in Stoughton, Mass. Attended Emerson Col. Bdwy debut 1924 in "Innocent Eyes," followed by "Music in May," "New Moon," "Ziegfeld Follies," "Mexican Hayride," "As the Girls Go," "70, Girls, 70."

LEARY, DAVID. Born Aug. 8, 1939 in Bklyn. Attended CCNY. Debut Off-Bdwy 1969 in "Shoot Anything with Hair that Moves," followed by "Macbeth."

LeCLAIR, HENRY. Born July 27 in Cranston, RI. Appeared in "Flora, The Red Menance," "A Time For Singing," "Wonderful Town" (CC'67), "1776."

LEE, BIG. Born Aug. 15, 1939 in Cleveland, O. Bdwy debut 1970 in "Lovely Ladies, Kind Gentlemen."

LEGIONAIRE, ROBERT. Born Nov. 3, 1926 in Rock Island, Ill. Attended Piscator's Workshop. Debut Off-Bdwy 1959 in "Three for Tonight," followed by Bdwy's "Andersonville Trial," "Antigone" (LC).

LEHMAN, SUSAN. Born Feb. 4, 1940 in Ft. Wayne, Ind. Graduate Northwestern. Bdwy debut 1962 in "I Can Get It for You Wholesale," Off-Bdwy in "Secret Life of Walter Mitty," "Show Me Where the Good Times Are," "Shoestring Revue" (ELT).

LENS, PATRICIA. Born May 3, 1947 in Philadelphia. Attended Northwestern U. Bdwy debut 1969 in "Celebration," followed by "Man of LaMancha."

Le ROUX, MADELEINE. Born May 28, 1946 in Laramie, Wyo. Graduate U Cape Town. Debut Off-Bdwy 1969 in "The Moondreamers," followed by "The Dirtiest Show in Town."

LeROY, GLORIA. Born in Bucyrus, O. Attended Neighborhood Playhouse. Bdwy debut in "This Was Burlesque," Off-Bdwy in "Boy on a Straight-Back Chair," "Show Me Where the Good Times Are."

LeROY, KEN. Born Aug. 17, 1927 in Detroit. Attended Neighborhood Playhouse. Appeared in "The American Way," "Morning Star," "Anne of England," "Oklahoma!," "Carousel," "Brigadoon," "Call Me Madam," "Pajama Game," "West Side Story," "Fiddler On The Roof."

LESTER, BARBARA. Born Dec. 27, 1928 in London. Graduate Columbia U. Bdwy debut 1956 in "Protective Custody," followed by "Legend of Lizzie," "Luther," "Inadmissable Evidence," "Johnny No-Trump," "Grin and Bare It," Off-Bdwy in "Electra," "Queen after Death," "Summer of the 17th Doll," "Richard II" and "Much Ado About Nothing" (NYSF), "One Way Pendulum," "Abelard and Heloise."

LEVENE, SAM. Born Aug. 28, 1905 in NYC. Graduate AADA. Bdwy bow 1927 in "Wall Street," followed by "3 Men on a Horse," "Dinner at 8," "Room Service," "Margin for Error," "Sound of Hunting," "Light Up the Sky," "Guys and Dolls," "Hot Corner," "Fair Game," "Make A Million," "Heartbreak House," "Good Soup," "Devil's Advocate," "Let It Ride," "Seidman & Son," "Cafe Crown," "Last Analysis," "Nathan Weinstein, Mystic, Conn.," "The Impossible Years," "3 Men on a Horse" ('69), "Paris Is Out," "A Dream Out of Time" (OB).

LEVIN, MICHAEL. Born Dec. 8, 1932 in Minneapolis. Graduate U. Minn. Bdwy debut 1965 in "Royal Hunt of the Sun," followed by "End of All Things Natural" (OB), LC's "Camino Real" "Operation Sidewinder," and "Good Woman of Setzuan."

LEWIS, ABBY. Born Jan. 14, 1910 in Mesilla Park, N Mex. Graduate N Mex U. Bdwy debut 1934 in "Richard III," followed by "You Can't Take It with You," "Macbeth," "The Willow and I," "The Chase," "Four Winds," "Howie," "Riot Act," "Life with Father" (CC'67), "70,Girls, 70."

LEYDEN, LEO. Born Jan. 28 1929 in Dublin, Ire. Attended Abbey Theatre School. Bdwy debut 1960 in "Love and Libel," followed by "Darling of the Day," "The Mundy Scheme," "The Rothschilds."

LICHTERMAN, MARVIN. Born May 12, 1938 in Brooklyn. Graduate Bklyn, Col., Yale. Off-Bdwy in "Anthology of Love," "Saturday Night," "Adaptation," "Steambath," on Bdwy in "Happiness Is Just A Little Thing Called A Rolls Royce," "Lovers and Other Strangers," "Dr. Fish."

LINDEN, HAL. Born Mar. 20, 1931 in NYC. Attended CCNY, Am. The. Wing. Appeared in "Strip for Action," "Bells Are Ringing," "Wildcat," "Subways Are for Sleeping," "Anything Goes" (OB), "Something More," "The Apple Tree," "Education of Hyman Kaplan," "The Rothschilds."

LINDFORS, VIVECA. Born Dec. 29, 1920 in Upsala, Swed. Attended Stockholm Royal Acad. Bdwy debut 1952 in "I've Got Sixpence," followed by "Anastasia," "King Lear" (CC), "Postmark Zero," Off-Bdwy in "Miss Julie," "Golden Six," "Brecht on Brecht," "Niggerlovers," "Pal Joey" (CC), "Cuba, Si," "Guns of Carrar," "Dance of Death."

LINDIG, JILLIAN. Born Mar. 19, 1944 in Johnson City, Tex. Graduate U. Tex. Debut Off-Bdwy 1969 in "The Brownstone Urge," followed by "AC/DC."

LINDSAY, KEVIN-JOHN. Born Sept. 7, 1957 in NYC. Debut 1970 in "The Me Nobody Knows."

LINN, MARGARET. Born Aug. 21, 1934 in Richmond, Ind. Attended Northwestern U., Denver U. Off-Bdwy credits: "Pale Horse Pale Rider," "The Room," "Billy Liar," "Huui, Huui," "The Disintegration of James Cherry" (LC), "House of Blue Leaves," on Bdwy in "How's The World Treating You?," "Halfway Up The Tree."

| George Loros | Susan Long | Peter MacLean | Renata Mannhardt | Ric Mancini |

LiPARI, MARJORIE. Born June 1, 1945 in Brooklyn. Bdwy debut 1968 in "Hair."

LIPSON, CLIFFORD. Born Feb. 10, 1947 in Providence, RI. Attended Neighborhood Playhouse, AMDA. Off-Bdwy credits: "Great Scot!," "Hooray, It's A Glorious Day," "The Indian Wants the Bronx," "Salvation," Bdwy bow 1970 in "Hair."

LIPSON, PAUL. Born Dec. 23, 1913 in Brooklyn. Attended Ohio State, American Theatre Wing. Bdwy bow 1942 in "Lily of the Valley," followed by "Heads or Tails," "Detective Story," "Remains to Be Seen," "Carnival in Flanders," "I've Got Sixpence," "The Vamp," "Bells Are Ringing," "Fiorello" (CC), "Sound of Music," "Fiddler on the Roof."

LITTLE, CLEAVON. Born June 1, 1939 in Chickasha, Okla. Attended San Diego State U, AADA. NY bow Off-Bdwy 1967 in "MacBird," followed by "Hamlet" (NYSF), "Someone's Coming Hungry," "The Ofay Watcher," "Scuba Duba," Bdwy debut 1968 in "Jimmy Shine" followed by "Purlie."

LOANE, MARY. Born Dec. 7 in Lake Bluff, Ill. Attended Russell Sage Col. Bdwy debut 1927 in "Cradle Snatchers," followed by "3 Men on a Horse," "The Women," "Affair of Honor," "Life with Father," "All Summer Long," "Sherry," "Scratch."

LOMBARD, MICHAEL. Born Aug. 8, 1934 in Brooklyn. Graduate Bklyn Col., Boston U. Off-Bdwy in "King Lear," "Merchant of Venice," "Cages," "Pinter Plays," "LaTurista," "Elizabeth the Queen" (CC), "Room Service," on Bdwy in "Poor Bitos," "Gingerbread Lady."

LONG, SUSAN. Born Feb. 1, 1947 in Salina, Kan. Graduate U Colo. Debut Off-Bdwy 1971 in "Do It Again!"

LONGO, PEGGY. Born Oct. 1, 1943 in Brooklyn. Graduate Ithaca Col. With NYC Opera before 1967 Bdwy debut in "Fiddler on the Roof."

LOROS, GEORGE. Born Jan. 9, 1944 in NYC. Attended Neighborhood Playhouse. Debut Off-Bdwy 1967 in "Nighthawks," followed by "Happiness Cage."

LOWRY, JUDITH. Born July 27, 1890 in Morristown, NJ. Bdwy debut 1915 in "Romeo and Juliet," followed by many productions. Currently in "The Effect of Gamma Rays on Man-in-the-Moon Marigolds" (OB).

LUPINO, PANDORA BRONSON. Born in Minnesota, Cal. Bdwy debut 1970 in "Conduct Unbecoming."

LUPINO, RICHARD. Born Oct. 29, 1929 in Hollywood, Cal. Attended LACC, RADA. Bdwy debut 1956 in "Major Barbara," followed by "Conduct Unbecoming."

LUSTIK, MARLENA. Born Aug. 22, 1944 in Milwaukee, Wisc. Attended Marquette U. Bdwy debut 1966 in "Pousse Cafe," followed by "Effect of Gamma Rays on Man-in-the-Moon Marigolds" (OB).

LYDIARD, BOB. Born Apr. 28, 1944 in Glen Ridge, NJ. Attended Atlantic U., Wayne State U. NY bow 1968 Off-Bdwy in "You're A Good Man, Charlie Brown," followed by "A Round with Ring," "Johnny Johnson."

LYNCH, RICHARD. Born Feb. 12, 1940 in Bklyn. Member Actors Studio. Bdwy bow 1965 in "The Devils," Off-Bdwy in "Live Like Pigs," "One Night Stands of a Noisy Passenger," "Things That Almost Happen."

LYNDECK, EDMUND. Born Oct 4, 1925 in Baton Rouge, La. Graduate Montclair State Col., Fordham U. Bdwy debut 1969 in "1776."

MacGOWRAN, JACK. Born Oct. 13, 1918 in Dublin, Ire. Trained at Abbey Theatre. Bdwy debut 1958 in "Juno," followed by Off-Bdwy "Gandhi," "MacGowran in the Works of Beckett."

MACKENZIE, WILL. Born July 24, 1938 in Providence, RI. Graduate Brown U. Off-Bdwy credits include "Wonderful Town," "Put It In Writing," "Morning Sun," "Brigadoon" (CC), on Bdwy in "Half A Sixpence," "Hello, Dolly!," "Sheep on the Runway," "Scratch."

MacLEAN, PETER. Born Jan. 2, 1936 in Dorchester, Mass. Graduate Emerson Col. Bdwy bow 1969 in "Fire!," followed by "Indians," "Child's Play."

MacMAHON, ALINE. Born May 3, 1899 in McKeesport, Pa. Attended Barnard Col. Bdwy debut 1921 in "Madras House," followed by "Green Ring," "Exciters," "Grand Street Follies," "Beyond the Horizon," "Maya," "Once in a Lifetime," "Heavenly Express," "Eve of St. Mark," "Confidential Clerk," "A Day by the Sea," "I Knock at the Door," "Pictures in the Hallway," "All the Way Home," LCRep in "The Alchemist," "Yerma," "East Wind," "Galileo," "Walking to Waldheim," "Tiger at the Gates," "Cyrano," "Pictures in the Hallway."

MACY, WILLIAM. Born May 18, 1922 in Revere, Mass. Graduate NYU. Bdwy bow 1959 in "Once More With Feeling," followed by "And Miss Reardon Drinks A Little," Off-Bdwy in "Threepenny Opera," "Machinal," "The Balcony," "America Hurrah," "Cannibals," "The Guns of Carrar," "Oh! Calcutta!," "Awake and Sing."

MADDEN, DONALD. Born Nov. 5, 1933 in NYC. Attended CCNY. Bdwy debut 1958 in "Look Back in Anger," followed by "First Impressions," "Step on a Crack," "One by One," "Black Comedy," Off-Bdwy in "Julius Caesar" for which he received a THEATRE WORLD Award, "Lysistrata," "Pictures in a Hallway," "Henry IV," "She Stoops to Conquer," "Octoroon," "Hamlet," "Ceremony of Innocence," "Henry VI," "Richard III," "A Doll's House," "Hedda Gabler."

MAGGART, BRANDON. Born Dec. 12, 1933 in Carthage, Tenn. Graduate U. Tenn. Off-Bdwy in "Sing, Muse!," "Like Other People," "Put It In Writing" for which he received a THEATRE WORLD Award, Bdwy debut 1965 in "Kelly," followed by "New Faces of 1968," "Applause."

MAITLAND, MICHAEL. Born Aug. 27, 1956 in Ft. Lauderdale, Fla. Debut Off-Bdwy 1963 in "Trojan Women," followed by Bdwy roles in "Music Man," "Mame," "The Rothschilds."

MALLORY, VICTORIA. Born Sept. 20, 1948 in Virginia. Graduate AMDA. NY debut 1968 in "West Side Story" (LC), followed by "Carnival" (CC'68), "Follies."

MALONE, NANCY. Born Mar. 19, 1935 in Queens Village, NY. Bdwy debut 1952 in "Time Out for Ginger," followed by "Major Barbara," "Makropoulos Secret" (OB), "A Touch of the Poet," "Trial of the Catonsville 9" (OB).

MANCINI, RIC. Born Apr. 16, 1933 in Bklyn. Attended Bklyn Col. Debut Off-Bdwy 1966 in "A View from the Bridge," followed by "All My Sons," "Night of the Iguana," "5 Finger Exercise," Heloise" (ELT).

MANDAN, ROBERT. Born Feb. 2, 1932 in Clever, Mo. Attended Pomona Col. Appeared in "Debut," "Speaking of Murder," "No Exit" (OB), "Maggie Flynn," "But Seriously," "Applause."

MANNHARDT, RENATA. Born Nov. 20 in Barmen-Wuppertal, Ger. Graduate U Munich. Debut 1971 in "Stag Movie." (OB)

MANNING, JACK. Born June 3, 1916 in Cincinnati, O. Graduate Cinn U. Bdwy bow 1941 in "Junior Miss," followed by "Great Big Doorstep," "Harriet," "Mermaids Singing," "Alice in Wonderland," "Man and Superman," "Billy Budd," "Tender Trap," "Say, Darling," "Do I Hear A Waltz?," "The Boy Friend."

Leila Martin   Peter Marklin   Katherine McGrath   Benjamin Masters   Molly McKesson

MANSON, ALAN. Born in NYC. Bdwy bow 1940 in "Journey to Jerusalem," followed by "This Is The Army," "Call Me Mister," "Southern Exposure," "Angels Kiss Me," "The Ponder Heart," "Maybe Tuesday," "Tenth Man," "Gideon," "Nobody Loves an Albatross," "Funny Girl," "A Place for Polly," "40 Carats," Off-Bdwy in "Dr. Jekyll and Mr. Hyde," "A Midsummer Night's Dream," "Oh Say Can You See L.A.?," "The Other Man."

MARCHAND, NANCY. Born June 19, 1928 in Buffalo, NY. Graduate Carnegie Tech. Debut in "The Taming of the Shrew" (CC), followed by "Merchant of Venice," "Much Ado About Nothing," "The Balcony" (OB), with APA in repertory, "Three Bags Full," "After The Rain," LCRep's "The Alchemist," "Yerma," and "Cyrano," "Forty Carats," "And Miss Reardon Drinks A Little."

MARKLIN, PETER. Born Dec. 22, 1939 in Buffalo, NY. Graduate Northwestern U. Appeared in "The Brig (OB), "Fiddler on the Roof."

MARKUS, THOMAS B. Born Oct. 28, 1934 in Evanston, Ill. Graduate Tulane U. Debut 1970 Off-Bdwy in "Gandhi."

MARTIN, LEILA. Born Aug. 22, 1932 in NYC. Bdwy debut 1944 in "Peepshow," followed by "Two on the Aisle," "Wish You Were Here," "Guys and Dolls," (CC), "Best House in Naples," "Ernest in Love" (OB), "Henry Sweet Henry," "The Wall," "Visit to a Small Planet," "The Rothschilds."

MARTIN, RON. Born June 23, 1947 in NYC. Attended Queens Col. Bdwy debut 1968 in "Red, White and Maddox," followed by "Child's Play," "Sensations" (OB).

MASCOLO, JOSEPH. Born Mar. 13, 1935 in Hartford, Conn. Appeared in "Night Life," "A View from the Bridge," NYSF, "Dinner at 8," "To Clothe the Naked" (OB), LCRep's "The Time of Your Life" "Camino Real," "Good Woman of Setzuan."

MASIELL, JOE. Born Oct. 27, 1939 in Bklyn. Off-Bdwy in "Cindy," "Jacques Brel Is Alive...," "Sensations," Bdwy debut 1969 in "Dear World."

MASON, MARSHA. Born Apr. 3, 1942 in St. Louis. Debut Off-Bdwy 1967 in "Deer Park," followed by "It's Called the Sugar Plum," "Happy Birthday, Wanda June."

MASSI, BERNICE. Born Aug. 23 in Camden, NJ. Bdwy debut 1952 in "South Pacific," followed by "Wish You Were," "By The Beautiful Sea," "Can-Can," "The Vamp," "Two For The Seesaw," "Beg, Borrow or Steal," "No Strings," "What Makes Sammy Run?," "Man of La Mancha," "How the Other Half Loves."

MASTERS, BENJAMIN. Born May 6, 1947 in Corvallis, Ore. Graduate U Ore. Debut 1970 Off-Bdwy in "Boys in the Band", followed by "What the Butler Saw."

MATHEWS, MARK. Born Nov. 9, 1943 in Los Angeles. Debut 1970 Off-Bdwy in "Greenwillow" (ELT).

MATTHEWS, ART. Born in NYC. Debut Off-Bdwy with American Savoyards, followed by "Leave It To Jane" on Bdwy in "Mame," "Ari."

MAY, WINSTON. Born Feb. 3, 1937 in Mammoth Spring, Ark. Graduate Ark. State U., Am. Th. Wing. Debut Off-Bdwy 1967 in "Man Who Washed His Hands," followed by "King Lear," "Candida," "Trumpets and Drums," "Otho the Great," "Uncle Vanya."

MAYER, JERR. Born May 12, 1941 in Waterloo, Iowa. Graduate NYU. NY bow 1968 in "Cyrano" (LC), followed by "Alice in Wonderland" (OB).

MAYRO, JACQUELINE. Born Apr. 2, 1948 in Philadelphia. Bdwy debut 1959 in "Gypsy," followed by "Bye Bye Birdie," "Cindy" (OB), "Ben Franklin in Paris," "Who's Who Baby" (OB), "Ari."

MAZZA, ALFRED. Born June 25, 1946 in Reno, Nev. Attended AADA. Debut Off-Bdwy 1970 in "You're a Good Man, Charlie Brown."

McCARTHY, KEVIN. Born Feb. 15, 1914 in Seattle, Wash. Attended U Minn. Bdwy bow 1938 in "Abe Lincoln in Illinois," followed by "Flight to the West," "Winged Victory," "Truckline Cafe," "Joan of Lorraine," "Death of a Salesman," "Anna Christie," "Deep Blue Sea," "Red Roses for Me," "The Day the Money Stopped," "Two for the Seesaw," "Advise and Consent," "Something about a Soldier," "Three Sisters," "Warm Body," "Cactus Flower," "Happy Birthday, Wanda June".

McCARTY, MARY. Born 1923 in Kan. Bdwy debut 1948 in "Sleepy Hollow" for which she received a Theatre World Award, followed by "Small Wonder," "Miss Liberty," "Bless You All," "A Rainy Day in Newark," "Follies."

McCOWEN, ALEC. Born May 26 in Tunbridge Wells, Eng. Attended RADA. Debut 1952 in "Antony and Cleopatra" and "Caesar and Cleopatra," followed by "King Lear" and "Comedy of Errors" at LC ('64), "After The Rain," "Hadrian VII," "The Philanthropist."

McDONALD, JAMES. Born June 23 in Jersey City, NJ. Attended Rutgers U. Off-Bdwy in "The Trojan Women," "White Devil," "Fortune and Men's Eyes," Bdwy bow 1970 in "Fiddler on the Roof."

MCGRATH, KATHERINE. Born Dec. 11, 1944 in Winchester, Mass. Attended Boston Conserv., RADA. Debut Off-Bdwy in "The Bacchants" (LC), followed by "Perry's Mission" (NEC).

McGUIRE, BIFF. Born Oct. 25, 1926 in New Haven, Conn. Attended Mass. State Col. Appeared in "Make Mine Manhattan," "South Pacific," "Dance Me A Song," "The Time of Your Life" (CC&LC), "A View from the Bridge," "Greatest Man Alive," "The Egghead," "Triple Play," "Happy Town," "Beg, Borrow or Steal," "Finian's Rainbow" (CC), "Beggar on Horseback" (LC), "Father's Day," "Trial of the Catonsville 9."

McGUIRE, MITCHELL. Born Dec. 26, 1936 in Chicago. Attended Goodman Th. School, Santa Monica City Col. Off-Bdwy in "The Rapists," "Go, Go, Go, God Is Dead," "Waiting for Lefty," "The Bond," "The Guns of Carrar," "Oh, Calcutta."

McHATTIE, STEPHEN. (formerly Stephen Smith). Born Feb. 3 in Antigonish, Nova Scotia. Graduate Acadia U, AADA. With NYSF in "Henry IV," on Bdwy in "The American Dream" ('68), OB in "Richard III," "The Persians," "Pictures in The Hallway" (LC).

McHENRY, DON. Born Feb. 25, 1908 in Paterson, NJ. Attended Rutgers U. Bdwy bow 1938 in "Don't Throw Glass Houses," followed by "Medea," "Tower Beyond Tragedy," "The Crucible," "Fanny," "Destry Rides Again," "Tovarich," "Elizabeth the Queen" (CC'66), "King Lear" and "A Cry of Players" (LC), "Hamlet" (OB).

McKECHNIE, DONNA. Born Nov. 1944 in Detroit. Bdwy debut in "How To Succeed . . . ," followed by "Promises, Promises," "Company."

McKENNA, SIOBHAN. Born May 24, 1922 in Belfast, Ire. Graduate Ntl. U., Dublin. Bdwy debut 1955 in "Chalk Garden" followed by "St. Joan," "Hamlet" (OB-title role), "Rope Dancers," "Here Are Ladies" (OB).

McKESSON, MOLLY. Born May 6, 1947 in Des Moines, Iowa. Graduate Northwestern. Bdwy debut 1970 in "Paul Sill's Story Theatre."

| Eda Reiss Merin | Jered Mickey | Betty Miller | Steve Mills | Jan Miner |

McMARTIN, JOHN. Born in Warsaw, Ind. Attended Columbia. Debut Off-Bdwy 1959 in "Little Mary Sunshine" for which he received a Theatre World Award, followed by (Bdwy bow 1968) "The Conquering Hero," "Blood, Sweat and Stanley Poole," "Children from Their Games," "Rainy Day in Newark," "Too Much Johnson" (OB), "Sweet Charity," "Follies."

McNAMARA, DERMOT. Born Aug. 24, 1925 in Dublin, Ire. Bdwy bow 1959 in "A Touch of the Poet," followed by "Philadelphia, Here I Come," Off-Bdwy in "The Wise Have Not Spoken," "3 by Synge," "Playboy of the Western World," "Shadow and Substance," "Happy as Larry," "Sharon's Grave," "A Whistle in the Dark," "Pictures in The Hallway" (LC).

McVEY, PATRICK. Born Mar. 17, 1913 in Ft. Wayne, Ind. Graduate Ind. Law School, Pasadena Playhouse. Appeared in "State of The Union," "Detective Story," "Hold It," "Bus Stop," "Catch Me If You Can," "On Vacation" (OB), "The Transgressor Rides Again" (OB), LC Rep's "Camino Real" and "The Time of Your Life," "Sunday Dinner" (OB).

MEARS, DeANN. Born in Ft. Fairfield, Me. Attended Westbrook Col. Debut 1961 Off-Bdwy in "The Decameron," followed by "Ernest in Love," "A Sound of Silence," "House of Blue Leaves," Bdwy bow 1963 in "Too True to Be Good," with ACT in "Tiny Alice," "Abelard and Heloise."

MENKEN, FAYE. Born Feb. 19, 1947 in NYC. Graduate NYU. Bdwy debut 1969 in "Fiddler On The Roof."

MERCER, MARIAN. Born Nov. 26, 1935 in Akron, O. Graduate U. Mich. Bdwy debut 1960 in "Greenwillow," followed by "Fiorello!," "Promises, Promises" for which she received a THEATRE WORLD Award, "A Place For Polly," "Hay Fever," Off-Bdwy in "Little Mary Sunshine," "Hotel Passionato," "Your Own Thing."

MERIN, EDA REISS. Born July 31 in NYC. Attended Hunter Col. Bdwy debut 1939 in "My Heart's in the Highlands," followed by "Trio," "Lovers," "Sophie," "A Flag Is Born," "A Far Country," OB in "Private Life of the Master Race," "Tower Beyond Tragedy," "Square in the Eye," "Huui, Huui," LC's "Inner Journey" and "Good Woman of Setzuan," "A Doll's House," "Hedda Gabler."

MERMAN, ETHEL. Born Jan. 16, 1912 in Astoria, NY. In vaudeville before 1930 Bdwy debut in "Girl Crazy," followed by "George White's Scandals," "Take A Chance," "Anything Goes," "Red, Hot and Blue," "Stars In Your Eyes," "Panama Hattie," "Something For The Boys," "Annie Get Your Gun," "Call Me Madam," "Happy Hunting," "Gypsy," "Hello, Dolly!"

MEYERS, MARTIN. Born Dec. 26, 1934 in NYC. Attended Am. The. Wing. Bdwy bow 1961 in "Mandingo," followed by "Lady of the Camellias," "The Guide," "Zorba," "Gandhi" (OB).

MICHAEL, MEYERS. Born Aug. 11, 1960 in Queens, NY. Debut 1971 in "Enemy of the People" (LC).

MICHAELS, LAURA. Born Nov. 17, 1953 in NYC. Attended HB Studio. Bdwy debut 1962 in "Sound of Music," followed by "Roar Of The Greasepaint . . . ," "A Time For Singing," NYSF, ASF, "The Me Nobody Knows."

MICHELL, KEITH. Born Dec. 1, 1926 in Adelaide, Aust. Attended Aust. School of Arts. Bdwy debut 1960 in "Irma La Douce," followed by "The Rehearsal," "Man of La Mancha," "Abelard and Heloise."

MICKEY, JERED. Born July 29, 1934 in Moscow, Idaho. Graduate Carnegie-Mellon U. Bdwy bow 1963 in "Andorra," followed by "Barefoot in the Park," "The Homecoming," Off-Bdwy in "Boys in the Band," "House of Blue Leaves."

MIDDLETON, RAY. Born Feb. 8, 1907 in Chicago. Graduate U. Ill., Juilliard. Bdwy bow 1933 in "Roberta," followed by "Knickerbocker Holiday," "George White's Scandals," "Annie Get Your Gun," "Love Life," "South Pacific," "Too True To Be Good," "Man of LaMancha."

MILANA, VINCENT. Born Apr. 11, 1939 in Newark, NJ. Graduate Carroll U., Neighborhood Playhouse. With APA, OB in "Abe Lincoln in Illinois," "Taming of the Shrew," "Color of Darkness," "Cannibals," "Now Is the Time" (ELT).

MILGRIM, LYNN. Born Mar. 17, 1944 in Philadelphia. Graduate Swarthmore, Harvard. Debut 1969 Off-Bdwy in "Frank Gagliano's City Scene," followed by "Crimes of Passion," "Macbeth," "Charley's Aunt."

MILLER, BETTY. Born Mar. 27, 1925 in Boston. Attended UCLA. Off-Bdwy in "Summer and Smoke," "Cradle Song," "La Ronde," "Plays for Bleecker St.," "Desire under the Elms," "The Balcony," "The Power and the Glory," "Beaux Stratagem," NYSF, "Gandhi," "Girl on the Via Flaminia," with APA in "You Can't Take It with You," "Right You Are," "The Wild Duck," "Cherry Orchard."

MILLER, KATHLEEN. Born July 1, 1945 in Los Angeles. Attended U Cal., AADA Debut Off-Bdwy in "House of Leather," followed by Bdwy bow (1970) in "Butterflies Are Free."

MILLER, MICHAEL. Born Sept. 1, 1931 in Los Angeles. Attended Bard Col. 1961 Off-Bdwy debut in "Under Milk Wood," followed by "The Lesson," "A Memory of 2 Mondays," "Little Murders," "Tom Paine," on Bdwy in "Ivanov," "Black Comedy," "Trial of Lee Harvey Oswald," "Morning, Noon and Night," "Enemy of the People" (LC).

MILLER, TOD. Born Sept. 15, 1944 in Quincy, Ill. Attended Pasadena Playhouse. Bdwy bow 1967 in "Mame," followed by "Here's Where I Belong," "Cabaret," "Canterbury Tales," "Stag Movie" (OB).

MILLS, STEVE. Born Oct. 9, 1895 in Boston. Appeared in burlesque and vaudeville, on Bdwy in "3 Little Girls," "A Wonderful Night," "Pleasure Bound," "A Lady Says Yes." "This Was Burlesque," "70, Girls, 70."

MINER, JAN. Born Oct. 15, 1919 in Boston. Debut Off-Bdwy in "Obligato," followed by "Decameron," "Dumbbell People," "Autograph Hound," on Bdwy in "Viva Madison Avenue," "Lady of the Camellias," "Freaking out of Stephanie Blake," "Othello."

MISITA, MICHAEL. Born Jan. 10, 1947 aboard HMS Queen Mary, Graduate Boston Cons. Bdwy debut 1968 in "Fig Leaves Are Falling," followed by "Mame," "Applause," "Follies."

MITCHELL, CAMERON. Born Nov. 4, 1918 in Dallastown, Pa. Attended Franklin-Marshall Col. Off-Bdwy debut 1938 in "At a Certain Hour," followed by "Peace and Plenty," on Bdwy in "Jeremiah," "Death of a Salesman" for which he received a THEATRE WORLD Award, "Southern Exposure," "Les Blancs."

MITCHELL, GARRY. Born Mar. 22, 1938 in Medicine Hat, Can. Graduate U Alberta. Debut 1968 Off-Bdwy in "Moon for The Misbegotten," followed by Bdwy in "We Bombed In New Haven," "Nobody Hears A Broken Drum," "Les Blancs."

MOFFAT, DONALD. Born Dec. 26, 1930 in Plymouth, Eng. Attended RADA. Bdwy bow 1957 in "Under Milk Wood," followed by "Much Ado about Nothing," "The Tumbler," "Duel of Angels," "Passage to India," "The Affair," "Father's Day," OB in "The Bald Soprano," "Jack," "The Caretaker," "Misalliance," with APA in "You Can't Take It with You," "War and Peace," "Right You Are," "The Wild Duck," "The Cherry Orchard," "Cock-a-doodle Dandy," and "Hamlet."

MOORE, CHARLES. Born May 22 in Cleveland, O. On Bdwy in "Jamaica," "Kwamina," "The Zulu and The Zayda," "Les Blancs." Off-Bdwy in "Ballad for Bimshire," "House Of Flowers," "Billy Noname."

| Roger Morden | Jennifer Moore | Fred Morsell | Joanne Nail | Stephen D. Newman |

MOORE, JENNIFER. Born May 18, 1944 in Johannesburg, SA. Attended Bennington Col. Debut 1961 Off-Bdwy in "Moon in the Yellow River," followed by "The Living Room," "A Month in the Country," on Bdwy in "The Promise," "Portrait of a Queen," "Abelard and Heloise."

MOORE, JONATHAN. Born Mar. 24, 1923 in New Orleans. Attended Piscator's Workshop. Debut 1961 Off-Bdwy in "After The Angels," followed by "Dylan," "1776."

MOORE, MELBA . Born 1945 in NYC. Graduate Montclair State Col. Bdwy debut 1968 in "Hair," followed by "Purlie" for which she received a THEATRE WORLD Award.

MORDEN, ROGER. Born Mar. 21, 1939 in Iowa City, Iowa. Graduate Coe Col., Neighborhood Playhouse. Off-Bdwy debut 1964 in "Old Glory," followed by "Man of LaMancha"(Bdwy), "3 by Ferlinghetti"(OB).

MORENO, RITA. Born Dec. 11, 1931 in Humacao, PR. Bdwy debut 1945 in "Skydrift," followed by "West Side Story," "Sign in Sidney Brustein's Window," "Last of the Red Hot Lovers."

MOREY, ARTHUR. Born Oct. 7, 1941 in Portland, Ore. Attended Harvard, U Chicago. Debut 1970 Off-Bdwy in "The Dirtiest Show in Town."

MORRIS, GARRETT. Born Feb. 1, 1944 in New Orleans. Graduate Dillard U. Off-Bdwy in "Bible Salesman," "Slave Ship," "Transfers," "Operation Sidewinder" (LC), "In New England Winter," "Basic Training of Pavlo Hummel," on Bdwy in "Porgy and Bess," "Hallelujah, Baby," "I'm Solomon," "The Great White Hope."

MORSE, RICHARD. Born May 31 in Brookline, Mass. Attended Principia Col., Neighborhood Playhouse. NY bow 1955 Off-Bdwy in "Teach Me How To Cry," followed by "Thor With Angels," "The Makropoulis Secret," "All Kinds of Giants," on Bdwy in "Mother Courage," "Fiddler On The Roof."

MORSELL, FRED A.. Born Aug. 3, 1940 in NYC. Graduate Dickinson Col. NY debut 1971 Off-Bdwy in "Any Resemblance to Persons Living or Dead."

MORTON, BROOKS. Born Oct. 3, 1932 in Ky. Attended Northwestern. NY bow 1962 Off-Bdwy in "Riverwind," followed by "Sunday Dinner," "Beyond The Fringe," "Marathon '33," "The Three Sisters," "Ivanov," "The Prime of Miss Jean Brodie," "Her First Roman," at CC in "West Side Story" and "Say, Darling!," "The Penny Wars."

MOSS, ARNOLD. Born Jan. 28, 1910 in Bklyn. Attended CCNY, Columbia. With LeGallienne's Repertory Co., on Bdwy in "Fifth Column," "Hold on to Your Hats," "Journey to Jerusalem," "Flight to the West," "The Land Is Bright," "The Tempest," "Front Page," "Twelfth Night," "King Lear," "Measure for Measure," "Follies."

MULLIGAN, RICHARD. Born Nov. 13, 1932 in The Bronx. Bdwy bow 1961 in "All the Way Home," followed by "Nobody Loves an Albatross," "Never Too Late," "Mating Dance," for which he received a THEATRE WORLD Award, "Hogan's Goat"(OB), "How the Other Half Loves."

MURCH, ROBERT G.. Born Apr. 17, 1935 in Jefferson Barracks, Mo. Graduate Wash. U. Bdwy bow 1966 in "Hostile Witness," followed by "The Harangues" (NEC), "Conduct Unbecoming," OB in "Charles Abbott & Son," "She Stoops to Conquer."

MURPHY, GERRY. Born Aug. 14, 1934 in Portland, Ore. Columbia graduate. Debut 1962 Off-Bdwy in "Portrait of the Artist...," followed by "Hop Signor," "Barroom Monks," ASF, "Trial of the Catonsville 9."

MURPHY, ROSEMARY. Born Jan. 13, 1927 in Munich, Ger. Attended Neighborhood Playhouse, Actors Studio. Bdwy debut 1950 in "Tower Beyond Tragedy," followed by "Look Homeward, Angel," "Period of Adjustment," "Any Wednesday," "A Delicate Balance," "Weekend," "Death of Bessie Smith," "Butterflies Are Free."

MURRAY, PEG. Born in Denver, Colo. Attended Western Reserve U. Off-Bdwy in "Children Of Darkness," "A Midsummer Night's Dream," and "Oh, Dad, Poor Dad . . . ," on Bdwy in "The Great Sebastians," "Gypsy," "Blood, Sweat and Stanley Poole," "She Loves me," "Anyone Can Whistle," "The Subject Was Roses," "Something More," "Cabaret," "Fiddler On The Roof."

MYERS, PAMELA. Born July 15, 1947 in Hamilton, O. Graduate Cincinnati Cons. of Music. Appeared at "Upstairs At The Downstairs" before Bdwy debut 1970 in "Company."

MYLES, LYNDA. Attended Mich. State Col. Columbia. Off-Bdwy in "Two Gentlemen of Verona," "The Trojan Women," "Rocking Chair," "No Exit," and "Iphigenia in Aulis," on Bdwy in "Plaza Suite."

NAIL, JOANNE. Born June 3, 1947 in Spokane, Wash. Graduate Wash. State Col. Bdwy debut 1971 in "Scratch."

NAPOLI, JOSEPH. Born Aug. 1940 in New Orleans. Attended Fordham, Tulane, Sorbonne, ACT. Debut Off-Bdwy 1971 in "One Flew Over the Cuckoo's Nest."

NASTASI, FRANK. Born Jan. 7, 1923 in Detroit. Graduate Wayne U., NYU. Off-Bdwy in "Bonds of Interest," "One Day More," "Nathan the Wise," "The Chief Things," "Cindy," "Escurial," "Shrinking Bride," "Macbird," on Bdwy in "Lorenzo," "Avanti!."

NATWICK, MILDRED. Born June 19, 1908 in Baltimore, Md. Bdwy debut 1932 in "Carrie Nation," followed by "The Wind And The Rain," "The Distaff Side," "End Of Summer, "Love From A Stranger," "Candida," "Star Wagon," "Missouri Legend," "Blithe Spirit," "Playboy Of The Western World," "Grass Harp," "Coriolanus," "Waltz Of The Toreadors," "Day The Money Stopped," "The Firstborn," "Critic's Choice," "Barefoot In The Park," "Our Town," "Landscapes" (LC), "70, Girls, 70."

NAUGHTON, JAMES. Born Dec. 6, 1945 in Middletown, Conn. Graduate Brown, Yale. Debut Off-Bdwy 1971 in "Long Day's Journey into Night" for which he received a THEATRE WORLD Award.

NELSON, GAIL. Born March 29 in Durham, NC. Graduate Oberlin, New Eng. Conserv. Bdwy debut 1968 in "Hello, Dolly!," followed by "Applause," "Six"(OB).

NELSON, GENE. Born Mar. 24, 1920 in Seattle, Wash. Bdwy debut 1942 in "This Is the Army," followed by "Lend an Ear" for which he won a THEATRE WORLD Award, "Follies."

NELSON, KENNETH. Born March 24, 1930 in Rocky Mt., NC. Attended Baylor U. Bdwy bow 1951 in "Seventeen," followed by "The Fantasticks"(OB), "Stop the World . . . ," "Half a Sixpence," "Boys in the Band"(OB), "Lovely Ladies, Kind Gentlemen."

NEWMAN, MARTIN. Born Dec. 23, 1924 in NYC. Attended Cornell, U NC. Bdwy debut 1950 in "Julius Caeser," followed by "Borned in Texas," "The Shrike," "My Foot, My Tutor"(OB).

NEWMAN, STEPHEN D. Born Jan. 20, 1943 in Seattle, Wash. Stanford Graduate. NY debut 1971 in Judith Anderson's "Hamlet," followed by "School for Wives."

| Mary Ann Niles | Michael Nouri | Marcia O'Brien | Ron O'Neal | Estelle Omens |

NILES, MARY ANN. Born May 2, 1933 in NYC. Attended Miss Finchley's and Ballet Acad. Bdwy debut in "Girl From Nantucket," followed by "Dance Me A Song," "Call Me Mister," "Make Mine Manhattan," "La Plume de Ma Tante," "Carnival," "Flora The Red Menace," "Sweet Charity," "George M!," Off-Bdwy in "The Boys From Syracuse," "Little Brown Road," "Big Spender," "Your Sister Rose," "Wonderful Town"(CC'67), "Carnival" (CC'68), "No, No, Nanette."

NOBLE, JAMES. Born Mar. 5, 1922 in Dallas, Tex. Attended SMU. Bdwy bow 1949 in "The Velvet Glove," followed by "Come of Age," "A Far Country," "Strange Interlude," "1776," Off-Bdwy in "Wilder's Triple Bill," "Night of The Dunce," "Rimers of Eldritch," "The Acquisition," "A Scent of Flowers."

NOURI, MICHAEL. Born Dec. 9, 1945 in Washington, DC. Debut Off-Bdwy 1964 in "The Crucible," followed by "40 Carats" on Bdwy 1968.

NUCHTERN, JEAN. Born Nov. 20, 1939 in NYC. Graduate Hofstra. Debut in "The King and I" (LC '64), followed by Off-Bdwy in "Our Play on the Future . . . ," "Greenwillow."(ELT).

NYBERG, PETER. Born Apr. 2, 1939 in Ft. William, Can. Graduate San Jose State. Bdwy debut Off-Bdwy in "White Devil," followed by LCRep's "The Alchemist," "Yerma," "East Wind," "Galileo," "Caucasian Chalk Circle," "Playboy of the Western World," and "Good Woman of Setzuan."

NYE, GENE. Born Feb. 23, 1939 in Bklyn. Graduate Hofstra U. Off-Bdwy in "Too Much Johnson," "Elizabeth the Queen," (CC'66), "Trelawny of the Wells."

NYPE, RUSSELL. Born Apr. 26, 1924 in Zion, Ill. Attended Lake Forest Col. Bdwy bow 1949 in "Regina," followed by "Call Me Madam" for which he received a THEATRE WORLD Award. "Tender Trap," "Tunnel of Love," "Wake Up, Darling," "Carousel"(CC), "Goldilocks," "Brigadoon"(CC), "Brouhaha" (OB), "The Owl And The Pussycat," "Girl in the Freudian Slip," "Private Lives"(OB), "Hello, Dolly!."

OAKES, GARY. Born Feb. 22, 1936 in North Adams, Mass. Attended Columbia, Neighborhood Playhouse. Debut OB 1963 in "Boys from Syracuse", followed by "Shoemaker's Holiday," on Bdwy in "1776."

O'BRIEN, MARCIA. Born Mar. 17, 1934 in Ind. Graduate Ind U. Bdwy debut 1970 in "Man of LaMancha," followed by "Now Is the Time for All Good Men" (ELT).

O'BRIEN, SYLVIA. Born May 4, 1924 in Dublin, Ire. Debut 1961 Off-Bdwy in "O Marry Me," followed by "Red Roses For Me," "Every Other Evil," "3 By O'Casey," "Essence of Women," on Bdwy in "The Passion of Josef D," "The Right Honourable Gentleman," "The Loves of Cass McGuire," "Hadrian VII," "Conduct Unbecoming."

O' DONNELL, ANNE. Born June 8 in Philadelphia. Attended Chestnut Hill Col. Debut 1970 Off-Bdwy in "Greenwillow"(ELT).

O'HARA, JENNY. Born Feb. 24 in Sonora, Cal. Attended Carnegie Tech. Bdwy debut 1964 in "Dylan," followed by "Fig Leaves Are Falling," "Criss-Crossing," "Promises, Promises," Off-Bdwy in "Hang Down Your Head and Die," "Play With A Tiger," "Arms And The Man," "Sambo," "My House Is Your House."

O'HARA, JILL. Born Aug. 23, 1947 in Warren, Pa. Attended Edinburgh State Teachers Col. Off-Bdwy in "Hang Down Your Head And Die," and "Hair," before Bdwy debut 1968 in "George M!" followed by "Promises, Promises," for which she received a THEATRE WORLD Award.

OLSON, DALE. Born June 16, 1943 in Jackson, Wyo. Attended Northwestern, Brigham Young U. NY bow 1971 in "Heloise"(ELT).

OMENS, ESTELLE. Born Oct. 11, 1928 in Chicago. Graduate U Iowa. Off-Bdwy in "Summer and Smoke," "Grass Harp," "Legend of Lovers," "Plays of Bleecker Street," "Pullman Car Hiawatha," "Brownstone Urge," "Gandhi," Bdwy debut 1969 in "The Watering Place."

O'NEAL, RON. Born Sept. 1, 1937 in Utica, N.Y. Attended Ohio State U. Debut 1968 Off-Bdwy in "American Pastoral," followed by "No Place To Be Somebody" for which he received a THEATRE WORLD Award, "Dream on Monkey Mt."(NEC)

O'NEIL, TRICIA. Born Mar. 11, 1945 in Shreveport, La. Graduate Baylor U. Bdwy debut 1970 in "Two by Two" for which she received a THEATRE WORLD Award.

O'NEILL, DICK. Born Aug. 29, 1928 in The Bronx. Attended Utica Col. Bdwy bow 1961 in "The Unsinkable Molly Brown," followed by "Skyscraper," "Have I Got One For You"(OB), "Promises, Promises."

ORBACH, JERRY. Born Oct. 20, 1935 in NYC. Attended U.Ill., Northwestern. Bdwy bow 1961 in "Carnival," followed by "Guys and Dolls"(CC), LC revivals of "Carousel" and "Annie Get Your Gun," "The Natural Look," "Promises, Promises," Off-Bdwy in "Threepenny Opera," "The Fantasticks," "The Cradle Will Rock," "Scuba Duba."

ORFALY, ALEXANDER. Born Oct. 10, 1935 in Brooklyn. Appeared in "South Pacific"(LC), "How Now, Dow Jones," "Ari," Off-Bdwy in "The End Of All Things Natural," "Mahagonny," "Johnny Johnson."

OSBORNE, KIPP. Born Oct. 17, 1944 in Jersey City, NJ. Attended U Mich., Neighborhood Playhouse. Bdwy debut 1970 in "Butterflies Are Free" for which he received a THEATRE WORLD Award.

OSTERWALD, BIBI. Born Feb. 3, 1920 in New Brunswick, NJ. Attended Catholic U. Bdwy debut 1945 in "Sing Out, Sweet Land," followed by "3 to Make Ready," "Sally," "Gentlemen Prefer Blondes," "Golden Apple," "The Vamp," "Look Homeward, Angel," "New Girl in Town," "A Family Affair," "Hello, Dolly!."

O'SULLIVAN, MAUREEN. Born May 17, 1911 in Roscommon, Ire. Bdwy debut 1962 in "Never Too Late," followed by "The Subject Was Roses," "Keep It in the Family," "Front Page," "Charley's Aunt."

OTTO, LIZ. Born in Coral Gables, Fla. Graduate U. Fla. Debut 1963 Off-Bdwy in "The Plot against the Chase Manhattan Bank," followed by "I Dreamt I Dwelt in Bloomingdale's."

OWENS, ELIZABETH. Born Feb. 26, 1938 in NYC. Attended New School, Neighborhood Playhouse. Debut 1955 Off-Bdwy in "Dr. Faustus Lights the Lights," followed by "The Lovers"(Bdwy), "Chit Chat on a Rat," "The Miser," "The Father," "The Importance of Being Earnest," "Candida," "Trumpets and Drums," "Oedipus," "Macbeth," "Not Now Darling"(Bdwy), "Uncle Vanya."

PAGE, GERALDINE. Born Nov. 22, 1924 in Kirksville, Mo. Attended Goodman Theatre. Off-Bdwy in "7 Mirrors," "Summer and Smoke," "Macbeth," Bdwy debut 1953 in "Midsummer" (for which she received a THEATRE WORLD Award), followed by "The Immoralist," "The Rainmaker," "The Innkeepers," "Separate Tables," "Sweet Bird of Youth," "Strange Interlude," "Three Sisters," "P.S. I Love You," "The Great Indoors," "White Lies," "Black Comedy," "The Little Foxes," "Angela."

PAISNER, DINA. Born in Bklyn. Bdwy debut 1963 in "Andorra," OB in "Cretan Women," "Pullman Car Hiawatha," "Lysistrata," "If 5 Years Pass," "Troubled Waters," "Sap of Life," "Cave at Machpelah," "Threepenny Opera," "Montserrat," "Blood Wedding," "Gandhi."

| Bernie Passeltiner | Susan G. Pearson | Don Perkins | Holly Peters | Michael Petro |

PARSONS, ESTELLE. Born Nov. 20, 1927 in Lynn, Mass. Attended Boston U., Conn. Col., Actors Studio. Off-Bdwy in "Threepenny Opera," "Automobile Graveyard," "Mrs. Dally Has A Lover" for which she received a THEATRE WORLD Award, "In the Summer House," "Monopoly," "Peer Gynt"(CP), "Mahagonny," with LC Rep in "East Wind" and "Galileo," on Bdwy in "Happy Hunting," "Whoop-Up!" "Beg, Borrow or Steal," "Ready When You Are, C.B." "Malcolm," "The Seven Descents of Myrtle," "A Way of Life," "And Miss Reardon Drinks a Little."

PASSANTINO, ANTHONY. Born July 9, 1945 in Brooklyn. Attended Hofstra U. Appeared in NYSF's "Hamlet" and "Othello," Bdwy bow 1969 in "Henry V," Off-Bdwy in "Macbeth."

PASSELTINER, BERNIE. Born Nov. 21, 1931 in NYC. Graduate Catholic U. Off-Bdwy in "Square in the Eye," "Sourball," "As Virtuously Given," "Now Is the Time for All Good Men," on Bdwy in "The Office"('66).

PATTERSON, PHIL. Born Mar. 7, 1952 in Queens, NY. Debut Off-Bdwy 1971 in "Red, White and Black."

PATTERSON, WILBUR, JR.. Born May 25, 1946 in NYC. Attended AMDA. Debut Off-Bdwy 1971 in "One Flew over the Cuckoo's Nest."

PAUL, STEVEN. Born May 16, 1959 in NYC. Attended AADA. Debut Off-Bdwy in "Lyle," followed by "Lemon Sky," "Happy Birthday, Wanda June."

PAYTON-WRIGHT, PAMELA. Born Nov. 1, 1941 in Pittsburgh. Graduate Birmingham Southern Col., RADA. Bdwy debut 1967 with APA in "The Show-Off," "Exit The King," and "The Cherry Orchard," "Jimmy Shine," Off-Bdwy in "The Effect of Gamma Rays on Man-in-the-Moon Marigolds."

PEARSON, SCOTT. Born Dec. 13, 1941 in Milwaukee. Attended Valparaiso U., U. Wisc. Bdwy debut 1966 in "A Joyful Noise," followed by "Promises, Promises."

PEARSON, SUSAN G. Born Jan. 3, 1941 in Minneapolis. Attended U. Minn. Debut 1969 in "No Place to Be Somebody."

PEARSONS, LYLE. Born Dec. 8, 1947 in St. Johnsbury, Vt. Graduate Boston U. NY debut 1971 Off-Bdwy in "Kiss Now."

PENDLETON, AUSTIN. Born Mar. 27, 1940 in Warren, O. Attended Yale. Appeared with LCRep(1962-3), in "Oh, Dad, Poor Dad . . . ," "Fiddler on the Roof," "Hail Scrawdyke," "The Little Foxes," "Last Sweet Days of Isaac" (OB).

PENDLETON, WYMAN. Born Apr. 18, 1916 in Providence, RI. Graduate Brown U. Off-Bdwy credits: "Gallows Humor," "American Dream," "Zoo Story," "Corruption In The Palace of Justice," "The Giant's Dance," "The Child Buyer," "Happy Days," "The Butter and Egg Man," on Bdwy in "Tiny Alice," "Malcolm," "Quotations From Chairman Mao Tse-Tung," "Happy Days," "Henry V," "Othello."

PENNOCK, CHRISTOPHER. Born June 7, 1944 in Jackson Hole, Wyo. Attended Hobart, Col., AADA. Debut 1966 in "The Rose Tatto"(CC), Bdwy bow 1969 in "A Patriot for Me," followed by "Abelard and Heloise."

PENTECOST, GEORGE. Born July 15, 1939 in Detroit. Graduate Wayne State, U. Mich. With APA in "Scapin." "Lower Depths," "The Tavern," "School for Scandal," "Right You Are," "War and Peace," "The Wild Duck," "The Show-Off," "Pantagleize," and "The Cherry Orchard," "The Boys in the Band"(OB), "School for Wives."

PENZNER, SEYMOUR. Born July 29, 1915 in Yonkers, NY. Attended CCNY. Off-Bdwy in "Crystal Heart," "Guitar" on Bdwy in "Oklahoma," "Finian's Rainbow," "Call Me Madam," "Paint Your Wagon," "Can-Can," "Kean," "Baker Street," "Man of La Mancha."

PERKINS, ANTHONY. Born Apr. 4, 1932 in NYC. Attended Rollins Col., Columbia. Bdwy debut 1954 in "Tea and Sympathy" for which he received a THEATRE WORLD Award, followed by "Look Homeward, Angel," "Greenwillow," "Harold," "Star Spangled Girl," "Steambath"(OB) which he directed.

PERKINS, DON. Born Oct. 23, 1928 in Boston. Graduate Emerson Col. Off-Bdwy in "Drums under the Window," "Henry VI," "Richard III" (CP) Bdwy bow 1970 in "Borstal Boy."

PERRY, JOHN BENNETT. Born Jan. 4, 1941 in Williamston, Mass. Graduate St. Lawrence U. Debut Off-Bdwy 1967 in "Now Is the Time for All Good Men," followed by "A Month of Sundays," "Ballad of Johnny Pot."

PETERS, BERNADETTE. Born Feb. 28, 1948 in Jamaica, NY. Off-Bdwy in "Penny Friend," "Curley McDimple," "Most Happy Fella" (CC), "Dames At Sea," "Nevertheless, They Laugh," Bdwy debut 1967 in "The Girl In The Freudian Slip," followed by "Johnny No Trump," "George M" for which she received a THEATRE WORLD Award, "La Strada."

PETERS, HOLLY. Born Apr. 16, 1946 in Hamburg, Ger. Attended HB Studio. Bdwy debut 1970 in "The Engagement Baby."

PETERSON, KURT. Born Feb. 12, 1948 in Stevens Point,. Wisc. Attended AMDA. Appeared in "An Ordinary Miracle"(OB) "West Side Story"(LC'68), Bdwy debut 1969 in "Dear World," followed by "Dames at Sea"(OB), "Follies."

PETRO, MICHAEL. Born July 1, 1944 in Westfield, NY. Graduate Slippery Rock Col., HB Studio. Bdwy debut 1971 in "Fiddler on the Roof."

PHALEN, ROBERT. Born May 10, 1937 in San Francisco. Attended CCSF., U. Cal. With LCRep in "Danton's Death." "The Country Wife," "Caucasian Chalk Circle," "The Alchemist," "Yerma," "Galileo," "St. Joan," "Tiger At The Gates," "Cyrano," "King Lear," "A Cry of Players," "In The Matter of J. Robert Oppenheimer," "Operation Sidewinder," "Beggar on Horseback," "Good Woman of Setzuan," "Birthday Party," and "Silence."

PHILLIPS, MARY BRACKEN. Born Aug. 15, 1946 in Kansas City, Mo. Attended Kansas U. Debut 1969 Off-Bdwy in "Perfect Party," followed by Bdwy bow in "1776," "Look Where I'm At" (OB).

PIACENTINI, ANNE. Born in Rochester, NY. Debut Off-Bdwy 1970 in "Greenwillow" (ELT).

PINCUS, WARREN. Born Apr. 13, 1938 in Bklyn. Attended CCNY. Off-Bdwy in "Miss Nepertiti Regrets," "The Circus," "The Magician," "Boxcars," "Demented World," "Give My Regards," "The Electronic Nigger," "The Last Pad," "Waiting for Godot."

PIZZI, DONNA. Born Aug. 12, 1945 in San Francisco. Attended SF State Col. Debut Off-Bdwy 1966 in "Sunset," followed by "Gandhi."

PLAYTEN, ALICE. Born Aug. 28, 1947 in NYC. Attended NYU, Bklyn. Col. Debut 1959 in Met's "Wozzeck," Bdwy bow 1960 in "Gypsy," followed by "Oliver," "Hello, Dolly!," "Henry, Sweet Henry" for which she received a THEATRE WORLD Award, "George M'", Off- Bdwy in "Promenade", "The Last Sweet Days of Isaac."

| Don Potter | Marion Ramsey | Paul B. Price | Mimi Randolph | Remak Ramsay |

PLESHETTE, JOHN. Born July 27, 1942 in NYC. Attended Brown U. Bdwy bow 1966 in "The Zulu and the Zayda," followed by "Jimmy Shine," Off-Bdwy in "A Sound of Silence," NYSF, "Macbird," "It's Called the Sugar Plum," "The Shrinking Bride."

PLIMPTON, SHELLEY. Born 1947 in Roseburg, Ore. Debut Off-Bdwy 1967 in "Hair."

PLUMLEY, DON. Born Feb. 11, 1934 in Los Angeles. Graduate Pepperdine Col. Debut Off-Bdwy 1961 in "The Cage," followed by NYSF's "Midsummer Night's Dream," "Richard II," and "Much Ado About Nothing," "Saving Grace," "A Whistle in the Dark," "Operation Sidewinder" and "Enemy of The People" (LC), "Back Bog Beast Bait."

POE, GARY. Born Apr. 6, 1947 in Elizabeth, NJ. Attended Kent State, AADA. With NYSF 1968 in "Henry IV," and "Romeo and Juliet," "The People vs Ranchman" (OB), "Othello."

POINTER, PRISCILLA. Born in NYC. With LCRep from 1965, in "Summertree," "An Evening For Merlin Finch," "Inner Journey," "The Disintegration of James Cherry," "The Time of Your Life," "Camino Real," "Amphitryon," "Good Woman of Setzuan," "Scenes from American Life," "Play Strindberg."

POLITO, PHILIP. Born Feb. 17, 1944 in Hackensack, NJ. Graduate Ill. Wesleyan U., Yale. Bdwy debut 1969 in "1776."

POLLICK, TENO. Born July 14, 1935 in NYC. Attended LACC. Bdwy debut 1954 in "Peter Pan," followed by "Much Ado About Nothing," "Steambath" (OB).

PONAZECKI, JOE. Born Jan. 7, 1934 in Rochester, NY. Attended Rochester U., Columbia. Bdwy bow 1959 in "Much Ado About Nothing," followed by "Send Me No Flowers," "A Call On Kuprin," "Take Her, She's Mine," "The Dragon" (OB), "Fiddler On The Roof," "Xmas In Las Vegas," "3 Bags Full," "Love In E-Flat," "90 Day Mistress," "Muzeeka" (OB), "Witness" (OB), "Harvey," "Trial of The Catonsville 9."

POOLE, ROY. Born Mar. 31, 1924 in San Bernardino, Cal. Graduate Stanford. Credits: "Now I Lay Me Down To Sleep," "St. Joan" ('56), "The Bad Seed," "I Knock At The Door," "Long Day's Journey Into Night," "Face of A Hero," "Moby Dick," "Poor Bitos," "1776," "Scratch."

POPE, PEGGY. Born May 15, 1929 in Montclair, NJ. Attended Smith Col. Appeared in "The Doctor's Dilemma" (1955), "Volpone," "The Rose Tattoo," "Muzeeka" (OB), "The Front Page," "School for Wives," "House of Blue Leaves." (OB)

PORTER, STAN. Born July 1, 1928 in Brooklyn. Bdwy debut 1967 in "Hello, Solly!," Off-Bdwy in "Jacques Brel Is Alive and Well . . ."

POTTER, DON. Born Aug. 15, 1932 in Philadelphia. Debut 1961 Off-Bdwy in "What A Killing," followed by "Sunset," "You're A Good Man, Charlie Brown."

PRICE, GILBERT. Born Sept. 10, 1942 in NYC. Attended Am. Th. Wing. Bdwy bow 1965 in "The Roar of the Greasepaint . . .," Off-Bdwy in "Kicks & Co.," "Fly Blackbird," "Jerico-Jim Crow" for which he received a THEATRE WORLD Award, "Promenade," "Slow Dance on the Killing Ground," "Six."

PRICE, PAUL B. Born Oct. 7, 1933 in Carteret, NJ. Attended Pasadena Playhouse. NY bow 1960 in "Dead End" (OB), followed by "A Cook for Mr. General," "Banquet for the Moon," "O Say Can You See," "Dumbwaiter," "Live Like Pigs," "Medea," "4H Club," "Waiting for Godot."

PROFANATO, GENE. Born Dec. 9, 1964 in NYC. Bdwy debut 1970 in "Lovely Ladies, Kind Gentlemen."

PURNELL, ROGER. Born June 11, 1943 in Spartanburg, SC. Graduate Middlebury Col., Yale. Bdwy debut 1970 in "Sleuth."

QUAYLE, ANTHONY. Born Sept. 7, 1913 in Ainsdale, Eng. Attended RADA. Bdwy debut 1936 in "Country Wife," followed by "Tamburlaine the Great," "The Firstborn," "Galileo" (LC) "Halfway up the Tree," "Sleuth."

RACHINS, ALAN. Born Oct. 3, 1942 in Brookline, Mass. Attended U. Pa. Bdwy debut 1967 in "After The Rain," followed by "Hadrian VII," "Oh! Calcutta!"

RADD, RONALD. Born Jan. 22, 1929 in Durham, Eng. Bdwy bow 1957 in "Hotel Paradiso," followed by "My Fair Lady," "Ivanov," "Abelard and Heloise."

RALSTON, TERI. Born Feb. 16, 1943 in Holyoke, Colo. Graduate SF State Col. Debut 1969 Off-Bdwy in "Jacques Brel Is Alive . . .," Bdwy bow 1970 in "Company."

RAMSAY, REMAK. Born Feb. 2, 1937 in Baltimore, Md. Princeton graduate. Off-Bdwy in "Hang Down Your Head and Die," Bdwy bow 1965 in "Half a Sixpence," followed by "Sheep on the Runway," "Lovely Ladies, Kind Gentlemen."

RAMSEY, MARION. Born May 10, 1947 in Philadelphia. Bdwy bow 1969 in "Hello, Dolly!," followed by Off-Bdwy's "The Me Nobody Knows," "Soon," "Do It Again."

RANDOLPH, JOHN. Born June 1, 1915 in the Bronx. Attended CCNY, Actors Studio. Bdwy bow 1937 in "Revolt of the Beavers," followed by "The Emperor's New Clothes," "Capt. Jinks," "No More Peace," "Coriolanus," "Medicine Show," "Hold on to Your Hats," "Native Son," "Command Decision," "Come Back, Little Sheba," "Golden State," "Peer Gynt," "Paint Your Wagon," "Seagulls over Sorrento," "Grey-Eyed People," "Room Service," "All Summer Long," "House of Flowers," "The Visit," "Mother Courage and Her Children," "Sound of Music," "Case of Libel," "Conversation at Midnight," OB in "An Evening's Frost," "My Sweet Charlie," "The Peddler and the Dodo Bird", "Our Town," "Line."

RANDOLPH, MIMI. Born Dec. 26, 1922 in Montreal, Can. Debut Off-Bdwy 1962 in "All in Love," followed by "Jo," "Pocketwatch," on Bdwy in "Dear Me, the Sky Is Falling," "Fiddler on the Roof."

RATCLIFFE, SAMUEL D. Born Mar. 30, 1945 in Eagle Lake, Fla. Graduate Birmingham Southern Col. Debut 1969 Off-Bdwy in "The Fantasticks," followed by Bdwy bow in "Fiddler on the Roof."

RATHBURN, ROGER. Born Nov. 11, 1940 in Perrysburg, O. Attended Ohio State, Neighborhood Playhouse. Bdwy debut 1971 in "No, No, Nanette" for which he received a THEATRE WORLD Award.

RAY, JAMES. Born July 4, 1932 in Calgra, Okla. Attended Okla. A&M. Bdwy debut 1957 in "Compulsion," followed by "J.B.," "The Wall," "Dylan," "The Glass Menagerie" ('65), "All Over," Off-Bdwy in "The Creditors," "The Collection," "Love's Labour's Lost" (CP), "Henry IV" (CP), "The Basement," "Sensations," with ASF from 1961, LC Rep's "Disintegration of James Cherry," and "Amphitryon."

REAMS, LEE ROY. Born Aug. 23, 1942 in Covington, Ky. Graduate U. Cinn. Cons. Bdwy debut 1966 in "Sweet Charity," followed by "Oklahoma!" (LC), "Applause."

REARDON, NANCY. Born June 28, 1942 in NYC. Bdwy debut 1964 in "Poor Bitos," followed by "Right Honourable Gentleman," "The Odd Couple," "Black Comedy," "The Unknown Soldier and His Wife," (LC), "Arturo Ui," OB in "Charles Abbott & Son" and "She Stoops to Conquer."

REDWOOD, JOHN HENRY. Born Sept. 10, 1942 in Bklyn. Attended U Kan. Debut Off-Bdwy 1970 in "Cartouche," followed by "One Flew over the Cuckoo's Nest."

| Jon Richards | Cathryn Roskam | Jerry Rodgers | Ann Boothby Ross | Jamie Ross |

REILEY, ORRIN. Born Aug. 12, 1946 in Santa Monica, Cal. Graduate UCLA. Bdwy debut 1969 in "Dear World," followed by "Man of La Mancha," "Applause."

RESTIFO, GARY. Born Dec. 4, 1948 in Schenectady, NY. Graduate SUNY, HB Studio. Debut Off-Bdwy 1971 in "Life in Bed."

REY, ANTONIA. Born Oct. 12, 1927 in Havana, Cuba. Graduate Havana U. Bdwy debut 1964 in "Bajour," followed by "Yerma" (OB), "Mike Downstairs," "Fiesta In Madrid" (CC), "Engagement Baby," "Camino Real" (LC), "Back Bog Beast Bait" (OB).

RHODES, ERIK. Born Feb. 10, 1906 in El Reno, Okla. Graduate UOkla. Bdwy bow 1928 in "A Most Immoral Lady," followed by "First Little Show," "Hey, Nonny, Nonny," "Gay Divorce," "Great Campaign," "Dance Me a Song," "Collector's Item" "Can-Can," "Shinbone Alley," "Jamaica," "How to Make a Man," "A Funny Thing Happened on the Way to the Forum," "My Fair Lady" (CC'68), "Colette" (OB).

RICHARDS, JON. Born in Wilkes Barre, Pa. Appeared in "Tobacco Road," "Arsenic and Old Lace," "Love or Money," "Gramercy Ghost," "Bad Seed," "Leave It to Jane" (OB), "Sunrise at Campobello," "Sail Away," "The Last Analysis," "A Very Rich Woman," "Roar like a Dove," "Elizabeth the Queen," "3 Bags Full," "Woman Is My Idea," "Does a Tiger Wear a Necktie?," "One Flew over the Cuckoo's Nest" (OB).

RICHARDS, PAUL. Born Aug. 31, 1934 in Bedford, Ind. Graduate Ind. U. Bdwy debut 1960 in "Once Upon A Mattress," followed by "Camelot," "Superman," "A Joyful Noise," "1776."

RICHARDSON, RALPH. Born Dec. 19, 1902 in Cheltenham, Eng. Toured U.S. 1935, Bdwy bow with Cornell in "Romeo and Juliet," followed by "Henry IV," "Oedipus," "The Critic," "Uncle Vanya," "Waltz of the Toreadors," "Home."

RILLEY, JAMES. Born July 9, 1947 in Port Chester, NY. Studied at HB Studio. Debut Off-Bdwy 1970 in "Greenwillow" (ELT), followed by "Heloise" (ELT).

ROBBINS, REX. Born in Pierre, S.Dak. Yale graduate. Bdwy debut 1964 in "One Flew over the Cuckoo's Nest," followed by "Scratch," Off-Bdwy in "Servant of Two Masters," "Alchemist," "Arms and the Man," "Boys in the Band."

ROBERTS, ANTHONY. Born Oct. 22, 1939 in NYC. Graduate Northwestern. Bdwy bow 1962 in "Something About A Soldier," followed by "Take Her, She's Mine," "The Last Analysis," "The Cradle Will Rock" (OB), "Never Too Late," "Barefoot In The Park," "Don't Drink The Water," "How Now, Dow Jones," "Play It Again, Sam," "Promises, Promises."

ROBERTS, DAVIS. Born Mar. 7, 1917 in Mobile, Ala. Attended U Chicago, UCLA, Actors Lab. Debut 1971 in "Trial of the Catonsville 9."

ROBERTS, DORIS. Born in St. Louis, Mo. Attended Neighborhood Playhouse, Actors Studio. Off-Bdwy credits: "Death of Bessie Smith," "American Dream," "Color of Darkness," "Don't Call Me By My Rightful Name," "Christy," "Boy in the Straightback Chair," "A Matter of Position," "Natural Affection." Bdwy debut 1956 in "The Desk Set," followed by "Have I Got A Girl for You," "The Time of Your Life" (CC), "Malcolm," "Marathon '33," "Under the Weather," "The Office," "The Natural Look," "Last of the Red Hot Lovers."

ROBERTSON, JANE. Born May 17, 1948 in Bartlesville, Okla. Attended U Okla. Debut Off-Bdwy 1970 in "Shoestring Revues" (ELT).

ROBERTSON, WILLIAM. Born Oct. 9, 1908 in Portsmouth, Va. Graduate Pomona Col. Bdwy debut 1936 in "Tapestry in Grey," followed by "Cup of Trembling," "Liliom," "Our Town" (1969) Off-Bdwy in "Uncle Harry," "Shining Hour," "The Cenci," "Aspern Papers," "Madame Is Served," "Tragedian in spite of Himself," "The Kibosh," "Sun-Up," "The Last Pad."

ROBINSON, ANDY. Born Feb. 14, 1942 in NYC. Graduate New School, London AMDA. Debut 1967 Off-Bdwy in "MacBird," followed by "The Cannibals," "Futz," "The Young Master Dante," "Operation Sidewinder" (LC), "Subject to Fits."

RODD, MARCIA. Born July 8 in Lyons, Kan. Attended Northwestern, Yale. Off-Bdwy in "Oh Say Can You See," "Cambridge Circus," "Mad Show," "Madame Mousse," "Love and Let Love," "Your Own Thing," Bdwy debut 1964 in "Oh What A Lovely War," followed by "Love in E-Flat," "Last of the Red Hot Lovers."

RODGERS, JERRY. Born Aug. 20, 1941 in Stockton, Cal. Graduate U Portland. Debut 1971 Off-Bdwy in "Miss Lizzie," followed by "Shakuntala," "Life in Bed."

ROERICK, WILLIAM. Born Dec. 17, 1912 in NYC. Bdwy bow 1935 in "Romeo and Juliet," followed by "St. Joan," "Hamlet," "Our Town," "Importance of Being Earnest," "The Land Is Bright," "Autumn Hill," "This Is the Army," "Magnificent Yankee," "Tonight at 8:30," "Burning Glass," "Right Honourable Gentleman," "Marat/deSade," "Homecoming," "We Bombed in New Haven," "Elizabeth the Queen" (CC'66), OB in "Madam, Will You Walk," "Come, Slowly Eden," "A Passage to E. M. Forster."

ROLLE, ESTHER. Born Nov. 8 in Pompano Beach, Fla. Attended Hunter Col. Bdwy debut 1964 in "Blues For Mr. Charlie," followed by "Purlie Victorious," "The Amen Corner," Off-Bdwy in "The Blacks," "Happy Ending," "Day of Absence," NEC's "Evening of One Acts," "Man Better Man," "Brotherhood," "Okakawe," "Rosalee Pritchett," "Dream on Monkey Mt.," "Ride a Black Horse."

RONAN, ROBERT. Born Feb. 17, 1938 in Richmond Hills, NY. Attended Hofstra U. Off-Bdwy in "Dr. Faustus," "Colombe," in NYSF's "Love's Labour's Lost," "All's Well That Ends Well," "Comedy of Errors," "Twelfth Night" and "Henry IV," "The Memorandum," "Invitation To A Beheading," "Trelawny of the Wells."

ROSE, GEORGE. Born Feb. 19, 1920 in Bicester, Eng. NY bow with Old Vic 1946 in "Henry IV," followed by "Much Ado About Nothing," "A Man For All Seasons," "Hamlet" ('64), "Royal Hunt of the Sun," "Walking Happy," "Loot," "My Fair Lady" (CC'68), "Canterbury Tales," "Coco."

ROSKAM, CATHRYN. Bowrn May 30, 1943 in Hempstead, NY. Graduate Middlebury Col. Debut Off-Bdwy 1970 in "Gandhi."

ROSQUI, TOM. Born June 12, 1928 in Oakland, Calif. Graduate Col. of Pacific. With LCRep in "Danton's Death," "Condemned of Altona," "Country Wife," "Caucasian Chalk Circle," "Alchemist," "Yerma," and "East Wind," Off-Bdwy in "Collision Course," NEC's "Day of Absence" and "Brotherhood," "What the Butler Saw," "Waiting for Godot."

ROSS, ANN BOOTHBY. Born in Chicago. Graduate Barnard, Old Vic. Debut Off-Bdwy 1970 in "Summertime," followed by "Motel," "Chronicle of 9," "Man's a Man," "Corrupters," "False Confessions" (ELT).

ROSS, JAMIE. Born May 4, 1939 in Markinch, Scot. Attended RADA. Bdwy debut 1962 in "Little Moon of Alban," followed by "Moon Beseiged," "Penny Friend" (OB), "Ari."

257

| Jane Russell | Robert Rovin | Marie Santell | Hoshin Seki | Marilyn Saunders |

ROSS, LARRY. Born Oct. 18, 1945 in Brooklyn. Attended AADA. Bdwy debut 1963 in "How to Succeed in Business . . . ," followed by "Fiddler on the Roof," "Frank Merriwell."

ROSS, MARTIN. Born July 9, 1938 in NYC. Off-Bdwy in "We're Civilized," "Look Where I'm At," on Bdwy in "Milk and Honey," "Once for the Asking," "The Yearling," "Pousse Cafe," "Cabaret," "Ari."

ROTH, LILLIAN. Born Dec. 13, 1910 in Boston. In vaudeville with "The Roth Kids," Bdwy debut 1917 in "Inner Man," followed by "Penrod," "Betrothal," "Shavings," "Padlocks of 1927," "Earl Carroll's Vanities," "Midnight Frolics," "I Can Get It for You Wholesale," "Funny Girl," "70, Girls, 70."

ROUNDS, DAVID. Born Oct. 9, 1938 in Bronxville, NY. Attended Denison U. Off-Bdwy in "You Never Can Tell," "Money," Bdwy debut 1965 in "Foxy" followed by "Child's Play" for which he received a THEATRE WORLD Award, "The Rothschilds."

ROUNSEVILLE, ROBERT. Born Mar. 25, 1919 in Attleboro, Mass. Attended Tufts U. Bdwy bow 1937 in "Babes In Arms," followed by "Two Bouquets," "Knickerbocker Holiday," "Higher and Higher," "Up In Central Park," "Show Boat" ('54), "The Merry Widow," "Candide," "Brigadoon" (CC), "Man of La Mancha."

ROVIN, ROBERT H. Born May 30 in Chicago. Graduate Northwestern. Debut Off-Bdwy 1965 in "Hotel Passionato," followed by "Futz," "House of Leather," on Bdwy in "Pousse Cafe," "Abelard and Heloise."

ROZAKIS, GREGORY. Born Jan. 30, 1943 in NYC. Bdwy bow 1963 in "Natural Affection," followed by "Royal Hunt of the Sun," "What Did We Do Wrong?," OB in "Cannibals," "Orestes."

RULE, JANICE. Born Aug. 15, 1931 in Norwood, O. Bdwy debut 1949 in "Miss Liberty," followed by "Great to Be Alive," "Picnic," "Flowering Peach," "Carefree Tree" (OB), "Night Circus," "Happiest Girl in the World," "The Homecoming" (OB).

RUSSEL, MARK. Born June 21, 1948 in Bklyn. Attended Bklyn Col. Debut 1970 with NYSF, followed by "Dirtiest Show in Town" (OB).

RUSSELL, JANE. Born June 21, 1921 in Bemidji, Minn. Attended Max Reinhardt Sch. Bdwy debut 1971 in "Company."

RUSSOM, LEON. Born Dec. 6, 1941 in Little Rock, Ark. Attended Southwestern U. Off-Bdwy in "Futz," "Cyrano" (LCRep), "The Boys In The Band," "Oh! Calcutta!," "Trial of the Catonsville 9," "Henry VI," "Richard III."

RUYMEN, AYN. Born July 18, 1947 in Bklyn. Attended HB Studio. Bdwy debut 1970 in "The Gingerbread Lady" for which she received a THEATRE WORLD Award.

RYAN, CHARLENE. Born in NYC. Bdwy debut 1964 in "Never Live Over A Pretzel Factory," followed by "Sweet Charity," "Fig Leaves Are Falling," "Coco."

RYAN, ROBERT. Born Nov. 11, 1913 in Chicago. Attended Dartmouth. Bdwy bow 1941 in "Clash By Night," followed by "Coriolanus" ('53OB), "Mr. President," "The Front Page" ('69), "Long Day's Journey into Night" (OB).

SALT, JENNIFER. Born Sept. 4, 1944 in Los Angeles. Graduate Sarah Lawrence Col. Bdwy debut 1970 in "Watercolor," followed by "Father's Day" for which she received a THEATRE WORLD Award.

SAND, PAUL. Born Mar. 5, 1935 in Santa Monica, Calif. Attended CCLA. Bdwy bow 1961 in "From the Second City," followed by "Story Theatre," "Metamorphoses," OB in "Journey to the Day," "Wet Paint," "Hotel Passionato," "Mad Show."

SANTELL, MARIE. Born July 8 in Brooklyn. Bdwy debut 1957 in "Music Man," followed by "A Funny Thing Happened on the Way . . . ," "Flora, the Red Menace," Off-Bdwy in "Hi, Paisano!," "Boys from Syracuse," "Peace," "Promenade," "The Drunkard," "Sensations."

SANTORO, DEAN. Born Jan. 30, 1938 in Johnstown, Pa. Graduate Penn. State. Debut with APA in "War and Peace" and "Man and Superman," followed by "Philosophy In The Boudoir" (OB), "Hadrian VII," "Borstal Boy," "Trelawny of the Wells" (OB).

SAPPINGTON, MARGO. Born July 30, 1947 in Baytown, Tex. NY debut 1965 with Joffrey Ballet, Bdwy debut in "Sweet Charity," followed by "Oh! Calcutta!"

SARANDON, CHRIS. Born July 24, 1942 in Beckley, WVa. Graduate UWVa., Catholic U. Bdwy debut 1970 in "The Rothschilds."

SAUNDERS, MARILYN. Born Apr. 28, 1948 in Brooklyn. Attended Bklyn Col. Off-Bdwy in "Dames at Sea," Bdwy debut 1970 in "Company."

SCHAAL, RICHARD. Born May 5 in Chicago. Attended Northwestern. Off-Bdwy in "Second City," "Harry, Noon and Night," on Bdwy in "Kelly," "Little Murders," "Story Theatre," "Metamorphoses."

SCHACHT, SAM. Born Apr. 19, 1936 in The Bronx. Graduate CCNY. Off-Bdwy in "Fortune and Men's Eyes," "The Cannibals," "I Met a Man," "The Increased Difficulty of Concentration" (LC), "One Night Stands of a Noisy Passenger."

SCHALLERT, WILLIAM. Born July 6, 1925 in Los Angeles. Graduate UCLA. Debut Off-Bdwy 1971 in "Trial of the Catonsville 9."

SCHEIDER, ROY R. Born Nov. 10, 1935 in Orange, NJ. Graduate Franklin-Marshall Col. Bdwy bow 1965 in "The Chinese Prime Minister," Off-Bdwy in "The Alchemist" (LC), "Sjt. Musgrave's Dance," "Stephen D," "The Year Boston Won the Pennant" (LC), "The Nuns."

SCHROCK, ROBERT. Born June 28, 1945 in Wolf Lake, Ind. Attended Goodman Sch. Debut Off-Bdwy 1970 in "The Dirtiest Show in Town."

SCOTT, BRUCE. Born Nov. 22, 1947 in NYC. Attended Actors Studio. Bdwy debut 1966 in "Lion in Winter," followed by "Turn of the Screw" (CC), "Antony and Cleopatra" (Met), "Your Own Thing" (OB), "Ballad for a Firing Squad" (OB), "Does a Tiger Wear a Necktie?," "Sensations" (OB).

SCOTT, HAROLD. Born Sept. 6, 1935 in Morristown, NJ. Harvard graduate. Off-Bdwy in "Land Beyond the River," "I, Too, Have Lived in Arcadia," "The Egg and I," "Deathwatch," "God's Trombones," "Jackass," "Program One," "Death of Bessie Smith," "The Blacks," "Trials of Brother Jero," "The Strong Breed," "Boys in the Band," LCRep's "After the Fall," "Marco Millions," "But for Whom Charlie," "The Changeling," and "Incident at Vichy," on Bdwy in "Cool World," "Cuban Thing," "Les Blancs."

SEBASTIAN, PAUL. Born Jan. 12, 1943 in NYC. Debut 1971 in "Heloise" (ELT).

SEKI, HOSHIN. Born Mar. 21, 1941 in NYC. Attended URI, Harvard. Debut 1971 Off-Bdwy in "Basic Training of Pavlo Hummel."

SELDES, MARIAN. Born Aug. 23, 1928 in NYC. Attended Neighborhood Playhouse. Bdwy debut 1947 in "Medea," followed by "Crime and Punishment," "That Lady," "Tower Beyond Tragedy," "Ondine," "High Ground," "Come of Age," "Chalk Garden," "The Milk Train Doesn't Stop Here Anymore," "The Wall," "A Gift of Time," "A Delicate Balance," "Before You Go," "Father's Day," Off-Bdwy in "Diff'rent," "Ginger Man," "Mercy St."

258

Susan Sharkey

Mario Siletti

Ivy Siegler

Norwood Smith

Lilia Skala

SERON, ORIE. Born Apr. 2, 1945 in Joliet, Ill. Graduate Northwestern. Debut 1970 Off-Bdwy in "Adaptation/Next."

SHAKAR, MARTIN. Born in Detroit, Jan. 1, 1940. Attended Wayne State U. Off-Bdwy in "Lorenzaccio," "Macbeth," "The Infantry," "Americana Pastoral," "No Place To Be Somebody," "The World of Mrs. Solomon," "And Whose Little Boy Are You?," Bdwy bow 1969 in "Our Town."

SHARKEY, SUSAN. Born Dec. 12, 1943 in NYC. Graduate U Ariz. Debut Off-Bdwy 1968 in "Guns of Carrar" and "Cuba Si," with LCRep in "Playboy of the Western World," "Good Woman of Setzuan," and "Enemy of the People."

SHARMA, BARBARA. Born Sept. 14, 1942. Off-Bdwy in "Boy Friend," "Italian Straw Hat," "Cole Porter Revisited," Bdwy in "Fiorello," "Little Me," "Sweet Charity," "Hallelujah, Baby," "Her First Roman," "Come Summer," "Last of the Red Hot Lovers."

SHAWN, DICK. Born Dec. 1 in Buffalo, NY. Attended U Miami. Bdwy debut 1948 in "For Heaven's Sake, Mother," followed by "A Funny Thing Happened on the Way to the Forum," "The Egg," "Peterpat," "Fade Out-Fade In," "I'm Solomon," "Room Service" (OB).

SHAWN, MICHAEL. Born July 3, 1944 in Springfield, Ill. Bdwy debut 1968 in "Golden Rainbow" followed by "Promises, Promises."

SHEA, PATRICK. Born Oct. 7, 1946 in NYC. Graduate AADA. 1969 with NYSF in "Peer Gynt" and "Twelfth Night," Bdwy bow 1970 in "Child's Play."

SHELLEY, CAROLE. Born Aug. 16, 1939 in London. Bdwy debut 1965 in "The Odd Couple," followed by "The Astrakhan Coat," "Loot," "Noel Coward's Sweet Potato," "Little Murders" (OB), "Hay Fever."

SHELLY, NORMAN. Born May 3, 1921 in Denver, Colo. Attended New School. Bdwy bow 1950 in "Peter Pan," followed by "Daughter of Silence," "Promises, Promises."

SHELTON, SLOANE. Born Mar. 17, 1934 in Asheville, NC. Attended Berea Col., RADA. Bdwy bow 1967 with NRT in "Imaginary Invalid," "A Touch of the Poet," and "Tonight at 8:30," followed by "I Never Sang for My Father," OB in "Androcles and the Lion," "The Maids," "Way of the World," "Dark of the Moon," "Basic Training of Pavlo Hummel."

SHEPARD, RED. Born Aug. 20, in Martinez, Cal. Bdwy debut 1970 in "Hair."

SHEPHERD, ELIZABETH. Born Aug. 12, 1936 in London. Graduate U Bristol. Debut 1970 Off-Bdwy in "The Jumping Fool," followed by "Conduct Unbecoming" (Bdwy 1970).

SHERWOOD, MADELEINE. Born Nov. 13, 1926 in Montreal, Can. Attended Yale. Off-Bdwy in "Brecht on Brecht," "Medea," "Hey You, Light Man," Bdwy in "The Chase," "The Crucible," "Cat on a Hot Tin Roof," "Invitation to a March," "Camelot," "Arturo Ui," "Do I Hear a Waltz?," "Inadmissible Evidence," "All Over."

SHERWOOD, WAYNE. Born in Olivia, Minn. Graduate UOre. Bdwy bow 1955 in "Catch a Star," followed by "Wonderful Town" (CC), OB in "Jacques Brel Is Alive . . . ," "Johnny Johnson."

SHIMIZU, DANA. Born Apr. 10, 1958 in NYC. In CC's "South Pacific" (65-67), "The King and I" ('68), Bdwy debut 1970 in "Lovely Ladies, Kind Gentlemen."

SHIMONO, SAB. Born in Sacramento, Cal. Graduate U Cal. NY bow 1965 in "South Pacific" (CC), followed by "Mame," "Lovely Ladies, Kind Gentlemen."

SHUTTA, ETHEL. Born Dec. 1, 1896 in NYC. Appeared in "Ziegfeld Follies," "Passing Show of 1923," "Marjorie," "Louis XIV," "Whoopee," "My Dear Public," "Jennie," "Follies."

SHYRE, PAUL. Born Mar. 8, 1926 in NYC. Attended UFla., AADA. Off-Bdwy in "Purple Dust," "I Knock at the Door," "Pictures in the Hallway" (LC).

SIDNEY, SUZAN. Born June 10, 1946 in Philadelphia. Attended Carnegie Tech. NY bow in "Oklahoma" (CC'65), followed by Bdwy 1967 "Canterbury Tales," "Ruddigore" (ELT).

SIEBERT, CHARLES. Born Mar. 9, 1938 in Kenosha, Wisc. Graduate Marquette U., LAMDA. Appeared in "Richard III" (CP), "Galileo" (LC), on Bdwy in "Jimmy Shine," "Gingerbread Lady."

SIEGLER, IVY. Born in Cleveland, O. Studied at Cleveland Playhouse, HB Studio. Debut 1970 in "Greenwillow" (ELT).

SILETTI, MARIO. Born Nov. 27, 1935 in NYC. Studied with Stella Adler. Debut Off-Bdwy 1955 in "Out of This World," followed by "Queen after Death," "Little Mary Sunshine," "He Who Gets Slapped," "The Alchemist," Bdwy bow 1971 in "School for Wives."

SILVER, JOE. Born Sept. 28, 1922 in Chicago. Attended U Wisc., Am. Th.Wing. Bdwy bow 1942 in "Tobacco Road," followed by "Doughgirls," "Heads or Tails," "Nature's Way," "Gypsy," "The Heroine," "The Zulu and the Zayda," "You Know I Can't Hear You When the Water's Running," "Lenny," OB in "Blood Wedding," "Lamp at Midnight," "Joseph and His Brethren," "The Victors," and "Shrinking Bride."

SILVERS, PHIL. Born May 11, 1911 in Bklyn. In vaudeville before 1939 Bdwy bow in "Yokel Boy," followed by "High Button Shoes," "Top Banana," "Do Re Mi," "How the Other Half Loves."

SILVIA, LESLIE. Born Dec. 11, 1958 in NYC. Bdwy debut 1967 in "Fiddler On The Roof."

SIMON, HERB. Born Sept. 18, 1946 in Hyannis, Mass. Attended Carnegie Tech. Debut Off-Bdwy 1971 in "Godspell."

SINGLETON, SAM. Born Feb. 11, 1940 in Charleston, SC. Attended Dramatic Workshop. Off-Bdwy in "Aria Da Capo," "The Dumb Waiter," "Beautiful Dreamer," "Great Goodness Of Life," "Life and Times," "Jazznite."

SKALA, LILIA. Born in Vienna; Graduate UDresden. Bdwy debut 1941 in "Letters to Lucerne," followed by "With a Silk Thread," "Call Me Madam," "Diary of Anne Frank," "Threepenny Opera" (CC'65), "Zelda," "40 Carats."

SLAUGHTER, HARRIET. Born Apr. 2, 1937 in Ft. Worth, Tex. Graduate U Tex. Bdwy debut 1960 in "The Hostage," followed by "Fiddler On The Roof."

SMALL, NEVA. Born Nov. 17, 1952 in NYC. Bdwy debut 1964 in "Something More," followed by "The Impossible Years," "Henry, Sweet Henry," "Frank Merriwell," Off-Bdwy in "Ballad For A Firing Squad," "Tell Me Where The Good Times Are," "How Much, How Much?"

SMITH, ALEXIS. Born June 8, 1921 in Penticton, Can. Attended LACC. Bdwy debut 1971 in "Follies."

SMITH, LOIS. Born Nov. 3, 1930 in Topeka, Kan. Attended UWash. Appeared in "Time Out for Ginger," "The Young and Beautiful," CC's "Wisteria Trees" '55, and "Glass Managerie" ('56), "Orpheus Descending," "Sunday Dinner" (OB).

SMITH, NORWOOD. Born Apr. 18, 1915 in San Francisco. Attended UCLA. Bdwy debut 1950 in "Guys and Dolls," followed by "Can-Can," "Silk Stockings," "Music Man," "Ari."

| Lois Smith | Bob Spencer | Pat Stevens | Jeremiah Sullivan | Laura Stuart |

SMITH, SHEILA. Born Apr. 3, 1933 in Conneaut, O. Attended Kent State U., Cleveland Playhouse. Bdwy debut 1963 in "Hot Spot," Off-Bdwy in "Taboo Revue," "Anything Goes," and "Sweet Miani," "Fiorello" (CC'62). "Mame" for which she received a THEATRE WORLD Award, "Follies."

SNYDER, ARLEN DEAN. Born Mar 3, 1933 in Rice, Kan. Graduate U Tulsa, U Iowa. Bdwy bow 1965 in "The Family Way," followed Off-Bdwy in "Benito Cereno," "Hogan's Goat," "Miss Pete," "Open 24 Hours," "Candyapple."

SNYDER, DREW. Born Sept. 25, 1946 in Buffalo, NY. Graduate Carnegie Tech. Bdwy debut 1968 with APA in "Pantagleize," "Cocktail Party" "Cock-a-doodle Dandy," and "Hamlet," followed by NYSF's "Henry VI," "Richard III."

SOMACK, JACK. Born Sept. 14, 1918 in Chicago. Graduate Northwestern, Chicago U. Off-Bdwy in "A View from the Bridge," "The Kitchen," "Country Girl" (CC'66), "Cannibals," "Shrinking Bride."

SOMMER, JOSEF. Born June 26, 1934 in Greifswald, Ger. Graduate Carnegie Tech. Bdwy bow 1970 with ASF's "Othello."

SPENCER, BOB. Born May 4, 1938 in Chicago. Bdwy bow 1960 in "Bye Bye Birdie," followed by "Enter Laughing," Off-Bdwy in "Sing, Muse," "The Fantasticks," "Manhattan Arrangement."

SPIELBERG, DAVID. Born Mar. 6, 1940 in Mercedes, Tex. Graduate UTex. Debut 1963 Off-Bdwy in "A Man's a Man," followed by "Two Executioners," "Funnyhouse of a Negro," "MacBird," "The Persians," "Trial of the Catonsville 9."

SPINETTI, VICTOR. Born Sept. 2, 1932 in South Wales. Attended Cardiff Drama Col. Bdwy debut 1960 in "The Hostage," followed by "Oh, What a Lovely War" for which he received a THEATRE WORLD Award, "La Grosse Valise," "The Philanthropist."

SPRUNG, SANDY. Born Nov. 23, 1937 in Bklyn. Attended NYU. Off-Bdwy debut 1969 in "Of Thee I Sing," followed by "Shoestring Revues" (ELT), "Goldilocks."

STADLEN, LEWIS J. Born Mar. 7, 1947 in Brooklyn. Attended Neighborhood Playhouse, Stella Adler Studio. Bdwy debut 1970 in "Minnie's Boys" for which he received a THEATRE WORLD Award, followed by "Happiness Cage" (OB).

STANLEY, FLORENCE. Born July 1 in Chicago. Graduate Northwestern. Off-Bdwy in "Machinal," "Electra," Bdwy debut 1965 in "Glass Menagerie," followed by "Fiddler On The Roof."

STAPLETON, MAUREEN. Born June 21, 1925 in Troy, NY. Attended HB Studio. Bdwy debut 1946 in "Playboy of The Western World," followed by "Antony and Cleopatra," "Detective Story," "The Bird Cage," "The Rose Tattoo" for which she received a THEATRE WORLD Award, "The Emperor's Clothes," "The Crucible," "Richard III," "The Seagull," "27 Wagons Full of Cotton," "Orpheus Descending," "The Cold Wind And The Warm," "Toys In The Attic," "The Glass Menagerie" ('65), "Plaza Suite," "Norman, Is That You?", "Gingerbread Lady."

STARK, SALLY. Born May 28, 1938 in Riverhead, NY. Attended St. Elizabeth Col. Debut 1967 Off-Bdwy in "Babes In Arms," followed by "Your Own Thing," "Dames At Sea."

STEELE, DAVID. Born Feb. 23, 1944 in The Bronx. Bdwy Debut 1970 in "Lovely Ladies, Kind Gentlemen."

STERNHAGEN, FRANCES. Born Jan. 13, 1932 in Washington, DC. Vassar graduate. Off-Bdwy in "Admirable Bashful," "Thieves' Carnival," "Country Wife," "Ulysses in Nighttown," "Saintliness of Margery Kemp," "The Room," "A Slight Ache," "Displaced Person," "Playboy of the Western World" (LC), Bdwy in "Great Day In the Morning," "Right Honourable Gentleman," with APA in "Cocktail Party" and "Cock-a-doodle Dandy."

STEVENS, PAT. Born in Linden, NJ. Attended HB Studio. Bdwy debut 1967 in "Hello, Dolly!," followed by "Manhattan Arrangement" (OB).

STEVENS, TONY. Born May 2, 1948 in St. Louis, Mo. Debut 1967 CC revival of "Wonderful Town," followed by "The Fig Leaves Are Falling," "Billy," "Jimmy," "The Boy Friend," "Ballad of Johnny Pot" (OB).

STEWART, PATRICK. Born July 13, 1940 in Mirfield, Eng. Attended Bristol Old Vic. Bdwy debut 1971 with RSC in "A Midsummer Night's Dream."

STRITCH, ELAINE. Born Feb. 2, 1925 in Detroit, Mich. Attended Dramatic Workshop. Bdwy debut 1946 in "Loco," followed by "Made In Heaven," "Angel In The Wings," "Call Me Madam," "Pal Joey," "On Your Toes," "Bus Stop," "The Sin Of Pat Muldoon," "Goldilocks," "Sail Away," "Who's Afraid Of Virginia Woolf?," "Wonderful Town" (CC), "Private Lives" (OB), "Company."

STRONG, MICHAEL. Born Feb. 8, 1923 in NYC. Graduate Bklyn Col., Neighborhood Playhouse. Bdwy debut 1941 in "Spring Again," followed by "Russian People," "Counter-Attack," "Eve of St. Mark," "Men to the Sea," "Whole World Over," "Detective Story," "Anastasia," "Firstborn," "Gypsy," "A Far Country," "Rhinoceros," "Emperor's Clothes," "Enemy of the People," with LCRep in "After the Fall," "Incident at Vichy," "But for Whom Charlie," and "Marco Millions," OB in "A Month in the Country," "Dance of Death."

STUART, LAURA. Born May 26, 1938 in Philadelphia. Attended Catholic U. Off-Bdwy in "Electra," "The Trojan Women," "The Women At The Tomb," Bdwy debut 1968 in "Fiddler On The Roof."

SULLIVAN, JEREMIAH. Born Sept. 22, 1937 in NYC. Harvard graduate. Appeared in "Compulsion" (1957), "Ardele" (OB), "The Astrakhan Coat," "Philadelphia, Here I Come!," "The Lion In Winter," "Hamlet," "A Scent Of Flowers" (OB), "House of Blue Leaves" (OB).

SULLIVAN, JOSEPH. Born Nov. 29, 1918 in NYC. Attended Fordham, Am. Theatre Wing. Appeared in "Sundown Beach," "Command Decision," "The Live Wire," "Country Girl," "Oh, Men! Oh, Women!," "The Rainmaker," "Best Man," "Fiddler On The Roof."

SWAIN, ELIZABETH. Born Aug. 6, 1941 in Eng. Attended London Sch. of Eco. Bdwy debut 1968 in "The Crucible," followed by "Tango" (OB), "Charley's Aunt."

SWEARINGEN, JOHN. Born July 23, 1935 in Knob Noster, Mo. Graduate Central Mo. State, Guildhall Drama School in London. Bdwy debut 1963 in "A Man For All Seasons," followed by "Me And Juliet" (ELT), "Immaculate Misconception" (OB).

SYMINGTON, DONALD. Born Aug. 30, 1925 in Baltimore, Md. NY bow 1947 in "Galileo," followed by CC's "Caesar and Cleopatra," "Dream Girl," and "Lute Song," "A Girl Can Tell," OB in "Suddenly Last Summer," "Lady Windermere's Fan," "Rate of Exchange," "Shrinking Bride."

SYMONDS, ROBERT. Born Dec. 1, 1926 in Bristow, Okla. Attended Tex. U, U Mo. With LC Rep in "Danton's Death," "Country Wife," "The Alchemist," "Galileo," "St. Joan," "Tiger At The Gates," "Cyrano," "A Cry of Players," "Inner Journey," "The Miser," "The Time Of Your Life," "Camino Real," "The Disintegration Of James Cherry," "Silence," "Landscape," "Amphitryon," "Birthday Party," "Landscape," "Silence," "Scenes from American Life," "Play Strindberg."

Carl Thoma	**Barbara Tarbuck**	**Peter Thompson**	**Nancy Tribush**	**John Tremaine**

TANDY, JESSICA. Born June 7, 1909 in London. Attended Greet Acad. Bdwy debut 1930 in "The Matriarch," followed by "The Last Enemy," "Time And The Conways," "The White Steed," "Geneva," "Jupiter Laughs," "Anne of England," "Yesterday's Magic," "A Streetcar Named Desire," "Hilda Crane," "The Fourposter," "The Honeys," "A Day By The Sea," "The Man In The Dog Suit," "Triple Play," "5 Finger Exercise," "The Physicists," "A Delicate Balance," "Camino Real" (LC), "Home," "All Over."

TANNER, TONY. Born July 27, 1932 in Hillingdon, Eng. Attended Webber-Douglas Drama School. Bdwy debut 1966 in "Half A Sixpence," followed OB by "Little Boxes," "The Homecoming."

TARBUCK, BARBARA. Born Jan. 15, 1942 in Detroit, Mich. Graduate U Mich., LAMDA. NY debut 1970 in LC's "Landscape," "Silence."

TARLOW, FLORENCE. Born Jan. 19, 1929 in Philadelphia. Graduate Hunter Col. Off-Bdwy credits: "Beautiful Day," "Istanbul," "Gorilla Queen," "America Hurrah," "Red Cross," "Promenade," Bdwy debut 1968 in "The Man In The Glass Booth," "Good Woman of Setzuan" (LC).

TARPEY, TOM. Born June 3, 1943 in NYC. Attended Carnegie-Mellon U, LAMDA. Debut 1969 Off-Bdwy in "The Glorious Ruler," followed by "Crimes Of Passion," "Othello" (Bdwy '70).

TATE, DENNIS. Born Aug. 31, 1938 in Iowa City, Iowa. Attended Iowa U. Off-Bdwy in "Black Monday," "The Blacks," "The Hostage," "Bohikee Creek," "The Happy Bar," "Trials of Brother Jero," "The Strong Breed," "Goa," "The Electronic Nigger," "Black Quartet," "Life and Times . . . ," "Jazznite," Bdwy bow 1970 in "Les Blancs."

TAYLOR, CLARICE. Born Sept 20, in Buckingham County, Va. Attended New Theater School. Debut 1943 Off-Bdwy in "Striver's Row," followed by "Major Barbara," "Family Portrait," "Trouble In Mind," "The Egg And I," "A Medal For Willie," "Nat Turner," "Simple Speaks His Mind," "Gold Through The Trees," "The Owl Answers," with NEC in "Song of The Lusitanian Bogey," "Summer Of The 17th Doll," "Kongi's Harvest," "Daddy Goodness," "God Is A (Guess What?)," "An Evening Of One Acts," "5 On The Black Hand Side," "Man Better Man," "Day of Absence," "Brotherhood," "Akokawe," and "Rosalee Pritchett."

TAYLOR, GEOFFREY. Born July 1, 1945 in Washington, Iowa. Attended UIowa. Debut Off-Bdwy in "You're a Good Man, Charlie Brown," followed by "The Fantasticks."

THOMA, CARL. Born Aug. 29, 1947 in Manila, PI. Attended SUNY at Buffalo. Debut 1970 in "The Me Nobody Knows."

THOMAS TONY. Born in Atlanta, Ga. Attended Temple U. Off-Bdwy in "Cities in Bezique," "The Pig Pen," Bdwy bow 1969 in "Henry V."

THOMPSON, EVAN. Born Sept. 3, 1931 in NYC. Graduate U Cal. Bdwy bow 1969 in "Jimmy" followed by "Mahagonny" (OB).

THOMPSON, PETER. Born in Carnegie, Okla. Attended U Okla. Bdwy bow 1970 in ASF's "Othello."

THOMPSON, REBECCA. Born Apr. 14, 1942 in Dover, NH. Graduate Penn State U. Debut 1961 Off- Bdwy in "Love's Old Sweet Song," followed by "St. Joan," "Red Roses For Me," "Shakespeare's Hamlet Revisited," "The White Rose And The Red," "Hedda Gabler."

THOMPSON, REX. Born Dec. 14, 1942 in NYC. Appeared in "Alive and Kicking," "Wisteria Trees," "The King and I," "Escapade," "King of Hearts," "First Love," "Charley's Aunt."

THOMPSON, SADA. Born Sept. 27, 1929, in Des Moines, Iowa. Graduate Carnegie Tech. Debut Off-Bdwy 1953 in "Under Milk Wood," followed by "The Clandestine Marriage," "Murder In The Cathedral," "The White Devil," "The Carefree Tree," "The Misanthrope," "USA," "River Line," "Ivanov," "The Last Minstrel," "An Evening For Merlin Finch," "The Effect of Gamma Rays On The Man-In-The-Moon Marigolds," on Bdwy in "Festival," "Juno," "Johnny No-Trump," "The American-Dream," "Happy Days."

TILLINGER, JOHN. Born June 28, 1938 in Tabriz, Iran. Attended U Rome. Bdwy debut 1966 in "How's The World Treating You?," followed by "Halfway Up The Tree," "Othello," "Hay Fever," Off-Bdwy in "Tea Party," "Pequod," "A Scent Of Flowers," "Crimes Of Passion."

TOBIN, MATTHEW. Born Aug. 10, 1933 in Indianapolis, Ind. Carnegie Tech graduate. Debut Off-Bdwy 1959 in "The Hasty Heart," followed by "Boys from Syracuse," "Mad Show," "Boys in the Band," "Empire Builders," "Lyle," "Survival of St. Joan," "Any Resemblance to Persons Living or Dead," Bdwy bow 1960 in "Redhead."

TORN, RIP. Born Feb. 6, 1931 in Temple, Tex. Graduate U Tex. Bdwy bow 1956 in "Cat On A Hot Tin Roof," followed OB by "Chaparral" for which he received a THEATRE WORLD Award, "Sweet Bird Of Youth," "Daughter Of Silence," "Strange Interlude" ('63), "Blues For Mr. Charlie," "The Country Girl," (CC'66), OB in "The Cuban Thing," "The Kitchen," "Deer Park," "Dream Of A Blacklisted Actor," "Dance of Death," "Macbeth."

TOWERS, CONSTANCE. Born May 20, 1933 in Whitefish, Mont. Attended Juilliard, AADA. Bdwy debut 1965 in "Anya," followed by "Show Boat" (LC), CC's "Carousel," "Sound Of Music," and "King And I," "Engagement Baby," "Ari."

TRACEY, PAUL. Born June 5, 1939 in Durban, SA. Attended Malvern Col. Bdwy debut 1966 in "Wait a Minim!," followed by "The Rothschilds."

TREMAINE, JOHN. Born Aug. 16, 1946 in Santa Monica, Cal. Attended U Cal., Actors Studio. Bdwy debut 1971 in "Abelard and Heloise."

TRESKO, ELSA. Born Oct. 1 in Vienna. Graduate Vienna Acad. Performing Arts. Off-Bdwy debut 1970 in "The Dirtiest Show in Town."

TRIANA, RAFAEL. Born Sept. 27, 1947 in NYC. Attended St. John's U., AADA, Debut 1970 with New York Shakespeare Festival, followed by "Yerma" (OB).

TRIBUSH, NANCY. Born Dec. 18, 1940 in NYC. Graduate Bklyn. Col. Bdwy debut 1961 in "Bye, Bye, Birdie," followed by "Happily Never After," Off-Bdwy in "Riverwind," "Hang Down Your Head And Die," "Oh, Calcutta."

TRONTO, RUDY. Born July 14, 1928 in Peekskill, NY. Bdwy debut 1960 in "Irma La Douce," followed by "Carnival," "Man of LaMancha," OB in "Boys from Syracuse," "Secret Life of Walter Mitty."

TUCCI, MARIA. Born June 19, 1941 in Florence, Italy. Attended Actors Studio. Off-Bdwy in "Corruption In The Palace of Justice," "Five Evenings," "The Trojan Women," "The White Devil," "Horseman, Pass By," with NYSF, "Yerma" (LC Rep), "Shepherd Of Avenue B," On Bdwy in "The Milk Train Doesn't Stop Here Anymore," "The Rose Tattoo" ('66), "The Little Foxes" ('67,) "The Cuban Thing," "The Great White Hope," "School for Wives."

TYSON, TARA. Born July 19 in NYC. Graduate AADA. Debut Off-Bdwy 1970 in "Foreplay."

261

Herve Villechaize Dolores Vanison Lee Wallace Glory Van Scott Josef Warik

URICH, TOM. Born Mar. 26 in Toronto, O. Attended Cin. Cons. Off-Bdwy in "The Streets Of New York," "The Fantasticks," "Shoemaker's Holiday," Bdwy bow 1970 in "Applause."

VACCARO, BRENDA. Born Nov. 18, 1939 in Bklyn. Attended Neighborhood Playhouse. Bdwy debut 1961 in "Everybody Loves Opal" for which she received a THEATRE WORLD Award, followed by "The Affair," "Children from Their Games," "Cactus Flower," "The Natural Look," "How Now, Dow Jones," "The Goodbye People," "Father's Day."

VAN, BOBBY. Born Dec. 6, 1930 in The Bronx. Bdwy debut 1950 in "Alive and Kicking," followed by "On Your Toes," "No, No, Nanette."

VAN ARK, JOAN. Born June 16, 1943 in NYC. Attended Yale, Actors Studio. Bdwy debut 1965 in "Barefoot in the Park," followed by "School for Wives" for which she received a THEATRE WORLD Award.

VANDIS, TITOS. Born Nov. 7, 1917 in Athens, Greece. Attended Ntl. Theatre Drama School. Bdwy bow 1965 in "On A Clear Day You Can See Forever," followed by "Illya, Darling," "The Guide," "Look to the Lilies," "Man of La Mancha."

VANISON, DOLORES. Born Mar. 25, 1942 in Lynchburg, Va. Graduate Bklyn Col., LIU. Bdwy debut 1969 in "Hello, Dolly!," followed by "Greenwillow" (ELT).

VAN SCOTT, GLORY. Attended Goddard Col. In CC revivals of "Carmen Jones," "Porgy and Bess," and "Show Boat," Off-Bdwy in "Fly Blackbird," "Prodigal Son," "Who's Who, Baby?," "Billy NoName, "Don't Bother Me, I Can't Cope," Bdwy in "House of Flowers," "Kwamina," American Ballet Theatre, "The Great White Hope."

VAUGHAN, DAVID. Born May 17, 1924 in London. Attended Wadham Col. Bway debut 1957 in "The Country Wife," followed by "Epitaph For George Dillon," "Minnie's Boys," Off-Bway in "The Boy Friend," "The Fantasticks," "The Way of The World," "The Wedding," "Madrigal of War," "The Promenade," "In Circles," "Peace."

VELIE, JAY. Born May 16, 1892 in Denver, Colo. Attended Fealy Drama Sch. Bdwy debut 1923 in "Little Jessie James," subsequently among others "The Perfect Fool," "The Fabulous Invalid," "Carousel," "Call Me Madam," "Happy Hunting," "Sound of Music," "Jennie," "70, Girls, 70."

VENTANTONIO, JOHN. Born Aug. 13, 1943 in Orange, NJ. Attended AADA. Bdwy debut 1969 in "Our Town," followed by "Othello" (ASF).

VESTOFF, VIRGINIA. Born Dec. 9, 1940 in NYC. Off-Bdwy credits: "The Boy Friend," "Crystal Heart," "Fall Out," "New Cole Porter Revue," "Man With A Load of Mischief," "Love and Let Love," on Bdwy in "From A To Z" (1960), "Irma La Douce," "Baker Street," "1776."

VILLECHAIZE, HERVE. Born Apr. 23, 1943 in Paris. Debut 1969 Off-Bdwy in "Moondreamers," followed by "Young Master Dante," "Honest-to-God Schnozzola," Bdwy bow 1970 in "Gloria and Esperanza."

VON FURSTENBERG, BETSY. Born Aug. 16, 1931 in Westphalia, Ger. Bdwy debut 1951 in "Second Threshold," followed by "Dear Barbarians," "Oh, Men! Oh, Women!," "Chalk Garden," "Child of Fortune," "Nature's Way," "Wonderful Town," "Mary, Mary," "Paisley Convertible," "Gingerbread Lady," OB in "The Making of Moo," "Season of Choice," "Measure for Measure."

VON SCHERLER, SASHA. Born Dec. 12 in NYC. Bdwy debut 1959 in "Look after Lulu," followed by "Rape of the Belt," "The Good Soup," "Great God Brown," "First Love," "Alfie," "Harold," Off-Bdwy in "The Admirable Bashville," "The Comedian," "Conversation Piece," "Good King Charles' Golden Days," "Under Milkwood," "Plays for Bleecker Street," "Ludlow Fair," "Twelfth Night" (CP), "Sondra," "Cyrano" (LC), "Crimes of Passion," "Henry VI," "Trelawny of the Wells."

VOSKOVEC, GEORGE. Born June 19, 1905 in Sazava, Czech. Graduate Dijon U. NY bow 1945 in "The Tempest," followed by "The Love of 4 Colonels," "His and Hers," "The Seagull," "Festival," "Uncle Vanya" (OB), "A Call On Kuprin," "The Tenth Man," "Big Fish, Little Fish," "Do You Know The Milky Way?," "Hamlet," "Brecht On Brecht" (OB), with LCRep in "The Alchemist," "East Wind," and "Galileo," "Oh, Say Can You See L.A." (OB) "Cabaret," "The Penny Wars," "Room Service" (OB), "All Over."

WAGER, MICHAEL. Born Apr. 29, 1925 in NYC. Harvard graduate. Bdwy bow 1949 in "Streetcar Named Desire," followed by "Small Hours," "Bernardine," "Merchant of Venice," "Misalliance," "Remarkable Mr. Pennypacker," "Othello," "Henry IV," "St. Joan," "Firstborn," "The Cradle Will Rock," "Three Sisters," "The Cuban Thing," OB in "Noontide," "Brecht on Brecht," "Sunset," "Penny Friend," "Trelawny of the Wells."

WALKEN, CHRISTOPHER. Born Mar. 31, 1943 in Astoria, NY. Attended Hofstra U. Bdwy debut 1958 in "J.B.," followed by "Best Foot Forward" (OB), "High Spirits," "Baker Street," "The Lion In Winter," "Measure For Measure" (CP), "The Rose Tattoo" (CC'66) for which he received a THEATRE WORLD Award, "The Unknown Soldier and His Wife," "Iphigenia In Aulis" (OB), "Rosencrantz and Guildenstern Are Dead," "Lemon Sky" (OB), "Scenes from American Life," (LC).

WALKER, SYDNEY. Born May 4, 1921 in Philadelphia. Attended Conservatoire Nationale, Paris. Bdwy bow 1960 in "Becket," Off-Bdwy in "Volpone," "Julius Caesar," "King Lear," "The Collection," "A Scent of Flowers," "The Nuns," with APA in "You Can't Take It With You," "War and Peace," "Right You Are," "School for Scandal," "We Comrades Three," "The Wild Duck," "Pantagleize," "The Cherry Orchard," "The Misanthrope," "The Cocktail Party," and "Cock-A-Doodle Dandy," "Blood Red Roses," with LCRep in "Playboy of the Western World," "Good Woman of Setzuan," "Enemy of the People," and "Antigone."

WALLACE, LEE. Born July 15, 1930 in NYC. Attended NYU. Debut Off-Bdwy 1966 in "Journey of the Fifth Horse," followed by "Saturday Night," "Evening with Garcia Lorca," "Macbeth" (NYSF), "Booth Is Back in Town," "Awake and Sing," "Shepherd of Avenue B," "Basic Training of Pavlo Hummel."

WARD, JANET. Born Feb. 19 in NYC. Attended Actors Studio. Bdwy debut 1945 in "Dream Girl," followed by "Anne of the Thousand Days," "Detective Story," "King of Friday's Men," "Middle of the Night," "Miss Lonelyhearts," "J.B.," "Cheri," "The Egg," "The Impossible Years," "Of Love Remembered," Off-Bdwy in "Chapparal," "The Typists" and "The Tiger," "Summertree," "Dream of a Blacklisted Actor," "Cruising Speed 600 MPH," "One Flew over the Cuckoo's Nest."

WARIK, JOSEF. Born in McKeesport, Pa. Attended Carnegie Mellon U. NY bow 1969 Off-Bdwy in "Crimes of Passion," Bdwy debut 1970 in "Othello" (ASF).

WARRICK, RUTH. Born June 29 in St. Louis, Mo. After film career, made Bdwy debut 1957 in "Miss Lonelyhearts," followed by "Single Man at a Party" (OB), "Take Me Along," "Any Resemblance to Persons Living or Dead" (OB).

Fredricka Weber   George M. Welbes   Anne Wedgeworth   Donn Whyte   Kate Wilkinson

WARRINER, FREDERIC. Born June 2, 1916 in Pasadena, Cal. Graduate Pasadena Playhouse. Bdwy debut 1950 in "King Lear," followed by "Speak of the Devil," "Mr. Pickwick," "Taming of the Shrew," "Getting Married," "St. Joan," "A Pin to See the Peepshow," "Wayward Saint," "Caligula," "Major Barbara," "Time Remembered," "Oliver," "Man for All Seasons," "Portrait of a Queen," OB in "Invitation to a Beheading," "Trelawny of the Wells."

WASHBOURNE, MONA. Born Nov. 27, 1903 in Birmingham, Eng. Bdwy debut 1957 in "Nude with Violin," followed by "Present Laughter," "Home."

WATERSTON, SAM. Born Nov. 15, 1940 in Cambridge, Mass. Graduate Yale. Bdwy bow 1963 in "Oh, Dad, Poor Dad . . . ," followed by "First One Asleep Whistle," "Halfway Up The Tree," "Indians," "Hay Fever," Off-Bdwy in "As You Like It," "Thistle In My Bed," "The Knack," "Fitz," "Biscuit," "La Turista," "Posterity For Sale," "Ergo," "Muzeeka," "Red Cross," "Henry IV" (CP), "Spitting Image," "I Met A Man," "Brass Butterfly," "Trail of the Catonsville 9."

WATSON, SUSAN. Born Dec. 17, 1938 in Tulsa, Okla. Attended Juilliard. Off-Broadway: "The Fantasticks," "Lend An Ear," "Follies of 1910," "Carousel" (LC), CC revivals of "Oklahoma!," "Where's Charley?," on Bdwy in "Bye Bye Birdie," "Carnival," "Ben Franklin In Paris," "A Joyful Noise," "Celebration," "Beggar on Horseback" (LC), "No, No, Nanette."

WATTERS, HAL. Born Feb. 20, 1943 in Oklahoma City. Graduate UOkla, Juilliard. Bdwy debut 1969 in "Celebration," followed by "Six" (OB).

WEAVER, FRITZ. Born Jan. 19, 1926 in Pittsburgh. Graduate U. Chic. Off-Bdwy credits: "The Way of The World," "The White Devil," "The Doctor's Dilemma," "Family Reunion," "The Power and The Glory," "Great God Brown," "Peer Gynt," "Henry IV," "My Fair Lady" (CC'68), on Bdwy in "Chalk Garden" for which he received a THEATRE WORLD Award, "Protective Custody," "Miss Lonelyhearts," "All American," "Lorenzo," "The White House," "Baker Street," "Child's Play."

WEBB, ALYCE ELIZABETH. Born June 1, 1934 in NYC. Graduate NYU. Bdwy debut 1946 in "Street Scene," followed by "Lost in the Stars," "Finian's Rainbow," "Porgy and Bess," "Show Boat," "Guys and Dolls," "Kiss Me, Kate," "Wonderful Town," "Hello, Dolly!," "Purlie," Off-Bdwy in "Simply Heavenly," "Ballad of Bimshire," "Trumpets of the Lord."

WEBER, FREDRICKA. Born Dec. 22, 1940 in Beardstown, Ill. Attended Northwestern. Bdwy debut 1965 in "Those That Play the Clowns," followed by "Upstairs at the Downstairs", Off-Bdwy in "The Last Sweet Days of Isaac" for which she received a THEATRE WORLD Award.

WEBSTER, BYRON. Born June 14, 1933 in London. Debut Off-Bdwy 1960 in "Feast of Panthers," followed by "Ticket-of-leave Man," on Bdwy in "Camelot," "Ben Franklin in Paris," "On a Clear Day You Can See Forever," "Sherry," "My Fair Lady" (CC) "Abelard and Heloise."

WEDGEWORTH, ANN. Born Jan. 21 in Abilene, Tex. Attended UTex. Bdwy debut 1958 in "Make A Million," followed by "Blues for Mr. Charlie," "Last Analysis," OB in "Chaparral," "The Crucible," "Days and Nights of Beebee Fenstermaker," "Ludlow Fair," "Line."

WEIL, ROBERT E. Born Nov. 18, 1914 in NYC. Attended NYU. Bdwy bow in "New Faces of 1942," followed by "Burlesque," "Becket," "Once Upon A Mattress," "Blood, Sweat and Stanley Poole," "Night Life," "Arturo Ui," "Love Your Crooked Neighborhood" (OB), "Beggar on Horseback" (LC), "Lenny."

WELBES, GEORGE M. Born Sept. 14, 1934 in Sioux Falls, SD. Graduate USD. Debut 1968 Off-Bdwy in "Oh Say Can You See L.A.," followed by "The Other Man," "Oh, Calcutta."

WELCH, CHARLES. Born Feb. 2, 1921 in New Britain, Conn. Attended Am.Th.Wing. Bdwy bow 1948 in "Cloud 7," followed by "Make a Million," "Donnybrook," "Golden Boy," "Breakfast at Tiffany's," "Married Alive," "Darling of the Day," "Dear World," "Follies."

WELDON, CHARLES. Born June 1, 1940 in Wetumka, Okla. Bdwy debut 1969 in "Big Time Buck White," followed by "Ride a Black Horse" (OB).

WELLS, MARY K. Born in Omaha, Neb. Attended BH Studio. Bdwy debut 1958 in "Interlock," followed by "Any Wednesday," "Everything in the Garden," "3 Men on a Horse," "40 Carats."

WESTON, GRAHAM. Born Sept. 10, 1944 in Birmingham, Eng. Studied at Birmingham Rep.Th. Sch. Bdwy debut 1970 in "Home."

WESTON, JIM. Born Aug. 2, 1942 in Montclair, NJ. Attended Manchester Col., AADA. Bdwy debut 1969 in "Red, White and Maddox," followed by "She Loves Me," "Lovely Ladies, Kind Gentlemen," "Ballad of Johnny Pot" (OB).

WHEEL, PATRICIA. Born in NYC. Has appeared in "Cyrano," "The Tempest," "Arms and the Man," "Little Brown Jug," "Stars Weep," "Browning Version," "Cry of the Peacock," "Gertie," "Sacred Flame," "Soldiers," "Butterflies Are Free."

WHITE, PENNY. Born Oct. 28 in Pensacola, Fla. Graduate Northwestern. Bdwy debut 1971 in "Metamorphoses," Off-Bdwy in "Second City," "Some Other Time" (LC), "Inside My Head," "Telemachus Clay," "Bag of Flies."

WHITELEY, LARRY. Born Mar. 14, 1936 in Minneapolis, Minn. Bdwy bow in "Pickwick," Off-Bdwy in "Now," "Americana Pastoral," "Of Thee I Sing," "Skye."

WHITESIDE, ANN. Born in Philadelphia. Attended Chestnut Hill Col. Bway debut 1955 in "A Roomful of Roses," followed by "Wake Up, Darling," "Jumping Fool" (OB), "Olathe Response" (OB).

WHYTE, DONN. Born Feb. 23, 1941 in Chicago. Attended Northwestern. Debut 1969 Off-Bdwy in "The Brownstone Urge," followed by "Foreplay."

WIEST, STAN. Born Aug. 23, 1943 in NYC. Graduate Hofstra U. Debut Off-Bdwy 1971 in "Stag Movie."

WILBUR, CLAIRE. Born June 8, in NYC. Studied with Stella Adler. Debut Off-Bdwy 1970 in "Dark of the Moon," followed by "Score."

WILDER, IAN. Born July 27, 1939 in Norwalk, Conn. Attended AADA. Bdwy debut 1965 in "Beyond the Fringe," followed by "False Confessions" (ELT).

WILKINSON, KATE. Born Oct. 25 in San Francisco. Attended San Jose State Col. Bdwy debut 1967 in "Little Murders," followed by "Johnny No-Trump," "Watercolor," "Postcards," Off-Bdwy in "La Madre," "Earnest in Love," "Story of Mary Surratt" (ELT), "Bring Me a Warm Body," "Child Buyer," "Rimers of Eldritch," "A Doll's House," "Hedda Gabler."

WILLIAMS, EMLYN. Born Nov. 26, 1905 in Mostyn, Wales. Bdwy debut 1927 in "And So to Bed," followed by "Criminal at Large," "Night Must Fall," "Montserrat," "Bleak House," "A Boy Growing Up," "Daughter of Silence," "Man for All Seasons," "The Deputy," "Readings from Charles Dickens."

Demond Wilson   **Lee Wilson**   **Stuart Craig Wood**   **Iva Withers**   **Mark Zeller**

WILLIAMS, JENNIFER. Born in Houston, Tex. Debut Off-Bdwy 1969 in "Geese," on Bdwy 1971 in "Frank Merriwell."

WILLIAMS, JOHN. Born Apr. 15, 1903 in Chalfont, Eng. Bdwy bow 1924 in "The Fake," followed by "Ghost Train," "Mixed Doubles," "The High Road," "Ten Minute Alibi," "Dodsworth," "Call It a Day," "No Time for Comedy," "Claudia," "Anne of the Thousand Days," "Velvet Glove," "Venus Observed," "Dial 'M' for Murder," "The Dark Is Light Enough," "Ross," "Chinese Prime Minister," "Hay Fever."

WILLIAMS, RICO. Born May 11, 1963 in NYC. Debut 1970 with LCRep in "Good Woman of Setzuan."

WILLISON, WALTER. Born June 24, 1947 in Monterey Park, Calif. Bdwy debut 1970 in "Norman, Is That You?," followed by "Two by Two" for which he received a THEATRE WORLD Award.

WILLS, LOU. Born 1928 in NYC. Bdwy debut 1941 in "Best Foot Forward," followed by "One Touch of Venus," "Laffing Room Only," "Are You with It?," "Make Mine Manhattan," "A Tree Grows in Brooklyn," "South Pacific" (CC), "Lovely Ladies, Kind Gentlemen."

WILSON, DEMOND. Born Oct. 13, 1946 in NYC. Hunter graduate. Bdwy bow 1951 in "Green Pastures," Off-Bdwy in "Obsidian," "5 on the Black Hand Side," "Ceremonies in Dark Old Men," "Jazznite."

WILSON, EARL, JR. Born Dec. 1, 1942 in NYC. Graduate Bucknell U. Debut Off-Bdwy 1971 in "A Day in the Life of Just about Everyone" which he wrote and composed.

WILSON, ELIZABETH. Born Apr. 4, 1925 in Grand Rapids, Mich. Attended Neighborhood Playhouse. Appeared in "Picnic," "The Desk Set," "The Tunnel of Love," "Big Fish, Little Fish," "Sheep on the Runway." Off-Bdwy in "Plaza 9," "Eh?," "Little Murders," "Good Woman of Setzuan" (LC).

WILSON, LEE. Born Jan. 23, 1948 in Wilmington, Del. Attended HB Studio. Debut 1967 in "Hello, Dolly!," followed by "Here's Where I Belong," "How Now Dow Jones," "La Strada," "Oklahoma!" (LC), "You're a Good Man, Charlie Brown."

WILSON, MARY LOUISE. Born Nov. 12, 1936 in New Haven, Conn. Graduate Northwestern. Off- Bdwy in "Our Town," "Upstairs At The Downstairs," "Threepenny Opera," "A Great Career," "Whispers on the Wind," Bdwy in "Hot Spot," "Flora, The Red Menace," "Criss-Crossing," "Promises, Promises."

WINSTON, HATTIE. Born Mar. 3, 1945 in Greenville, Miss. Attended Howard U. Off-Bdwy in "Prodigal Son," "Day of Absence," "Pins and Needles," "Weary Blues," "Man Better Man" (NEC), "Billy Noname," "Sambo," "The Me Nobody Knows."

WINTER, EDWARD. Born June 3, 1937 in Roseburg, Ore. Attended U. Ore. With LCRep. in "The Country Wife," "Condemned of Altona," and "The Caucasian Chalk Circle," "Waiting for Godot," Bdwy in "Cabaret," "The Birthday Party," "Promises, Promises."

WITHERS, IVA. Born July 7, 1917 in Rivers, Can. Bdwy debut 1945 in "Carousel," followed by "Oklahoma!," "As The Girls Go," "Make A Wish," "Guys and Dolls," "Redhead," "The Unsinkable Molly Brown," "Rattle of A Simple Man," "High Spirits," "I Do! I Do!," "The Happy Time," "40 Carats."

WOMBLE, ANDRE. Born Feb. 11, 1940 in Brooklyn. Attended NYU. Has appeared in "Miss Julie" (OB), "Slow Dance On The Killing Ground," "The Zulu and The Zayda," "The Little Foxes" ('67), "To Be Young, Gifted and Black," and "Akokawe" (OB).

WOOD, STUART CRAIG. Born Oct. 3, 1945 in Washington, DC. Graduate Carnegie Tech, Wayne State U. Debut Off-Bdwy 1968 in "Young Abe Lincoln," Bdwy bow 1970 in "Lovely Ladies, Kind Gentlemen."

WOOD, PEGGY. Born Feb. 9, 1894 in Brooklyn. Bdwy debut 1910 in "Naughty Marietta," followed by "Lady of the Slipper," "Love O' Mike," "Maytime," "Candida," "Trelawny of the Wells," "Merchant of Venice," "Bitter Sweet," "Old Acquaintance," "Blithe Spirit," "The Happiest Years," "Getting Married," "Charley's Aunt," "Girls in 509," Off-Bdwy in "Transposed Heads," "Opening Night," "Pictures in a Hallway," "A Madrigal for Shakespeare," "Madwoman of Chaillot," "Passage To E.M. Forster."

WOODS, ALLIE. Born Sept. 28, 1940 in Houston, Tex. Graduate Tex. Southern. Off-Bdwy in "The Blunderers," and with NEC in "Song of The Lusitanian Bogey," "Kongi's Harvest," "Daddy Goodness," "God Is A (Guess What?), " "Man Better Man," "Brotherhood" and "Day of Absence," "Akokawe."

WOODS, JAMES. Born Apr. 18, 1947 in Vernal, Utah. Graduate Mass. Inst. Tech. Bdwy debut 1970 in "Borstal Boy," followed by "Saved" (OB), "Conduct Unbecoming."

WOODS, RICHARD. Born May 9, 1930 in Buffalo, NY. Graduate Ithaca Col. Appeared in "Beg, Borrow or Steal," "Capt. Brassbound's Conversion," "Sail Away," Off-Bdwy in "The Crucible," "Summer and Smoke," "American Gothic," "Four-In-One," "My Heart's In The Highlands," "Eastward In Eden," "The Long Gallery," "The Year Boston Won The Pennant" (LC), "In The Matter of J. Robert Oppenheimer" (LCRep), with APA from 1962 in "You Can't Take It With You," "War and Peace," "School For Scandal," "Right You Are," "The Wild Duck," "Pantagleize," "Exit The King," "The Cherry Orchard," "Cock-A-Doodle Dandy," and "Hamlet," "Coco."

WRIGHT, BOB. Born 1911 in Columbia, Mo. Attended U. Mo. Bdwy bow 1948 in "Make Mine Manhattan," followed by "Kiss Me, Kate," "Hit The Trail," "South Pacific" (CC'57), "Tall Story," "The Merry Widow" (LC), "The Sound of Music" (CC'67), "Man of La Mancha."

WRIGHT, TERESA. Born Oct. 27, 1918 in NYC. Bdwy debut 1938 in "Our Town," followed by "Life with Father," "The Dark at the Top of the Stairs," "Mary, Mary," "I Never Sang for My Father," OB in "Who's Happy Now?," "A Passage to E. M. Forster."

YOHN, ERICA. Born in NYC. Off-Bdwy in "Agammemnon," "Circle of Chalk," "Ascent of F6," "Dream of Love," "Lysistrata," "Middle Man What Now," "Heel of Achilles," "Empire Builders," LCRep's "Yerma," "Caucasian Chalk Circle," and "Danton's Death," on Bdwy in "That Summer, That Fall," "Lenny."

ZANG, EDWARD. Born Aug. 19, 1934 in NYC. Graduate Boston U. Off-Bdwy in "The Good Soldier Schweik," "St. Joan" (LCRep), "The Boys In The Band," "AC/DC."

ZARIT, PAM. Born Mar. 7, 1944 in Chicago. Attended Denver U., Northwestern. Bdwy debut 1969 in "Promises, Promises."

ZELLER, MARK. Born Apr. 20, 1932 in NYC. Attended NYU, Juilliard. Bdwy debut 1956 in "Shangri-La," followed by "Happy Hunting," "Wonderful Town" (CC 58), "Saratoga," "Ari."

ZIMMERMANN, ED. Born Mar. 30, 1935 in NYC. Graduate Columbia. Off-Bdwy in "20 Poems of E. E. Cummings," "Hamlet," "Tea Party" and "The Basement," on Bdwy in "Luther," "The Right Honourable Gentleman," "Venus Is," "A Day in the Death of Joe Egg," "A Patriot for Me," "Not Now Darling," "The Philanthropist."

OBITUARIES

ARCHIBALD, WILLIAM, 53, actor, dancer, playwright, died in NYC of infectious hepatitis on Dec. 27, 1970. Born in Trinidad, BWI, made Bdwy debut with Humprey-Weidman Co., followed by "One for the Money," "Two for the Show," "All in Fun," "Dancing in the Streets," "Laffing Room Only," "Concert Varieties." Wrote "Carib Song," "Far Harbour," "The Innocents," "Portrait of a Lady," "The Crystal Heart," and "The Cantilevered Terrace." Also choreographed, directed, and appeared in clubs. Surviving are 2 brothers and 2 sisters.

BENZELL, MIMI, 47, singer, actress, died of cancer in Manhasset, NY, on Dec. 23, 1970. Was member of Metropolitan Opera from 1944-50, singing 60 roles. Became night club performer, and appeared on Bdwy in "Milk and Honey." Was hostess for a daily radio show, and appeared on tv. Surviving are her husband, Walter Gould, a son and daughter.

BRADY, ELEANOR, 73, former actress, died in Washington, D.C., on Mar. 26, 1971. She appeared in several productions, including "Lightnin" and "The Goose Hangs High" before her marriage and retirement. Was a graduate of AADA. Survived by a son, and was the widow of Joseph Sandeman.

BROOKS, HELEN, 60, actress, died in Nice, France on Apr. 6, 1971. Had lived in Europe for 20 years, but had appeared in several productions on Bdwy during the 1940's, including "Arsenic and Old Lace," "First Lady, " and "The Vinegar Tree.," Survived by her husband, James W. Wise, and a daughter.

BURNS, DAVID, 68, actor, collapsed on stage and died of a heart attack at the Forrest Theatre in Philadelphia, on Mar. 12, 1971. He was performing in "70, Girls 70." Career began in 1920, and among his many credits are "Irene," "Polly Preferred," "Wonder Boy," "Dinner at 8," "Face the Music," "Them's the Reporters," "They Came by Night," "Hide and Seek," "Bobby Get Your Gun," "The Man Who Came to Dinner," "Pal Joey," "Oklahoma!," "Dear Public," "Billion Dollar Baby," "Make Mine Manhattan," "Heaven on Earth," "Alive and Kicking," "Out of this World," "South Pacific," "Two's Company," "Men of Distinction," "Catch a Star," "The Music Man" "Do Re Mi," "A Funny Thing Happened on the Way to the Forum," "Hello, Dolly!," "The Price," and "Sheep on the Runway." He received Tony's for "Music Man," and "Funny Thing . . . " His widow suvives.

CALVERT, CATHERINE, 80, retired actress, died after a stroke in Uniondale, NY, on Jan. 18, 1971. Born Catherine Cassidy in Baltimore, she was the widow of playwright Paul Armstrong who wrote for her "Alias Jimmy Valentine," "The Deep Purple," and "The Escape." She also appeared opposite Otis Skinner in "Blood and Sand." Her second husband, Col. George Carruthers, a Canadian millionaire, was also deceased. A son survives.

CARMINATI, TULLIO, 77, stage and film actor, died of a stroke in Rome, Italy on Feb. 26, 1971. Of noble Dalmatian birth, he ran away from home and became leading man for Maria Carmin and Eleanora Duse. Came to the U.S. and appeared in "The Command to Love," "Strictly Dishonorable," "Great Lady," "Music in the Air," "Saint Joan," and in many films. No survivors.

CICERI, LEO, 46, Canadian-born actor, died Aug. 10, 1970 following an automobile accident near Stratford, Ont., where he was teaching and appearing in the Festival productions for his 11th season. Had appeared on Bdwy in "Tiger at the Gates" for which he received a THEATRE WORLD Award, and in "The Lark." Surviving are his mother, sister and brother.

CLEMENT, DONALD, 29, actor, was accidentally electrocuted in his NYC apartment on July 28, 1970. He was appearing in "The Boys in the Band." Surviving are his parents and 2 brothers.

COLEMAN, FRANK 3rd, 35, actor-singer, died Dec. 5, 1970 in Cooperstown, NY. He had appeared in "Kismet," and "Sacco-Vanzetti." His wife and son survive.

DALL, JOHN, 54, stage, and screen actor, died of a heart attack in his Hollywood home on Jan. 15, 1971. Had appeared in "Janie," "R.U.R," "Eve of St. Mark," "Dear Ruth," "Red Gloves," and "The Champagne Complex." A brother survives.

DARRELL, J. STEVAN, 65, stage, radio, film and tv character actor, died of a brain tumor in Hollywood on Aug. 14, 1970. His last stage performance was in "Born Yesterday." His widow survives.

DAY, EDITH, 75, Minneapolis-born musical comedy star who became the toast of London in the 1920's and remained there, died in London on May 1, 1971. Starred on Bdwy in "Going Up," "Irene" for 670 performances, "Orange Blossoms," and "Wildflower." Moved to London in 1920 and starred in "Irene," "Rose Marie," "Show Boat," and "Desert Song." She was a widow and left no known survivors.

Mimi Benzell   1961

David Burns   1970

John Dall   1949

Glenda Farrell   1939

Nathaniel Frey   1955

Tyrone Guthrie   1969

DELON, JACK, 42, singer-actor, died of a stroke in Queens, NY, on June 29, 1970. He had appeared in "Candide," "Body Beautiful," "Most Happy Fella," "The Good Soldier Schweik," "Green Willow," "Family Affair," "Street Scene," "Ballad of Baby Doe," "The Crucible," and "Mahagonny," His mother survives.

DURIEUX, TILLA, 90, grand old lady of the German theatre, died after an operation on Jan. 26, 1971 in Berlin. Her career began in 1901, and she appeared in NY in "The Shadow," and "Fedora." She had just completed a role in the film "The Last Bridge."

ERVINE, ST. JOHN, 87, playwright, died in London on Jan. 24, 1971. A native of Ireland, his plays include "The Magnanimous Lover," "Mixed Marriage," "The First Mrs. Fraser," "Anthony and Emma," "Robert's Wife," "Mary, Mary Quite Contrary," "The Ship," "Jane Clegg," "John Ferguson." In 1929 was drama critic for NY World. His wife died in 1965.

FARMER, FRANCES, 56, stage and film actress, died of cancer in Indianapolis, Ind., on Aug. 1, 1970. She had appeared on Bdwy in "Golden Boy," had been hostess on a tv program, and at the time of her death was actress-in-residence at Purdue Univ. Three times married and divorced, she leaves a sister and brother.

FARRELL, GLENDA, 66, stage, film, and tv star, died in her NYC home after a long illness on May 1, 1971. Made NY stage debut in 1928 in "Skidding," followed by "Divided Honors," "Love, Honor and Betray," "On the Spot," "Life Begins," "Separate Rooms," "The Life of Reilly," "Stage Door," "The Overtons," "Mrs. Gibbons' Boys," "Home Is the Hero," "Masquerade," and "Forty Carats." Appeared in 122 films, and received an Emmy for "A Cardinal Act of Mercy" on tv. Surviving are her second husband, Dr. Henry Ross, and actor-son Tommy Farrell. Interment was at West Point.

FLIPPEN, JAY C, 70, stage, film and tv actor, died on the operating table in Los Angeles on Feb. 3, 1971. Had appeared in minstrel shows, vaudeville, and made Bdwy debut in 1920 in "Broadway Brevities," followed by "The Great Temptations," "Padlocks of 1927," and "June Days," Went to Hollywood after WWII. Surviving is his widow, writer Ruth Brooks.

FREY, NATHANIEL, 57, stage, film and tv actor, died of cancer in NYC on Nov. 7, 1970. Had appeared in "Barefoot Boy with Cheek," "High Button Shoes," "Touch and Go," "Call Me Madam," "A Tree Grows in Brooklyn" "Wonderful Town," "Damn Yankees," "Goldilocks," "Harold," "She Loves Me," and "The Odd Couple." Surviving are his wife and son.

GORDON, GAVIN, 69, actor, singer, composer, died of coronary thrombosis in London on Nov. 18, 1970. Had appeared in NY in "Romeo and Juliet," "Annie Dear," "The Celebrity," "Lady in Love," "Sh! The Octopus," "Crashing Through," "Gentleman from Athens," "Metropole," "The Devil's Disciple," "Buy Me Blue Ribbons," His wife survives.

GRAVEY, FERNAND, 65, Belgian-born stage and film actor, died in Paris on Nov. 2, 1970. Appeared on Bdwy in 1964 in "Beekman Place," and in over 100 films, and 60 plays. He was divorced from actress Jane Renouardt. In the U.S. was billed as Fernand Gravet.

GUTHRIE, TYRONE, 70, actor, author, director, and producer, died May 15, 1971 at his home in Newbliss, Ire. He had been involved with theatres around the world for nearly half a century. Acted with Oxford Repertory Theatre for 5 years before becoming a director and producer. Had been inspirational associate in such organizations as Scottish National Theatre, Cambridge Festival, Old Vic, Stratford, (Ont.) Shakespeare Festival, and the Minnesota Theatre Co. in Minneapolis whose theatre was named for him. He was knighted in 1961 for his contributions to the theatre. Among his NY productions were "The Matchmaker," "Candide," "The First Gentleman," "Six Characters in Search of an Author," "The Tenth Man," "Gideon," "Mary Stuart," and "House of Atreus." His Widow survives.

HAMPER, GENEVIEVE, 82, retired actress, died in NYC after a long illness on Feb. 13, 1971. She was the widow of the Shakespearean actor Robert B. Mantell, and appeared as his leading lady from 1916 to 1928. She retired in 1933. Surviving is her second husband, actor John Alexander.

HART, TEDDY, 74, comedian of stage and screen, died in Los Angeles on Feb. 17, 1971. Made Bdwy debut in 1917, subsequently appearing in "Guns," "Inspector General," "East of Broadway," "3 Men on a Horse," "Room Service," "Boys from Syracuse," "See My Lawyer," "New Moon," "The More the Merrier," "The Man Who Came to Dinner," and "One Touch of Venus." He was the brother of lyricist Lorenz Hart. Surviving are his widow and son.

HARVEY, JOHN, 53, stage and film actor, and talent representative, died of a heart attack in NYC on Dec. 25, 1970. Had appeared in "Kiss and Tell," "Open House," "The Growing Paynes"(tv series), and over 50 films. He is survived by his wife, actress Judy Parrish, and a daughter.

HAYWARD, LELAND, 68, publicist, agent, producer, died of a stroke after surgery in Yorktown Heights, NY., on Mar. 18, 1971. His productions include "A Bell for Adano," "State of the Union," "Mister Roberts," "Anne of the Thousand Days," "South Pacific," "Call Me Madam," "The Wisteria Trees," "Sound of Music," "Gypsy," "A Shot in the Dark," and his last, "The Trial of the Catonsville 9." Surviving are his third wife, a son and daughter.

HENDERSON, RAY, 74, composer, died of a heart attack in his Greenwich, Conn., home on Dec. 31, 1970. He contributed to such musicals as "George White's Scandals," "Manhattan Mary," "Good News," "Hold Everything," "Three Cheers," "Follow Through," "Flying High," "Hot Cha," "Greenwich Village Follies," and "Strike Me Pink," and to numerous films, including "Sonny Boy" for Al Jolson. He is survived by his widow, a son, and two daughters.

HERNANDEZ, JUANO, 74, stage, radio, and film actor, died from a cerebral hemorrhage in San Juan, P.R., on July 17, 1970. On Bdwy had appeared in "Show Boat," "Strange Fruit," and "Set My People Free." He had roles in over 30 films. Married three times, four children survive.

HINES, ELIZABETH, 76, musical comedy star, and radio serial actress, died in her Lake Forest, Ill., home on Feb. 19, 1971. Among her vehicles were "See Saw," "O'Brien Girl," "Little Nellie Kelly," "Marjorie," "Manhattan Mary." She played the lead in radio serials "Helen Trent" and "I Love a Mystery." She retired in 1927 when she married Quaker Foods executive, Frank Warton, and moved to Chicago. A son and daughter survive.

HORTON, EDWARD EVERETT, 83, stage, film, and tv actor, died of cancer in his San Fernando Valley, Calif., home on Sept. 30, 1970. In a career that spanned over 60 years, he became famous for his double-take and comic jitteriness. He made more than 150 films, and appeared in the play "Springtime for Henry" more than 3000 times. Other Bdwy credits include "The Man Who Stood Still," "The Cheater," and "Carousel, " Also appeared in many touring companies, and summer theatres. A sister and two brothers survive.

JAMESON, HOUSE, 68, stage, radio, and tv actor, died Apr. 23, 1971 in Danbury, Conn. Made Bdwy debut in 1923 in "St. Joan," followed by "Goat Song," "Grand Street Follies," "Garrick Gaities," "An American Tragedy," "The Dark Hours," "We, The People," "Judgement Day," "In Time To Come," "The Patriots," "Requiem for a Nun," "Never Too Late," "The Great Indoors," and "Don't Drink the Water." Appeared on radio and tv in "Renfrow of the Mounted," and "The Aldrich Family." His widow survives.

KAUFMAN, WOLFE, 65, writer, drama critic, and press agent, died of a heart attack in Paris on Nov. 24, 1970. Before moving to Paris in 1954, he served as president of the Association of Theatrical Press Agents and Managers. His widow survives.

KING, DENNIS, 73, English-born stage and screen actor-singer, died of a heart ailment in NYC on May 21, 1971. After appearing in Eng., came to Bdwy in 1921 in "Clair de Lune" and soon became a matinee idol, appearing in "Back to Methuselah," "Romeo and Juliet," "Antony and Cleopatra," "Rose Marie," "Vagabond King," "Three Musketeers," "Peter Ibbetson," "Show Boat," "Petticoat Fever," "A Doll's House," "I Married an Angel," "Three Sisters," "Searching Wind," "Dunnigan's Daughter," "He Who Gets Slapped," "Medea," "Edward, My Son," "Winslow Boy," "Second Man," "Devil's Disciple," "Music in the Air," "The Strong are Lonely," "Lunatics and Lovers," "A Day by the Sea," "Affair of Honor," "Shangri-la," "Hidden River," "Greatest Man Alive," "Love and Libel," "Photo Finish," "Minor Miracle," "Loves of Cass McGuire," "Portrait of a Queen," and his last role in 1969 in "A Patriot for Me." Became U.S. citizen in 1953. Surviving are two sons, actors Dennis, Jr., and John Michael King.

KING, JANE. 75, retired vaudeville and musical comedy performer, died May 23, 1971 of a heart attack in Arlington, Va. With sister Mary, the King Sisters appeared in vaudeville and on Broadway in "Irene," "Jim Jam Jems," "I'll Say She Is," among others. Retired in 1924 when she married Leslie H. Baker, a Washington broker. Survivors besides her husband are her sister, a son, and daughter.

KIRKHAM, SAM, 48, singer-actor, died of a heart attack in NYC on Oct. 30, 1970. Made Bdwy debut in 1946 in "Cyrano de Bergerac," followed by "South Pacific," "Alive and Kicking," "That's the Ticket," "Stalag 17," "Marat/deSade," "Don't Drink the Water," "Hello, Dolly!," and "Oklahoma!" at City Center. A brother survives.

Elizabeth Hines   1921

Edward Everett Horton   1934

Dennis King   1956

Winnie Lightner 1930

Edmund Lowe 1932

Chester Morris 1969

KOLLMAR, RICHARD, 59, former actor, was found dead in his NYC home on Jan. 7, 1971 apparently of a heart attack. Had appeared on Bdwy in "Knickerbocker Holiday," "Too Many Girls," "Crazy with the Heat," and "Early to Bed." Co-produced "By Jupiter," "Early to Bed," "Dream with Music," "Are You with It?" "Plain and Fancy," "Body Beautiful," and was Boston Blackie on radio for a decade. With his late wife Dorothy Kilgallen, appeared for 18 years on radio in "Breakfast with Dorothy and Dick." Surviving are his second wife, designer Anne Fogarty, 2 sons and a daughter.

KRAFT, JILL, 39, former actress, died of cancer in Chicago on June 25, 1970. Had appeared in "Goodbye, My Fancy," "Gigi," "Time Out for Ginger," "The Importance of Being Earnest," "Cyrano de Bergerac," "A View from the Bridge," "Blue Denim," "Cheri," and "Dear Me, the Sky Is Falling." Surviving is her third husband, Herman Leonard, a son and daughter.

LATHAM, JOSEPH W., Sr, 80, stage, radio, and tv actor, died in Nyack, NY, on Oct. 10, 1970. Among his many Bdwy plays were "Waltz Song," "Vagabond King," "Remains to Be Seen," "By the Beautiful Sea," and "No Time for Sergeants." Survived by his widow, a son and daughter.

LIGHTNER, WINNIE, 71, former vaudeville, musical comedy, and film actress, died of a heart attack in her Sherman Oaks, Calif., home on Mar. 5, 1971. She appeared at the Palace, and on Bdwy in "George White's Scandals of 1923," and "Gay Paree." She retired after her second marriage to film director Roy Del Ruth, who survives, as does a son.

LINDSAY, LEX, 69, retired stage and screen actor, died after a short illness in Doylestown, Pa., on Apr. 24, 1971. Had appeared in such plays as "Rebound," "Personal Appearance," "Glamour Preferred," "Chalked Out," "Kiss the Boys Goodbye." Surviving is his widow, former Ziegfeld girl, Naomi Sehaub.

LOWE, EDMUND, 79, stage and film actor, died after a long illness on Apr. 3, 1971 in Hollywood. Made Bdwy debut in 1918 in "The Brat," followed by "The Walk-offs," "Roads of Destiny," "The Son-Daughter," "The Right to Strike," "Trilby," "Desert Sands," and "The Ryan Girl" in 1945. Had been in over 100 films. He was married three times, but left no survivors.

LOWE, K. ELMO, 71, former actor, and director of Cleveland Play House (1921-'69), died after a stroke in Cleveland, Ohio, on Jan. 26, 1971. Survivors include his widow, actress Dorothy Paxton, and actress-daughter Stanja.

MAPLE, AUDREY, 72, retired musical comedy actress, died in her NYC home after a long illness on Apr. 18, 1971. She retired in 1940 when she married Ernest A. Zadig. Among the productions in which she appeared were "Katinka," "Naughty Riquette," "Angela," "The Orchid Lady," and several Shubert musicals. Her husband survives.

MEIGHAN, JAMES E., JR., 66, retired stage and radio actor, died June 20, 1970 in his Huntington, NY, home. Had appeared in such productions as "My Maryland," and "Under the Gaslight," and on radio in "Just Plain Bill," "Meet Miss Julie," and "Special Agent." His widow and daughter survive.

MILLER, FLOURNOY, 84, comedian, died June 6, 1971 after a long illness in Hollywood. With the late Aubrey Lyles, was popular team in the 1920's. Produced and appeared in "Sugar Hill," wrote and appeared in "Shuffle Along" in 1933 and 1952. Appeared at the Palace in 1955 in vaudeville. No reported survivors.

MONTEREY, CARLOTTA. 82, retired actress, and widow of Eugene O'Neill, died in Westwood, N.J., on Nov. 18, 1970 after a long illness. She appeared in O'Neill's "The Hairy Ape" and was the inspiration for characters in his "Strange Interlude" and "Mourning Becomes Electra." He became her fourth husband in 1929, and for the remainder of their lives excluded almost everyone, including their children. A daughter by her second marriage survives.

MORRIS, CHESTER, 69, stage, film, and tv actor, died in New Hope, Pa., on Sept. 11, 1970 of an overdose of barbiturates. He was appearing at the Bucks County Playhouse in "The Caine Mutiny Court Martial." Born to a theatrical family, he made his acting debut at 9, appearing in over 85 films, and on stage in "The Copperhead," "Turn to the Right," "Thunder," "The Exciters," "Extra," "The Home Towners," "Yellow," "Crime," "Whispering Friends," "Fast Life," "Fifth Season," "Girl of the Golden West," "Blue Denim," "Advise and Consent," and "The Subject Was Roses." Survived by his widow, a daughter, and 2 sons.

MOTYLEFF, ILYA. 76, former associate of Stanislavksi in Moscow, and a director, died in NY on Nov. 28, 1970 after suffering a cerebral hemorrhage. A brother and sister survive.

NICHOLS, BEATRICE, 78, retired stage, film, and tv character actress, died in NYC on Sept. 26, 1970. Began career in 1950's and appeared in such plays as "Polly Preferred," "Moonbirds," "Waltz of the Toreadors," and "Never Too Late." She also appeared in over 100 tv shows. Two sons and a daughter survive.

O'BRIEN, DONNELL, age unreported, actor-singer, died in NYC after a long illness on July 27, 1970. Had appeared in vaudeville, tv, in films, and on stage in "Excess Baggage," "Hold Your Horses," "Detective Story," "Student Prince," and "Room Service." A sister survives.

OLIVETTE, NINA, 63, retired singer-actress, died after a heart attack in NYC on Feb. 21, 1971. Made Bdwy debut in 1925 in "Captain Jinks," subsequently appearing in such productions as "Hold Everything" and "The Matchmaker." Survived by husband, actor Harry Stockwell.

OLSEN, GEORGE, 78, retired bandleader, died Mar. 18, 1971 in his Paramus, NJ, home. He and his band were featured in such Bdwy musicals as "Kid Boots," "The Girl Friend," "Whoopee," "Good News," and "Sunny." His widow and 2 sons survive.

PARKER, CECIL, 73, stage and film actor, died Apr. 20, 1971 in his Brighton, Eng., home. Had appeared on Bdwy in "Daphne Laureola," and in many films.

PERRY, MARY, 83, stage, film, and tv actress, died in NYC on Mar. 6, 1971. During her 50 years in theatre, had appeared in "Bury the Dead," "Out West of Eighth," "Let Freedom Ring," "Brother Rat," "Hell-bent fer Heaven," "Traveling Lady," and "All the Way Home." No known survivors.

RAMBEAU, MARJORIE, 80, stage and screen actress whose career spanned 70 years, died after a long illness in her Palm Springs, Calif., home on July 6, 1970. Had appeared in NY in "Kick In," "Sadie Love," "Cheating Cheaters," "Eye of Youth," "Where Poppies Bloom," "The Fortune Teller," "Daddy's Gone A-hunting," "The Goldfish," "As You Like It," "The Road Together," and "Valley of Content." In 1930 she went to Hollywood and remained there to make numerous films through the 1950's. Married and divorced 3 times, she left no immediate survivors.

REINER, ETHEL LINDER, 65, producer, died in Barbados on Feb. 8, 1971 after a long illness. She was associated with such productions as "Four Saints in Three Acts," "Masterpieces of the 20th Century," "Camino Real," "The Rainmaker," "Candide." In recent years had lived in London. A son and a daughter survive. Burial was in England.

ROGERS, CYNTHIA, 62, actress, died in her NYC home on May 2, 1971. Had appeared in "Houseparty," "Garrick Gaieties," "Modern Virgin," "Money in the Air," "Dangerous Corner," "Mary of Scotland," "By Your Leave," "Lost Horizon," "Dance Me a Song," and "The Big Knife." Surviving is her actor-playwright husband, Robert Wallsten.

RUGGLES, CHARLES, 84, stage, screen and tv actor, died of cancer in Santa Monica, Calif., on Dec. 23, 1970. Made NY stage debut in 1906, subsequently appearing in "Help Wanted," "Rolling Stones," "Canary Cottage," "Battling Butler," "Passing Show of 1918," "Queen High," "Spring is Here," "Tumble In," "The Girl in the Limousine," "Ladies Night," "Demi-Virgin," "White Collars," "The Pleasure of His Company," for which he won a Tony, "The Captains and the Kings," and "Roar Like a Dove" in 1964. Appeared in over 80 movies and in the tv series "The Ruggles," and "The World of Mr. Sweeney." His second wife survives.

SERLIN, OSCAR, 70, producer, died in his NYC home on Feb. 27, 1971 after a long illness. His productions include "Skidding," "Broken Dishes," the long-running "Life with Father" and its sequel "Life with Mother," "The Moon Is Down," and the "American National Theatre Album." Became inactive in 1951. Surviving are his widow, 2 sons and a daughter.

SHANNON, RAY, 76, stage and radio comedian, died Jan. 1, 1971 in Cincinnati, Ohio. Had appeared with Stan Laurel, W. C. Fields, Al Jolson, and on Bdwy in "Simple Simon" and "Flying High." Retired in 1935.

SHELTON, GEORGE, 87, burlesque, vaudeville, stage and radio comedian, long teamed with Tom Howard, died in NYC on Feb. 12, 1971 as a result of burns. He appeared in "Rain or Shine," and on radio and tv in "It Pays to Be Ignorant." His widow survives.

SILVERA, FRANK, 56, actor, director, and producer, was accidentally electrocuted in his home on June 11, 1970. Born in Jamaica, made NY stage debut in 1945 in "Anna Lucasta," followed by "Nat Turner," "Camino Real," "Mademoiselle Colombe," "A Hatful of Rain," "The Skin of Our Teeth," "Jane Eyre," "Semi-Detached," "King Lear" (NYSF), "Lady of the Camellias," and "The Amen Corner." Appeared in over 40 films, and co-founded the Theater of Being in Los Angeles. A son and daughter survive.

Marjorie Rambeau   1946

Charles Ruggles   1964

Frank Silvera   1965

Menasha Skulnik   1961

Lenore Ulric   1940

Eugene R. Wood   1968

SKULNIK, MENASHA, 78, comedy star of Yiddish theatre and Broadway, died in NYC on June 4, 1970 after a short illness. Warsaw born, he came to the U.S. at 17 and became active in Yiddish theatres throughout the country. He was a permanent star for 35 years at the Second Avenue Theatre in NYC. Appeared on Bdwy in "The Fifth Season," "The Flowering Peach," "Uncle Willie," "The 49th Cousin," "Come Blow Your Horn," and "The Zulu and the Zayda." He was also a familiar character on the radio serial "The Goldbergs" for 19 years. Surviving are his second wife, actress Anna Roman, and 2 daughters.

STEWART, FRED, 63, actor, producer, director, died at the Actors Studio in NYC on Dec. 5, 1970. Career began in Atlanta at 18. Made Bdwy debut in 1931 in "Ladies of Creation," followed by "Experience Unnecessary," "200 Were Chosen," "Excursion," "Robin Landing," "Washington Jitters," "The Devil and Daniel Webster," "Night Music," "Retreat to Pleasure," "Land's End," "Whole World Over," "Brigadoon," "The Crucible," "Cat on a Hot Tin Roof," "Girls in 509," "Romulus," "Strange Interlude," "Galileo," "More Stately Mansions." Was a regular on the tv series "Love of Life." Two sisters and a brother survive.

STRATTON, CHESTER, 57, stage, film, radio, and tv actor, died of a heart attack in his Los Angeles home on July 7, 1970. On radio he starred in "The O'Neills" for 10 years, in "Pepper Young's Family," and "Ace of the Airways." Appeared on Bdwy in "Tomorrow's Harvest," "Red Harvest," "Whiteoaks," "Kiss the Boys Goodbye," "A Connecticut Yankee," "The Barretts of Wimpole Street," "The Live Wire," "Man and Superman," "Richard II," and "Island Fling." His widow survives.

TAYLOR, MABEL, stage, radio, and tv actress, age unreported, died in NYC on July 7, 1970. Appeared in "Come of Age," "The Crippen Case," "This Rock," "Outrageous Fortune," "Lovers and Friends," and "Gently Does It." Also appeared in England and Australia. Her husband, actor Lloyd Taylor, survives.

TERRISS, ELLALINE, 100, actress and musical comedy star of the 1890's, died June 16, 1971 in London. With her late husband, actor-manager Sir Seymour Hicks, became famous husband and wife team in New York as well as London. Among her many successes were "Two Roses," "David Garrick," "The Shop Girl," "Cinderella," "Alice in Wonderland," "Bluebell in Fairyland," "Quality Street," "The Amazons," and her last in 1935 "The Miracle Man."

TIHMAR, DAVID, 61, dancer, actor, director, died after a heart attack in Oklahoma City on Apr. 16, 1971. Had appeared with Ballet Russe de Monte Carlo, and in "Oklahoma!." and "Follow the Girls." More recently had been directing and choreographing in regional theatres. A sister and brother survive.

TRACEY, SID, 70, vaudeville and Broadway performer, died Sept. 21, 1970 in Los Angeles of complications from a fall. He was a dance act with his wife Bessie Hay, and appeared in a number of Bdwy productions including "Ziegfeld Follies," "Gingham Girl," and "Blue Train." Surviving are his wife and a daughter.

ULRIC, LENORE, 78, retired stage and film star, died Dec. 30, 1970 in Rockland State Hospital where she had been a patient for several years. One of Belasco's and Bdwy's brightest stars from 1916 to 1930, she appeared in "Bird of Paradise," "The Heart of Wetona," "Tiger Rose," "The Son-Daughter," "Lulu Belle," "The Harem, "Mima," "Pagan Lady," "The Social Register," "Nona," "Her Man of Wax," "The Fifth Column," and "Antony and Cleopatra." Her marriage to Sidney Blackmer ended in divorce. A sister survives.

VILAR, JEAN, 59, actor-director who dominated theatre in France for a generation, died May 28, 1971 of a heart attack in Sete, France. Founded and directed Theatre National Populaire and appeared with company on Bdwy in 1958 in "Le Triomphe de L'Amour," "Le Cid," and "Don Juan." Surviving are his widow and 3 children.

WALL, GERALDINE, 57, former stage and film actress, died of pneumonia following a heart attack in Woodland Hills, Calif., on June 22, 1970. She had appeared in "Heat Lightning," "3 Men on a Horse," "3 Blind Mice," and "The Love Nest." Two sisters, actresses Lucille and Mildred Wall, survive.

WOOD, EUGENE R., 67, stage, film, and tv actor, and former teacher at Ithaca College, died of a heart attack on Jan. 22, 1971 while appearing in "The Vinegar Tree" with Shirley Booth in West Palm Beach, Fla. He had appeared in "The Crucible," "Kiss Me, Kate," "Porgy and Bess," "Pajama Game," "Look Homeward, Angel," "Subways Are for Sleeping," "West Side Story," "The Devils," and "The Great White Hope." A brother survives.

WYNN, NAN, 55, stage and screen actress, and night club singer, died of cancer in her Santa Monica, Calif., home on Mar. 21, 1971. She had appeared in "The Seven Lively Arts," and "Finian's Rainbow." A daughter survives.

INDEX

276

279

281

283

285